# Alexander the Great:
# The Invisible Enemy

# Alexander the Great:
# The Invisible Enemy

## A biography

John Maxwell O'Brien

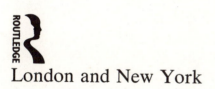

**London and New York**

First published in 1992 by Routledge

First published in paperback 1994
by Routledge
11 New Fetter Lane, London EC4P 4EE

Simultaneously published in the USA and Canada
by Routledge
29 West 35th Street, New York, NY 10001

© 1992, 1994 John Maxwell O'Brien

Typeset in 10 on 12 point Times by
Intype, London

Printed in Great Britain by
TJ Press (Padstow) Ltd, Padstow, Cornwall

*British Library Cataloguing in Publication Data*
A catalogue record for this book is available from the British Library

*Library of Congress Cataloging in Publication Data*
A catalogue record for this book has been requested

ISBN 0–415–10617–6

For Dorothy Peluso O'Brien, whose love and strength of character enabled me to endure this labor

# Contents

*Preface*                                           ix
*Acknowledgments*                                   xi
*Frequently cited sources in the text*              xiii
*List of maps*                                      xiv

Prologue                                            1

1 The coming of age in Macedonia                    5
  *Dionysus in the Royal Tombs*                     5
  *Macedonian drinking*                             6
  *Philip and Alexander*                            8
  *Olympias and Alexander*                          12
  *The Dionysiac cult in Macedonia*                 14
  *Olympias, Philip, and Alexander*                 16
  *The Gardens of Midas (343–340 BC)*               19
  *Heroic models*                                   21
  *Regent (340 BC)*                                 23
  *The battle of Chaeronea (338 BC)*                24
  *Athens (338 BC)*                                 26
  *The wedding of Philip II and Cleopatra (337 BC)* 28
  *The Pixodarus affair (336 BC)*                   31
  *The assassination of Philip II (336 BC)*         34

2 A Homeric king                                    43
  *The accession (336 BC)*                          43
  *Alexander in Greece (336 BC)*                    46
  *Northern campaigns (335 BC)*                     49
  *The destruction of Thebes (335 BC)*              52
  *Dium (335 BC)*                                   55
  *Alexander's sexuality*                           56
  *Alexander at the Hellespont (334 BC)*            59
  *The battle of the Granicus River (334 BC)*       62
  *Asia Minor (334 BC)*                             65
  *The Gordian knot (333 BC)*                       70

*The battle of Issus (333 BC)*                                      75
*Phoenicia (333–332 BC)*                                            79
*The siege of Tyre (332 BC)*                                        82
*Egypt (332 BC)*                                                    86
*Alexandria (331 BC)*                                              87
*The journey to Siwah (331 BC)*                                     87
*The battle of Gaugamela (331 BC)*                                  91
*Babylon and Susa (331 BC)*                                        97

3 The metamorphosis                                               101
*The signs of change*                                             101
*The burning of Persepolis (330 BC)*                               105
*Orientalization*                                                  111
*The Philotas affair (330 BC)*                                     117
*The death of Cleitus (328 BC)*                                    128
*Proskynesis*                                                      142
*Callisthenes*                                                     143
*The pages' conspiracy (327 BC)*                                   145
*Nysa and Aornus (327 BC)*                                         148

4 The ambivalent victor                                           155
*Into "India" (326 BC)*                                            155
*The battle of the Hydaspes (Jhelum) River (326 BC)*               157
*"Mutiny" at the Hyphasis (Beas) River (326 BC)*                   164
*Ocean (325 BC)*                                                   170
*The Gedrosian Desert (325 BC)*                                    179
*Carmania (325–324 BC)*                                            184
*Persis (324 BC)*                                                  192
*Cyrus' tomb (324 BC)*                                             194
*Susa (324 BC)*                                                    197
*Deification (324 BC)*                                             201
*The Opis "mutiny" (324 BC)*                                       204
*The death of Hephaestion (324 BC)*                                210

5 Death in Babylon                                                217
*The last plans (323 BC)*                                          217
*The death of Alexander (323 BC)*                                  223

*Epilogue*                                                         229
*Appendix A: The Royal Tombs*                                      231
*Appendix B: Attributes of wine in Alexander the Great's readings* 233
*Postscript*                                                       239
*Key to abbreviations of frequently cited journals*                240
*Notes*                                                            241
*List of topics in the Bibliography*                               278
*Bibliography*                                                     279
*Index*                                                            323

# Preface

Early in his illustrious career, Alexander the Great faced the challenge of attempting to undo the Gordian knot. Legend had it that the man who could accomplish this feat would rule all of Asia (i.e., the Persian Empire). The knot, however, had no visible ends, and it remained intact, despite the resolute efforts of resourceful men. In the most familiar account of Alexander's endeavor at Gordium, the king, utterly frustrated, raises his sword and slashes straight through the knot. In another version, however, Alexander utilizes an oblique stratagem. He simply removes the dowel holding the knot in place, exposes a loose end, and unties it.

This book examines Alexander's personality in a manner that evokes the alternative version of the Gordium incident. The enigma of Alexander the man is the formidable knot that unravels when the dowel – the god Dionysus – is removed. This work will direct the reader's attention to those interludes in Alexander's life when his path crossed that of the wine god. Enough loose ends surface in the process to justify a fresh look at certain aspects of Alexander's personality that have thus far defied explanation.

The most perplexing of all such considerations is Alexander's metamorphosis. Even as he performed one epic deed after another, this superb warrior began to exhibit a disturbing personal transformation. During the last seven years of his life Alexander became increasingly unpredictable, sporadically violent, megalomaniacal, and suspicious of friends as well as enemies. What could have caused such a lamentable transformation? This book explores that question in a way that requires the reader's forbearance until exposed threads begin to reveal patterns in Alexander's behavior.

The elusive god Dionysus, who is profiled in the Prologue, plays an important role in this book. His character is fleshed out as the text develops and his burgeoning impact on Alexander becomes more apparent. The respect Dionysus required in antiquity has been extended to him here. The god will manifest himself in various forms, and is therefore treated as a real, vital force in Alexander's life.

Alexander is said to have slept with a copy of Homer's *Iliad* under his pillow. He emulated its hero, Achilles, from boyhood. The young king also demonstrated a particular interest in Greek drama, and especially in the plays of Euripides. He quoted from that tragedian's *Bacchae* extemporaneously. Excerpts from these two masterpieces are interspersed throughout the text. Removed from their original context, virtually stripped of punctuation, and used in an unorthodox fashion, they serve, in some ways, as a Greek chorus, providing commentary on the action, and expressing thoughts that may have echoed through Alexander's own mind on occasion. The excerpts are also employed to illustrate and intensify the heroic and Dionysiac dimensions of Alexander's experience. As the reader progresses through this work, it will become evident that it is the precarious balance of these elements that lends a tragic quality to the man's life.

This book has been written with the general reader in mind and with an eye to students and scholars. Military matters and political considerations have been kept to a bare minimum because of the focus on Alexander's personality, but interested parties can pursue these questions through the Notes and Bibliography. I have reluctantly declined to include an analysis of the ancient sources because of the nature of the present work and the fact that so many of these studies (particularly the impressive contributions of A. B. Bosworth) are now readily available.

I must make it clear that a definitive study of Alexander's personality is unattainable because of the fragmentary and contradictory nature of the sources. All efforts to fathom the man remain little more than educated guesses, colored by the investigator's interests and presuppositions. Most of the assertions made here, however, have the advantage of being rooted in the ancient sources, both apologetic and critical. These assertions, I believe, would have been intelligible to Alexander and his contemporaries. To those who object to the way in which the great conqueror is portrayed, I commend the words of his tutor, Aristotle, who reminds us that "no one is able to attain the truth adequately, while, on the other hand, no one fails entirely, but every one says something true about the nature of things" (*Metaph.* 993ᵇ).

# Acknowledgments

This research was supported (in part) by a grant from the City University of New York PSC–CUNY Research Award Program. The Interlibrary Loan units at Queens College and Teikyo Post University were instrumental in my efforts to complete this work. The book has profited inestimably from the criticisms and suggestions of scholars who were kind enough to read portions of the manuscript at various stages in its evolution: Thomas W. Africa, Beate Hein Bennett, A. B. Bosworth, Elizabeth D. Carney, Ernst A. Fredricksmeyer, J. R. Hamilton, Waldemar Heckel, J. Donald Hughes, Harry Gene Levine, Paul R. Lonigan, Robert Emmet Meagher, R. D. Milns, J. M. Mossman, Robin Room, Wolfgang Zeev Rubinsohn, Edward-David E. Ruiz, Frank Salvidio, Alan R. Schulman, Sheldon C. Seller, David Sider, and last, but by no means least, Robert S. Tilton. I accept exclusive responsibility for any residual defects. Non-specialists contributed with unfathomable generosity. The Herculean efforts of Anita T. Bello, Barney Rickenbacker, Sondra Rosenberg, and Karen Salomone have humbled me with gratitude. Other splendid people have also made significant contributions to this volume: Marjorie Adler, Stuart Astor, Goldie Baron, Thea Bergere, Lewis Beshers, Gina Bianchi, Nora Bird, William H. Bohner, Alessandro Boselli, Thomas Brennan, M.D, Thomas J. Byrne, Suzanne Chemtob, Karen Conroy, Marianne Conti, Deanna Crooks, Andreana Filiotis, Basile Filiotis, Georgia Filiotis, Vasiliki Filiotis, Eleanor Friedman, Dennis Galik, Edythe B. Gardner, Colette Golinski, Gertrude Halpern, Thomas Heckman, Dorothy Higgins, R. D. R. Hoffmann, Doug Jamieson, Patricia Jamieson, Ingrid Jewsick, Eric Johnson, Gertrude Kallinger, Susan Kane, Suzanne Katz, Joseph Krachie, Raymond Lampe, William L. Lawson, Daria Lewis, Chris McGarrigal, James McLandish, Mary McLoughlin, Emmett McSweeney, Aaron N. Maloff, Morgan Manley, the inimitable D. H. Murdoch, Aida Nema, Marie Nulty, my daughter Christine O'Brien, my daughter Lillian Catherine O'Brien, my son William James O'Brien, Dolores Orsi, Robert Page, Pat Parisi, John W. Price, Wladyslaw Roczniak, Doris Sherrow, Aprajita Sikri, JoAnn Soldano-Rush, Riva Sossman, Jesse Spilka, Izabella Taler, Leon Thaler, Mary Tracy, Susan Vaccarrelli, Joyce Weinstein, Brigitte

Winkler, and Marlene Yahalom. Richard Stoneman, Heather McCallum, and Sue Bilton of Routledge have been gracious and supportive in this mutual enterprise. Rita A. Sweeney edited this work with genius and efficiency.

I am indebted to the following individuals and publishers for permission to quote from copyrighted materials: excerpts from *The Iliad* by Homer, translated by Richmond Lattimore, copyright © The University of Chicago Press, 1951. Excerpts from *The Bacchae* by Euripides in *Euripides V*, translated by William Arrowsmith, copyright © The University of Chicago Press, 1959. Excerpts reprinted by permission of the publishers and The Loeb Classical Library from Arrian: *Anabasis Alexandri* and *Indica*, Vols. 236, 269, translated by P. A. Brunt, Cambridge, Mass.: Harvard University Press, 1976, 1983. Excerpts reprinted by permission of the publishers and The Loeb Classical Library from Diodorus Siculus: *Library of History*, vol. 422, translated by C. B. Welles, Cambridge, Mass.: Harvard University Press, 1970. Excerpts from *The Age of Alexander* by Plutarch, translated by Ian Scott-Kilvert (Penguin Classics, 1973), translation and notes copyright © Ian Scott-Kilvert, 1973, introduction copyright © G. T. Griffith, 1973. Excerpts from *The History of Alexander* by Quintus Curtius Rufus, translated by John Yardley (Penguin Classics, 1984), translation copyright © John Yardley, 1984, introduction, notes and additional material © Waldemar Heckel, 1984. Excerpts from my article "Alexander and Dionysus: the Invisible Enemy" in *The Annals of Scholarship* (1980). Excerpts from my article, "The Grand Elixir 2,300 Years Removed: Attributes of Wine in Alexander the Great's Reading," *Drinking and Drug Practices Surveyor* (1980).

# Frequently cited sources in the text

A. = Arrian's *Anabasis Alexandri*. A.*Ind.* = Arrian's *Indica*. Line citations and quotations are from P. A. Brunt's Loeb edition.

P. = Plutarch's *Life of Alexander*. P.*Mor.* = Plutarch's *Moralia*. Line citations are from Bernadotte Perrin's Loeb edition of *Alexander*, but quotations are from Ian Scott-Kilvert's Penguin translation. All quotations from the *Moralia* are the work of various translators in the Loeb edition.

D. = Diodorus Siculus' *Library of History*. Line citations and quotations are from C. Bradford Welles' Loeb edition.

C. = Curtius' *History of Alexander*. Line citations are from John C. Rolfe's Loeb edition, but quotations are from John Yardley's Penguin translation.

J. = Justin's epitome of the *Philippic Histories* of Pompeius Trogus. Line citations are from the Teubner edition of O. Seel, but quotations are from J. S. Watson's translation in Bohn's Libraries.

S. = Strabo's *Geography*. Line citations and quotations are from Horace Leonard Jones' Loeb edition.

*Ba.* = Euripides' *Bacchae*. Line citations are from Arthur S. Way's Loeb edition, but quotations are from William Arrowsmith's University of Chicago translation.

*Il.* = Homer's *Iliad*. Line citations are from A. T. Murray's Loeb edition, but quotations are from Richmond Lattimore's University of Chicago translation.

Please consult the Bibliography for a more complete description of these works.

N.B. All dates in the following pages are BC unless otherwise indicated.

# Maps

The Greek World 336 BC                     xv
Alexander's Campaigns 334–323 BC           xvi
From Pella to Susa 334–330 BC              xviii
India and Ocean 326–325 BC                 xx

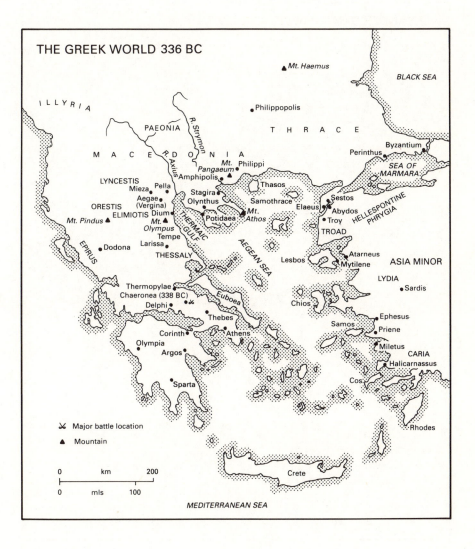

THE GREEK WORLD 336 BC

ILLYRIA

BLACK SEA

▲ Mt. Haemus

• Philippopolis

PAEONIA

T H R A C E

MACEDONIA

R. Strymon

Axius

Byzantium •
Perinthus •

SEA OF
MARMARA

LYNCESTIS
Mieza • • Pella
Aegae •
(Vergina)
ORESTIS
ELIMIOTIS Dium •
Mt. ▲
Olympus
Tempe

Mt. • Philippi
Pangaeum •
Amphipolis • ▲
Stagira •
Olynthus •
Thasos •
Samothrace •
Potidaea • Mt.
Athos

Sestos •
Elaeus • Abydos •
Troy •
TROAD

HELLESPONTINE
PHRYGIA

EPIRUS
Mt. Pindus ▲

THERMAIC GULF

• Dodona
Larissa •
THESSALY

AEGEAN SEA

Lesbos • Atarneus •
Mytilene •

ASIA MINOR

LYDIA
Sardis •

Thermopylae
Chaeronea (338 BC)
Delphi •
Thebes •
Corinth •
Olympia •
Argos •

Euboea

Chios •

Athens •

Samos •

Ephesus •
Priene •
Miletus •
CARIA
Halicarnassus •

Sparta •

Cos •

Rhodes •

⚔ Major battle location

▲ Mountain

| 0 | km | 200 |
| 0 | mls | 100 |

Crete

MEDITERRANEAN SEA

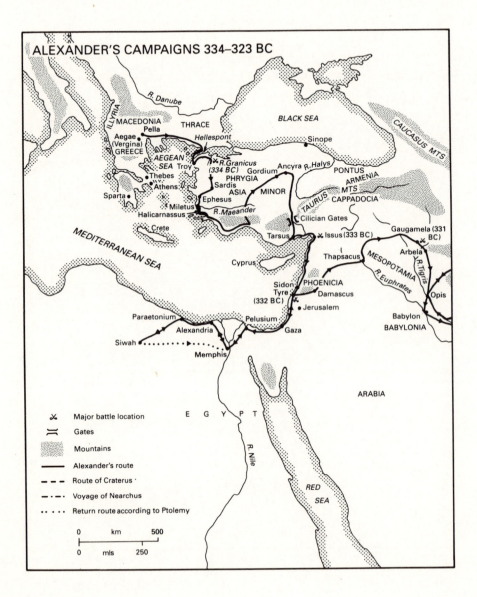

**ALEXANDER'S CAMPAIGNS 334–323 BC**

ILLYRIA
R. Danube
MACEDONIA
THRACE
BLACK SEA
CAUCASUS MTS
Pella
Aegae (Vergina)
GREECE
Hellespont
Sinope
AEGEAN SEA
Troy
R. Granicus (334 BC)
Gordium
Ancyra  R. Halys
PONTUS
ARMENIA
PHRYGIA
Thebes
Sardis
ASIA  MINOR
MTS
Athens
Ephesus
TAURUS
CAPPADOCIA
Sparta
R. Maeander
Miletus
Cilician Gates
Halicarnassus
Gaugamela (331 BC)
Crete
Tarsus
Issus (333 BC)
Arbela
MEDITERRANEAN SEA
R. Tigris
Thapsacus
MESOPOTAMIA
Cyprus
R. Euphrates
Opis
Sidon
PHOENICIA
Tyre (332 BC)
Damascus
Jerusalem
Babylon
BABYLONIA
Paraetonium
Pelusium
Alexandria
Gaza
Siwah
Memphis
ARABIA

E  G  Y  P  T

Major battle location

Gates

Mountains

Alexander's route

Route of Craterus

Voyage of Nearchus

Return route according to Ptolemy

R. Nile

RED SEA

0        km        500

0        mls        250

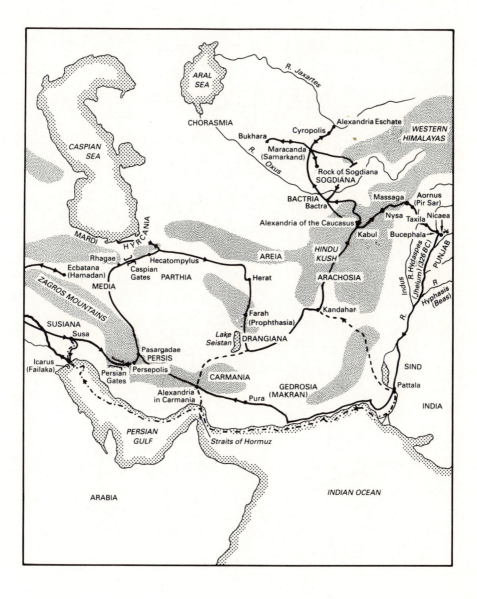

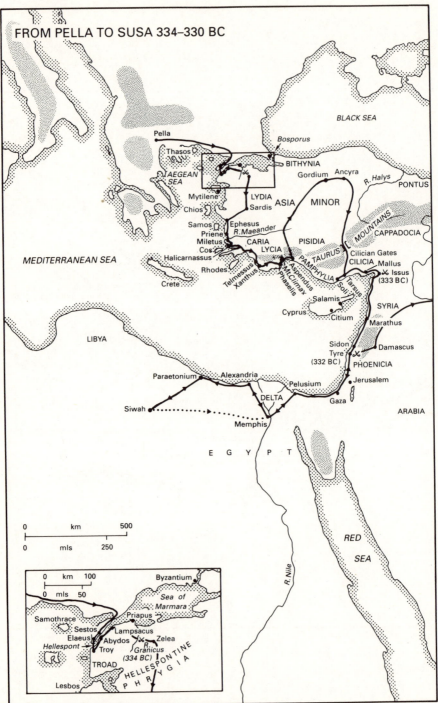

# FROM PELLA TO SUSA 334–330 BC

BLACK SEA

Pella

Thasos

*AEGEAN SEA*

*Bosporus*

BITHYNIA

Mytilene

Chios

LYDIA

Sardis

Gordium   Ancyra

ASIA   MINOR

*R. Halys*

PONTUS

Samos

Priene

Miletus

Cos

Ephesus

*R. Maeander*

CARIA

LYCIA

PISIDIA

CAPPADOCIA

TAURUS

MOUNTAINS

Cilician Gates

CILICIA

Halicarnassus

Rhodes

Telmessus

Xanthus

Aspendus

Mt. Climax

Phaselis

PAMPHYLIA

Soli

Tarsus

Mallus

Issus
(333 BC)

Crete

MEDITERRANEAN SEA

Salamis

Cyprus

Citium

SYRIA

Marathus

Damascus

Sidon

Tyre
(332 BC)

PHOENICIA

LIBYA

Paraetonium

Alexandria

Pelusium

DELTA

Jerusalem

Gaza

ARABIA

Siwah

Memphis

E G Y P T

*R. Nile*

RED
SEA

0        km        500

0        mls        250

0     km     100

0     mls     50

Byzantium

*Sea of Marmara*

Samothrace

Sestos

Elaeus

*Hellespont*

Priapus

Lampsacus

Abydos

Troy

Zelea

*R. Granicus*
*(334 BC)*

HELLESPONTINE

P H R Y G I A

TROAD

Lesbos

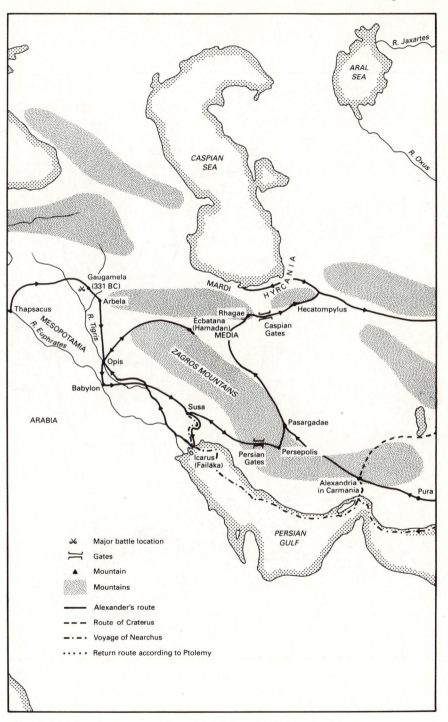

ARAL
SEA

R. Jaxartes

R. Oxus

CASPIAN
SEA

MARDI

HYRCANIA

Gaugamela
(331 BC)

Arbela

Thapsacus

MESOPOTAMIA

R. Euphrates

R. Tigris

Rhagae

Ecbatana
(Hamadan)

MEDIA

Caspian
Gates

Hecatompylus

Opis

ZAGROS MOUNTAINS

Babylon

ARABIA

Susa

Pasargadae

Icarus
(Failaka)

Persian
Gates

Persepolis

Alexandria
in Carmania

Pura

PERSIAN
GULF

✄    Major battle location

)(    Gates

▲    Mountain

      Mountains

———    Alexander's route

- - -    Route of Craterus

-·-·-    Voyage of Nearchus

· · · ·    Return route according to Ptolemy

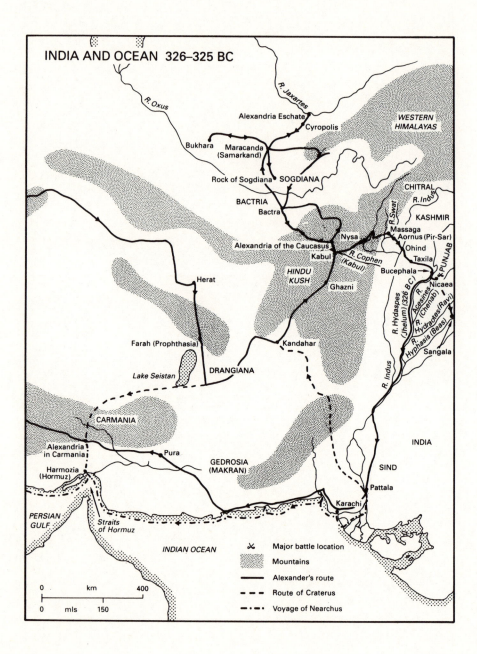

Dionysos, dieu des illusions, de la confusion et du brouillage incessant entre la réalité et les apparences, la vérité et la fiction
J.-P. Vernant and P. Vidal-Naquet,
*Mythe et tragédie en Grèce ancienne II*, 42

Tragedy presupposed an awareness of the intersection of the Dionysian and heroic spheres
C. Kerényi, *Dionysos*, 329

# Prologue

The god of everything that blossomed and breathed, Dionysus could surface in the moisture on a rose, bellow majestically through a raging bull, or imperceptibly shed old skin for new in the guise of a snake. He was the divine patron of the theater with an empty mask as his emblem, the god of a thousand faces who epitomized metamorphosis, and could transform mortals at will. Armed with ecstasy and madness, this paradoxical deity would smile at human determination and laugh at logic. In league with death as well as life, his realm reached beyond the grave to the murky waters of the netherworld.[1]

The Greeks of classical antiquity assumed that Dionysus had come to them from a distant land.[2] He was an enigmatic alien, who used might and magic to establish his cult in Hellas. He was a newcomer, a stranger, an exotic intruder who usurped his place among the twelve Olympians and became an incongruous thirteenth god.

By the age of Alexander the Great Dionysus had displaced the goddess Hestia and sat as a latecomer among the greater gods. He was now regarded primarily as the god of wine, although this was only one of the many roles he continued to play. Dionysus (Bacchus)[3] was often portrayed brandishing his distinctive drinking cup (*cantharus*) amidst a lush profusion of vine leaves and grapes. Crowned with ivy and laurel, he undertook long journeys across the world to distribute his joyous gift to mankind.

The gift he brought was himself, for Dionysus was not just the god of wine; he was the wine itself. The presence of Dionysus could be felt through the liquid fire of the grape, and this celestial potation enabled mortals to partake of his divinity. The drinker became an inspired recipient of Dionysus' benefits, and had the god within (*entheos*) in a literal sense.

The most welcome of all of wine's benefactions was its ability to distort reality and make human existence palatable.

> For filled with that good gift, suffering mankind forgets its grief; from it comes sleep; with it oblivion of the troubles of the day. There is no other medicine for misery. And when we pour libations to the gods,

we pour the god of wine himself that through his intercession man may
win the favor of heaven.

(*Ba.* 280–5)

Dionysus proffered himself through wine, and mortals revealed his personality (as well as their own) through drinking and drunkenness. A number
of the god's epithets describe his attractive attributes or praise the benefits
to be culled from his precious gift.[4] He is a relaxer of the mind, a healer
of sorrow, a dispeller of care, a provider of joy, a merrymaker, and a
lover of laughter. Other epithets refer to his less admirable characteristics,
and simultaneously serve as a reminder of the potential destructiveness of
his earthly agent. He is a disturber of the soul, a mind-breaker, a bestower
of envy, a dispenser of anger, a chaser of sleep, a noise-maker, and a liar.

The visible effects of wine unmasked the fundamental ambivalence of
the god and revealed a kindred quality in mortals. Wine exalted the spirit,
but it also had the capacity to unleash primordial impulses. Under its
influence a veneer of sophistication might disappear abruptly, and civility
could be transformed into uncontrollable rage. The wine god disclosed
reason's uneasy sway over emotion, and served as a chilling reminder of
bestiality at the core.

In Greek antiquity the Bacchic cult elicited images of maniacal women
and hysteria, rather than excellence (*arete*) and epic deeds. Thus, aspiring
heroes had a tendency to neglect this god – except, of course, in his
potable mode. This neglect was a dangerous path to take, however, since
those who withheld the libation from Dionysus or were remiss in acknowl-
edging his power and importance were likely to become the object of
divine retribution.

Dionysus was capable of altering the perceptions of mortals and ultimately maddening them.[5] Those afflicted would undergo profound changes
that manifested themselves in uncharacteristic behavior. The deity's prey
were sometimes left bearing a peculiar likeness to the god they had
offended, while remaining sublimely unaware that their impiety had stirred
the darker side of an omnipresent and invisible enemy.

This process is perhaps most eloquently portrayed in Euripides' *Bacchae*, in which Pentheus, the king of Thebes, becomes a sacrificial victim
of Dionysus.[6] Pentheus is described as an ambitious young man, who is
intent upon establishing his reputation as a ruler of singular distinction.
Although he possesses the requisite qualities for the attainment of heroic
stature – an impressive lineage, lofty aspirations, perseverance, and courage[7] – some unheroic attributes begin to emerge as the play unfolds.

Pentheus is plagued by insecurities. These breed a compulsion to be
successful at all times and a need to be universally honored for his unique
excellence. His obsession with the enhancement and defense of his own
reputation surfaces in grandiosity, self-righteous anger, and a curious

preoccupation with those capable of disclosing his deficiencies. Disproportionately cerebral, he is a victim of his own unintegrated personality.[8]

Pentheus attempts to suppress the irrational in himself, but is fascinated by its expression elsewhere. More adolescent than adult, he is fearful of unloosing the floodgates of his own emotions. Pentheus is old enough to be king, but remains unmarried and womanless, thereby ignoring the cardinal obligation to produce an heir to the throne. Immature and self-centered,[9] this beardless hero channels his abundant energies into activities that elevate his stature, but also contribute to his megalomaniacal tendencies.

The moments of triumph in the life of this troubled hero are overshadowed by his inability to achieve inner harmony or a sense of well-being. Sporadic outbursts of ungovernable anger belie the aura of stability and control he wishes to project. Pentheus forges ahead in his frenzied efforts to accumulate as many laurels as possible.

Dionysus raises the veil and reveals the king's true nature. The god arrives in Thebes disguised as a man with the intention of establishing his cult there. He perplexes and disturbs Pentheus by refusing to allow the king to impose his will upon him. Older and wiser men implore the king to alter his attitude toward Dionysus, but he disregards their advice and is determined to uproot the Dionysiac "disease." Pentheus is unable to accept the fact that he is powerless in the presence of this "man." Frustrated in his efforts to achieve control over Dionysus, Pentheus instead finds himself controlled by the god.

Dionysus, whose divine plan is to convert a reluctant suppliant into one of his own devotees and then sacrifice him, utilizes his adversary's intense curiosity to lure him into observing the cult in action. Pentheus is beguiled into wearing the garb of a female disciple of Dionysus. This act of robing provides the prelude to his victimization. The king then undergoes a metamorphosis which leaves him bearing a striking resemblance to the god to whom he has been condescending and impious. Unwittingly, Pentheus has become the antithesis of everything he intended to personify.

Spellbound by a deity who blurs distinctions and finds humor in the rigidity of the heroic outlook, Pentheus discovers that his categorical thinking is in utter disarray. The confused ruler completely surrenders to the Bacchic influence, and commingles notions that he had previously believed to be mutually exclusive: the Hellene and the Asiatic, the hunter and the hunted, male and female, man and beast, mortal and immortal.[10] Gradually, but ineluctably, Dionysus moves his quarry from the realm of the tangible to the domain of the chimerical. Perception becomes delusion, sanity is usurped by madness, and vitality gives way to extinction.

The very name Pentheus promises suffering (*penthos*) and suggests *pathos*,[11] but its significance is lost on its bearer. He is said to be experiencing the type of insanity that drugs cannot cure. This king, who has been promised glory reaching to the heavens by Dionysus, is persuaded to spy on the revels of the Dionysiac women from atop a tree. He is discovered, pulled to the ground, and torn to pieces by Agave, his own mother. Fleetingly, Pentheus becomes aware of what is happening to him, but this revelation occurs too late to be of any use to him.

As the *Bacchae* draws to a close, the king's severed head looms as a grotesque symbol of a man divided against himself.[12] It also serves as a grim reminder of the empty but smiling mask of Dionysus.[13]

a certain Dionysus
whoever
he
may
be
(*Ba.* 220)

# 1 The coming of age in Macedonia

## DIONYSUS IN THE ROYAL TOMBS

In 1977 the Greek archaeologist Manolis Andronicos began unearthing three ancient tombs at Vergina in Macedonia, two of which had miraculously escaped pillage.[1] When Andronicos removed the keystone from the vault at the back end of Tomb II, he gazed upon a repository of magnificent artifacts *in situ* from over 2,300 years ago. His discovery confirmed the suspicion of N. G. L. Hammond that Vergina was once Aegae, the ancestral capital city of Macedonia and the traditional burial ground for its rulers.[2]

The contents of Tomb II were particularly impressive. The sarcophagus located in the main chamber held a 24-pound gold chest with a Macedonian starburst (or sunburst) emblazoned on its cover.[3] Inside the chest was a golden oak wreath, representing the tree sacred to Zeus, complete with delicately wrought branches, oak leaves, and golden acorns. Beneath the wreath lay the cremated remains of a man in his mid-forties who had taken his last breath during the fourth century BC. Traces of the purple cloth that had covered him were still evident.

The tomb itself was constructed some time between 350–310 BC, and since Alexander III (the Great) had been entombed in Alexandria, there were only two Macedonian kings to whom these bones could be attributed. Andronicos, the discoverer of the tomb, and a number of historians, including Hammond, have argued that this is, in all likelihood, the tomb of Philip II (359–336), the father of Alexander the Great. Other scholars have suggested Philip Arrhidaeus, the half-brother of Alexander the Great who ruled as Philip III (323–317), as a more plausible candidate.[4] The absence of any identifying inscription prevents a final word on this matter, but in either case, the occupant was a blood relative and a contemporary of Alexander the Great.

The burnt bones of a young woman in her twenties were found wrapped in a gold and purple cloth placed in a smaller gold chest in the antechamber of Tomb II. Vestiges of a male teenager were uncovered in Tomb III. Tomb I, which had been denuded by grave robbers, contained the skeletal deposits of a woman, a man, and what may have been a newborn infant. These bones, and other human remains from the Royal Tombs at Vergina, continue to inspire speculation and impassioned controversy among researchers.[5] The identities of the occupants of these tombs will probably never be established conclusively.

Within the walls of the unpillaged tombs, however, there lurked another tenant, whose wraithlike presence is indisputable, striking, and ubiquitous: Dionysus. This god, who could appear as a subterranean (*chthonios*) deity cloaked in a black goatskin (*melanaigis*),[6] must have been at ease under the huge mound that crowned these burial vaults for over two millennia, for he was no stranger to death. Here, in the unlooted tombs at Vergina, Dionysus manifested himself as the god of wine. Tomb II contained an appreciable number and variety of drinking cups (see Appendix A). It also housed both large and small wine jars, a bucket to transport the sacred liquid, a mixing bowl, a spoon, a ladle, and a strainer – in short, all of the paraphernalia necessary for an epic drinking party other than the wine itself and the presence of a few live quaffers. The findings at Vergina are therefore consistent with Eugene N. Borza's assertion that "thus far, the archaeological evidence seems to support the notion that the Macedonian gentry was a hard-drinking lot." [7]

## MACEDONIAN DRINKING

> In their midst
> stand bowls
> brimming
> with
> wine
> (*Ba.* 221–2)

In a surviving fragment from his lost *On the Death of Alexander and Hephaestion*, Ephippus, an Olynthian scandal-monger who joined Alexander on his Asian expedition, characterizes the Macedonians as a people who "never understood how to drink in moderation."[8] Ephippus claims that they drank so much at the beginning of a feast that they were drunk by the time the first course was served. In Plato's *Gorgias*, one of the disputants, Polus, accuses Archelaus of usurping the Macedonian throne by hosting his rivals, getting them drunk, carrying them off in a wagon, and murdering them.[9] Such tales strain credulity, but corroborate the fact that the Macedonians were singled out as a people who drank excessively. Ancient Greeks diluted their wine with water – possibly for economy, but certainly to discourage intemperance.[10] Moderation was the hallmark of the civilized, while gulping was for the vulgar, and drunkenness was the way of the barbarian. The Greeks were highly critical of Macedonians, who, like barbarians, drank wine undiluted and in prodigious amounts.[11]

And the prototypical Macedonian drinker was Philip II, the father of Alexander the Great.

The Athenian orator Demosthenes and the historian Theopompus of Chios, both of whom knew King Philip II, provide us with graphic descriptions of his drinking. Demosthenes likens Philip to a sponge;[12] Theopompus claims that the Macedonian king not only got drunk on a daily basis, but was often in this same state when he rushed into battle.[13] Political and personal biases permeate these accounts, but there is no question that Philip's drinking was, as J. R. Hamilton claims, "notorious."[14] Philip gave protracted drinking parties, engaged in drinking bouts, and got drunk with predictable regularity.[15] His drinking seems to have followed the pattern of a reward cycle: great expenditures of energy on the battlefield were followed by raucous celebrations and the consumption of huge quantities of "uncut" wine.[16] Theopompus rightly characterized Philip, who was rumored to sleep with a gold drinking cup under his pillow, as a *philopotes*, a lover of drink.[17]

For most of his life this extraordinarily successful man appears to have been a rather genial drunk who accepted criticism, laughed at himself, and even modified his deportment when admonished. In one incident an aggrieved woman complained about one of Philip's decisions, and he asked to whom she appealed. She stated, with clear reference to his condition, that her appeal was to a sober Philip. The king quickly came to his senses, reconsidered the case, and decided in the woman's favor.[18] After his great victory at Chaeronea in 338 "Philip downed a large amount of unmixed wine and . . . paraded through the midst of his captives, jeering all the time at the misfortunes of the luckless men" (D.16.87.1). When the Athenian captive Demades shouted that Philip acted more like the Homeric anti-hero Thersites than Agamemnon, the king abandoned his revelry and freed Demades in reward for his courageous reprimand.

Philip's drinking prowess had its advantages. In a warrior society, where epic toping was a source of admiration and intemperance a virtue, the cavalier and extravagant way Philip carried on must have contributed to his personal mystique. He kept boon companions, comedians, and musicians close at hand for impromptu drinking parties, and seemed to favor those who drank as he did. Theopompus claimed that Philip spent most of his time with these men "because of their love of drinking and their vulgarity, and with them he used to hold deliberations on the most important matters."[19]

While it appears that some temperate drinkers with essential skills also became members of his court, they could easily become targets of the king's sardonic humor. For instance, Philip's abstemious general Antipater was once singled out in the king's ritualistic announcement of his intention to get drunk: "Now we must drink; for it is enough that Antipater is sober."[20] It is clear from this reference that his nondrinking companions were few.

Heavy drinking was also admired by some non-Macedonians, and in this respect Philip's virtuosity was to his advantage. Theopompus claimed that Philip won over most Thessalians "by parties rather than by presents."[21] Catering to those with an appetite for wine similar to his own, Philip used his great capacity as an instrument of diplomacy. There must have been difficult moments, however, for those who failed to share his gargantuan appetite for drink at all hours. One might imagine the look of stoic resignation on the faces of Athenian envoys bracing for free-flowing wine at the crack of dawn.[22]

It is not surprising that Philip's son attempted to emulate the royal tippler *par excellence*. When holding his own at a drinking party (symposium), Alexander's drinking probably elicited almost as much admiration from his men as his heroics on the battlefield. It also served to confirm in an odd but significant way that this boy was his father's son and a worthy successor. It is ironic that Alexander, who would see so little of Philip during his boyhood and who was determined to distinguish himself from him, would in this and a multitude of other ways come to replicate so many of his father's attitudes and actions.

## PHILIP AND ALEXANDER

Brilliant men rarely produce brilliant sons, and Alexander was fearful at an early age that the shadow cast by his father would eclipse his own ambitions.[23] He was incapable of sharing in Philip's glory, and became determined from the outset to make his own mark. His father was said to be "a man without precedent in Europe."[24] In war and peace, battles and celebrations, negotiations and philandering, Philip exhibited an irrepressible exuberance and a unique personality. These qualities, coupled with his intelligence and courage, and his succession of unparalleled victories on the battlefield, made him a folk hero among Macedonians. He was the savior of an imperiled country, a valiant warrior, second to none in fighting and drinking, and the idol of his battle-scarred veterans.[25] Alexander would have to demonstrate that he, too, was a man of singular distinction. Furthermore, he had to show the world that he was not merely the equal of, but actually superior to, his famous father.

Philip's early attitude toward Alexander offers every indication of paternal pride, affection, and a personal commitment to the boy's future. Plutarch, our main source for Alexander's youth, relates a story probably told many times over by Alexander himself.[26] When Alexander was nine or so,[27] his father was inspecting a Thessalian horse being offered for sale. This black stallion, with either a white patch on his forehead or an ox-head brand that earned him the name Bucephalas ("ox-head")",[28] proved to be unmanageable, and Philip ordered him to be taken away.

"What a horse they are losing, and all because they don't know how to handle him, or dare not try!" (P.6.2), declared Alexander. Philip asked his son if he found fault with his elders. Did he think he knew more than they? Could he handle a horse better? Alexander was quick to respond that at least he could handle this one better. Then Philip wanted to know if Alexander would be willing to set a value on his impertinent claim. Without hesitation, Alexander answered that he would pay the full price of the horse if he were proven to be wrong. This pronouncement drew a chorus of laughter. The selling price of the horse was said to be thirteen talents,[29] an astronomical sum, and no one expected young Alexander to succeed where accomplished horsemen had failed. Nevertheless, his father offered him the opportunity to prove his claim.

> They are difficult horses for mortal men to manage . . .
> all except Achilleus [Achilles]
> (*Il.* 10.402–4)

Alexander began by turning the head of Bucephalas toward the sun. With the perceptivity so characteristic of his later behavior on the battle-field, he had noticed that the horse shied away from his own shadow, and this simple maneuver eliminated an unsettling distraction. Alexander calmed the horse and trotted alongside him until the proper moment, when he gingerly leaped upon his back. Philip and his companions held their breath "until they saw Alexander reach the end of his gallop, turn in full control, and ride back triumphant and exulting in his success. Thereupon the rest of the company broke into loud applause, while his father, we are told, actually wept for joy, and when Alexander had dismounted, he kissed him and said, 'My boy, you must find a kingdom big enough for your ambitions. Macedonia is too small for you' " (P.6.8).

Demaratus of Corinth, a diplomat, purchased the horse and presented him as a gift to Alexander. Until Bucephalas was 30 years old he carried his master into some of Alexander's most celebrated battles. The king's fondness for this animal was such that later in life, on the banks of the Jhelum River in modern Pakistan, he honored his horse by founding the city of Bucephala in his memory.[30]

> the finest of all horses beneath the sun
> (*Il.* 5.266–7)

Philip must have appeared impressive and admirable to his young son on the one hand, yet imperious and intimidating on the other. The king's biting humor and jovial cynicism may have kept Alexander, as it had so many others, tentative and cautious when in his father's presence. A clue to the relationship between father and son is found in an anecdote recorded by Plutarch, who tells us that Alexander complained about Philip's siring of children by women other than the boy's mother. His quick-witted father ignored the accusation and adroitly transferred the problem to his son. "Well then, if you have many competitors for the kingdom, prove yourself honourable and good, so that you may obtain the kingdom not because of me, but because of yourself," he exclaimed.[31]

> And Peleus the aged was telling his own son Achilleus
> to be always best in battle
> and pre-eminent
> beyond
> all
> others
> (*Il*. 11.783–4)

From an early age Alexander was intensely concerned with the way in which he appeared to other people. Plutarch says he "valued his good name more than his life or his crown" (42.4), and "his passionate desire for fame implanted in him a pride and a grandeur of vision which went far beyond his years" (4.8). Arrian, the most authoritative of Alexander sources,[32] says that "he was fearfully mastered by love of fame" (7.2.2). He also makes the telling observation that "it was praise alone for which he was absolutely insatiate" (7.28.1). Seeking confirmation of his uniqueness from others, Alexander did little to discourage flatterers.

Philip had also been preoccupied with image and reputation, consciously striving to be above and beyond other men. His competitive nature exemplified the ethos of the Olympics: to do something well and conspicuously.[33] Philip's flair for singularity and predilection for challenge was translated into a staggering succession of victories. Demosthenes tells us that Philip was willing to sacrifice anything and everything in order to achieve honor and glory.[34] Philip's influence on Alexander in this respect is undeniable.

When Alexander heard that his father had taken an important city or enjoyed some other special triumph, he reacted with dismay rather than elation. He is said to have complained to friends that the king would preempt them in everything, and expressed the fear that his own generation would be deprived of a chance to show the world anything noteworthy: "And so every success that was gained by Macedonia inspired in Alexander the dread that another opportunity for action had been squandered on his father. He had no desire to inherit a kingdom which offered him riches, luxuries and the pleasures of the senses: his choice was a life of struggle, of wars, and of unrelenting ambition" (P.5.4–6).[35]

It was no small task to become great when measured against Philip of Macedon. Alexander, Arrian tells us, offered his own summary of Philip's accomplishments in a speech to his Macedonian soldiers at Opis in 324 BC:

> First of all, I shall begin my speech with Philip, my father, as is only fair. Philip took you over when you were helpless vagabonds, mostly clothed in skins, feeding a few animals on the mountains and engaged in their defence in unsuccessful fighting with Illyrians, Triballians and the neighbouring Thracians. He gave you cloaks to wear instead of

skins, he brought you down from the mountains to the plains; he made you a match in battle for the barbarians on your borders. . . . He made you city dwellers and established the order that comes from good laws and customs. . . . He annexed the greater part of Thrace to Macedonia . . . opened up the country to trade . . . made you the rulers of the Thessalians . . . gave you access into Greece. . . . instead of our paying tribute to the Athenians and taking orders from the Thebans . . . we . . . gave them security. He [gained] recognition as leader with full powers over the whole of the rest of Greece in the expedition against the Persians.[36]

(7.9.2–5)

Arrian's text relates that after paying the respects required by the circumstances, Alexander went on to minimize the significance of his father's contributions by contrasting them with his own. "These services which my father rendered you, great as they are when considered by themselves alone, are actually small in comparison with our own." He then offered a recitation of his achievements and the benefits he had conferred upon his troops (7.9.6–10.7).

Alexander was right. His conquests dwarfed those of his father. However, during his early years at Pella he could not have foreseen that he would enjoy such an astounding career, and the insecurities engendered during this difficult period echoed throughout his entire life. Long after Philip's death Alexander continued to be disturbed when people compared him unfavorably with his father. Determined to be seen as the better of the two, Alexander seized every opportunity to go one step beyond Philip.

In his attempts to surpass his father, however, he also imitated him. For instance, while Philip named Philippi and Philippopolis (Plovdiv) after himself, Alexander founded at least twenty-five (perhaps more than seventy) cities in his own name.[37] Philip was the first Macedonian king to reach the Danube, but Alexander was the first to cross it. Philip transferred populations throughout greater Macedonia. Alexander contemplated massive transfers between Europe and Asia. Philip punished Thebes. Alexander destroyed it. Philip dispatched a vanguard across the Hellespont, but Alexander crossed into Asia and conquered the Persian Empire. And while Philip only flirted with deification, Alexander arranged to have divine cult offered to him during his lifetime.

> some day
> let them say of him
> He is better
> by far
> than
> his
> father
> (*Il.* 6.479)

## OLYMPIAS AND ALEXANDER

Alexander followed in Philip's footsteps with such spectacular success that he escaped the anonymity with which children of famous parents are ordinarily burdened. The fact that he did not stand in his father's shadow, however, was an accomplishment in itself, due in no small part to the concerted efforts of his determined mother, Olympias.[38] This iron-willed woman did everything in her power to protect her son's interests and advance his career. She helped to instill in the boy the conviction that he would become an overwhelming success in his own right. The relationship between Alexander and his mother was an important, and to this day still is a mysterious, aspect of his life.

Sir William Tarn once wrote that Alexander "never cared for any woman except his terrible mother."[39] There is little doubt that she was one of the dominant influences in his early life. Even after Alexander had succeeded Philip, their relationship was always marked by affection and loyalty. When Alexander crossed the Hellespont to Asia in 334, Olympias remained in Europe as his redoubtable supporter. Throughout the vagaries of his monumental conquests and ultimate apotheosis (324), Alexander's profound dedication to his mother never wavered. Besieged by requests from his viceroy in Macedonia to curb her interfering and obstreperous ways, Alexander is said to have remarked "that Antipater did not understand that one tear shed by [my] mother would wipe out ten thousand letters such as this" (P.39.13).

While on the fringes of the known world, Alexander expressed a thought he had apparently been mulling over for some time: his mother's deification. He told close friends that "the greatest reward for my efforts and my labours will be if my mother Olympias be granted immortality on her departure from life" (C.9.6.26).

> Achilleus who was born of an immortal mother
> (*Il.* 10.404)

Most of Olympias' male contemporaries, however, found her to be overbearing. The Athenian orator Hyperides indicates that this could be true even at a distance. For instance, she wrote letters denouncing the Athenians for offering to make impressive enhancements to a temple at Dodona in her native Epirus. According to Hyperides, Olympias, a member of the royal Molossian family of Epirus, said in one letter: "This Molossian land in which the temple is, is mine, and it is not for you Athenians to lay a finger on a stone in that temple."[40] Her hectoring nettled Hyperides, and he made the observation that Olympias had donated a votive cup to the statue of a goddess in Athens, and that, after all, the Athenians had been commanded to undertake the renovations in question by Zeus himself through his oracle at Dodona. "And is Olympias, forsooth, to be allowed to adorn our temples, while we are not permitted to adorn those in Dodona even when the god himself has told us to do it?" he asked.[41]

Even Alexander's devotion was occasionally strained to its limits, and as king he found it necessary to reprove Olympias when her words or actions were incompatible with his designs. On one occasion he is said to have asserted that his mother was charging an awfully high rent for those few months she had lodged him during her pregnancy.[42]

It should be noted that Alexander's mother's name was not always Olympias. Justin's rendition of the events following Philip's assassination has Olympias consecrating the assailant's sword to Apollo "under the name of Myrtale, which was Olympias' own name when a child" (9.7.13). Grace Macurdy suggests that Olympias adopted the name at the urging of her husband Philip because their son's birth coincided so auspiciously with the victory of Philip's horse at the Olympic games in 356.[43] Nonetheless, we know for certain that she was the orphaned daughter of Neoptolemus, the late king of Epirus. After the death of Olympias' father, her uncle Arybbas assumed the throne and she became his ward.[44] As a royal princess she proved to be a valuable pawn in the political game of marriage.

Plutarch tells us that Philip fell in love with Olympias after their initiation into an ancient mystery cult on the island of Samothrace in the northern Aegean.[45] Philip arranged for a betrothal soon after their initial encounter. This seems to have occurred in the mid-to-late 360s, when Philip was no more than 20 and Olympias barely past pubescence. Their marriage took place several years later, probably in 357, when Olympias was 18 or so and Philip in his mid-twenties.

The cult into which Philip and Olympias were initiated was linked with the god Dionysus.[46] Olympias, however, apparently had a previous connection with Dionysus in Epirus, for as soon as the young bride arrived in Macedonia she was eager to instruct other Bacchantes in the art of snake-handling.[47] This skill firmly established Olympias' reputation among local Dionysiac enthusiasts. She led private bands of women in revelry, and may have become an official priestess in the god's public cult.[48]

Olympias was a proud Molossian whose ancestry could be traced to Achilles, the legendary hero of the Trojan War.[49] Neoptolemus, the son of Achilles, chose Andromache, the widow of Hector, as his prize after the fall of Troy. Their union produced Molossus, the founder of the royal dynasty in Epirus. Olympias' blood lines were also said to run to Helenus, a son of the Trojan king Priam.[50] Thus, she was able to claim the distinction of a lineage that included both Achilles and, at least indirectly, Hector, the two great adversaries of the Trojan War.

Alexander's belief that he was a descendant of Achilles through his mother had a profound effect on his attitude toward himself.[51] Thetis, the divine mother of Achilles, had bathed her son in the River Styx with the intention of making him immortal. According to legend, her grip shielded his heel from the sacred waters and the boy remained mortal after all. In a similar way, the emotional grip of Olympias may have contributed to the vulnerability of her own brilliant son.

## THE DIONYSIAC CULT IN MACEDONIA

Alexander's parents, both of whom were formidable influences in his life, each enjoyed a special relationship with the god Dionysus. Philip took pride in his drinking prowess, and Olympias showed uninhibited devotion to her god. As a young man Alexander seems to have been contemptuous of his father's excessive drinking, but it was a practice he would emulate later in life. And while he apparently raised no serious objections to his mother's zealousness as a Bacchante, the young Alexander was more interested in heroes such as Achilles and Heracles. As we shall see, Alexander the king would observe only minimal obligations toward Dionysus, and occasionally proved remiss even in that respect.

> Go worship your Bacchus
> but do not wipe
> your madness
> off
> on me
> (*Ba.* 343–4)

This was a curious trait for a ruler in whose realm Dionysus was exceptionally popular.[52] Admittedly, the god was commonly thought of in relation to the women of Macedonia, but he was also a favorite among Alexander's troops, who had learned to appreciate his rich bounty through rural celebrations.[53] Perhaps at the urging of Olympias, Philip had increased the god's representation on his coinage, and even added a *cantharus*, the cup of Dionysus, to the customary image of Heracles.[54] Dionysus was also said to be found among ancestors in the royal family tree.[55] The worship of Bacchus, together with other traditional rites observed by the ruling Argead dynasty, formed the nucleus of the king's cultic practices.[56] The influence of Dionysus at the highest levels of society in ancient Macedonia has become evident through recent archaeological finds in northern Greece, and his imposing presence in the royal tombs at Vergina (see Appendix A) offers eloquent testimony to his authority in this region.

"I am Dionysus, the son of Zeus . . . . My mother was . . . Semele," the deity announces in Euripides' *Bacchae* (1–3). In Greek mythology Semele, pregnant with Dionysus, is consumed in flames when Zeus is manipulated by his wife Hera into appearing before his lover in all of his unbearable majesty. In the standard version, Zeus snatches the fetus from Semele's burnt body and houses the prematurely born Dionysus in his own thigh until the divine child can be born again at full term. He survives this unusual gestation unscathed, and later, upon learning that his mother had disappeared into the underworld, retrieves her and establishes her on Mount Olympus.

Dionysus can be found in the company of loyal women throughout his mythological career. As a child he is given over to Ino, the sister of Semele, who nurses and guards him. Ino and her husband Athamas raise Dionysus as a girl in order to disguise and protect him from Hera. Irate over her consort's infidelity with Semele, Hera maddens the god's adoptive parents, who then murder their own children. Zeus intervenes, however, rescues Dionysus from the carnage by turning him into a wild goat, and has Hermes shuttle him off to Asia, where the young god enjoys sanctuary among the nymphs of Nysa. Eventually Hera manages to afflict Dionysus with madness, and the god, in turn, displays a proclivity for driving mortals insane.

Plutarch says it is apparent that in Macedonia "from very ancient times all the women . . . [were] initiates of the Orphic religion and of the orgiastic rites of Dionysus" (2.7). The observances in Macedonia, he claims, were extravagant and superstitious, like those practiced in Thrace. Euripides wrote the *Bacchae* in Macedonia (*c.* 407–6), and may well have been influenced by what he had witnessed there about a half-century before Olympias' arrival.[57] The following excerpts from the play describe the physical appearance of the rituals associated with the Bacchantes.

A startled herdsman relates what he saw:

> First they let their hair fall loose, down over their shoulders, and those whose straps had slipped fastened their skins of fawn with writhing snakes that licked their cheeks. Breasts swollen with milk, new mothers who had left their babies behind at home nestled gazelles and young wolves in their arms, suckling them. Then they crowned their hair with leaves, ivy and oak and flowering bryony. One woman struck her thyrsus [staff] against a rock and a fountain of cool water came bubbling up. Another drove her fennel in the ground, and where it struck the earth, at the touch of god, a spring of wine poured out.
>
> (695–707)

Pastoral women are transformed into revelers possessed by a divine madness (maenads) from whom the herdsmen flee in order to avoid "being torn to pieces" (734). These maniacal women then attack the herdsmen's cattle with their bare hands:

> Unarmed, they swooped down upon the herds of cattle grazing there on the green of the meadow. And then you could have seen a single woman with bare hands tear a fat calf, still bellowing with fright, in two, while others clawed the heifers to pieces. There were ribs and cloven hooves scattered everywhere, and scraps smeared with blood hung from the fir trees. And bulls, their raging fury gathered in their

horns, lowered their heads to charge, then fell, stumbling to the earth, pulled down by hordes of women and stripped of flesh and skin more quickly, sire, than you [Pentheus] could blink your royal eyes.

(735–47)[58]

The promise of life after death was one of the great attractions of the cult,[59] and a prototype for resurrection was to be found in one version of the story of the god himself. The infant Dionysus, it was said, was slain by Titans, who proceeded to cook his flesh. The roast was already under way when Zeus appeared and burned the assailants to a crisp. Dionysus was born again after his limbs were reassembled, and mankind, we are told, arose from the smoking residue of Titans.[60] Mortals were warned to purge the Titanic and exalt the Dionysiac in themselves.

> [Dionysus] desires his honor
> from all mankind
> He wants
> no one
> excluded
> from his
> worship
> (*Ba.* 208–9)

Olympias' intense participation in the Dionysiac *orgia*, as well as her penchant to excel in the more esoteric aspects of the cult, is mentioned by Plutarch.[61] Sexual encounters with men may have characterized some Dionysiac festivals, but in the *Bacchae* no such activity is recorded. Macedonian women may have formed their own societies and restricted ecstatic possession and the higher rites to initiates of their own sex.[62] Euripides implies that virtuous women, each insulated by her own moral fiber, could choose to remain chaste despite the fundamental amorality of the cult.[63] All things considered, it seems unlikely that Olympias would have engaged in promiscuity through worship. This would have endangered her status and compromised Alexander's legitimacy. There is no evidence that links Olympias with any man other than Philip.

Despite the impressive number of women who appear in the tales of Dionysus, sexual encounters are rare for him, and fatherhood is not an attribute of his character. The god's sexual attitudes, in stark contrast to those of Zeus, are neither menacing nor predatory toward women. Instead, Dionysus, who is androgynous by nature, offers a divine archetype for those who would be both feminine and powerful.[64]

## OLYMPIAS, PHILIP, AND ALEXANDER

In the interval between their first meeting and his marriage to Olympias, Philip seems to have married three other wives, each of whom happened to suit a particular political purpose at home or abroad. According to Satyrus, a Greek biographer, Philip first married Audata (*c.* 359), the daughter of a troublesome Illyrian king on Macedon's northwestern frontier.[65] His subsequent marriage to Phila (*c.* 358), a Macedonian princess from Elimiotis, was perhaps arranged to help him consolidate affairs within his own realm. Satyrus goes on to report that Philip, hoping to establish his claim to the Thessalian nation, also married Philinna of Larisa (*c.* 358).[66]

Philip's marriage to Olympias, the fourth by this count, may also have been inspired more by opportunity than romance. Satyrus is explicit in emphasizing the political nature of the match.[67] It enabled Philip to avoid entanglement on Macedon's southwestern frontier and to concentrate his efforts on his drive eastward.

Each new wedding also occasioned fresh hopes for a son and successor.[68] Audata had given birth to a daughter, Cynane, and Phila died childless. Philinna gave birth to a son, Philip Arrhidaeus, but he was "half-witted."[69] Plutarch tells us that "as a boy he had shown an attractive disposition and displayed much promise, but Olympias was believed to have given him drugs which impaired the functions of his body and irreparably injured his brain" (77.8). While Olympias may be the victim of someone's slander here, there is no question that she was capable of the act. It was certainly on her order that Philip Arrhidaeus was executed in 317.[70]

The status of a royal wife in the women's quarters at Pella, the Macedonian capital, was contingent upon the production of children, preferably male. Olympias lost no time in establishing her ascendant position among Philip's other wives. Alexander was born within a year (*c.* 20 July 356),[71] and his sister Cleopatra appeared soon afterwards (*c.* 355).[72] Healthy, intelligent, and attractive, Alexander was treated by his father and the court as the heir to the throne perhaps from birth, and his high standing assured his mother a preeminent role among the royal wives.[73]

Subsequent marriages to Nicesipolis of Thessaly (*c.* 353) and Meda, a Danubian princess (*c.* 339), probably mirrored Philip's interests in those areas.[74] Fortunately, from Olympias' point of view, no male child seems to have survived from these marriages, or at least none appeared before Alexander reached maturity. Olympias protected her son's interests with unfaltering vigilance and exercised influence on his behalf whenever the opportunity presented itself.

Despite the absence of competitors with Alexander for the position of heir, Olympias' position at the Macedonian court would remain precarious until her son became king. During Alexander's youth she influenced his early schooling by providing a number of tutors from either Epirus or a region under Molossian influence. The most important of these was Leonidas, a kinsman of Olympias.[75] Alexander's bittersweet recollections of Leonidas suggest that this mentor may have been just as demanding and austere as his namesake, who was famous for sacrificing himself and his fellow Spartans at Thermopylae in 480. For instance, in southern Asia Minor in 334, Alexander, then in his early twenties, was offered the services of some of the most accomplished chefs of that region. The king's response "was that he did not need them, because his tutor Leonidas had provided him with better cooks than these, that is a night march to prepare him for breakfast, and a light breakfast to give him an appetite for supper. 'This same Leonidas . . . would often come and open my chests of bedding and clothes, to see whether my mother had not hidden some luxury inside' " (P.22.8–10).[76] Olympias seems to have recommended a harsh taskmaster who treated the boy as if he were a little man, and Alexander's tutelage under Leonidas may have had a profound effect on him in later years.

> His own mother
> like a priestess
> with her
> victim
> (*Ba.* 1114)

The self-denial, perseverance, and astounding feats of endurance exhibited by Alexander in adulthood were surely developed during this time in an atmosphere of scrutiny and testing, further testing, and then more testing. Long after Alexander had advanced beyond formal instruction, he continued to test himself, and often proved to be his own most rigorous critic.

Callisthenes, Alexander's court historian, is said to have boasted on one occasion that Alexander's share in divinity (see Chapters 3–4) did not depend on Olympias' invention about her son's birth, but rather on his own account of the conqueror's exploits.[77] This seems to confirm the assertion that Olympias claimed the cooperation of a divine partner in Alexander's conception.[78] When her son left for Asia, Olympias is said to have reminded him to be worthy of his divine parentage.[79]

The magnitude of Alexander's conquests and the exceptional demands he made upon himself are best understood in light of the fierce competitiveness that characterized his early years. By example and injunction his parents encouraged the boy to entertain lofty expectations of himself. Arrian's perceptive observations on Alexander's career reflect this telling influence:

> [N]one of Alexander's plans were small and petty . . . no matter what he had already conquered, he would not have stopped there quietly, not even if he had added Europe to Asia and the Britannic Islands to Europe, but that he would always have searched far beyond for something unknown, in competition with himself in default of any other rival.

> (7.1.4)

To take Arrian a step further, the dominant influences of Alexander's early life – his incredibly successful father and overly demanding mother – seem to have fostered insecurities that often left him in competition with himself, regardless of whether an external challenge actually existed.

## THE GARDENS OF MIDAS (343–340 BC)

"Philip had noticed that his son was self-willed, and that while it was very difficult to influence him by force, he could easily be guided toward his duty by an appeal to reason, and he therefore made a point of trying to persuade the boy rather than giving him orders" (P.7.1). Philip may have had this in mind when, after Alexander had turned thirteen in 343, Aristotle was selected as his tutor. The authority and encyclopaedic knowledge of the philosopher, it was hoped, might supply Alexander with the "rudder's guidance and the curb's restraint"[80] required at such a restless age (P.7.2).

Aristotle was in his early forties at the time and had not yet written the great works that are the basis of his reputation today.[81] Nevertheless, he had been an outstanding student at Plato's Academy, and had undoubtedly by this time attained some recognition for his intellectual abilities. Philip's selection, however, may also have involved considerations other than academic credentials. Aristotle's father Nicomachus had been the family physician to Amyntas III, Philip's father, and so Aristotle and Philip may have been boyhood companions at the Macedonian court.

During the ensuing years, while Aristotle was studying in Athens, Philip destroyed the young philosopher's birthplace, Stagira, while on his march eastward. However, the Macedonian king pledged a reconstruction of the city and restoration of its citizenry if Aristotle would return to Pella to instruct Alexander.[82] His offer, undoubtedly sweetened with handsome emoluments, was accepted without hesitation.

Aristotle's recent residency in Asia Minor may have been another factor in Philip's choice. In 347, shortly before his death, Plato had chosen his own nephew instead of Aristotle to succeed him as head of the Academy. Aristotle, perhaps seeing himself as a victim of nepotism, accepted a position at the court of Hermias of Atarneus in the Troad and ultimately became his son-in-law.[83] This ruler controlled territory on the coast of Asia Minor that could be of great strategic importance during Philip's contemplated invasion of the Persian Empire.[84]

Philip's grand enterprise certainly required as much support as he could marshal from Asia, and Aristotle may have served as a liaison of sorts between the two rulers.[85] Indeed, he may have been instrumental in the negotiation of an agreement involving the use of this Anatolian territory as a bridgehead for the Macedonian invasion.[86] This possibility ended abruptly in 341, however, when Hermias was captured by agents of the Persian king and crucified in Susa for his treasonous correspondence with

Philip.[87] The outcome for Aristotle was more favorable. By this time he had begun to orchestrate Alexander's education in Macedonia.

Philip settled Aristotle and his students at Mieza,[88] a quiet retreat with grottoes and shady walks in the eastern foothills of the Bermium mountain range, away from the clamor and intrigue of the Macedonian court. This locale, sometimes called the Precinct of the Nymphs, was situated in an area referred to as the Gardens of Midas. It included the entire wine-growing region surrounding modern Naoussa, where the legendary king Midas was supposed to have mixed wine with sacred water in order to capture Silenus and learn the secret of life from him. In Aristotle's rendition of the tale, which is preserved in a fragment, an ensnared Silenus utters the uninspiring revelation that life is full of grief and birth a misfortune.[89] In a later and more imaginative version, the hoodwinked Silenus is ransomed by Dionysus, who promises an unthinking Midas that everything he touches will turn to gold.

Plutarch informs us that Alexander greatly admired Aristotle and grew closer to him than to his own father, "for the one, he used to say, had given him the gift of life, but the other had taught him how to live well" (8.4). One can only imagine Alexander's exhilaration while sitting at the feet of a scholar whose wide interests matched his own boundless curiosity. A physician's son, Aristotle was trained in medicine and evidently passed these skills on to his most famous pupil. Later in life Alexander was known to tend to his soldiers' wounds, prescribe cures for friends, and advise doctors.[90] Aristotle also seems to have lectured on zoology and botany at Mieza, and Alexander maintained a lifelong interest in these subjects. The spirit of inquiry encouraged by Aristotle suited Alexander's pragmatic cast of mind. Be wary of assumptions, Aristotle cautioned. Treat each situation as unique, and draw conclusions only after all of the evidence has been assembled and analyzed. Alexander would ultimately use this training, along with his gift for spontaneity, to accomplish one incredible military victory after another.

The execution of Hermias occurred while Alexander was still in Aristotle's company at Mieza. It inspired the philosopher to compose a "Hymn to Virtue," in which he celebrated the *arete* (excellence) evidenced in his father-in-law's life. Although tortured, Hermias refused to reveal anything that might have been damaging to others, and is said to have asked that his friends be told that he had done nothing to disgrace philosophy. Aristotle paid tribute to this exceptional virtue by placing Hermias in the company of heroes whose *arete* was universally recognized: Ajax, Heracles, the Dioscuri (Castor and Polydeuces), and Achilles.

> Arete, you whom the mortal race wins by much toil,
> the fairest prey in life,
> for the beauty of your form, maiden,
> it is an enviable lot in Hellas both to die

and to endure toils violent and unceasing.
On such fruits do you set the mind:
equal to the Immortals, better than gold,
and noble ancestors and languid-eyed sleep.
For your sake Heracles, the son of Zeus,
and Leda's youths [Castor and Polydeuces]
endured much in their deeds
hunting after your power.
Through longing [*pothos*] for you, Achilles and Ajax
came to the house of Hades.
Because of the gracious beauty of your form the nursling
[Hermias] of Atarneus forsook the sun's rays.
Therefore the Muses will exalt him, famous in song for
his deeds and immortal.[91]

## HEROIC MODELS

Aristotle's reference to Achilles was likely to draw special attention from Alexander, who believed that this hero's blood ran through his own veins. Alexander intended to live up to his ancestor's reputation, and encouraged comparisons between himself and his legendary forebear. In the days before Mieza, a self-styled pedagogue named Lysimachus ingratiated himself with Alexander by addressing the boy as Achilles and Philip as Peleus, the hero's mortal father, and referring to himself as Phoenix, Achilles' tutor.[92] Lysimachus would later accompany Alexander on his expedition to Asia, and, as king, Alexander would risk his own life to save this aging flatterer who called him Achilles.[93]

Homer's epic was a source of great inspiration to Alexander. As noted in the Preface, in Asia he is said to have slept with a copy of the *Iliad* (personally annotated by Aristotle) underneath his pillow.[94] After discovering a precious casket among the Persian king's belongings that had been part of the spoils from an important victory, Alexander asked the opinions of his friends concerning what use should be made of it.[95] He listened attentively to every suggestion made, but in the end decided to deposit his copy of Homer's masterpiece in the casket, thus designating it as his most valuable possession. The *Iliad* was Alexander's guide to the art of war, and its hero, Achilles, his exemplar of heroic virtue.[96]

Arrian tells us of an emulative "rivalry" with Achilles that lasted a lifetime.[97] Echoes of the Homeric hero may be heard throughout Alexander's career: at the crossing of the Hellespont, on the plains of Troy, in his style of warfare, and in his reaction to the death of a beloved friend. The mythicized career of Achilles and the "lives" of other heroes provided models for the way in which Alexander wished to be remembered. His seemingly impossible challenge was to live a life that equalled or surpassed their fictionalized patterns of behavior.

Achilles, the most influential of Alexander's mythological role models, is attractive, magnanimous, honest, and loyal. Ordinarily tactful, courteous, and considerate, he is also religious, strong, swift, and courageous, a noble warrior whose *arete* is matchless. Achilles chooses a glorious early death over a long but uneventful life.

Though magnificent on the battlefield and undaunted in the face of death, Achilles is less able to cope with situations that he cannot resolve by violence.[98] This becomes most evident when his reputation appears threatened, and he is unable to resolve the situation through force. Agamemnon's unjust appropriation of the woman Briseis, Achilles' war prize, drives the offended hero to self-righteous distraction. His ungovernable anger becomes the focus of the *Iliad*. He bristles at criticism, resents authority, and even broods over the fate he has chosen for himself. When emotion clouds his judgment, Achilles becomes the "most terrifying of all men" (*Il.* 1.146), willing to take on no less an opponent than Apollo in human guise. This noble warrior is a great hero whose fear of disgrace overshadows mere death. The fact that he is largely responsible for his own destruction is obscured by his success and the intensity of his commitment.

> the proud heart
> feels not terror
> nor turns to run
> and it
> is
> his own courage
> that
> kills
> him
> (*Il.* 12.45–6)

It is only in the underworld, after experiencing the tedium of eternity, that Achilles questions the wisdom of the choice he has made.[99]

The inglorious monotony of death could be overcome, however, and it was Heracles, another of Alexander's forebears, who had shown how it might be accomplished. This intrepid hero, cited by Aristotle in his "Hymn to Virtue," became a god. He accomplished this through *arete* and labors bravely endured, and thereby showed that a seat on Mount Olympus could be the reward for one with a sacred lineage who performed superhuman acts with regularity. Heracles became what Pindar called a *heros theos*, who bridged the gap between hero and god.[100] Heracles was worshipped throughout Macedonia because of his special relationship with the ruling family.

The Macedonian royal family claimed descent from the Temenid kings of Argos, who traced their origins to Heracles.[101] King Alexander worshiped his ancestor as both a hero and a god. He is said to have taken a miniature statue of Heracles on his great expedition, where it graced the royal table without unduly overshadowing the king.[102] Heracles was supposed to have traveled beyond the earth's encircling Ocean in the west, and established the Pillars of Heracles at Gibraltar *en route*. At the eastern limits of his own odyssey, Alexander ordered the construction of a dozen colossal towers in honor of the Twelve Immortals (see Chapter 4). Thus, he bequeathed a splendid counterpart to the weighty mementos deposited by Heracles at the other end of the world.

> If I could only
> be called
> son
> to Zeus.
> (*Il.* 13.825–6)

The god Dionysus was also counted among the ancestors of Macedonian kings, but his name is absent from Aristotle's honor roll of the particularly virtuous. This omission is hardly surprising. Although there are sporadic traces of heroism in the mythological life of Dionysus – he travels extensively and boasts Triumph as an epithet – his image is expressly unheroic in attitude and action, and his cult became a refuge for those without honorable lineage or impressive deeds. Arrian has Alexander tell his own men, rather apologetically, "Even Dionysus, a more delicate god than Heracles, had not a few labours to perform" (5.26.5).

The most elaborate reference to Dionysus in the *Iliad*, where he appears marginally and is ignored by the great warriors, describes him as a child shivering with terror who retreats from an enemy by diving into the surf, where Thetis clutches him to her bosom (*Il.* 6.135–7). What a far cry he was from the newborn Heracles, who strangled serpents in his crib; and Achilles, who slew lions at the age of 6. Skittish and unpredictable, Dionysus was a god to be cajoled and enjoyed, especially in his liquid semblance, and not one to be taken all that seriously, at least by men of heroic disposition.

> But let the truth be told
> there is
> no god greater
> than
> Dionysus
> (*Ba.* 776–7)

## REGENT (340 BC)

Alexander's formal schooling came to an end in 340, when he was 16.[103] At that time Philip's drive eastward had brought him to the Hellespont, the gateway to Asia. He was there to punish Byzantium and Perinthus for their refusal to assist him in a campaign against the Athenian settlements along the Thracian coast. Finding himself too far removed from Pella to govern effectively, Philip decided to place Alexander in charge of the Royal Seal, and so appointed him regent. This first opportunity to act as a ruler was a testament to the time and effort Philip had spent on his son's grooming, and Alexander eagerly accepted the responsibility.

In Philip's absence the Maedi, a belligerent Thracian tribe, rebelled against Macedonian overlordship.[104] Alexander promptly led a punitive expedition to the Upper Strymon, where he subdued the rebels, captured their center of operations, and reestablished it as a Macedonian colony. He then called it Alexandropolis in imitation of a similar situation two years earlier when his father had founded Philippopolis in Thrace. This was the first city Alexander named after himself, and it would not be the last.

> I . . . shall lie still
> when I am dead
> Now
> I must
> win excellent glory
> (*Il.* 18.121)

Philip, after unsuccessful attempts to capture Byzantium and Perinthus, headed north toward the Danube, hoping for a more profitable encounter with the Scythians. At some point Alexander, with Antipater remaining behind as regent, was summoned to join Philip and the main body of the army. He no doubt brought fresh troops, but perhaps more important was that he was given the opportunity to acquire more experience in the art of war under the direction of a master.

This time Philip's efforts were rewarded with victory and an impressive amount of booty. During his return, however, the Macedonian force was surprised by the fierce Triballians. This Thracian tribe seized Philip's cattle and slaves, and gave the king a severe leg wound that left him temporarily immobilized and permanently lame. Around this time Alexander is said to have courageously saved Philip's life in battle.[106] In 338, after they had overcome Theban and Athenian resistance at Chaeronea, Macedonian ascendancy would be established over most of Greece.

## THE BATTLE OF CHAERONEA (338 BC)

The role assigned to Alexander at Chaeronea confirmed his status as crown prince and spoke of Philip's confidence in his son's ability to lead men. This battle resulted in the foundation of a Macedonian hegemony among the Greek city-states (other than Sparta). A victory here was also a prerequisite for the waging of war against the Great King of Persia. Thebes and Athens provided the main opposition.

The plan at Chaeronea was for Philip to lead his infantry on the right of the Macedonian line and execute a feigned retreat.[107] Alexander, in command of the Companion Cavalry on the left, was instructed to lead the decisive charge against the enemy's right wing as soon as the flank of the Theban Sacred Band was exposed by Philip's maneuver. The Sacred Band, a fabled unit of 300 crack infantrymen, was the heart of the Greek allied forces.

Philip's plan worked well. At the crucial moment, "Alexander, his heart set on showing his father his prowess and yielding to none in will to win . . . succeeded in rupturing the solid front of the enemy line . . . striking down many" (D.16.86.3). But Philip joined in the rout "well in front and not conceding credit for the victory even to Alexander" (D.16.86.4). Nonetheless, it was Philip's son and the Companion Cavalry who delivered the *coup de grâce* at Chaeronea by annihilating the Sacred Band.[108] Alexander, at 18 years of age, was a hero.

> winning for my own self
> great glory
> and
> for
> my
> father
> (*Il.* 6.446)

One thousand Athenians fell at Chaeronea, and 2,000 more were captured.[109] Demosthenes, who had been fulminating against Philip since 351 and warning compatriots of the "barbarian's" intention to sack their city and enslave its population, had fled from the disaster at Chaeronea. The inhabitants of Athens braced themselves for the worst.

Philip's first order of business, however, was to celebrate his triumph. He raised a trophy of victory and sacrificed to the gods in appreciation for the outcome. He rewarded those who had distinguished themselves, including, no doubt, Alexander. Diodorus tells us that after dinner, Philip, having drunk a great deal of unmixed wine, formed a Dionysiac comus – an ancient, tipsy, Conga line, which had its origins in the rural Dionysia – with his comrades "in celebration of the victory [and] paraded through the midst of his captives, jeering all the time at the misfortunes of the luckless men" (16.87.1).

Instead of destroying Athens, Philip sent home one of the prisoners, Demades, to discuss a peace treaty and an alliance. Thebes was punished for its presence at Chaeronea, but Athens was spared. Athenian captives were to be returned to Athens without ransom, and Macedonian troops would not set foot on Attic soil. The king's only "request" was for an alliance, and this was agreed to with bewilderment and relief.

Philip may have been equally relieved, for his true objective in Greece was to establish a general peace that would enable him to march on Asia without concern about the threat of imminent rebellion in Europe, or the need to maintain a significant force there. His plan was to embark for Asia on a Panhellenic crusade with authorization from a league, which all Greek states would be "invited" to join. With a mandate from the so-called Corinthian League,[110] and a representative contingent of its troops, who also served as hostages, Philip would become the agent of retribution for the Persian sacrilege on the Acropolis in 480. Even Philip, a devout cynic, would have found it difficult to sponsor this fiction if, in victory, he had treated Athens in a manner reminiscent of the Persians. There is every reason to believe that Philip, who appreciated Greek culture, wished to be accepted by the Greek world rather than be viewed as the instrument of its destruction. The supremacy he had established at Chaeronea afforded him the opportunity to display magnanimity and enjoy a fleeting moment of Athenian gratitude, if not respect. A statue of the benevolent victor was erected in the agora of Athens, and Philip and Alexander were granted Athenian citizenship.[111]

## ATHENS (338 BC)

Philip decided not to conduct the negotiations in person. Instead, it was Alexander and Antipater who would escort the ashes of the dead Athenians back to their native city.[112] The king may have surmised that his son would make a better impression in Athens. Philip himself was covered with scars from head to toe, had an empty socket instead of a right eye, and limped on a maimed leg.[113] He would have served as a caricature of the most unflattering Athenian assumptions about Macedonians.

Despite the fact that Macedonians were of Greek stock, most Greeks perceived them to be barbarians.[114] Macedonian aristocrats were known for their hunting, fighting, gambling, and drinking. It was said by the Greeks that a Macedonian nobleman was not entitled to recline at his own symposium until he had killed a wild boar,[115] and that a Macedonian could not wear a belt until he had killed another man in battle.[116]

Macedonian aristocrats spoke Attic Greek in Philip's day, but their native tongue, although Greek, was incomprehensible to an Athenian.[117] Greek poets, painters, and philosophers had been lured to Pella since the reign of the Macedonian king Archelaus (*c.* 413–399). Socrates had declined the invitation, and Plato's name is not to be found in the guest register at the court.[118] The rhetorician Thrasymachus captured the general sentiment: "Shall we, being Greeks, be slaves to Archelaus, a barbarian?"[119] Given this prevailing attitude, most Athenians in the fourth century probably agreed with Demosthenes' pronouncement that " 'he [Philip] is not [a] Greek, nor related to the Greeks,' "[120]

Yet Alexander did fit the Greek mold. He was attractive, youthful, courteous and intelligent, and he had been a student of Aristotle, the most celebrated product of Plato's Academy. Alexander was also inquisitive and knowledgeable. He may have surprised the Athenians with both his questions and his polished remarks. He was capable of capturing the attention of the local sages by reciting obscure quotations from Homer or the Attic tragedians, and his devotion to Athena, the patron goddess of their city, must have impressed even the most supercilious of his hosts.

These actions were not just for show, however. Athena played a major role in the religious observances of the Macedonian royal family. As king Alexander would sacrifice to Athena with impressive regularity.[121] He also held contests in honor of the goddess, built altars in her name, dedicated a temple to her, and later sacrificed to Athena at Troy.[122] There he exchanged his armor for equipment said to have been used during the Trojan War.

Had Alexander peered over the southern slope of the Acropolis, he would certainly have seen the ancient shrine of Dionysus and the theater attached to it. Alexander's appetite for drama had been cultivated by Aristotle, who claimed that the origins of "the tragic pleasure" were found in the dithyramb, a choral song to Dionysus.[123] Subjects relating directly to Dionysus, however, rarely provided a focus for tragedy. Instead, men and women of heroic stature were depicted on stage in a pageant of unfolding tension and conflict. It was the members of the audience who were transferred into the Dionysiac realm by exchanging their own reality for theatrical illusion.

Later, as king, Alexander patronized playwrights, sponsored theatrical competitions, and imported troupes of actors from the Dionysiac guild.[124] Far away in Persia, Alexander asked his treasurer Harpalus to send him something to read. Harpalus, who presumably knew Alexander's tastes in literature, packaged the plays of Aeschylus, Sophocles, and Euripides, along with some dithyrambic poetry and Philistus' *History of Sicily*, and sent them off to his king (P.8.3–4).

Alexander had a special interest in tragedy. He quoted Euripides on a number of occasions,[125] and this may reflect a preference. Euripides was bold and original, a master of illusion, surprise, and the grand gesture. His psychological insights were keen, and he recognized emotion as a silent partner in the intellectual process. Euripides etched a tableau of private fury raging beneath public decorum, and denigrated heroes who justified their actions by distorting the truth. He wrote: "You are mad, you who seek glory in combat, among weapons of war, thinking in your ignorance to find a cure for human misery there" (*Hel.* 1151–4).

While in Athens as an ambassador, Alexander surely heard the story of how the Persian king Xerxes had stolen the statues of the tyrant slayers, Harmodius and Aristogeiton, and had transported them back to Susa. Years later, when Alexander occupied the Persian capital, he retrieved these statues and arranged to have them returned to Athens.[126] He would learn, however, that elegant gestures of this type would not alter Athenian hostility toward him. Some Athenians purposefully remembered Chaeronea and the citizens who perished there, and chose to ignore the fact that their world had changed now that Macedonian influence could be felt throughout Hellas.

## THE WEDDING OF PHILIP II AND CLEOPATRA (337 BC)

After Chaeronea, Philip authorized the construction of a *tholos* (circular building) at Olympia called the Philippeum. This structure resembled its counterpart at Delphi and would eventually encircle portrait statues of Philip, Olympias, Alexander, and Philip's parents (Amyntas III and Eurydice).[127] This statue group was sculpted in gold and ivory, media usually reserved for the gods, and the sculptor was the Athenian Leochares, whose work would later be commissioned by Alexander.[128] Soon after the original work on the *tholos* had begun, however, the relationship between Philip, Olympias, and Alexander would undergo a profound alteration.

Philip returned to Pella in the spring of 337. Once again he celebrated a marriage. Since he had accumulated wives on a regular basis, Philip may never have anticipated the uproar that followed his marriage to this new wife. The biographer Satyrus places this marriage in a special category: "After all these women he married Cleopatra [called Eurydice by Arrian (3.6.5)], with whom he had fallen in love . . . and by bringing her home to supplant Olympias, he threw the entire course of his life into utter confusion."[129] Arrian states unequivocally that "there was a lack of confidence between Alexander and Philip after Philip took Eurydice to wife, and disgraced Olympias, the mother of Alexander" (3.6.5).

> [He] dishonoured
> his own wife
> my
> mother
> (*Il.* 9.450–1)

The wedding was a boisterous affair. Alexander was present; Olympias was not. In Plutarch's version of the feast, Attalus, the intoxicated uncle of the bride, raised his cup and appealed to the gods for a legitimate heir to the throne. Alexander, the crown prince, leaped to his feet shouting, "Villain, do you take me for a bastard, then?" (9.8).[130] He hurled his drinking cup, a *skyphos*, at the speaker. Philip, who was quite drunk, drew his sword and lunged at his apparently sober son, only to stumble and sprawl headlong on the floor. Alexander is reported to have looked down contemptuously at his father and remarked: "Here is the man who was making ready to cross from Europe to Asia, and who cannot even cross from one table to another without losing his balance" (P.9.10).

> Then I took it into my mind
> to cut him down
> with the sharp bronze

but some one of the immortals
checked my anger
reminding me of rumour
among the people
and men's maledictions repeated
that I
might not
be called
a
parricide
(*Il.* 9.458–61)

This whole episode was a nightmare for Alexander and Olympias. The derogatory remarks of Attalus were totally unacceptable, and Philip's failure to defend Alexander's honor was humiliating. The king had drawn his sword, but instead of using it to attack the man sputtering insults, he had turned the weapon on his own son. In his besotted state, Philip may have held Alexander responsible for the disruption of the celebration. Whatever the case, the king must have awakened the next day in rueful disquiet over the situation he had created.

Even if the occasion had been devoid of drunken histrionics, Olympias would have felt threatened by this wedding. She had resigned herself to several other marriages over the previous twenty or so years, perhaps because the necessity of each could be explained in terms of pressing political considerations. Until now, however, the other wives were also considered to be foreigners, and they probably enjoyed little or no support at court. These rivals may have been distracting, but remained politically innocuous unless they produced a healthy male child. None did.

Philip's new bride, Cleopatra, however, was a full-blooded Macedonian aristocrat. This perhaps sharpened the bite of her uncle's provocative toast at the wedding. She is described by Plutarch as "a girl with whom Philip had fallen in love and whom he had decided to marry, although she was far too young for him" (9.6). Philip was 46 and Cleopatra was perhaps thirty years his junior.

While it is true that Philip's mother was half-Illyrian,[131] he had proved himself to be a "genuine Macedonian." Olympias, however, was not, and her enemies probably saw her as an interloper on Macedonian soil. Alexander's own abilities, precocity, and station must also have earned him a fair share of envy and enmity. One might infer from Attalus' slur at the wedding that it may have been fashionable to refer to the "exceptional" (i.e., non-Macedonian) character of Alexander in an uncomplimentary way. In such cases his less attractive characteristics were probably attributed to his mother.

Immediately after the altercation at his father's wedding, Alexander collected his mother and headed for Macedonia's western frontier. Olym-

pias was deposited in Epirus at her brother's court. Alexander then travelled north to take refuge with the Illyrians.[132] This new situation was
potentially dangerous for mother and son, but also for Philip. Olympias,
for instance, might prevail upon her brother to defend the family's honor
and avenge the outrageous insults to which she had been subjected. Also,
with his customary astuteness, Alexander had placed himself among Macedonia's stalwart enemies, where he was in a position, if necessary, to
launch an invasion against Philip.

What prompted Philip to follow a course of action that guaranteed
Olympias' hostility and risked the alienation of his son and successor? As
noted above, Plutarch says simply that Philip fell in love with Cleopatra.
Satyrus, who, it may be recalled, emphasized political considerations when
discussing Philip's other marriages, also speaks of love in this instance.[133]
It may be that despite, or because of, the marked disparity in age between
the two, Philip became smitten by an attractive younger woman.[134] Eros,
it was said, loosens the limbs and damages the mind, and Philip may well
have been the victim of Eros in this case.

It is difficult to imagine Philip relying exclusively on his emotions,
however, in a matter affecting affairs of state at such a critical stage in
his career. He was a methodical planner, and there was one aspect of the
forthcoming invasion of Asia that he was unlikely to ignore. This very
consideration may have convinced him of the necessity of this seemingly
ill-advised marriage. Alexander would not have accepted another regency
while glory of untold magnitude awaited him in Asia, and Philip, under
the circumstances, would never have left him behind. Philip and Alexander would cross the Hellespont together, and while they were both
renowned for courage, both also took unnecessary risks in battle. What
if neither of them survived the invasion? In such a scenario civil war
would have been likely in Macedonia unless Philip had produced another
legitimate heir to the throne before his departure. A thoroughbred Macedonian boy, particularly one fathered by the man who had unified Macedonia and brought it to preeminence, would help in averting such turmoil.

Despite the underlying reasons for the marriage, it is reasonable to
assume that Philip never anticipated this imbroglio because of the steps
he took to ameliorate the situation. Demaratus of Corinth, who had
acquired Bucephalas for Alexander, visited Pella while the king's son was
still dwelling among the Illyrians.[135] When Philip asked about affairs in
Greece, Demaratus answered: "It is all very well for you to show so much
concern for the affairs of Greece, Philip. How about the disharmony you
have brought about in your own household?" (P.9.13). Philip responded to
this rebuke by asking Demaratus to go to Illyria and negotiate Alexander's
return.

Alexander did show reluctance in returning to Macedonia, but Demaratus finally succeeded with his entreaties and Alexander returned before
the year 337 ended.[136] Philip must have assured Alexander in no uncertain

terms that he was still the heir to the throne. As devoted as he was to his mother, though, Alexander apparently had to abandon her cause for the time being, since she remained, it seems, in Epirus. Philip presumably had no intention of subjecting his new wife to any of Olympias' invectives, and although an accord had been reached between father and son, its tentative nature would soon be put to the test.

## THE PIXODARUS AFFAIR (336 BC)

Philip's plans for his invasion of Asia continued to gain momentum. On the diplomatic level he received overtures for an alliance from Pixodarus of Caria, a dynast in southern Asia Minor.[137] The likelihood of a full-scale Macedonian invasion had encouraged Pixodarus, whose satrapy was part of the Persian Empire, to seek an independent alliance with Philip. Preliminary discussions revolved around the arrangement of a marriage between the satrap's daughter and Philip's son Arrhidaeus.

Alexander reacted to this prospect with considerable dismay. He apparently became convinced that the marriage was of far greater importance than Philip saw fit to disclose, and was persuaded, perhaps by Olympias and his close friends, that it signified Arrhidaeus' replacement of him as heir apparent.

> And now my prize
> you threaten
> in person
> to strip
> from me
> (*Il.* 1.161)

An alarmed Alexander sent a certain Thessalus[138] to engage in private negotiations with Pixodarus. Thessalus was a prominent actor who, more than once, had been awarded first prize at the Dionysia in Athens. Like Philip, Alexander was employing an actor in a diplomatic capacity. Thessalus was instructed to persuade Pixodarus to insist upon Alexander as the bridegroom in any dynastic marriage. Philip became infuriated when informed of what his son had done: "When Philip discovered this, he went to Alexander's room, taking with him Philotas the son of Parmenio, one of the prince's companions. There he scolded his son and angrily reproached him for behaving so ignobly and so unworthily of his position as to wish to marry the daughter of a mere Carian, who was no more than the slave of a barbarian king" (P.10.3).

> How I wish
> at this moment
> the earth
> might

open
beneath
him
(*Il.* 6.281–2)

Philip may have been informed of Alexander's activities by Parmenio, who would have learned about them in Asia Minor, or by his son, Philotas.[139] In any event, Philotas was there to hear the charge and witness the chastisement. This whole business must have been humiliating for Alexander, discomforting for Philotas, and exasperating for Philip. But it was more than an embarrassment and a source of consternation: Alexander's unauthorized diplomacy could very well have been interpreted as high treason.[140] If Philip had ever intended to remove Alexander as his inheritor, this situation would have presented him with a golden opportunity to do so.

Philip was deeply concerned about both his son's anxiety and his apparent unreliability, but this was a condition for which the father had to bear some of the responsibility. Philip had always enjoyed confusing others about his true intentions. Now he had misled his own son, and he was confronted with that son's unfathomable behavior.

The king wrote to Corinth demanding that the actor Alexander had sent to Caria be brought back to Macedonia in chains as a reflection of the seriousness with which he viewed this man's mission. Philip also sent several of Alexander's closest friends – notably Harpalus, Nearchus, and Ptolemy – into exile as a result of their collusion in the Pixodarus affair.[141] Later Thessalus would join Alexander on his Asian expedition, participating in tragic contests and enjoying special consideration and gratitude from his patron for the dangerous undertaking on behalf of the troubled prince. After his father's death, Alexander recalled all of his exiled friends and elevated each of them to an influential position.[142]

By 336 Alexander's clique of friends had also become a source of concern to Philip. It was to be expected, of course, that Alexander would develop a group of close associates who enjoyed special relationships with him. His charisma and personal valor assured such associations. Philip himself was partly responsible for his son's popularity through his own willingness to share the limelight with him. The very special loyalty that Alexander evoked in his companions, however, may have been more than his father had anticipated or desired. In fact, their steadfast allegiance may have been construed by Philip as a threat. His son's entourage may also have distressed Philip because it seemed prematurely royal in complexion and function; Alexander was after all only the crown prince, not the king.

Plutarch suggests that Alexander had been poorly advised by both his mother "and his friends" during the Pixodarus affair (10.1). As we shall see, this is not the only occasion when Alexander was depicted as following the bad advice of his friends with troublesome results. While competing for his favor each was highly sensitive to anything that might be perceived as a threat, and was equally anxious for any opportunity to display his own fidelity and usefulness.[143] Although the poor counsel referred to in the sources can often be explained as a device on the part of apologists to absolve Alexander of complete blame for his mistakes, enough of his critics allude to it for it to warrant consideration. Alexander's friends may actually have played on his insecurities in order to draw attention to their own vigilance and devotion to him. Leonnatus, Perdiccas, and Attalus[144] (not Cleopatra's uncle, later Perdiccas' brother-in-law) can be counted among those close, personal friends who, for whatever reason, were not exiled. The first two would figure prominently in Alexander's later exploits and plans.

Leonnatus was a member of Alexander's inner circle of friends and later became one of his Royal Bodyguards, an elite corps of seven men who guarded the king. He served him well on numerous occasions, helped bring a conspiracy to murder Alexander to the king's attention in 327, risked his own life to save Alexander's in 325, and was awarded a golden crown for distinguished service in 324. Perdiccas, another member of the king's inner circle, eventually became a Royal Bodyguard as well. He too played an important role in response to a plot against Alexander's life. The name Perdiccas appears on a list of friends at whose houses Alexander drank during the last year of his life in Ecbatana, and he is also recorded as having been present at Alexander's last drinking party. While awaiting death Alexander handed his royal ring over to Perdiccas to ensure that the king's business would continue to be conducted.[145]

Philotas was drawn into the Pixodarus episode but escaped banishment, perhaps because it might have been imprudent for the king to discipline Philotas severely at this juncture. If the general's son had been privy to Alexander's dealings, he may have been pardoned for his role as an informer or because his father Parmenio was instrumental in Philip's immediate plans. Moreover, should further misunderstandings have developed between Philip and Alexander concerning their respective rights and privileges, Philotas could be called upon to quote Philip's admonitions to his son by chapter and verse. In any event, Philotas' role in this affair, whatever its nature, would not have endeared him to Alexander.

In the end, Pixodarus of Caria decided to forsake all efforts to develop a *rapprochement* with Philip. Realizing that any arrangements made under these uneasy circumstances might ultimately be hazardous, Pixodarus elected to throw his lot in with Darius III and the new Persian regime. Philip's reconciliation with Alexander, however, which had been fragile from the outset, soon began to show further signs of deterioration.

## THE ASSASSINATION OF PHILIP II (336 BC)

A series of violent incidents, which were eventually felt at the very highest levels, occurred at the Macedonian court around this time. Jealousy, homosexuality, suicide, drunkenness, revenge, rape, and assassination were among the elements involved in this drama that would alter the course of Alexander's life.[146] Diodorus describes the lurid prelude to these events:

> There was a Macedonian Pausanias who came of a family from the district Orestis. He [was a] bodyguard of the king [Philip] and was beloved by him because of his beauty. When he saw that the king was becoming enamoured of another Pausanias (a man of the same name as himself), he addressed him with abusive language, accusing him of being a hermaphrodite and prompt to accept the amorous advances of any who wished. Unable to endure such an insult, the other kept silent for the time, but, after confiding to Attalus, one of his friends, what he proposed to do, he brought about his own death voluntarily and in a spectacular fashion. For a few days after this, as Philip was engaged in battle with Pleurias, king of the Illyrians, Pausanias stepped in front of him and, receiving on his body all the blows directed at the king, so met his death. The incident was widely discussed and Attalus [the same man at whom Alexander had flung his *skyphos*], who was a member of the court circle and influential with the king, invited the first Pausanias to dinner and when he had plied him till drunk with unmixed wine, handed his unconscious body over to the muleteers to abuse in drunken licentiousness. So he presently recovered from his drunken stupor and, deeply resenting the outrage to his person, charged Attalus before the king with the outrage. Philip shared his anger at the barbarity of the act but did not wish to punish Attalus at that time because of their relationship, and because Attalus's services were needed urgently. He was the nephew [actually uncle] of the Cleopatra whom the king had just married as a new wife and he had been selected as a general of the advanced force being sent into Asia, for he was a man valiant in battle. For these reasons, the king tried to mollify the righteous anger of Pausanias at his treatment, giving him substantial presents and advancing him in honour among the bodyguards.
>
> (16.93.3–9)

While all of this was unfolding Philip was concentrating on his plans for the invasion of the Persian Empire. In the spring of 336 he sent an advance force of 10,000 troops across the Hellespont led by Parmenio, his finest general, and Alexander's adversary Attalus, a popular and capable commander, who had recently become Parmenio's son-in-law.[147] The crossing was unopposed, and the invading forces quickly established their bridgehead in Asia. News of their progress raised the spirits and expectations of everyone at Pella; or, rather, almost everyone.

Meanwhile Pausanias, who was seeking royal justice for the atrocities inflicted upon him, managed to evoke only sympathy and evasiveness from the king. Philip attempted to palliate his anguish with a military promotion, but Pausanias found this to be inadequate recompense for the humiliations he had suffered. The acclaim earned by Attalus in Asia Minor only added insult to his injury.

Philip's adroit handling of another problematic situation, however, appeared to be something of a *coup d'éclat*. The disposition of Epirus, whose hostility could scarcely be afforded at this time, was in question because of Olympias' disaffection.[148] Philip ingeniously decided to alter the circumstances by offering his daughter, Cleopatra, in marriage to her uncle Alexander of Epirus (Olympias' brother).

> You are an old hand
> at cunning
> I see
> (*Ba.* 824)

The king of the Molossians would find it difficult to refuse this betrothal without offending Philip, and such a marriage must have seemed an attractive alternative to war with Philip of Macedon. The young Epirote king had, in fact, secured his throne through the efforts of Philip, and their relationship had been anything but hostile.[149]

Olympias may have seen this marriage as a ploy on Philip's part to deprive her of the weapon of revenge that her brother might sponsor. Through her brother she had hoped to regain her position in Macedonia. Nonetheless, it was conceivable that the entire scenario might, in the end, yield generous returns. Should anything happen to Philip after the wedding, her son would predictably succeed his father as the Macedonian king, and her daughter and brother would rule in Epirus. Olympias would thus emerge as the most powerful and prestigious woman in the Greek-speaking world.

In the meantime, Philip, seeking divine approbation, inquired at Delphi concerning the prospects of his imminent invasion. The oracle, through whom Apollo, a god favored by Philip, was presumed to speak, announced: "Wreathed is the bull. All is done. There is also the one who will smite him" (D.16.91.2). Philip considered the answer ambiguous. Assuming that the bull symbolized Persia, however, "he thought that the gods supported him and . . . that Asia would be made captive under the hands of the Macedonians" (D.16.91.4).

The wedding between Alexander of Epirus and Cleopatra took place at Aegae during the autumn of 336.[150] It was designed to serve as a glorious overture to Philip's departure for Asia. This event was arranged to celebrate his own unparalleled success as well as his daughter's marriage.

Magnificent sacrifices to the gods and lavish entertainments were prepared, and Philip was presented with golden crowns by representatives of
the Greek city-states. The Athenian herald, while offering his gift to the
king, proclaimed ominously that anyone who dared plot against Philip
would be denied sanctuary in Athens and would be delivered to Macedonia.

Diodorus tells us that on the first day of the festivities, Philip, at the
state banquet, ordered an actor by the name of Neoptolemus to quote
verses apropos of the upcoming campaign.[151] Neoptolemus, who was thinking of the Persian king, spoke the following prescient words:

> Your thoughts reach higher than the air;
> You dream of wide fields' cultivation.
> The homes you plan surpass the homes
> That men have known, but you do err,
> Guiding your life afar.
> But one there is who'll catch the swift,
> Who goes a way obscured in gloom,
> And sudden, unseen, overtakes
> And robs us of our distant hopes –
> Death, mortals' source of many woes.
>
> (16.92.3)

Diodorus continues: "Finally the drinking was over and the start of the
games set for the following day" (16.92.5). The guests gathered in the
theater at sunrise and an impressive procession was formed on the grounds
outside. Statues of the twelve gods "adorned with a dazzling show of
wealth to strike awe in the beholder" were escorted into the theater with
pomp and circumstance. The assembled dignitaries were then surprised
by the appearance of a thirteenth statue, one of Philip himself, "suitable
for a god." Through this startling gesture, Diodorus claimed, "the king
exhibited himself enthroned among the twelve gods" (16.92.5).

> unwise
> are those who aspire
> who outrange
> the limits
> of
> man
> (*Ba.* 396)

The statues preceded Philip into the theater. His bodyguards were
instructed to follow him at a distance. This would enhance the drama and
serve as a graphic rebuttal to the charges that he was a tyrant, since tyrants
customarily surrounded themselves with bodyguards. Dressed in a white
cloak, Philip entered the theater accompanied by the two Alexanders, his
son and his new son-in-law.[152] While Philip halted momentarily at the

entrance to the arena, one of his own bodyguards drew a dagger and without warning rushed at the king. His dagger thrust forward. It penetrated the king's ribs and killed him instantly.

The bodyguard was Pausanias. He had finally avenged himself on the king for the injustices he had suffered. Pausanias ran toward the city gates, where horses had been stationed to facilitate his escape, but his boot became ensnared in a vine root. He fell, and several of his pursuers immediately skewered his body with javelins. "Such was the end of Philip, who had made himself the greatest of the kings in Europe in his time, and because of the extent of his kingdom had made himself a throned companion of the twelve gods" (D.16.95.1).

Philip was dead, but had he been killed by a lone assassin for personal retribution?[153] Aristotle, for one, said yes: "Philip, too, was attacked by Pausanias because he permitted him to be insulted by Attalus and his friends."[154] Aristotle had nothing further to say about the event. This lean reference is found in a discussion of rulers who were killed for personal rather than political reasons. One might argue that further elaboration would have obscured the point he was attempting to make. More cynical observers might say, however, that Aristotle, who enjoyed Macedonian patronage, chose to say as little as possible about an unsavory event that might place his benefactors in an unfavorable light.

Diodorus, who offers no evidence to contradict Aristotle, pictures Pausanias nursing his wrath and yearning for revenge "not only on the one who had done him wrong, but also on the one who failed to avenge him" (16.94.1). Diodorus asserts that Pausanias was inadvertently encouraged to commit regicide by his tutor Hermocrates. This sophist reportedly answered Pausanias' question about how one might become famous by saying "that it would be by killing the one who had accomplished most, for just as long as he was remembered, so long his slayer would be remembered also" (16.94.1).

Other ancient authorities insist that Pausanias was a mere instrument in the hands of more powerful individuals who harnessed his resentments to serve their own ends. Plutarch states that when Philip was slain by Pausanias, "It was Olympias who was chiefly blamed for the assassination, because she was believed to have encouraged the young man and incited him to take his revenge" (10.6). Justin declares that "It is even believed that he [Pausanias] was instigated to the act by Olympias . . . as Olympias had felt no less resentment at her divorce, and the preferment of Cleopatra to herself, than Pausanias had felt at the insults which he had received . . . . Olympias, it is certain, had horses prepared for the escape of the assassin" (9.7.1–9).

When Olympias learned that the king was dead, Justin explains, she hastened to the funeral. Upon her arrival she astonished everyone by paying ostentatious respect to the assassin's corpse rather than to Philip's.

Here Justin, ordinarily deemed an untrustworthy source, supplies such detailed information that his account deserves serious consideration:[155]

> [Olympias] put a crown of gold, the same night that she arrived, on the head of Pausanias, as he was hanging on a cross; an act which no one but she would have dared to do, as long as the son of Philip was alive. A few days after, she burnt the body of the assassin, when it had been taken down, upon the remains of her husband, and made him a tomb in the same place; she also provided that yearly sacrifices should be performed to his manes [spirit], possessing the people with a super-stitious notion for the purpose . . . . Last of all she consecrated the sword [or dagger], with which the king had been killed, to Apollo, under the name of Myrtale, which was Olympias's own name when a child. And all these things were done so publicly, that she seems to have been afraid lest it should not be evident enough that the deed was promoted by her.
>
> (9.7.10–14)

Plutarch, after also indicting Olympias, adds the statement that "a certain amount of accusation attached itself to Alexander also" (10.6).[156] Plutarch then recounts a story concerning Alexander and Pausanias in which Alexander listened to the woes of Pausanias and responded with a recitation of some verses from Euripides in which Medea threatened "[t]he father, bride and bridegroom all at once."[157] The passage refers to King Creon's concern over what the incensed Medea might do to him, his daughter, and his son-in-law (her children's father), after she had been rejected and shamed by her husband. The analogy is to Attalus, his niece Cleopatra, and Philip. Plutarch adds that Pausanias had been victimized by both Attalus and Cleopatra.[158]

An admirer of Alexander, and clearly uncomfortable at the implications this might have had for him, Plutarch reveals his own commitment to Alexander's innocence by reminding the reader that the new king "took care to track down and punish those who were involved in the plot" (10.8).

I

am not

responsible

but Zeus

is

and

Destiny

(*Il.* 19.86–7)

Justin, on the other hand, says that both Olympias and Alexander were "thought to have encouraged Pausanias, when complaining of his insults being left unpunished, to so atrocious a deed [as Philip's assassination]"

(9.7.8), and declares categorically that it was Olympias who had arranged to have horses waiting to aid in the assassin's escape. Satyrus provides Olympias' motive. In his opinion Philip brought Cleopatra "home to supplant Olympias,"[159] something Alexander's mother would never have accepted graciously. Beyond that, Olympias and Pausanias shared common grievances against Philip, Attalus, and Cleopatra.

Olympias' treatment of Philip's young widow after the assassination also reveals the depth of her resentment. Cleopatra's child was tortured to death in her presence, and the horrified mother was forced to hang herself.[160] Such actions make the case against Olympias in Philip's assassination, while perhaps insufficient for conviction beyond the shadow of a doubt, nevertheless seem quite persuasive.[161]

A quarter of a century ago, Ernst Badian, the *doyen* of Alexander scholars, published a challenging brief on the death of Philip that implicated Alexander in his father's assassination.[162] Arguing in the context of Alexander's "continued insecurity" from the time of Philip's marriage to Cleopatra, and owing to a faction at court that included Attalus and Parmenio, both of whom may have opposed Alexander's accession, Badian offers an ingenious exposition of the hypothesis that Alexander, in complicity with Antipater, was responsible for Philip's death. Placing the events involving Philip and Alexander against the background of Macedonian court politics and alluding to Alexander's future behavior as king, Badian draws the following conclusions: "As for Alexander, he never forgave his father for the danger and humiliation that he had inflicted on him. As soon as he felt strong enough, he insulted Philip's memory and even denied his paternity. As in other attested cases, his resentment did not stop at the grave he had helped to dig."[163] Badian's hypothesis has become the basis for a contention, developed and subscribed to by several scholars, that Alexander was guilty of patricide.[164]

There are diverse elements in this argument that merit consideration. From Alexander's point of view, Philip selected his latest bride from a most undesirable family. Also, criticism of any sort always disturbed Alexander, and so the insult from Attalus enraged him. The Pixodarus affair revealed the depth of Alexander's insecurities, as well as the illogical lengths to which he would go when fearful of being deprived of the opportunity to realize his own glory. The banishment of several of his most loyal supporters probably compounded Alexander's anxieties, and it did not help when the obnoxious Attalus was offered the opportunity to draw first blood in Asia. Even the marriage of Alexander's sister to the Molossian king could be construed as another unconscionable offense on Philip's part. Alexander perceived himself as the victim of circumstances, a role he found intolerable.

Alexander's fear of losing his right to assume the kingship is pivotal to the contention that he participated in a plot against his father. This argument involves questions of Alexander's legitimacy, his standing as heir apparent, the displacement of his mother by Philip, and the status of the child or children born to Philip's last wife. There is no convincing evidence that Philip ever questioned Alexander's legitimacy.[165] The bargain struck to ensure Alexander's return from Illyria must have included confirmations of his status and right of succession. If Philip had planned to replace Alexander, the Pixodarus affair offered a perfect opportunity, but the king's actions made it clear that he had no such intention. If, as reported, Alexander accompanied his father in a place of honor at Aegae, there is no reason to believe that Alexander's inheritance was in jeopardy. The question of how Alexander interpreted their relationship is, however, unanswerable.

Sometime before the assassination Philip arranged a marriage between his daughter Cynane and his nephew Amyntas.[166] Amyntas had been the child-heir to the Macedonian throne in 359. At that time Philip probably acted as the child's regent, but he subsequently replaced him as king. Alexander's cousin was about five years older than the crown prince and a potential candidate for the throne, if one accepts the theory that the assembly could choose any male member from the Argead family as their new king.[167] Either Amyntas or his son by Philip's daughter would qualify in this respect. Philip may have sponsored the marriage to supply one more candidate for the throne should he and Alexander perish, and his own marriage to Cleopatra fail to produce a surviving son. Whatever Philip's rationale, this move was yet another source of anxiety for Alexander.

Some scholars claim that Philip divorced Olympias[168] – an action that would certainly have alienated Alexander – but this assumption seems unwarranted. Macedonian kings customarily practiced polygamy, and there was no apparent reason for him to make an exception in Olympias' case. In fact, a divorce might have served to disaffect Alexander of Epirus and perhaps force him into an adversarial position. It would have been unnecessary and counterproductive to all of Philip's intentions.

The problem of the number and gender of the children produced by Philip's last wife is significant and puzzling. Plutarch ignores the question, but the marriage clearly resulted in at least one, and possibly two, offspring. Satyrus says that "Cleopatra, in her turn, bore to Philip a daughter, the one who was called Europa."[169] Europa (whose mythological brother was Cadmus, the mortal grandfather of Dionysus), is not mentioned by name elsewhere. Diodorus says simply that "Cleopatra had borne a child to Philip a few days before his death" (17.2.3). Justin speaks of a daughter,[170] but also of Alexander's brother Caranus, the son of his step-mother, as "a rival for the throne" (9.7.3).[171] Pausanias (the writer, not the assassin) makes reference to Philip's "infant son by Cleopatra."[172]

The evidence is confusing, but there is a possible explanation. There may have been two children: the first a girl, with whom Cleopatra could have been pregnant at her wedding; the second a boy, who was born shortly before the assassination.[173] The male infant may only have survived for a brief period of time, and this could be the reason that he was ignored by some ancient authorities. It has been pointed out by Robin Lane Fox that "babies are not invented in Macedonian history,"[174] and the name referred to in the sources for this boy is eminently credible – a king called Caranus was believed to be the founder of the Argead dynasty in Macedonia.[175] If one agrees that Alexander was in a state of high anxiety during this period, the birth of a royal son who was recognized as "legitimate" by an influential faction at the court – and called Caranus – would only serve to multiply his fears.

Those who allege Alexander's complicity in the death of his father emphasize the manner in which the assassin was handled. The unspecified number of bodyguards who apprehended Pausanias killed him with dispatch, thereby eliminating any explanation of the act by its perpetrator. The names of three of the bodyguards who killed Pausanias are mentioned by Diodorus. They are none other than Alexander's friends who had not been exiled in connection with the Pixodarus affair: Leonnatus, Perdiccas, and Attalus.[176] It has been claimed that they were Royal Bodyguards, but the evidence suggests that they probably served in Alexander's own cadre of personal bodyguards.[177]

Antipater plays a crucial role in the scholarly brief against Alexander.[178] He reportedly presented Alexander to the army for acclamation as king immediately after the assassination, and it was his son-in-law, Alexander the Lyncestian, who was the first to salute Alexander as the king. He was a senior diplomat and general, and an intellectual of sorts; his actions were crucial in the transference of power. This man was no stranger to the new king. He was apparently present when Alexander became regent at 16, certainly accompanied the young man on his diplomatic pilgrimage to Athens after Chaeronea, and then was appointed viceroy in Europe when Alexander left on his expedition. Antipater's motives for participating in the plot, it has been suggested, can be traced to his dissatisfaction with the growing power of the Parmenio–Attalus faction, and to his increased disenchantment with Philip, as the king increasingly flirted with his own deification.[179]

The prosecution's case against Alexander has been argued well. His relationship with Philip had certainly become embittered. He was infuriated over the callousness with which he and his mother had been treated, insecure over the question of succession, and probably resentful about the fact that it was his father and not he himself who was on the threshold of everlasting fame. After all, Philip, even at 47 was remarkably durable, and it might be twenty years or more before Alexander would get his chance to lead. There was even the remote possibility, at least in Alexander's mind, that such an opportunity would never come to pass.

Yet the ancients offer no hard evidence of Alexander's involvement in his father's murder. Plutarch merely states that some accusations had touched on Alexander.[180] Justin says that Pausanias had been instigated by Olympias "and that Alexander himself was not ignorant that his father was to be killed" (9.7.1). This rendition appears to be more credible than those that depict Alexander as an active conspirator.

If, in fact, Olympias was responsible for the assassination, it is highly unlikely that Alexander would have been ignorant of what was about to transpire.[181] Both mother and son had enemies, and it seems unreasonable to assume that Olympias would risk the possibility of permitting someone other than Alexander to seize the throne during the inevitable confusion of the aftermath. At the same time it would have been essential for Alexander to remain above reproach in the whole episode, and for not one shred of evidence to point in his direction. Suspicion would have to be deflected from the new king, and, in this context, the melodramatic glorification of Pausanias by Olympias becomes plausible. Accusations against Olympias were inevitable, but she could demonstrate her approval of the murder without necessarily admitting guilt, while simultaneously drawing attention to herself and away from her son. Should anyone have had enough temerity to demand that charges be brought against Olympias, Alexander, now king, could be counted on to act as her paladin. Alexander did officially designate those who were Pausanias' co-conspirators, and he brought them to justice.

No ancient source makes the assertion that Alexander played an active role in the assassination. In fact, the silence of his detractors testifies to his probable innocence in this brutal affair. Even the Roman historian Curtius, who enjoyed moralizing over Alexander's shortcomings, counts filial piety among his virtues.[182] Such praise from Curtius would be unimaginable had there been sufficient grounds to support any indictment. Alexander's religiosity and obsessive concern for the way in which he was seen by others would have prevented him from ever becoming an accomplice to such a heinous act. Patricide would sully his reputation forever. The prospect was unthinkable.

> the blameless
> son
> of
> Peleus
> (*Il.* 2.770)

# 2 A Homeric king

## THE ACCESSION (336 BC)

Among the most pressing of Alexander's state obligations was the arrang-
ing of his father's funeral. If the tombs at Vergina are a reflection of his
efforts, then Alexander attended to this duty with dispatch and consideration. The bones from Tomb II suggest that the deceased may have been
given a Homeric burial similar to that of Hector as described in the closing
verses of the *Iliad*:

> But when all were gathered to one place and
> assembled together, first with gleaming wine
> they put out the pyre that was burning, all
> where the fury of the fire still was in force,
> and thereafter the brothers and companions of
> Hektor gathered the white bones up, mourning,
> as the tears swelled and ran down their cheeks.
> Then they laid what they had gathered up in a
> golden casket and wrapped this about with soft
> robes of purple, and presently put it away in
> the hollow of the grave.
>
> (24.790–7)

The "sons of Aeropus" were accused of Philip's assassination, and two
of the three brothers were put to death at Aegae.[1] These men belonged
to the royal house that once governed Lyncestis, an upland region that
had been coerced into becoming a part of Macedonia. Justin says that the
murderers were executed at Philip's grave site.[2] If this is so, the burned
weapons found on the outside of the roof of Tomb II may have belonged
to the two brothers. Their role in the murder of Philip is reported with
tantalizing brevity by Arrian.[3]

Alexander, however, could have had other reasons for their elimination,
which the historian was unaware of or thought best not to elaborate upon.
The Lyncestians may have supported an Argead other than Alexander for
the kingship, or hoped to see a member of their own family enthroned.

Alexander, who was unsure of Lyncestian allegiance, might have seized the opportunity to rid himself of these powerful men of dubious loyalty. Speculation aside, Alexander's actions established an official position with respect to the assassination, and anyone who objected did so at his own peril.

The third brother, Alexander the Lyncestian, saved himself by being the first to hail Alexander as king.[4] He put on a breastplate and escorted his sovereign to the palace. His behavior, along with the fact that he was Antipater's son-in-law, was probably the decisive factor in Alexander's decision to grant him immunity. This reprieve also demonstrated that Macedonia's new king was discriminate with punishment and capable of clemency.

The Lyncestian house was also linked with Amyntas, the son of Perdiccas III and the brother and predecessor of Philip II.[5] This child-king, who had been put aside in favor of Philip in 359,[6] still possessed the credentials necessary to assert a claim to the throne. After Philip's death, Macedonia, Plutarch tells us, "was festering with revolt and looking toward Amyntas and the children of Aëropus" (P.*Mor*.327c).[7] Amyntas, who had lived at Philip's court without posing a threat, is said to have claimed the throne sometime after Alexander's accession. For this he was executed by Alexander.[8] Justin says that Caranus, the alleged son of Philip's last wife, was also killed shortly after Alexander came to power.[9]

The situation in Asia Minor was also troublesome. Attalus, Cleopatra's uncle and Alexander's *bête noire*, served there under Parmenio, his father-in-law and the most accomplished of Philip's generals. Shortly after the assassination, Attalus responded to subversive correspondence from Demosthenes without informing the king. When it became clear to Attalus that Alexander was securely established on the throne, he turned Demosthenes' letters over to Alexander as belated proof of his loyalty. The king, who was apparently aware of the entire situation, answered by sending a certain Hecataeus to Asia "under orders to bring back Attalus alive if he could, but if not, to assassinate him as quickly as possible" (D.17.2.5). Attalus and his relatives were soon liquidated.[10] Although Attalus was popular with his troops, and Parmenio was with him in Asia at this time, there was no uprising against Alexander. Ernst Badian has suggested that a deal was struck between Alexander and Parmenio that resulted in the latter's jettisoning of Attalus.[11] Parmenio's acquiescence in Attalus' elimination perhaps helps to explain the fact that on the brink of the invasion of Asia many of the senior command positions in the Macedonian army were occupied by members of the house of Parmenio.[12] This was a situation that Alexander would alter when Parmenio was no longer a necessary part of his plans.

Alexander began his reign, as his predecessors had begun theirs, with a purge. The king is credibly reported to have been disturbed by his mother's brutal treatment of Cleopatra while he was away from court.[13]

Alexander also spared Philip Arrhidaeus, who was a cause of grave concern at the time of the Pixodarus affair. It could be argued that the new king no longer saw his half-brother as an immediate threat to his position, and was therefore able to safeguard him, and coincidentally offer to posterity an example of his concern for the handicapped and vulnerable. The mentally deficient Arrhidaeus may have accompanied Alexander to Asia in 334, which would have prevented Alexander's unfortunate half-brother from becoming a focus for rebellion in Macedonia.[14]

Alexander declared that the change in kings was a change in name only, thereby assuring the Macedonian nobility of his intention to respect all of their rights and privileges.[15] In general, he stated that they could expect the state to be run on the same principles as those employed by Philip.

> at the same time
> a good king
> and a
> strong
> spearfighter
> (*Il.* 3.179)[16]

Also, although Alexander was badly in need of money, all Macedonian citizens, it was said, were henceforth exempt from direct taxation. This proclamation was designed to sway public opinion in the young king's favor. As expected, no one protested.

On the day of the assassination Greek representatives were reminded of the oaths of alliance that bound their *poleis* to Philip and his descendants through the Corinthian League. The delegates in attendance confirmed these oaths, but their fellow citizens back home were soon celebrating Philip's demise and anticipating the end of Macedonian control. Demosthenes, whose daughter had died only six days before, abandoned the traditional emblems of mourning and appeared in Athens dressed in a splendid robe and crowned with a garland.[17] The orator had received word from his agents in Macedonia about what had occurred there. He announced to a populace still unaware of Philip's death that it had been revealed to him in a dream that Athens would very shortly receive news of a great blessing. Predictably word would soon reach the city concerning what had happened at Aegae and confirming Demosthenes' revelation. A jubilant citizenry voted thanksgivings for the good news and consecrated a golden crown in memory of the dead assassin.

The Greeks assumed that because of his age and inexperience Alexander would soon be overwhelmed by both internal problems and by widespread revolt along his northern borders. They felt that the time was ripe to assert independence from Macedonia. Alexander's advisers agreed with the Greek assessment of the situation. They counseled him to ignore Greece and appease the rebellious barbarians until his succession was secure. Alexander, characteristically, "chose precisely the opposite course, and decided that the only way to make his kingdom safe was to act with audacity and a lofty spirit, for he was certain that if he were seen to yield even a fraction of his authority, all his enemies would attack him at once" (P.11.4).[18]

## ALEXANDER IN GREECE (336 BC)

The king's first challenge occurred at the vale of Tempe, a narrow river gorge in Thessaly that led southward into Greece proper. While the Thessalians, who enjoyed a strong defensive position between the massifs of Olympus and Ossa, mulled over Alexander's request to pass through, Alexander had his engineers cut steps around the seaward side of Mount Ossa. When negotiations resumed, the Thessalians were astonished to see a large portion of the Macedonian army positioned behind them.

Alexander capitalized on his upper hand by gently reminding his neighbors that they shared a common lineage from Heracles and Achilles, and that his father had been of no small service to Thessaly. Stunned by his stratagem, and even more so by his cordial disposition under the circumstances, the Thessalians permitted Alexander to succeed Philip as president (*tagos*) of their federation, and placed their cavalry, the best in Greece, at his disposal. Alexander also accepted the same revenue from Thessaly enjoyed by Philip, and exempted Thessalian Phthia, the birthplace of Achilles, from any and all taxation.[19]

At Thermopylae Alexander was confirmed as *hegemon* of the Hellenes, a prestigious position that had also been held by his father.[20] Alexander then marched on Thebes, where the Macedonian garrison had been expelled and where attempts to liberate Greece from Macedonian overlordship had found a rallying point. He appeared with such startling rapidity that Thebes was unprepared to resist effectively.[21] His appeals to be recognized as *hegemon* of the Corinthian League and for Macedonian troops to be reinstated were accepted without hesitation.[22]

An Athenian delegation soon appeared, expressed profound regrets over their tardy recognition of the new king, and announced that they had conferred honors on Alexander that were even greater than those they had bestowed upon Philip.[23] Alexander called a plenary meeting of the Corinthian League. He was declared its *hegemon* and granted the support he requested for a punitive expedition against the Persians.

A frequently told tale involving Alexander and Diogenes of Sinope, the famous Cynic philosopher, is set in Corinth at this time.[24] In Plutarch's version of the story, Diogenes, unlike most philosophers in the area, who were either curious or seeking a grant of some sort, chose to ignore Alexander's presence. The king, we are told, sought out Diogenes and found him sunbathing. During this encounter Diogenes just stared at Alexander until the king asked him if there was anything he might do for him. "Yes . . . you can stand a little to one side out of my sun" (14.4), the philosopher commented.

> the happiness of those for whom the day is blessed
> but doubly blessed the night
> whose
> simple wisdom
> shuns
> the thoughts
> of
> proud
> uncommon
> men
> (*Ba.* 425–9)

Plutarch continues by stating that Alexander was impressed by his independent spirit and is said to have remarked to friends who made unkind remarks about the surly philosopher: "You may say what you like, but if I were not Alexander, I would be Diogenes" (14.5). While this story may be fictitious, it does capture the character of both the philosopher and the king.

After completing his business at Corinth, Alexander consulted the oracle of Apollo at Delphi concerning his forthcoming war against Persia.[25] Unfortunately, he arrived there at a time when it was forbidden for Apollo's prophetess, the Pythia, to consider a question or utter a reply. When Alexander, who was determined to extract a response from this great authority, attempted to drag her off to the shrine, she is said to have exclaimed, "You are invincible, my son!" (P.14.7). Alexander then released her from his grip, saying that no further prophecy was required.

> such is my strength
> and my
> hand
> so
> invincible
> (*Il.* 8.450)

It was uncommon for Alexander to violate a sacred tradition. If anything, he was punctilious in observing religious protocol.[26] When necessity caused a conflict between action and orthodoxy, however, he would seek a solution that would accomplish his objective while keeping any religious penalties to a bare minimum. A perfect example of this behavior takes place before the battle of the Granicus River in 334 BC, when Alexander was faced with a situation which required creative religiosity.[27] He was determined to attack the Persians as soon as the opportunity presented itself, but it was the Macedonian month of Daisios (May), during which fighting was forbidden by custom. Applying the same imaginative approach for which he is famous on the battlefield, the king solemnly proclaimed that it was not Daisios at all, but a continuation of Artemisios, the preceding month. This manipulation of the calendar, which was undoubtedly approved by his seers, allowed him to engage in battle without (technically) violating the tradition.

Alexander's uncharacteristic behavior at Delphi in 336 is reminiscent of an encounter his mythical ancestor Heracles was once supposed to have had with the Pythia. Apollo was the god of purification, especially concerning homicide, and Heracles is said to have visited Delphi seeking a cure for the madness that made him kill. When the oracle refused to reply to his request, Heracles seized the tripod, the sacred seat of the prophetess, and threatened to establish his own oracle elsewhere. Apollo then rose to the defense of his priestess and struggled violently with his half-brother. Zeus had to separate his brawling sons with a thunderbolt, but Heracles eventually got the advice he was seeking. Members of this family shared an insistence on having things their own way, and Alexander, who thought of himself as a direct descendant of Heracles, was no exception.

Alexander seems to have appeared at Delphi shortly after Apollo had left for his annual sojourn among the Hyperboreans. In the god's absence, Dionysus, who had become Apollo's partner there, presided over the sanctuary. Therefore it would be Dionysus, and not Apollo, who was slighted by Alexander's rude behavior.

Plutarch, who was a priest of Apollo at Delphi and had been initiated into the mysteries of the cult of Dionysus, offers some revealing observations on the two gods: "Apollo the artists represent in paintings and sculpture as ever ageless and young, but Dionysus they depict in many guises and forms; and they attribute to Apollo in general a uniformity, orderliness, and unadulterated seriousness, but to Dionysus a certain variability combined with playfulness, wantonness, seriousness, and frenzy" (P.*Mor*.389b).

If Apollo symbolizes, in some ways, the rational element in human beings, "Dionysus represents the irrational element in man, and his myths the conflict between reason and social convention on one side, emotion on the other," says G. S. Kirk.[28] Although seemingly antithetical, Apollo and Dionysus were joined together symbiotically at Delphi long before Alexander's excursion there. Andrew Stewart describes an Attic red-figured *crater* (a bowl-shaped vase used for mixing wine and water) from the early fourth century that pictures "these two representatives of opposing yet complementary aspects of the human psyche as conjoined in an indissoluble bond."[29]

Alexander's physical intimidation of the Pythia, occurring it would seem while Dionysus was on watch at Delphi, was an act of violence (*hybris*) that a vengeful deity was not likely to forget. The king galloped north unmindful of the Apollonian maxims to "Know thyself" and "Do nothing in excess," while the divine sentinel unveiled his enigmatic smile.

He shall come
to
know
Dionysus
(*Ba.* 859–60)

## NORTHERN CAMPAIGNS (335 BC)

Alexander rushed back to Macedonia with the intention of stabilizing his northern frontiers as soon as possible.[30] In the early spring of 335 he led a strike force up from Amphipolis, past Philippi and Philippopolis to Mount Haemus. Perhaps Olympias, a devotee of Dionysus, advised her son that his behavior at Delphi was more serious than he realized.

Mankind young man possesses two supreme blessings
First of these is the goddess Demeter or Earth . . .
who gave to man . . . grain . . .
But after her there came
the son of Semele
who matched her present
by inventing
liquid
wine
as
his gift
to man
(*Ba.* 274–80)

Whatever his motivation, Alexander made a point of pausing to sacrifice to Dionysus at the god's sanctuary in northeastern Macedonia. The flames from his sacrifice reached such an unusual height that Alexander became alarmed.[31] The king's seers reassured him that this merely signified victory in the campaign ahead, and he appears to have been satisfied with this interpretation.

At the Trojan pass in the Balkan Mountains Alexander was confronted with Thracian wagons that were gathered at the top of a steep incline. He anticipated a cascade of descending wagons as a prelude to an enemy attack, and ordered his troops, when room was available, to sidestep the oncoming vehicles. When this was impossible, the soldiers were instructed to lie down and link their shields together so that the wagons would bound harmlessly over them. This spectacular tactic was followed by a Macedonian offensive that stunned the routed.

Soon after, Alexander defeated the Triballians, a tribe that had caused considerable problems for his father, and then continued his march toward the Danube (Ister). Philip had been the first Macedonian king to campaign as far north as the Danube, and Alexander was now presented with a chance to surpass his father.[32] Here, according to Arrian, Alexander felt a longing (*pothos*)[33] to cross this formidable river. *Pothos*, which appears in Aristotle's paean to Hermias, and intermittently throughout Arrian's account of Alexander's career, has been linked by a modern scholar with the conqueror's "longing for things not yet within reach, for the unknown, far distant, unattained."[34]

> Why
> are
> you
> so
> passionately
> curious?
> (*Ba.* 813)

Although the desire to outdo Philip was most likely the prime motive, other factors undoubtedly contributed to his decision to cross the Danube. Frustrated by the menacing Getae across the river, Alexander probably concluded that it was necessary to demonstrate that there was no safe retreat for any hostile force in the region. The transporting of his army across the Danube in the face of opposition was just the sort of major challenge Alexander excelled at. The hides from his troops' tents were stuffed with straw and converted into rafts, and these improvised vessels were joined with local dugout canoes to form a makeshift flotilla. Some five thousand men crossed the Danube overnight.

The enemy was astounded when the Macedonian infantry, presumed to be on the other side of the river, emerged out of a field of high-standing corn, flattening it with their fourteen-foot pikes held sideways. The Getae retreated in utter confusion, and soon tribes from throughout the surrounding area came to pay homage to this dashing young warrior who fought with such flair. Even the Celts, whose troop concentrations were some distance away on the Adriatic, arrived to pay their respects.

A conversation between Alexander and the Celts at a drinking session was reported by Ptolemy, who fought in this campaign.[35] Alexander, perhaps hoping to elicit a memorable compliment from them, asked the Celts what they dreaded most. They answered that their greatest fear was that the sky would fall. Alexander was puzzled and no doubt disappointed by their response. They did finally express admiration of some unspecified sort for him, and he in turn declared the Celts to be his friends and allies. As they departed, however, Alexander, having formed a somewhat different opinion from the one that he expressed, murmured, "What braggarts Celts are!" (A.1.4.8).[36]

In gratitude for his safe passage across the river, Alexander sacrificed to Zeus the Preserver, Heracles, and the Spirit of the Danube. He may also have privately acknowledged his indebtedness to a celebrated Athenian writer and general for this great feat. Xenophon, who helped lead the retreat of 10,000 Greeks out of Mesopotamia and across Asia Minor earlier in the fourth century, had left a record of this remarkable journey in his *Anabasis*. In this work, a treasure trove of detailed military, geographic, and ethnographic information about Persia, Xenophon describes a remarkably similar crossing of the Euphrates on rafts of stuffed skins.[37]

Alexander knew his Xenophon, and seems to have been particularly influenced by the *Cyropaedia*, a fictionalized and laudatory account of the life of Cyrus the Great (d. 529), the founder of the Persian Empire.[38] This work, written by an intelligent and pragmatic Athenian aristocrat, catalogues the virtues of an ideal leader, while addressing the questions of authority and imperial governance. Simon Hornblower points out that the theory of kingship found in this work, wherein a ruler earns his right to govern through his own exertions (*philoponia, askesis*) as a glorious servant of his people, has its model in Heracles.[39]

The *Cyropaedia* contains an imaginary conversation in which Xenophon has Cyrus tell his father Cambyses, "'that the ruler ought to surpass those under his rule not in self-indulgence, but in taking forethought and willingly undergoing toil.'"[40] Cambyses advises Cyrus that nothing is more important for a leader than winning the affection of his men, and this can be accomplished by sharing in their happiness, sorrow, pleasure, and pain. In war, Cambyses tells Cyrus, "'if they [the campaigns] fall in the summer time, the general must show that he can endure the heat of the sun better than his soldiers can, and that he can endure cold better than they if it be in winter; if the way lead through difficulties, that he can endure hardships better. All this contributes to his being loved by his men.'"[41]

Xenophon's Cyrus is a prototype of the ideal ruler, and Alexander was, as Strabo says, "a lover of Cyrus" (11.11.4).[42] To Xenophon the Persian monarch is an intrepid conqueror who consistently displays courage and a military inventiveness that confounds the enemy.[43] He keeps his troops on the march as much as possible, and sponsors competitive games when they are stationary. These games encourage an *esprit de corps*, advocate fitness, and cultivate a benign paternal image for the ruler who doles out rewards for excellence.[44] Cyrus memorizes the names of his officers,[45] pays special attention to his wounded,[46] and shows a deep, personal concern for the problems of his soldiers.[47] He constantly monitors their health, morale, and discipline.[48] He must learn "from the gods by the soothsayer's art,"[49] which will give him a special wisdom that is respected by his subjects. "For people are only too glad to obey the man who they believe takes wiser thought for their interests than they themselves do."[50]

Image is of the utmost importance, and appearance is sometimes more important than reality. We seem to learn from Cyrus, Xenophon says, that it is necessary for a successful ruler "to excel his subjects not only in point of being actually better than they, but that he ought also to cast a sort of spell upon them."[51] Cyrus may have had this in mind, Xenophon infers, when he adopted the Median dress "and persuaded his associates also to adopt it; for he thought that if any one had any personal defect, that dress would help to conceal it, and that it made the wearer look very tall and very handsome."[52] Xenophon also mentions a shoe to which an additional sole could be added without being obvious so that "the wearer can easily put something into the soles so as to make him look taller than he is."[53]

Xenophon would have admired the young Alexander's speed, determination, and peremptory analysis of one complex military situation after another. Through these efforts, Alexander was able to lend stability to his northern borders, and, into the bargain, offer his troops a sample of the type of military experiences they were destined to encounter in the years ahead.

Although he had been confronted by enemies from every direction upon his accession, Alexander dealt successfully with each in turn. Some, Diodorus tells us, he won over "by persuasion and diplomacy, others he frightened into keeping the peace, but some had to be mastered by force and so reduced to submission" (17.3.6). He did what was necessary to establish his authority as king, erasing any doubts in the minds of his troops that, at least on the battlefield, Alexander was a worthy successor to Philip.

## THE DESTRUCTION OF THEBES (335 BC)

While Alexander struggled to subdue his northern neighbors, Demosthenes fulminated against him in the Athenian Assembly. The orator referred to him as a boy, and, worse yet, a Margites – the anti-hero of a Homeric parody who never seemed to get anything straight, including his own parentage. Demosthenes urged Thebes to revolt, promised to supply the city with weapons purchased with Persian gold, and offered assurances that Athens would join the Thebans in a war against Macedon. It was rumored in Greece that Alexander had been killed among the barbarians, and Demosthenes went so far as to produce a wounded soldier who claimed to have participated in the battle in which Alexander fell.[54] Some Thebans, prompted by the return of exiles hostile to Macedon, killed two Macedonians who had ventured outside their fortress. Thebes was in open revolt.

Faced with the prospect of a general outbreak in Greece, Alexander led his troops southward through the pass at Thermopylae. He announced that because Demosthenes had called him a boy while he was among the Illyrians and Triballians, and a youth when he was in Thessaly, he would demonstrate to the orator before the walls of Athens that he was a man.[55] It was Thebes, however, and not Athens, that was his immediate consideration, and Alexander marched his troops some 250 miles in 13 days and established himself a few miles north of the city.[56] At first the Thebans found it impossible to believe that it was truly Alexander and not Antipater or some other Alexander who led the army. Their incredulity soon vanished.

Alexander stationed his troops outside the city at the Electra Gate, close to the precinct of Iolaus (named for the beloved companion of Heracles), where the road from Athens entered Thebes. Hoping that his presence would force the Thebans to reconsider their position, Alexander waited for signs of repentance and reconciliation. He asked for the surrender of two of the leaders of the revolt to match the Macedonian casualties, and offered amnesty for all those who were willing to separate themselves from the insurgents. With surprising insolence the Thebans countered with a demand that Alexander turn Philotas and Antipater over to them. They announced from a high overlook, Diodorus says, "that anyone who wished to join the Great King and Thebes in freeing the Greeks and destroying the tyrant of Greece should come over to them. This epithet stung Alexander. He flew into a towering rage and declared that he would pursue the Thebans with the extremity of punishment" (17.9.5–6).

Thebes offered a valiant defense, but the city was overwhelmed. Alexander, Arrian tells us, could be seen "now here, now there," (1.8.7) in the battle.

> No one could have stood up against him and stopped him
> except the gods
> when he burst in the gates
> and
> his eyes
> flashed
> fire
> (*Il.* 12.465–6)

The Macedonian juggernaut, supported by troops from local members of the Corinthian League, prevailed. Six thousand Thebans were slaughtered before the engagement was over, and afterwards the question arose of whether or not further punishment should be inflicted.

Through its revolt Thebes had violated the Common Peace established by the Corinthian League, of which it was a member. Alexander had acted in his official capacity as an agent of the League. Continuing to observe protocol, Alexander turned the fate of Thebes over to those members of the League who happened to be present. These members were, for the most part, from neighboring cities victimized by Thebes at some time in the past, and they recited a litany of unconscionable acts perpetrated in bygone days by this great power. Charges included the leveling of several cities and, perhaps more important to Alexander, Thebes' support of Persians against Greeks in the past. Justin says, "They brought forward also the fabulous accounts of their old crimes, with which they had filled every theatre, to make them odious not only for their recent perfidy, but for their ancient infamy" (11.3.11). What else might one expect of the city that produced the likes of Oedipus and Creon? It was solemnly decreed that the city was to be destroyed.

As *hegemon* of the Corinthian League, Alexander carried out the order. Thebes was leveled, and 30,000 of its inhabitants were sold into slavery. The king was careful to protect priests, priestesses, temples, holy places, and individuals who supported Macedon in one way or another. He also spared the family home of the poet Pindar, who had written one poem in honor of Alexander I of Macedon, and another speaking of "Herakles bravest in battle . . . the blood in him follows his father's tracks."[57]

Technically, Alexander had nothing to do with the decision of the League; he merely executed its mandate. There is no doubt, however, that he could have influenced the members' discussions had he chosen to.[58] Alexander seems to have complied so exactly with the League's directive because he expected that this action would "frighten the rest of the Greeks into submission by making a terrible example" (P.11.11). It did. In J. R. Hamilton's words, "It was a calculated act of terrorism on Alexander's part."[59]

Athens had waited to see how the Thebans would fare against the Macedonians before supplying the manpower it had promised. Now, fearing a similar fate for their own city, the Athenians sent a delegation to Alexander, congratulating him on his return from the north and cravenly condemning the Theban revolt. Plutarch says: "It may be that Alexander's fury had been sated with blood, like a lion's, or perhaps that he wished to efface his cruel and savage treatment of the Thebans by performing an act of clemency" (13.2). The king demanded only the surrender of ten (or eight) generals and citizens (including Demosthenes) who were instrumental in encouraging Thebes to revolt.[60] Instead Athens sent Demades, who had negotiated successfully with Philip, to appeal for a mitigation of what Alexander had asked. Since he was now as anxious as his father had been to launch the Asiatic adventure, Alexander merely insisted on the exile of a certain non-Athenian general in the service of the city. The Athenians willingly complied.

Philip's destruction of Olynthus in 348 had ended any resistance to Macedonian suzerainty in that region, and Alexander's destruction of Thebes accomplished the same objective in Greece. Yet Thebes was different. It boasted a rich tableau of mythological and historical figures that included Cadmus, Oedipus, Pelopidas, and Epaminondas. This city, it was said, was one of the two eyes of Hellas, and now that eye was gone.[61] Arrian admits that the act was viewed by all Greeks as a general calamity.[62] It certainly put to rest any hopes for a cordial relationship between Alexander and the mainland Greeks, and seems to have had a telling personal effect on the king.[63] Perhaps it occurred to him, amidst the rubble of the city, as he ruminated over Thebes' vanished supremacy and distinguished religious tradition, that this was, after all, the birthplace of Dionysus, the city chosen by the god in which to establish his cult.

> I was
> terribly
> blasphemed
> my name
> dishonored
> in
> Thebes
> (*Ba.* 1377–8)

Even if Alexander had forgotten all of this during those frenzied days of decision and clash of arms on the Boeotian plain, his mother was certain to have reminded him of the sacrilegious nature of his action once he returned to Pella.

Later in his career Alexander claimed that some of the most painful experiences in his life were acts of divine retribution for what he had done at Thebes. Plutarch writes: "Certainly he believed that the murder of Cleitus, which he committed when he was drunk, and the cowardly refusal of the Macedonians to cross the Ganges [Beas] and attack the Indians, which cut short his campaign and robbed him of its crowning achievement, were both caused by the anger of the god Dionysus, who wished to avenge the destruction of his favourite city" (13.4).

> By the clustered grapes
> I swear by Dionysus'
> wine
> someday
> you shall come to know
> the name
> of
> Bromius [Dionysus]
> (*Ba.* 534–6)

## DIUM (335 BC)

In November 335 Alexander presided over the annual festival in Macedonia in honor of Zeus Olympius and the Muses at Dium. This festival, which was held at the foot of Mount Olympus in Pieria, had been established by Archelaus and used by Philip to commemorate a number of victories, including the capture of Olynthus. It was a nine-day celebration, with each of the Muses being honored on a separate day. With delegates in attendance from all over Greece, it served, like Philip's fateful gathering at Aegae, to trumpet the king's planned crossing of the Hellespont during the upcoming spring. Wine flowed, and Alexander no doubt heard drinking songs similar to the one composed by Bacchylides for Alexander I in the preceding century:

> I hasten to send a golden feather of the Muses
>     to Alexander as an adornment for feasts
>     on twentieth days
>     when the sweet inducement of the moving cups
>     makes warm the tender heart of youths
>     and the anticipation of Cypris [Aphrodite],
>     mingled with gifts of Dionysus,
>     disturbs their senses
>     and sends men's thoughts on high.
> Then does one destroy the citadels of cities
>     and rule as monarch over all humanity.
>     His halls gleam with gold and ivory,
>     and over the radiant sea from Egypt
>     wheat-laden ships bring him vast wealth.
>     Such are the longings [*pothos*] of the drinker's heart.[64]

During this festival Alexander was informed that a local statue of Orpheus, who, like Pentheus, was said to have been attacked and dismembered by maenads, had begun to sweat profusely.[65] This would ordinarily be recognized as a bad omen. However, Aristander of Telmessus,[66] who had become Alexander's chief seer (and may have served Philip in the same capacity), interpreted it differently. He claimed that this phenomenon simply meant that poets would have to work themselves into a lather in order to do justice to Alexander's great deeds.[67] Aristander had a talent for transforming such disastrous omens into harbingers of good fortune. His revelations were good for morale, and, on an *ad hoc* basis, he proved to be remarkably accurate, thanks in part to his patron's ability to turn potential catastrophe into victory.

> You are
> an extraordinary young man
> and you go to an extraordinary experience
> You shall win a glory
> towering to heaven
> and
> usurping god's
> (*Ba.* 971–2)

## ALEXANDER'S SEXUALITY

When Alexander's advisers attempted to persuade him to marry and sire a son before his departure for the Orient, the young king flatly refused to consider the request, and remarked curtly that it was no time to remain at home "celebrating a marriage and awaiting the birth of children" (D.17.16.2). The child's birth, of course, would not have required Alexander's presence, and his response must have seemed illogical and vexing.

Alexander's minimization of the problem of succession was particularly baffling since the king and his advisers knew all too well the history of Macedonian civil wars over the question of legitimate succession. His decision to embark for Asia without even considering the need for a royal heir at home must have seemed bizarre, if not unconscionable, to many, and certainly raises questions concerning Alexander's attitude toward women and the nature of his sexuality.

Alexander held women in higher regard than did most of his contemporaries, including the intellectuals of the Greek-speaking world. His tutor Aristotle, for example, proclaimed the subordinate role of women in Hellenic culture as ordained by nature: a man's virtue was displayed through leading; a woman's, through following.[68] The philosopher pointed out with some pride, however, that the Greek, unlike the barbarian, did not treat a woman as if she were a slave. On the contrary, he boasted, Greek men showed a genuine appreciation for a woman's beauty, compliance, and capacity for work![69]

Alexander's attitude toward women was, for the most part, uncommonly considerate and appreciative. In Asia Minor he restored Queen Ada of Caria to her throne. Sisygambis, the Persian queen mother, was permitted to ride in splendor with the Macedonian king while he was still at war with her son. Alexander also addressed both Ada and Sisygambis as "mother." Thomas W. Africa has suggested that the proud Sisygambis served in Asia as "a surrogate Olympias without the sound and the fury."[70] This could very well have been the case.

During the sack of Thebes Alexander found it necessary to grant immunity to a certain Timocleia, who had murdered one of his officers after the drunken man had raped and robbed her.[71] In fact, Alexander apparently refused to take sexual advantage of any of the tens of thousands of women captured during his travels. Instead, he is said, for instance, to have walked past the most alluring of Persian women as if they were "lifeless images cut out of stone" (P.21.11).[72]

Alexander's unconventional behavior in the presence of women has been the source of abundant speculation concerning his sexuality.[73] Many scholars have assumed that Alexander and his lifelong friend Hephaestion were lovers, at least during their younger years. Alexander was fond of comparing them to Achilles and Patroclus in the *Iliad*, and since it was generally assumed in his own day that this celebrated Homeric relationship was homosexual, Alexander's encouragement of the analogy might very well indicate a similar bond between himself and Hephaestion.[74]

In 334 the king is reported to have crowned the tomb of Achilles at Troy, while Hephaestion placed a wreath on the tomb of Patroclus.[75] A year later, after the battle of Issus in 333, Sisygambis, presuming that the taller of the two men was the king, inadvertently made obeisance to Hephaestion rather than Alexander. King Alexander graciously reassured a mortified Sisygambis that she had made no mistake, "for Hephaestion was also an Alexander" (A.2.12.7).[76]

Through the vicissitudes of world conquest Alexander's *alter ego*, Hephaestion, remained unequivocally supportive of the king, and ultimately became his only real confidant.[77] Alexander permitted Hephaestion to read personal reports from his mother on the state of affairs in Europe, and we know that Hephaestion was close enough to Alexander to earn Olympias' suspicion and enmity. Hephaestion's loyalty to Alexander was rewarded with honors, culminating in his appointment as second in command. But Alexander's Patroclus would drink himself to death in 324 under circumstances remarkably similar to those that would surround the king's own demise. The loss devastated Alexander.

> my dear companion has perished
> Patroklos
> whom I loved beyond all other companions
> as well
> as my own life
> (*Il.* 18.80–2)

There is evidence of "institutionalized pederasty" in Macedonian court circles,[78] and so it would have been unlikely for either Olympias or Philip (who seems to have consorted with anything ambulatory) to object too strenuously to a youthful *affaire de cœur* between Alexander and Hephaestion. Parental concern would only arise if Alexander failed to show a sexual interest in women at the appropriate time. When he became king, Alexander would be expected to produce an heir to the throne. Any deficiency in this respect would be of serious concern to all. A curious anecdote attributed to Theophrastus, a disciple of Aristotle, who accompanied the philosopher to Macedonia and probably served as his assistant at Mieza, relates to Alexander's sexuality.[79] According to this account, both Olympias and Philip expressed concern over Alexander's indifference to women. They therefore arranged a sexual encounter between Alexander and a seductive Thessalian courtesan named Callixeina. Theophrastus says that "Olympias often begged him to have intercourse with Callixeina,"[80] apparently to no avail. Alexander himself is reputed to have said that "it was sleep and sexual intercourse which more than anything else, reminded him that he was mortal" (P.22.6).[81] He may simply have been an individual for whom sex was not an issue of paramount concern, or he may have suppressed his own sexual urge, or he may in fact have been homosexual.

Alexander's affair with Barsine, the first woman in whom he seems to have had a special interest, occurred when he was in his early twenties and resulted in the birth of an illegitimate son called Heracles.[82] Barsine, who was perhaps ten years the senior of Alexander, was the daughter of the Persian satrap Artabazus,[83] who would prove useful to Alexander in the future. This relationship, perhaps Alexander's first sexual experience with a woman, had been urged on by Parmenio, his chief adviser in Asia.[84]

Given all of the opportunity at his disposal, Alexander proved to be a reluctant heterosexual. His first marriage, to Roxane, did not take place until Alexander was 27 years old. Plutarch (47.7) calls it "a love match," but practical considerations involving Alexander's future plans were certainly at stake at the time. His second and third wives, both married during the year before he died, were relatives of former Persian kings, and his intentions were blatantly political. Alexander did not live to see his only legitimate heir born. Roxane gave birth to a boy called Alexander (IV) shortly after the king's death in 323.[85] Roxane, her teenage son Alexander, and the illegitimate Heracles would all perish during the wars of succession.

> you were lost young from life
> and have left me a widow in your house
> . . . [our] boy is only a baby
> . . . I think
> he
> will
> never
> come of age
> (*Il.* 24.725–8)

The wars came about in large part because of Alexander's inability to produce a successor during his own lifetime. A. R. Burn says of this,

> [O]ne cannot but reflect that this is the most crushing evidence of Alexander's irresponsibility. His ideals were purely self-centred. It gave him pleasure and served his great purpose – fame – to be munificent to his friends, attentive to his wounded, generous on occasion to a brave and attractive enemy; but his lifelong lack of interest in the succession, especially in view of his own recklessness, shows an utter carelessness of what happened to Asia, Greece or Macedon once he was gone.[86]

## ALEXANDER AT THE HELLESPONT (334 BC)

Alexander marched from Pella in the early spring of 334, having left Antipater as his viceroy in charge of Macedonian and Greek affairs. After passing below Mount Pangaeum, with its oracle of Dionysus, and skirting Amphipolis, Alexander began replicating, in reverse, the route taken by Xerxes in his invasion of Greece during the Persian Wars, thereby confirming Macedonian propaganda that this was a war of revenge.[87]

His expeditionary force of about 32,000 foot soldiers and 5,100 horsemen arrived in the Gallipoli peninsula after a twenty-day march of about

300 miles from Pella.[88] The main body of troops, under Parmenio, crossed from Sestos in Europe to Abydos in Asia, which had been Xerxes' point of departure in the fifth century BC. The king, however, observing his own priorities, proceeded down the southern tip of the peninsula to Elaeus, where Agamemnon is said to have sailed from Europe with his Greek armada in the Trojan War. Alexander had decided to genuflect at Troy before taking up arms against the Persians. The king, it seems, paid as much attention to Clio, the Muse of history, as he did to Calliope, the Muse of heroic epics. His historical consciousness in such matters was meticulous.

Particulars also reveal the comprehensiveness of Alexander's religiosity, as well as his passion to emulate the great heroes. Before setting sail he sacrificed in the Thracian Chersonese to Protesilaus, a Thessalian participant in the Trojan War, who enjoyed everlasting fame because he was the first to set foot on Asian soil. Protesilaus, however, had been killed on the spot, and Alexander sacrificed at his tomb in the hope of avoiding the same fate.

It was Alexander's turn on stage in the oscillating drama of conflict between Greeks and Asians. Fair-skinned, with blondish hair and a penetrating gaze, Alexander was clean-shaven and muscular, but slightly less than average in height.[89] His hurried gait and rapid speech exuded an aura of destiny and high adventure. Plutarch tells us: "The best likeness of Alexander which has been preserved for us is to be found in the statues sculpted by Lysippus, the only artist whom Alexander considered worthy to represent him. Alexander possessed a number of individual features which many of Lysippus' followers later tried to reproduce, for example the poise of the neck which was tilted slightly to the left, or a certain melting look in his eyes, and the artist has exactly caught these peculiarities" (4.1–2).

Xenocrates, who is associated with the Lysippean school, describes qualities in the work of the master that may help to explain his special appeal to Alexander:

> Lysippus is said to have contributed greatly to the art of bronze statuary by representing the details of the hair and by making his heads smaller than the old sculptors used to do, and his bodies more slender and firm, to give his statues the appearance of greater height . . . . he used commonly to say that whereas his predecessors had made men as they really were, he made them as they appeared to be.
>
> (Pliny *HN* 34.65)

This skill might have been particularly attractive to Alexander, who, as mentioned, was slightly shorter than most men, but who was also aware, like Xenophon's Cyrus, that illusion could compensate for reality.[90]

During the crossing the king sacrificed a bull to Poseidon and, like Xerxes, poured a libation from a golden cup. This libation was in honor of the Nereids, the sea-nymphs who were his ancestors through Olympias. At one point he took the helm of the royal flagship from Menoetius (who bore the same name as Patroclus' father in the *Iliad*), but as the coastline emerged he changed into a full suit of armor and was the first to leap from the ship and hurl his spear into the shore. He was announcing, in distinctly Homeric fashion, "that he received Asia from the gods as a spear-won prize" (D.17.17.2).[91]

Tyche, the goddess of fortune, was with him. The Persian fleet had not yet assembled for the sailing season, and the entire expeditionary force passed over unchallenged. Alexander landed in what was believed to be the old "harbor of the Achaeans" spoken of in the *Iliad*. He erected altars and sacrificed to Zeus of the Safe Landings (Apobaterios), Athena, and Heracles, – just as he had done on the European side. The young warrior was placing his invasion in the custody of these three deities.

> I bring this young man
> to a great ordeal
> The victor
> Bromius
> (*Ba.* 974–6)

Alexander went directly to Troy and sacrificed at the temple of Athena Ilias. There he dedicated his armor to the goddess and replaced it with relics said to have been used during the Trojan War.[92] Alexander also took the time to sacrifice to Priam at the altar of Zeus of the Enclosures (Herkeios), where Neoptolemus, the son of Achilles, had slain Priam during the sack of Troy. Was Alexander atoning for the sacrilege committed by his ancestor? Perhaps he was concerned that Priam's spirit might be waiting to strike back at one of his murderer's unwary descendants?[93] This king was taking no chances.

At Troy Alexander was asked by a trafficker in tourist items if he wished to see the lyre of Paris, who was also called "Alexander" in the *Iliad*. Offended by any linkage with this undistinguished fighter and womanizer who shared his name, Alexander indignantly rejected the suggestion, but said that he would not mind seeing the lyre of Achilles, who sang songs celebrating the glorious deeds of brave men.[94]

Xerxes had sacrificed 1,000 cows to Athena at Troy,[95] but Alexander could not afford to match the Great King's grand gesture. Alexander began his reign faced with a 500-talent deficit left by his father.[96] Four hundred and forty talents had been realized through the sale of captives at Thebes, and this helped somewhat, but his financial situation remained precarious because of his continuing obligation to meet the expenses incurred when maintaining a large army in the field. In a display of indifference to his own circumstances, Alexander turned over the royal estates and their revenues to his personal friends and Royal Companions.

When asked what he had left for himself, Alexander replied cavalierly, "My hopes!" (P.15.4).[97]

The fallen statue of a former satrap of Phrygia, which lay outside the temple of Athena at Ilium, moved Aristander to forecast a great triumph for his patron in the near future. This was a most welcome prediction. Alexander hurried to rejoin his main force and set out to confront the enemy. *En route* he came upon the city of Lampsacus, then under Persian rule, whose townsmen sent out Anaximenes, a native son and historian, to greet Alexander and attempt to persuade him to bypass the city. Pausanias' account says that Alexander anticipated the historian's mission and swore by the gods in the presence of the petitioner that he would do the opposite of whatever Anaximenes asked.[98] When the astute Anaximenes asked that the king destroy the city, Alexander, bound by his oath, and perhaps induced by handsome tribute, is said to have laughed and marched on. In gratitude his fellow citizens dedicated a statue to the historian at Olympia.

The next town in Alexander's southwestern line of march was Priapus, which was also under Persian control. Rather than risk having their city sacked, the inhabitants decided to throw in their lot with Alexander, and the king dispatched a small contingent to "liberate" those Greeks from Persian overlordship. The men assigned to the task must have been surprised and amused by the manner in which the city's divine namesake was represented. The most prominent attribute of this deity, who is referred to by Charles Seltman as probably "the oldest and most primitive of all Mediterranean wine-gods,"[99] was his gargantuan genitalia, which required a wheelbarrow when the divinity moved about. The cult of Priapus spread rapidly throughout the Mediterranean world after its discovery by Alexander's troops. This fertility god, who may have been associated with an earlier Greek version of Dionysus, was eventually incorporated into the Greek pantheon as his son.

## THE BATTLE OF THE GRANICUS RIVER (334 BC)

Memnon, a Greek mercenary from Rhodes in the service of Persia, was familiar with the efficiency of the Macedonian phalanx. He advised against a direct conflict with the Macedonians and proposed a "scorched-earth" strategy that would force Alexander to return home for lack of provisions. Memnon also urged that the war be pressed at sea, and that Macedonia itself should be attacked. The Persian satraps interpreted his suggestions as an implication of their military inferiority and stoutly proclaimed their refusal to relinquish any measure of imperial territory.

The Persians decided to put an immediate end to the invasion. They would wait for Alexander at the Granicus (Koçabas) River, which flowed northward from Mount Ida through Hellespontine Phrygia.[100] It was late in the spring, and the river afforded some steep and muddy defensive positions on the east bank. Alexander deployed about 13,000 foot soldiers and some 5,100 horsemen. This army outnumbered the enemy force of about 10,000 cavalry and 4,000–5,000 Greek mercenary infantry. The Persians stationed their 10,000 horsemen along the bank of the river.[101]

Diodorus pictures Alexander waiting to strike at dawn at an unopposed river crossing.[102] Arrian, in a contradictory account, has Parmenio appealing for such a delay but Alexander responding to his arguments by saying: "All this I know, Parmenio, but I should feel ashamed if after crossing the Hellespont easily, this petty stream . . . hinders us from crossing, just as we are. I consider this unworthy either of the prestige of the Macedonians or of my own celerity in dealing with dangers; I believe it would encourage the Persians to think themselves equal to fighting the Macedonians, since they have not experienced any immediate disaster to justify their alarm" (1.13.6–7). Alexander, as one might expect, prevailed.

After an initial cavalry charge in which twenty-five of the Companions of the king were killed, Alexander, conspicuous by the white plumage displayed on his helmet, joined in the assault.

> Over his mighty head he set the well-fashioned helmet
> . . . the plumes nodded terribly above it
> (*Il.* 16.137–8)

The Persians were intent on slaying Alexander straightaway, and they launched a series of cavalry charges aimed directly at him. The Persian nobility descended on Alexander, and a series of fierce personal encounters in the Homeric mold took place.

> if one is to win honour in battle
> he must by all means
> stand his ground strongly
> whether he be struck
> or
> strike down
> another
> (*Il.* 11.409–10)

Alexander's spear broke, but Demaratus of Corinth supplied the king with his own spear. Then Alexander, seeing Mithridates, the son-in-law of the Persian king, "charged out alone in advance of his own men, thrust his lance into Mithridates' face and hurled him to the ground" (A.1.15.7). Another Persian nobleman, Rhoesakes, sheared off part of Alexander's helmet with a blow from his scimitar, but he too was run through by the king. Spithridates, the brother of Rhoesakes, then approached Alexander from the rear with his scimitar poised to deliver a mortal blow when Cleitus, son of Dropides, who led the Royal Squadron of the Companion Cavalry, severed the Persian's arm with a timely stroke and saved the king's life.[103]

We shall still keep you safe

for this time

o

hard

Achilleus

(*Il.* 19.408)

Macedonian numbers, discipline, and superior weaponry eventually took their toll. A determined charge up the river bank resulted in a rout of the Persians. The Greek mercenaries on the Persian side were surrounded and asked for quarter, but Alexander, Plutarch says, "guided by passion rather than by reason," refused (16.14). A slaughter ensued. The 2,000 survivors, including an appreciable number of Athenians, were treated as traitors according to principles adopted by the Corinthian League. They were put in chains and sent off to Macedonia to work in the mines.[104]

On the following day Alexander, whose personal courage played a significant role in the victory, saw to it that his own dead were given magnificent burials. Diodorus relates that "he thought it important by this sort of honour to create in his men greater enthusiasm to face the hazards of battle" (17.21.6). Arrian tells us that Alexander personally tended to his wounded, "visiting each man himself, examining their wounds, asking how they were received, and allowing them to recount and boast of their exploits" (1.16.5). The king ordered Lysippus to sculpt bronze statues of the twenty-five Companions who had perished in the first attack. These were set up at Dium in a grouping that featured Alexander.[105] All parents and children of every Macedonian who died at the Granicus were granted lifetime exemptions from property taxes and personal services.

Fallen Persian commanders (even Greek casualties on the Persian side) were also buried with honor. To underline his role as avenger and *hegemon* of the Corinthian League, and perhaps in the hope that the Athenians would come to share in the fantasy of this as a war of revenge, Alexander selected 300 full sets of armor from dead Persians and ordered them to be sent back to Athens and dedicated to Athena on the Acropolis. The attached inscription read: "Alexander son of Philip and the Greeks, except the Lacedaemonians,[106] set up these spoils from the barbarians dwelling in Asia" (A.1.16.7).

Luxury items, including purple draperies and ornate drinking vessels that were probably intended for the Dionysia, were sent home to Olympias. In turn, his mother sent Alexander a sacrificer-cook, who was familiar with all of the king's ancestral religious rites, and his Bacchic obligations as well, probably as a reminder to her son not to neglect this powerful deity.[107]

we must

do honor

to
this
god
(*Ba.* 181–3)


## ASIA MINOR (334 BC)

The way had now been made clear for the invading force. Alexander appointed a Macedonian as satrap of Hellespontine Phrygia, and the army moved inland in a southwesterly direction. Sardis, the most important city in the satrapy of Lydia, surrendered to the king, who granted its citizenry their "freedom." Mithrines, the Persian commander who turned the city and its treasures over to Alexander, was treated with observable honor as an advertisement of the advantages of cooperating with the young king.

Alexander's guise of "liberator" was common during this phase of his conquests. At Sardis, he represented himself as a restorer of the ancient customs that had been abolished when Cyrus the Great defeated Croesus of Lydia 200 years before. Alexander's court historian, Callisthenes, reminded his audience that Cyrus was the last man to capture Sardis,[108] an indication that Alexander had no objection to being compared favorably to the founder of the Achaemenid Persian Empire. Alexander could also have claimed that his takeover of the region was a resumption of family responsibilities, since like most Greeks he probably believed that the Lydians were at one time ruled by descendants of Heracles.

Alexander inspected the citadel of Sardis and was thinking of building a temple to the Macedonian Zeus Olympius somewhere in the vicinity when a sudden thunderstorm and a particularly heavy downpour seemed to center on the area of the ancient Lydian kings' palace. Alexander interpreted this event to be a sign from heaven and determined that the temple and altar be constructed there.[109] Croesus and the other Lydian kings before the Persian conquest took pride in their Hellenization, and this gesture must have pleased the local population. Like his father, Alexander was a master at public relations.

An oligarchy protecting Persian interests at Ephesus in Ionia was overthrown as soon as the news of Alexander's victory reached that city. The inhabitants promptly established a democratic faction in power and began to massacre oligarchs until Alexander intervened. He put a stop to the slaughter and pledged to support the newly installed democratic regime. In Greece Alexander, like his father, ordinarily backed oligarchs and other antidemocratic elements because they were more likely to serve Macedonian interests. In Asia Minor, however, oligarchs customarily supported Persian policy, and so the king responded by establishing democracies wherever feasible.[110] Alexander's political policies, like those of his father, were pragmatic rather than ideological.

Alexander's interest in Ephesus, however, was not entirely practical.

The city's temple to Artemis, one of the wonders of the ancient world, had been put to the torch by a madman around the time Alexander was born. In fact, a rumor had been circulated that the goddess (who had assisted in the birth of her twin brother Apollo) had failed to protect her temple because she was off in Europe assisting at the delivery of Alexander when the disaster occurred.[111] The temple was still under renovation in 334, and Alexander graciously offered to underwrite the remaining costs. The proud Ephesians refused his offer. They did, however, agree to permit Alexander to enlarge the size of the sacred *temenos*, the area of asylum.[112] Heracles was said to have done this at one time, and Alexander accepted their offer in order to emulate the actions of his ancestor.

While in Ephesus Alexander arranged to sit for Apelles of Cos, the most renowned painter of his age. Pliny the Elder relates an interesting anecdote concerning the special relationship between the affable portraitist and Alexander:

> [Apelles] was on quite good terms with Alexander the Great who frequently came to his studio – for, as we said, he forbade by an edict that his portrait should be made by any other artist – but when Alexander used to discourse upon many aspects of painting even though he was not well informed, Apelles would politely advise him to be quiet, saying that he was being laughed at by the boys who were grinding the colors. So confident was he in the power of his privileged position even with a king who was otherwise of an irascible nature.
>
> (*HN* 35.85–6)[113]

The king was apparently displeased with the initial efforts of Apelles in Ephesus but gratified by the final product, which pictured him brandishing a thunderbolt in the fashion of Zeus.[114] Lysippus objected to the religious insensitivity of such a portrayal (*P.Mor.*360d), but Alexander rewarded Apelles with twenty talents, literally a fortune, and the painting was ceremoniously dedicated in the temple. This perhaps provides an early sign of the king's interest in the depiction of his superhuman attributes.

Memnon, a formidable adversary, managed to escape from the Persian *débâcle* at the Granicus. This man, whose namesake was slain by Achilles in the Trojan War,[115] was no stranger to the king. They had met when Alexander was still a boy. Memnon had shared the exile of the Persian satrap Artabazus at Pella. He and his older brother, Mentor, had helped Artabazus in his satrapy, Hellespontine Phrygia, and were rewarded with large estates in the Troad. Mentor married the satrap's daughter Barsine, and when he died, which was sometime before Alexander's invasion, Barsine was married to Memnon. This is the same Barsine who is said to have had an affair with Alexander and given birth to his son Heracles.

Memnon and the other survivors from the Granicus had found refuge at Miletus in Ionia, and Alexander marched southward toward this seaport. On the way he stopped at Priene to implement the policies he had established at Ephesus and to contribute to a newly constructed temple of Athena Polias, the divine patroness of the city. His donation proved sufficient to earn him the right to be recognized as the dedicator of the temple. The inscription, which can be seen in the British Museum today,[116] reads: "King Alexander set up this temple to Athena Polias." It may have provided some consolation for the earlier refusal he had experienced at Ephesus.

The Corinthian League's fleet of 160 ships reached the harbor at Miletus before the arrival of the 400–sail Persian navy. The Greek allies blockaded the entrance to the harbor, while the Persians tried to lure the numerically inferior Greek force into open conflict on the high seas. Parmenio was inclined to oblige them. He pointed out an eagle perched on the shore that he interpreted as a sign favorable for a naval engagement, and even personally volunteered to participate in the attack. Alexander, worried about the adverse effects of a major naval defeat, as well as the possibility of excessive losses in such an operation, suggested that Parmenio had misinterpreted the omen. The eagle was unquestionably on Alexander's side, but resting on shore. Therefore, he reasoned, it would be from the shore that the Persian fleet would be defeated.[117]

Alexander besieged Miletus while the Greek fleet prevented the Persian navy from providing any assistance to the defenders of the city. Miletus fell, and the foreigners who failed to escape were either killed or enslaved. Among those who escaped were 300 Greek mercenaries, who managed to flee to a nearby island and were prepared to fight to the last man. Arrian says that Alexander "was seized with pity for them, as fine, loyal soldiers, and made terms with them on which they should join his forces" (1.19.6). Alexander's appreciation of their valor is undoubtedly historical, but he must also have realized that his harsh treatment of Greek mercenaries at the Granicus had only encouraged stiffer resistance. It would clearly be more advantageous to encourage them to fight on his behalf. The Milesians were granted amnesty because their ancestors had played a critical role in the struggle against the Persians a century and a half before. It might have seemed embarrassingly inconsistent to punish a city whose resistance to the Great King helped to spark the Persian Wars.

Soon after his success at Miletus Alexander decided to disband the entire allied fleet. This critical decision was influenced by the fact that the fleet was expensive to maintain, yet too small to be effective against the Persians in open waters. Furthermore, the king seems to have been unsure of the loyalty of many of his Greek allies. He therefore dismissed all but a few transport ships, which included twenty Athenian vessels whose retention guaranteed that city's continued cooperation. Alexander decided to deal with the Persian navy by denying its ships access to any harbor and thus "to overcome the ships from dry land" (A.1.20.1). It was a calculated risk, predicated on Alexander's ability to control each and every port on the eastern shores of the Mediterranean.

On his march south to Halicarnassus (Bodrum), the capital of Caria, Alexander was met by Ada,[118] a member of the satrapal royal house and sister of the now dead Pixodarus. Ada, who had once been queen, had been deposed by Pixodarus. She now sought to regain her throne with Alexander's help. He unhesitatingly recognized her as queen and accepted her offer to adopt him as her son.[119] Their relationship became most friendly and there are reports of Ada sending delicacies and sweetmeats to the king – all remarkably reminiscent of Olympias' smugglings when Alexander was under the harsh tutelage of Leonidas. The restoration of Ada probably pleased most Carians, who had seen Pixodarus succumb to Persian control. This would make it possible for Alexander to assume the throne without opposition when Ada died. It was typical of his masterful diplomacy.

Halicarnassus appeared to be impregnable. It had three citadels, massive walls, a huge moat, and an unopposed fleet to supply its defenders. Alexander's forces filled in the moat but were subjected to spirited sorties from the city that were aimed at destroying Alexander's siege equipment. The king's men also experienced considerable difficulty in their attempts to breach the wall and enter the city. At one point, Arrian tells us, "[two soldiers of] Perdiccas' battalion . . . bivouacked and drinking together, were each boasting of his own prowess and actions: rivalry arose, assisted by the heating fumes of wine; so they armed themselves and attacked the wall" (1.21.1). The fighting was so ferocious that in its aftermath Alexander was forced to ask for a truce to remove and bury his dead, a rare occurrence during his career.[120]

In the final conflict outside the walls Alexander's troops were faced with disaster until they were joined by a hitherto inactive battalion of Philip's veterans, who reversed the outcome of the battle.[121] Memnon, who had been appointed admiral and commander-in-chief of the Anatolian coast, led the defense of the city with imagination and élan, but eventually he was forced to abandon it and leave his garrison in the last of the three citadels. Alexander installed his own garrison in the other two citadels by the harbor, but he was inclined to leave well enough alone rather than put his entire force through another long and demoralizing siege. He left a contingent of troops behind to deal with the remaining enemy. This operation dragged on into 332.

Ada, who had personally assisted in the siege of Halicarnassus and was called "Mother" by Alexander, was recognized as the satrap of Caria by him. Alexander became her adopted son and heir to the kingdom.

Those men who had married just before the invasion began were sent back home on leave by the king. Arrian claims that "Alexander gained as much popularity by this act among the Macedonians as by any other" (1.24.2). It was a brilliant tactic. These young heroes would, of course, be excellent disseminators of propaganda about Alexander's efforts in Asia, and could be counted upon to do their best to sire a fresh supply of Macedonians for future exploits. Accompanying officers were ordered to return with able-bodied Macedonians as well as additional troops from the Peloponnesus.

Parmenio was instructed to return to Sardis with the foreign detachments and to rejoin the king at Gordium in the springtime. The troops on furlough and the fresh recruits were scheduled to rendezvous in Gordium as well. Meanwhile Alexander, accompanied by a smaller mobile force, set out to establish control over the southern coast of Asia Minor as far as Cilicia. His winter was spent seizing harbors and subduing recalcitrant tribes in the region.

One day, while Alexander was napping at Halicarnassus, an incident occurred that the king thought serious enough to call to Aristander's attention. A twittering swallow had circled over Alexander's head, and then began lighting here and there on his bed and chattering loudly enough to disturb the king's sleep. The king waved his hand at the bird, but instead of flying away the swallow perched on Alexander's head and stayed there until he was fully awakened. Aristander suggested that this represented a conspiracy soon to come to light that would involve one of Alexander's friends.[122]

At Phaselis Alexander received alarming news from Parmenio that lent credence to Aristander's prophecy. Parmenio informed him that he had captured a messenger from the Persian king who was prepared to offer 1,000 gold talents and the Macedonian throne to Alexander the Lyncestian for murdering Alexander. When brought before the king, the messenger recited the same story he had told Parmenio. The Lyncestian had apparently been mentioned to the Great King as a willing assassin of the Macedonian king,[123] even though he had been held in high favor by Alexander since proclaiming him king on the day Philip was murdered. Now in charge of the Thessalian cavalry, he served under Parmenio. This was a serious matter. Alexander had already been warned about Alexander the Lyncestian by Olympias. The king summoned his close friends to hear their opinions regarding the situation. They registered profound distrust for this "son of Aeropus" and expressed alarm at his being placed in charge of the Thessalian cavalry. Their advice was to "get rid of him as soon as possible, before he became more popular with the Thessalians and secured their help for a revolution" (A.1.25.5). Alexander sent a Macedonian commander and some native guides to instruct Parmenio to arrest and imprison Alexander the Lyncestian. This was accomplished, but perhaps because he was the son-in-law of Antipater,[124] the accused was spared execution for approximately three years.

In the marketplace at Phaselis, Alexander noticed "a statue which had been erected in honour of Theodectas [a tragedian who had been a friend of Aristotle], a former citizen of the place. One evening after dinner when he [Alexander] had drunk well, he had the impulse to pay a convivial tribute to his [Theodectas'] association with Aristotle and with philosophy, and so he led a band of revellers to the statue and crowned it with a garland" (P.17.9).

He shall

come

to rue

his

merrymaking

(*Ba.* 357)

After Phaselis Alexander moved along the coast toward Pamphylia. At one juncture he sent most of his troops up the face of a mountain and across its heights by way of a new road, while he and a small party attempted to negotiate the coastline along the narrow ledges below. Without the strong northerly wind that shifted the water outward, thereby lowering the level of the sea enough to create a path along the water's edge, this route would have been impassable. However, at the critical moment the wind shifted and Alexander and his party were able to achieve their objective.[125] Good fortune continued to embrace him.

## THE GORDIAN KNOT (333 BC)

With his newlywed soldiers on furlough, Alexander kept his appointment with Parmenio and his reinforcements at Gordium (the capital of ancient Phrygia) sometime in the spring of 333. Several Athenian envoys also arrived with an appeal for the king to free the Athenians captured at the Granicus. Alexander refused to grant their request, but said that they might approach him again when circumstances were more favorable. Arrian says, "Alexander did not think it safe, with the Persian war still in progress, to relax intimidation of the Greeks who did not scruple to fight for the barbarians against Greece" (1.29.6).

Meanwhile, the Persian fleet under Memnon had begun a reconquest of the islands in the Aegean. This was designed to serve as the prelude to a direct attack on Macedonia. Memnon captured Chios and all of Lesbos except for Mytilene, which he was in the process of assaulting when he suddenly fell ill and died. Alexander had become so apprehensive over Memnon's activities that he assembled a new fleet of his own, and sent money home to bolster his country's defenses. Memnon's plans caused Alexander "no little anxiety" (D.17.31.4) because a large-scale invasion might result in the recall of the entire expedition in order to defend the homeland. Alexander was therefore enormously relieved to learn of this worthy opponent's demise. In his biography of the king, Ulrich Wilcken estimates that "[Memnon's] death at this moment was the greatest stroke of luck in Alexander's life, and no one recognised this more fully than Alexander."[126]

At Gordium Alexander "was seized with a longing" (*pothos*) to visit a legendary wagon on the acropolis dedicated to Zeus Basileus.[127]

> designed
> to make me
> curious
> (*Ba*. 475)

This vehicle was said to have carried Midas, the founder of the Phrygian dynasty, to Gordium shortly after an oracle had proclaimed that a new king would be brought to the Phrygians in just such a fashion. The wagon's yoke was bound to a pole with a large complex knot of cornel bark (or a vine twig) without visible ends. It was therefore virtually impossible to untie. According to local legend, the man who untied the knot would rule all of Asia, but to that point no one had been able to solve the problem. This consideration, and the coincidental personal ties to those who figured in the legend, made the Gordian knot an irresistible challenge to Alexander.[128]

> here is a man who wishes to be above all others
> who wishes to hold power over all
> and to be lord of all
> and give them their orders
> yet I think
> one
> will not
> obey
> him
> (*Il*. 1.287–9)

Macedonians believed that this same Midas once lived in the region where Alexander had studied under Aristotle. In the Macedonian tradition, Midas was displaced from the foothills of the Bermium range by Perdiccas I, one of Alexander's ancestors. Midas, then a refugee, led his "Brigians" to Asia where they became known as Phrygians. The migration itself is historical,[129] and the Phrygian connection must have heightened the king's interest, but his primary concern was undoubtedly the prestige to be gained from succeeding where all others had failed.

As mentioned in the Preface to this work, there are two different versions of the story of Alexander and the problem of the Gordian knot. In one account, which can be traced to Aristobulus, the king studies the problem and removes the dowel holding the knot in place.[130] This ingenious gambit exposes the rope-ends, enabling him to proceed with the unraveling. In the alternative, better-known version, an exasperated Alexander is unsuccessful in every legitimate attempt.[131]

> his whole body
> drenched with sweat
> while I
> sat nearby
> quietly
> watching
> (*Ba.* 620–2)

Faced with the specter of conspicuous failure, Alexander slashes the knot in two with his sword.

We cannot be certain if either of these versions is historical, but both are plausible, and each in its own way reveals something about the man. There is no question that Alexander possessed extraordinary powers of concentration and responded to "impossible" challenges with exceptional insight. Thus, the version told by Aristobulus is credible for a man of his ability.

> You are clever
> very
> but
> not
> where
> it
> counts
> (*Ba.* 655)

On the other hand, Alexander was a man incapable of shrugging his shoulders and walking away from an unsuccessful effort. If, as a result of several futile attempts, he was frustrated and angry, he might very well have decided that a sudden stroke of the sword would rescue him from public embarrassment.

Alexander was eager to be convinced that he had passed the test and fulfilled the oracle, and his courtiers were anxious to provide him with such reassurances. Thunder and lightning on the same evening was interpreted by Alexander and his seers as a signal of divine approbation, "so Alexander in thanksgiving offered sacrifice [the] next day to whatever gods had shown the signs and the way to undo the knot" (A.2.3.8).

Celestial flashes and rumblings are related to Dionysus as well as Zeus, however, and need not signify approval. Semele was cremated while bearing Dionysus, and the incendiary element is an integral part of his double birth. On the night before she was married to Philip, Olympias is said to have "dreamed that there was a crash of thunder, that her womb was struck by a thunderbolt, and that there followed a blinding flash from which a great sheet of flame blazed up and spread far and wide before it finally died away" (P.2.3). Philip might have interpreted this reverie as a testimony to his sexual prowess, but Olympias would have seen in it the divine origins of the male child she hoped to bear, who would thus enjoy a genesis similar to the god she worshipped.

> midwived by fire
> delivered
> by the lightning's blast
> (*Ba.* 3)

Phrygia was the heartland of Dionysiac worship in Asia. It was believed to be the lair of the god who enjoyed confounding heroes and mocking their self-assurance. Alexander thought he had triumphed and hoped that those around him would see his performance as divinely inspired. Indeed his invincibility seemed to remain intact, but Alexander's *hybris* (or subterfuge) violated the spirit of the enterprise.

After Gordium Alexander headed for Ancyra (modern Ankara), some 50 miles to the northeast, where emissaries from Paphlagonia submitted to him and requested that his army bypass their territory. Alexander agreed. He had not planned to conquer this area anyway because of its difficult terrain, but his decision had more to do with his intention to rush south for the Taurus passes and Cilicia.

Marching southeast from Ancyra, he passed through Cappadocia. While there he appointed a native as satrap. This action provided some relief for an already overburdened administrative staff and demonstrated Alexander's willingness to utilize native talent at high levels in his command structure. Like Philip, Alexander never let ethnocentric provincialism prevent him from achieving his objectives. However, his appointment of a barbarian must have raised the eyebrows of at least some of the old guard Macedonians.

As he looked forward to the upcoming conflict, Alexander probably recalled that Xenophon had written that the Cilician Gates were virtually impassable if they were manned.[132] The defile could have been defended indefinitely by a handful of men, but to Alexander's astonishment its Persian defenders fled at his approach. The cause of this tactic was most likely the experience of Arsames, the Persian satrap of Cilicia, at the Granicus. His experience had taught him to appreciate the wisdom of Memnon's advice to avoid direct confrontation with Alexander. Whatever the reason, the abandonment of the Gates allowed Alexander to descend into Cilicia and travel toward Tarsus at a brisk pace. Reports had reached Alexander that Arsames intended to sack the city and carry off the treasury. The king raced ahead to prevent Arsames from doing any damage, and entered the city in time. Another victory was his.

Before he could press on, however, he was to face an unexpected threat. It was July of 333, and Alexander – sweaty, exhausted, and perhaps suffering from an upper-respiratory infection – plunged into the icy waters of the Cydnus River to cleanse and refresh himself. The shock of the water, along with his poor health, brought on a chill that left the king sleepless with a violent fever.[133] Because of the gravity of his condition the court physicians were reluctant to suggest a remedy. Should the king die, they might be held responsible for his death. Only Philip the Acarnanian,[134] a man who Arrian says "was very much trusted in medical matters, and in general enjoyed honour in the army," came forward with a recommendation (4.8). Philip had looked after Alexander since the king was a boy, and when the physician proposed a strong purge, Alexander, who, according to Curtius, "could tolerate anything more readily than delay," accepted (3.6.3). While Philip was busy preparing his potion, a letter arrived from Parmenio warning Alexander that Philip had been bribed by the Persian king to poison him. When Philip returned, the king handed him that letter to read as Alexander drank from the cup. It was risky business, but superb panache on Alexander's part. Philip responded by advising the king that he would eventually recover if he followed his instructions.

Curtius tells us that after having drunk the medicine Alexander told Philip "I am as concerned about clearing your name as I am for my recovery" (3.6.12).[135] This sentiment seems dubious, but it was a grave illness and the physician certainly called upon all of his knowledge and experience to promote his patient's recovery. "Philip left nothing untried; he applied poultices to his body, and roused him when he was faint with the smell of food at one time, or wine at another. As soon as he saw Alexander conscious, he would continually remind him of his mother and sisters,[136] or again of the great victory that was coming to him" (C.3.6.14–15). This doctor knew his patient.

Arrian says that "The purge worked and eased the illness; and Alexander showed Philip that as his friend he trusted him, and his suite in general that he was resolute in refusing to suspect his friends and steadfast in the face of death" (2.4.11). This extraordinary display of confidence boosted everyone's morale at a time when Alexander the Lyncestian languished in prison, and the king's personal friend Harpalus had, without authorization, fled from his responsibilities to Megara in Greece.[137] It restored much-needed optimism and enthusiasm to the venture.

Alexander was forced to convalesce until September. He then sent Parmenio eastward to occupy the passes that lead from Cilicia to Syria. At the end of September he felt strong enough to resume campaigning in southwestern Cilicia. At Anchiale he discovered the remains of an ancient city said to have been founded by Sardanapalus the Assyrian. The founder's tomb was at the center of the city, and the Assyrian king (probably Ashurbanipal) was depicted on a memorial relief snapping the fingers on his right hand with an accompanying admonition to eat, drink, and copulate, for all else was worth no more than the gesture indicated.[138] Alexander is said to have reported this incident to Aristotle, who remarked that such an epitaph was equally applicable to a bull.[139]

Alexander continued on to Soli, where he sacrificed to Athena and

Asclepius, the god of healing, in gratitude for his recovery. This god, who was the son of Apollo, had also been connected with Dionysus,[140] and was a relative newcomer among Greek deities. Olympias, who was enormously relieved at her son's recovery, sent a dedication to Hygeia, the daughter of Asclepius and the personification of health, at Athens.[141] In Soli Alexander held a full-dress army processional (*pompe*), a torch relay race, and other athletic and literary competitions. Actors, singers, musicians, and sometimes the soldiers themselves engaged in contests (*agones*) that helped to reinvigorate the fighting force.

The king then led his infantry and the Royal Squadron of the cavalry to Magarsus (arriving in the autumn of 333), where he sacrificed to a local Athena. Magarsus was a harbor town attached to Mallus and claimed Argive foundation. Because of their alleged common descent from Heracles, Alexander exempted the townsmen from tribute. He also sacrificed to Amphilochus, an Argive hero who was said to have been at Troy and had become associated with healing.[142] Amphilochus, who possessed prophetic power, was supposed to have founded Mallus with another seer, Mopsus. Amphilochus visited Greece and upon his return had to battle Mopsus for control of the city. The seers killed each other in single combat. Apparently neither one had foreseen the outcome.

Finding the city in civic turmoil, Alexander quickly restored order and established the anti-Persian faction in power. He also learned at Mallus that the Persian king, Darius III, was encamped at Sochi on the Syrian plain, and his attention turned in that direction.

> come yourself
> and stand up against me
> so you
> can see
> what
> I
> am
> like
> (*Il.* 13.448–9)

## THE BATTLE OF ISSUS (333 BC)

Darius III was tall and had a reputation as a remarkable fighter. He was rumored to have personally killed a Cadousian rebel whom no one else had the courage to face.[143] A member of a collateral branch of the royal Achaemenid family, he had assumed the throne only in 336 with the support of the Vizier Bagoas, a eunuch who routinely poisoned his enemies. Soon after his accession Darius turned the tables on the Vizier and forced him to take a dose of his own medicine. Darius' abilities as a ruler or a general are difficult to assess because of the unattractive image espoused by European commentators seeking to justify his ultimate displacement by Alexander.[144]

By November 333 Darius had assembled his imperial army and was marching up from Susa in search of the Macedonian invader. He intended to defeat Alexander decisively in a pitched battle. Darius wanted to choose the battlefield on which he would defend his empire against the invading force, and he chose well. The broad plains at Sochi were ideal for the deployment of his numerically superior force (perhaps 50,000 to 75,000 men),[145] and especially for his *corps d'élite*, the Persian cavalry. Darius' advisers, however, attempted to persuade their leader that Alexander, whose illness had kept him inactive for some time, was avoiding him, and that the Great King should seek him out. Amyntas, a Macedonian exile at the Persian court who supported Darius and knew Alexander well, advised the Great King to ignore his other advisers and stay put. Amyntas said: "Your majesty need have no fears on that score. Alexander will march against you, in fact he is probably on his way now" (P.20.3).

Nonetheless, Darius abandoned his excellent position at Sochi and marched north into Cilicia to track down his enemy.[146] By now Alexander had established himself in a defensive position.[147] When he heard that the Persian army had taken an unexpected route and slipped in behind him, he sent some ships up the coast to confirm the report. It was true. Alexander had blundered and Darius was to the north at Issus. There the Persian king found the sick and wounded Macedonian soldiery who could not keep up with Alexander's southward pace. Darius interpreted their abandonment as evidence of Alexander's frantic efforts to avoid him. The stragglers were either massacred or had their hands chopped off, thereby rendering them incapable of ever fighting again.[148]

Issus was in the region where the Anatolian subcontinent meets the Phoenician coast. The second of Alexander's great battles would be fought somewhere within the confines of a narrow plain, with the sea on one side, mountains on the other, and the Pinarus River running between the two. Although the exact location of the battlefield remains in doubt, these features would make it difficult for the considerably larger Persian force to outmaneuver or encircle Alexander's army.[149]

On the eve of the battle Alexander, who could see the enemy illumined by thousands of flickering Persian campfires at the other end of the narrow coastal plain, prayed to Thetis, the Nereids, Nereus, and Poseidon, all of whom are sea divinities. This covered one flank. He also climbed, we are told, "to the top of a high ridge and by the light of several torches sacrificed to the tutelary gods of the area in [a] traditional manner" (C.3.8.22) – the other flank was therefore covered as well. Alexander was imploring the gods not to be the source of his misfortune. He had no fear if all things were equal.

Arrian has Alexander addressing his smaller force and arousing confidence in them through a skillful recitation of their advantages:[150] they had already demonstrated their superiority during their past victories over this enemy; the gods had given proof of their support by placing Darius in a position that was vulnerable to the Macedonian phalanx; Persian numbers were meaningless under such conditions; and Macedonian physique and morale were superior to those of the barbarian. Macedonian toughness, he maintained, would triumph over a people wallowing in luxury. It was a struggle between free men and slaves. Greeks will meet Greeks, he said, but our Greeks fight voluntarily, and theirs for pay – poor pay at that. Our barbarians are superior to theirs, and besides all this, "you have Alexander commanding against Darius" (2.7.5).

The king, Arrian states, recalled innumerable acts of past bravado. He either displayed an eidetic memory, or demonstrated that he, like Xenophon's Cyrus, had done the homework required for such an impressive rhetorical performance. Alexander also reminded his troops of the dangers he had faced and suggested that even the 10,000 Greeks who fought their way out of the Persian Empire a half-century before were inferior to his Macedonians. Now that the Great King was present on the battlefield, "nothing remained after this final struggle but to rule the whole of Asia and set an end to their long exertions" (2.7.6). Those in close proximity to the king clasped his hand and shouted appeals to be led on at once.

> and among them was standing warlike Achilleus
> and urged on the fighting men
> with their shields
> and the horses
> (*Il.* 16.166–7)

Leading the Companion Cavalry in an angled charge from the far right of his line, Alexander punched a hole in the Persian left, and then wheeled toward Darius' position at the Persian center. Parmenio stood his ground against a formidable Iranian cavalry on the Macedonian left, while the Macedonian phalanx struggled to hold its own at the center. Alexander charged directly at Darius in a spectacular scene that is apparently represented on the *Alexander Mosaic* from Pompeii.[151]

> From the other side
> the son of Peleus
> rose
> like a lion
> against him
> (*Il.* 20.164)

A tale told by Chares has Darius inflicting a thigh wound on Alexander before the Great King turned his chariot in headlong flight.[152] Alexander's wound is probable, and its infliction by Darius is suspect, but the Persian king's departure from the field is certain. After assisting his beleaguered troops elsewhere on the battlefield and otherwise making certain of the victory, Alexander furiously pursued Darius. The chase had to be abandoned when darkness intervened. Darius mounted a fresh horse and escaped at high speed. The royal chariot, however, empty except for the king's bow and a discarded mantle and shield, was taken back by Alexander and his Companions to the captured Persian camp, where the Macedonian Royal Pages had been busy preparing the Great King's captured tent for Alexander. He could not help but be impressed by the Persian opulence, but his public comments about it were all unflattering, as Plutarch reports:

> When Alexander entered the bath-room he saw that the basins, the pitchers, the baths themselves and the caskets containing unguents were all made of gold and elaborately carved, and noticed that the whole room was marvellously fragrant with spices and perfumes, and then passing from this into a spacious and lofty tent, he observed the magnificence of the dining-couches, the tables and the banquet which had been set out for him. He turned to his companions and remarked. "So this, it seems, is what it is to be a king."
>
> (20.13)

The king scrubbed himself down and had his wound tended to. It was time to celebrate, and Alexander, as Curtius tells us, "had invitations issued to his most intimate friends – no mere graze on the thigh could keep him from attending a banquet" (3.12.2).

Those assembled at the symposium were interrupted by wailings from an adjacent tent. Alexander was told that these sounds were the keens of Darius' female relatives, who assumed that their king was dead when they learned of the empty chariot and the fate of the royal insignia.[153] The victor sent Leonnatus to allay their grief by informing them that Darius was still alive, and by reassuring them there was nothing to fear from Alexander, who would honor their role and retain their privileges. The queen mother, Sisygambis, was told that she would be given a list of fallen Persian noblemen, and was free to arrange a proper burial for those who deserved special attention. Alexander gained possession of the families of the Persian high command. This would give him a decided advantage in future negotiations.

His actions confirmed the words he had transmitted. The royal women were protected from molestation and treated with ostentatious respect. The king grieved formally when Darius' beautiful wife, perhaps untouched by Alexander as Pantheia was untouched by Cyrus in the *Cyropaedia*,[154] died in childbirth. These women were, of course, priceless political commodities. Their good will would also be instrumental in the establishment of Alexander's rightful claim to the Persian throne. Nevertheless, one should not dismiss the genuine pity and compassion on Alexander's part in this episode, or underestimate the impact of his magnanimity and charm. The royal women were said to have praised him as the one man to whom it was right to lose an empire. Two actions by Sisygambis are telling in this regard. She is reported to have refused to be liberated by Persian troops during the battle of Gaugamela.[155] And her suicidal fast after Alexander's death further testifies to the type of loyalty that the chivalrous victor at Issus was capable of inspiring.[156]

After Issus Alexander erected altars and sacrificed to Zeus, Heracles, and Athena. Once again he also attended to the wounded, this time limping about in a manner reminiscent of his father. Displaying his own gash, he listened well to the elaborate explanations of how each man had acquired his own badge of courage.

The temptation was there to pursue Darius toward the upper reaches of the empire. He could perhaps settle all issues, or at least make it difficult for the Great King to regroup. With a Persian counteroffensive still under way in the Aegean, however, there were some other important considerations. Alexander sensed that any failure to implement the decision to conquer all available moorings along the southern lip of the Mediterranean might have serious repercussions. His presence might be required at any time in Asia Minor, the Aegean, or even Europe. Without the moorings all progress could come to an abrupt halt.

> We shall fight again
> until the divinity
> chooses between us
> and gives victory
> to one
> or
> the other
> (*Il.* 7.377–8)

## PHOENICIA (333–332 BC)

With this in mind Alexander marched in a southwesterly direction. He was determined to subjugate the Phoenician coast and force the defection of the Phoenician contingents of the Great King's navy. Badian, speaking of this decision, says that "Alexander tempered his opportunism with a firm grasp of what mattered. It is this that chiefly distinguishes him from mere royal adventurers like Demetrius the Besieger or Pyrrhus, who could probably never have conquered the Achaemenian empire."[157] His victory at Issus had laid open the route to Phoenicia. Alexander was greeted with a golden crown by the ruler of the port city of Marathus, and it was here that Alexander received the first peace offers from Darius. Envoys from the Great King carried a personal letter to Alexander and were instructed to appeal to him for the release of the royal captives. The letter, reported in Arrian, blamed Philip for the war and Alexander for the invasion that damaged their countries' "ancient friendship" (2.14.2). According to

Arrian's account it also stated that Darius accepted Issus as the will of some god, and professed the Great King's willingness to become a friend and ally of Alexander if the Persian royal family were returned to him.[158]

Diodorus claims, however, that the letter from Darius included significant details that were omitted in Arrian's version.[159] It offered, according to Diodorus, a large ransom for the captives and agreed to a cession of all imperial territory west of the Halys River. This was the entire area that Isocrates had hoped Philip would conquer. Also contained in this version is the assertion that Alexander, fearing that this overture might prove too attractive to his advisers and therefore blunt his more grandiose objectives, substituted a fictitious letter that was intolerably overbearing. The spurious document was, not surprisingly, rejected by his counselors.

The tone of Darius' letter, as it appears in Arrian, is curiously arrogant considering the circumstances, and may support Diodorus' claim of forgery. Later offers mentioned by Arrian are similar to the original proposal recorded by Diodorus, and this too tends to support the latter's claim. The concessions described by Diodorus involved that portion of the empire already under Alexander's control. The king's eye, however, had already become fixed on territory that remained unconquered. In the discussions between Alexander and the Macedonian high command during this period we see the first signs of disagreement about the aims and objectives of the invasion.

Whatever the true nature of the Persian king's proposals, they were flatly rejected by Alexander. He sent his own envoys to Darius with a letter that was to be delivered to the Great King, but not discussed with him. This letter, or a version of it that seems to have been recorded by Callisthenes and preserved by Arrian, provides a plausible justification of the invasion from the Macedonian point of view. It also sheds considerable light on the way in which Alexander wished to be seen:

> Your ancestors invaded Macedonia and the rest of Greece and did us great harm, though we had done them no prior injury; I have been appointed *hegemon* of the Greeks, and invaded Asia in the desire to take vengeance on Persia for *your* aggressions. For you assisted Perinthus, which wronged my father, and Ochus sent a force into Thrace, which was under our rule. My father was murdered by conspirators, whom you Persians organized, as you yourselves boasted in your letters to all the world; you assassinated Arses with the help of Bagoas, and seized the throne unjustly and in actual contravention of Persian law, doing wrong to Persians; you sent unfriendly letters to the Greeks about me, urging them to make war on me. You despatched sums of money to the Lacedaemonians and certain other Greeks, which no other city accepted but the Lacedaemonians. Your envoys destroyed my friends and sought to destroy the peace I had established in Greece. Although I marched against you, it was you that started the quarrel.

As I have conquered in battle first your generals and satraps, and now yourself and your own force, and am in possession of the country by the gift of heaven, I hold myself responsible for all of your troops . . . . You must then regard me as Lord of all Asia and come to me. If you fear that by coming you may receive some harm at my hands, send some of your friends to receive pledges. Ask for your mother, wife and children and what you will, when you have come, and you will receive them. You shall have whatever you persuade me to give. And in future when you send to me, make your addresses to the king of Asia, and do not correspond as an equal, but tell me, as lord of all your possessions, what you need; otherwise I shall make plans to deal with you as a wrongdoer. But if you claim the kingship, stand your ground and fight for it and do not flee, as I shall pursue you wherever you are.

(2.14.4–9)

Alexander ordered Parmenio to transport the spoils from Issus to Damascus and to seize the baggage train there. Parmenio followed orders and, to relieve the king's financial pressures, confiscated money and other precious objects, including the ornate casket that would house Alexander's annotated copy of the *Iliad* (P.26.1–2). Found among these impressive spoils were some 3,400 pounds of bejewelled drinking cups and seventeen bartenders in the service of the Great King.[160] Barsine, the widow of Memnon, was also discovered by Parmenio, and he suggested that this woman might also be a valuable asset to the king. Around the same time Parmenio informed the king that two Macedonians had been charged with seducing the wives of Greek mercenaries in Alexander's service. Alexander stated that if convicted, these men "should be put to death as wild beasts which are born to prey upon mankind" (P.22.4).

In addition, Parmenio came across Greek envoys who had arrived at Darius' court sometime before Issus. Alexander asked that they be sent directly to him. A Spartan, whose native city was openly hostile toward Alexander, was to be kept under house arrest until Sparta no longer posed a threat. Two Thebans, one of whom was called Dionysodorus ("the gift of Dionysus"), were released since they represented a state that no longer existed, and because Alexander felt compassion for their plight.[161]

These gestures coincided with the king's other attempts to improve his image in Hellas. For instance, the prisoner Iphicrates of Athens was the son of a prominent Athenian general of the same name who at one time had been of some service to Macedon. He was kept as an honored guest rather than a prisoner, and when he became ill and died, his remains were transported back to Athens for burial.

A number of cities along the Phoenician coast surrendered to Alexander without opposition. Sidon, which had been treated poorly by the Persians, transferred command of its fifty ships from Darius to Alexander. Also at Sidon Hephaestion was given his first important assignment: the responsibility of choosing a new king for the city. Hephaestion managed to locate and install the only local man who could claim royal blood. This man, Abdalonymus, was working as a gardener at the time.[162] He turned out to be an excellent king who had a sense of gratitude for his selection. His sarcophagus, which was constructed after the deaths of Hephaestion and Alexander and is now known as the *Alexander Sarcophagus*, features Alexander with a lion's head for a helmet and, it seems, Hephaestion battling against Persians.[163]

## THE SIEGE OF TYRE (332 BC)

At first it seemed as if Tyre had also submitted to Alexander. This was welcome news because this city promised to be even more difficult to besiege than Halicarnassus. The old port of Tyre had been abandoned for some time, and the Tyrians were now securely ensconced behind massive walls on an island that was a half-mile from the shore. Alexander decided to test their sincerity by announcing his intention to sacrifice to Heracles (the Tyrian Melcarth) inside the walls of the city.[164] He was told with apologies that Tyre would admit neither Persians nor Macedonians while hostilities between the two continued, and it was suggested that he worship Melcarth/Heracles at the temple in the old city. The furious king dismissed the representatives. He made one further attempt to negotiate an entrance into the city, but his Macedonian envoys were seized and unceremoniously hurled from the battlements. Alexander met with his advisers and pushed for a siege of the city.

He argued that it was especially dangerous to leave Tyre behind because of the state of affairs in Greece. Alexander conjectured that the Persians might "transfer the war into Greece, where the Lacedaemonians are openly at war with us, while Athens is kept in control for the present by fear rather than goodwill towards us" (A.2.17.2). Egypt, he noted, was the key. Greece and Macedon would no longer be vulnerable once Egypt and the Nile were theirs. Only then, he claimed, could they confidently resume their pursuit of Darius. The king's arguments were persuasive, and his opinion prevailed.

Alexander's determination to conduct the siege was reinforced by a dream he had in which Heracles stretched out his right hand to lead him up into the city.[165]

> for Herakles
> the godlike
> would not
> let go
> my
> spirit
> (*Il.* 15.24–5)

Curtius places the dream during the siege, and says that Alexander, who "was not inexperienced in dealing with the soldier's temperament," announced the dream to his troops in order to bolster their flagging support for the project (4.2.17). The dream was taken by Aristander to mean that Tyre would indeed be captured, but only through Herculean efforts. Philip had been successful in some sieges, but had failed at Perinthus and Byzantium, which were less imposing challenges than Tyre. An opportunity to outdo his father may have provided a further incentive for Alexander.

During the siege Alexander is said to have had another dream in which, Plutarch tells us, a satyr mocked him from a distance.[166] The satyr eluded his grasp at first, but was eventually captured. The seers, who were etymologists of sorts when the occasion demanded, divided the word *satyros* into *sa*, "yours," and *Tyros*, "Tyre," and told Alexander that the dream meant that Tyre would be his. A report of this dream and its interpretation was announced as an endorsement of the siege to the troops. As usual, public disclosure of encouraging omens like this was useful in refueling the army's enthusiasm whenever its resolve seemed to be faltering.

> Let no
> ill-omened words
> profane your tongues
> (*Ba.* 69–70)

Alexander began the siege, according to Diodorus, "determined to run every risk and make every effort to save the Macedonian army from being held in contempt by a single undistinguished city" (17.40.4). This commitment turned out to be far more exacting than Alexander could ever have imagined. The siege lasted from January through August of 332.[167] During it, Diodorus says, the king himself became so weary that he thought of giving up the whole business and marching on to Egypt.[168] But, characteristically, his determination and aversion to failure drove him to conjure up a more imaginative approach. He built a solid causeway over the water, a half-mile long and 200 feet wide, and then constructed siege towers that were more than 150 feet high, the tallest ever erected in antiquity. Unfortunately, the Tyrians responded to each and every stratagem with innovations of their own, which frustrated the efforts of the besiegers.

At one point the king's council, almost unanimously, advised him to abandon the assault. Alexander seems to have wavered, but "he changed his mind as he reflected that it would be disgraceful to leave the Tyrians with all the glory of the operation" (D.17.45.7).

Alexander was also not about to admit that he had labored in vain, nor was he willing to leave Tyre behind as a monument to his fallibility. Reinforced by ships from the Persian fleet that had defected to him in what was, perhaps, the decisive event of the siege, Alexander launched a varied assault on the city. Calling on the Macedonians "to dare no less than he," he personally led an attack on a breached section of the city's wall, while a battering ram brought it down elsewhere (D.17.46.1). After seven of the most exasperating months in his life, Alexander led his troops into the city.

The Macedonians, who during the siege had felt the sting of white-hot sand on their backs and seen comrades tossed from the walls of the city, slaughtered the inhabitants indiscriminately. Eight thousand Tyrians are said to have perished during the sack, and Curtius claims that 2,000 men of military age were crucified after the city was taken.[169] With his customary religious scrupulosity Alexander granted immunity to those Tyrian notables who had been fortunate enough to find sanctuary in the temple of Melcarth. The rest of the 30,000 or so inhabitants were sold into slavery. Thus Tyre, a city associated with Cadmus, the maternal grandfather of Dionysus, suffered a bloodbath.

> What blasphemy!
> Stranger
> have you
> no respect
> for
> heaven
> (*Ba*. 263)

Alexander sacrificed to Heracles in the temple of Melcarth and held a procession, a naval review, athletic games, and a torch-race in honor of his ancestor. He also paid his respects at a temple containing a colossal Greek statue of Apollo, which the Tyrians were said to have chained during the hostilities.[170] They feared, it was claimed, that Apollo might defect to Alexander.

During the siege, perhaps when it became apparent that the city would eventually be taken, the king received a second overture from Darius. This time the original proposal was made more attractive by an offer of 10,000 talents for the royal family, the granting of all territory west of the Euphrates, and the offer of a marriage alliance. It was under these circumstances that Parmenio is said to have commented that if he were Alexander, he would gladly accept such an offer. Alexander's famous retort, suggestive of his father's wit, was that he too would accept the offer if he were Parmenio.[171]

Instead, Alexander continued on toward Egypt, only to encounter a situation at Gaza that was hauntingly similar to his prolonged nightmare at Tyre.[172] The city stood on a high mound surrounded by deep sand, two-and-a-half miles from the sea, and Batis, the eunuch general in command of Gaza, refused to capitulate. Alexander's engineers, who contributed greatly to the king's victory at Tyre, concluded that Gaza was impossible to take because of the height of the mound. Arrian says, "Alexander thought, on the contrary, that the more impracticable it was, the more necessary was the capture; for the achievement would strike great terror into his enemies just because it was beyond calculation, while not to take it would be a blow to his prestige when reported to the Greeks and Darius" (2.26.3).

When the siege engines were finally placed against the wall, and Alexander was sacrificing, a bird reportedly flew and dropped a stone on the king's head.[173] Alexander asked Aristander what this signified, and was told that the city would be taken, but he must take special precautions with regard to his own safety. Alexander kept at a distance from the fighting until he saw his troops retreating and then instinctively joined in the mêlée. He was hit by a shot from a catapult, which penetrated his shield and corselet, and inflicted a severe shoulder wound. Curtius reports (4.6.18–20) that Alexander was bandaged by Philip the Acarnanian and "remained on his feet before the standards, either concealing or mastering his pain, until the blood . . . began to flow more copiously" (4.6.19). He collapsed and was taken back to the camp to recuperate. Batis, believing that Alexander was dead, prematurely celebrated a victory.

Alexander found solace in conjecturing that since his soothsayer's premonition about the wound was accurate, he was also probably right about the capture of the city. At Tyre, it may be recalled, Aristander had prophesied imminent victory when more time was needed to accomplish the task. Alexander then prolonged the month in order to keep Aristander's record intact.

> one who knew in his mind
> the truth of portents
> and whom
> the people
> believed
> in
> (*Il.* 12.228–9)

The siege at Gaza lasted for two months. It was successfully resolved with the help of sappers who dug under the walls and caused them to crumble. "Alexander himself led the advance troops and, as he approached somewhat recklessly, he was struck on the leg with a rock. He supported himself with his spear and, though the scab had still not formed on his first wound, kept fighting in the front line, goaded also by his anger at having received two wounds in besieging that particular city" (C.4.6.23–4). Arab mercenaries defended Gaza with conviction, but they too were finally overcome. The entire garrison was slaughtered, and all surviving women and children were sold into slavery.

Curtius recounts the unusually cruel punishment inflicted on Batis, who remained defiantly silent when brought before his adversary. Batis' refusal to acknowledge Alexander's victory enraged the king. The captive's feet, we are told, were pierced and thongs were inserted through the openings. His body was then attached to Alexander's chariot, and he was dragged behind it until he was dead. Curtius adds that "the king gloated at having followed the example of his ancestor Achilles in punishing his enemy [Hector]" (4.6.29).[174]

> In both of his feet at the back he made holes by the tendons . . .
>    and drew thongs of ox-hide through them and fastened them to
> the chariot so as to let the head drag and mounted the chariot and
> . . . whipped the horses to a run and they winged their way unreluctant
> (*Il.* 22.396–400)

## EGYPT (332 BC)

The ancient Greeks were fascinated by Egypt, where the cryptic artifacts made their own heralded monuments appear diminutive and recent. The historian and pioneer anthropologist Herodotus visited what he called "the gift of the Nile,"[175] and provides a lengthy disquisition on Egyptian culture and religion in his *Histories*. Herodotus came to the conclusion that the Egyptians were the most religious of all men.[176] This may, in part, help to explain the enthusiastic reception that Alexander, a conspicuously religious man, received there. The most important reason for their enthusiasm, however, was the fact that the Egyptians had strained under Achaemenid control for most of the two centuries before Alexander's appearance, and they were ready to be "liberated." After accepting Egypt from the Persian satrap, who did not have enough troops to offer effective resistance, Alexander marched across the Sinai Desert by way of Heliopolis, and entered Memphis as Egypt's triumphant deliverer in November 332.

As pharaoh,[177] Alexander publicly sacrificed to Apis the sacred bull, amidst his other celebrations. His sacrifice to a divinity for whom there was no counterpart in the Hellenic world was a masterful diplomatic stroke. It offered a vivid illustration of his respect for this distinctly Egyptian god, and served notice that he intended to meet his priestly obligations as pharaoh. Alexander ordered a renovation of the temples desecrated by the Persians at Luxor and Karnak. He showed himself worthy of the double crown and uraeus, and the crossed scepters of crook and flail that symbolized Egyptian kingship. Alexander was now the king of both Upper and Lower Egypt; Horus, the protector of the land and divine son of the sun-god Ra; and the beloved son of Ammon. He was also, at least in Egyptian eyes, the son of a god and a living god himself. Gossip would eventually have it that Alexander was really the son of Nectanebo II, the last native pharaoh, who, the story goes, had taken the form of a snake and slept with Olympias.[178]

## ALEXANDRIA (331 BC)

After holding the usual athletic and literary contests, Alexander sailed down the western arm of the Nile, searching for a suitable area on the coast where he might found a city. He cruised around the Delta until he discovered the ideal environment. It was situated between Lake Mareotis, which was inland, and the island of Pharos. Plutarch tells us that the inspiration for his selection originated in Homer's *Odyssey*, and that the lines in question were recited to Alexander in a dream.

> Out of the tossing sea where it breaks on the beaches of Egypt
> Rises an isle from the waters: the name that men give it is Pharos
> (4.354–5)

The king surveyed the area and personally chose the location, while commenting that Homer, who had many other qualities, was also a wise architect. The formal foundation of the city probably occurred after Alexander's visit to Siwah.[179]

It was an excellent choice. Close to the Delta, with a supply of fresh water, cool and free from malaria, defensible, and with a deep-water anchorage, it would become a model metropolis and the great Mediterranean trading center during the Hellenistic period. While Alexander was obviously thinking about its military and commercial advantages when planning the city, posterity was uppermost in his mind when he called it Alexandria. It was the first and most distinguished of the many cities to bear that name. Their proliferation testified to Alexander's preoccupation with being remembered.

> you are pleased
> when men stand outside your doors
> And the city glorifies
> . . . [your] name . . .
> and so the god
> he too delights
> in
> glory
> (*Ba.* 319–21)

## THE JOURNEY TO SIWAH (331 BC)

While in the coastal region, perhaps at Alexandria, Arrian relates that:

> [A] longing [*pothos*] seized Alexander to pay a visit to Ammon in Libya, for one reason to consult the god, since the oracle of Ammon was said to be infallible, and to have been consulted by Perseus . . . and by Heracles . . . . Alexander sought to rival Perseus and Heracles, as he was descended from them both; and in addition he himself traced

his birth in part to Ammon, just as the legends traced that of Heracles and Perseus to Zeus. In any case he set out for Ammon with this idea, hoping to secure more exact knowledge of his affairs, or at least to say he had secured it.

(3.3.1–2)

This excursion required 600 miles of travel through a hazardous desert region and took six weeks out of Alexander's life at a time when the enemy was collecting a force designed to destroy him. It was a curious pilgrimage, about which his advisers, if consulted, might have raised questions for which there were no persuasive answers.[180] They might have reminded him that Cambyses, the son of Cyrus the Great, had launched an expedition into the Libyan Desert that was swallowed up by a sandstorm.[181] But, Alexander might have replied, Cambyses was not Cyrus, and the son drank excessively and went mad when he thought that he would never be able to equal his father's exploits.[182]

This was *pothos* – a yearning, a Dionysiac urge to do something extraordinary. It eluded conventional analysis and could be utilized when the king wished to escape the restraints of parochial logic.[183] When he was in the power of *pothos*, any objections or reservations could be dismissed without consideration.

> Let counsels
> and the meditations of men
> be given to the flames then
> (*Il.* 2.340)

In Alexander's mind the undertaking made perfect sense. He was a religious man on the brink of the most important battle in his life, and so a consultation with a prestigious oracle was perfectly consistent with his priorities. The trip might be perilous, but for him that would be an incentive rather than a deterrent. Aristotle had spoken with respect about a pious pilgrim who made the journey.[184] The Greek world, whose opinion was always of concern to Alexander, ranked Siwah alongside Delphi and Dodona in the forefront of prophetic authorities.[185] Given the infallible reputation of its oracular pronouncements, approval at Siwah could lend *imprimatur* to whatever Alexander believed or wished to undertake.

Callisthenes, the king's historian, records that the official reason for this epic sojourn was Alexander's rivalry with Heracles and Perseus.[186] Arrian, as has been noted, offers the other important incentive for this demanding trip – Alexander's determination to clarify the question of his divine origin. Olympias, it may be recalled, is said to have told Alexander that his father was a god. The Egyptians had already accepted him as both the son of a god and a god in his own right, but among Macedonians and Greeks these issues had to be treated with sensitivity and tact. The authority of the oracle could be decisive with any such claim made in the future.

When Alexander emerged from the desert at Siwah he was greeted by the chief priest at the oasis as either the son of Ammon or, as Callisthenes said, the son of Zeus. The Greeks identified Ammon with Zeus, their supreme god, and Alexander probably shared this view. When Alexander later swore by both Zeus of the Greeks and Ammon of the Libyans, he was speaking essentially of the same god in different modes. Separate manifestations imply distinctions, however, and Alexander seems to have been more defensive about being called the son of Ammon than being referred to as the son of Zeus.[187]

There is evidence to suggest the god Ammon became increasingly important to Alexander after Siwah, and even an indication that he wished to be buried at the deity's oracle in the Libyan Desert.[188] After his death the men who knew him well would incorporate the horn of Ammon into the canonical iconography of Alexander.[189]

> Horns
> have sprouted
> from
> your head
> (*Ba.* 921)

Of utmost importance to Alexander at the time of the visit, however, was that his divine descent be acknowledged by a religious figure of unimpeachable authority. Wilcken's claim that the salutation Alexander received at Siwah "must have entered his soul like a flash of lightning and caused the deepest emotion"[190] seems exaggerated. If Alexander was recognized as pharaoh, he had every right to expect such a greeting.

The new pharaoh was offered the select privilege of communing with the oracle within the sacred precinct of the sanctuary, where he alone was entitled to pose questions. Other than the fact, later corroborated, that Alexander was told to which gods he should pay special attention, we do not know what happened inside the shrine. Alexander is also said to have asked if he would rule over the entire world and been told that he would, but this appears to be the invention of a later age.

He is also reported to have asked if any of his father's murderers remained unpunished.

> why does this man
> who is
> guiltless
> suffer his sorrows
> for no reason
> (*Il.* 20.297–8)

This is a much more specific question, "reported," as A. R. Burn tells us, "very credibly."[191] The priest responded by chastising the king for making an inquiry that was blasphemous, since Alexander's father was not mortal. Alexander then, we are told, rephrased the question by asking whether or not all of Philip's murderers had been brought to justice. He was told that Philip had been fully avenged. Alexander must have been delighted by such a pronouncement, and it was unlikely that he would keep it to himself. A revelation of this sort would be well suited for what Fritz Schachermeyr has suggested were official leaks, authorized at the highest level.[192]

Arrian merely says that within the holy of holies[193] Alexander "received the answer his heart desired" (3.4.5). In a letter to Olympias, which some historians dismiss as spurious and others accept as genuine,[194] Alexander is said to have told her that he had received secret information that he would reveal to her alone when he returned home. He would not, in fact, ever return home, but his news was, in all likelihood, a confirmation that a divine partner supplied the seed for Alexander's conception. Or, perhaps, it was the recognition that his mother, like the mother of Achilles, would also enjoy divine status.

Like Perseus and Heracles, Alexander would settle for no one less than Zeus or Ammon to be his divine father. This notion would be flattering to Olympias as well, even if she might originally have implicated Dionysus, as some scholars have speculated.[195] Dionysus was, after all, the child of Zeus and a mortal mother, while the Zeus Olympias knew at Dodona seems to have been associated with Ammon.[196] The authenticity of the king's letter to his mother aside, Alexander's belief that he was the son of Ammon had certainly become common knowledge among his officers by 328, when it figured prominently in his drunken quarrel with Cleitus. Also, any acknowledgment of such divine filiation by the king himself, even in the form of an authorized leak, might have encouraged Olympias to conjure up ways of circulating this news in her own sphere of influence. This would supply a plausible explanation for the cheerful complaint of Olympias that her son was slandering her to Hera.[197]

Paradoxically, Alexander's divine engendering did not require the abandonment of his mortal father. Greek heroes such as Heracles and the Dioscuri had shown that dual paternity was possible.[198] Whenever it was necessary Alexander could continue to refer to Philip as his father, and, in fact, he often did just that. Nonetheless, Alexander's new pedigree implied a subordinate paternal role for his mortal father, and lent credence to his mother's claims concerning his origin. This proof of his divine filiation might also have served, like the words ascribed to Olympias before her son left for Asia, to raise Alexander's already unrealistic expectations of himself even higher.

There were more mundane considerations in this matter that required discretion. Imprudent emphasis on his divine father might prompt the question of whether or not Alexander was truly Philip's son, and such allegations of illegitimacy could become the spur of a conspiracy. Wisely, Alexander did not insist on his divine descent to the degree that it caused any of his subjects to doubt that he was Philip's son. In fact, his continuing sacrifices to Heracles (his ancestor through Philip) served to confirm the notion that Alexander was a legitimate Argead.[199] Even his trek into the desert, at least in the emulative aspect so clearly emphasized in the official account, underlined Alexander's royal, mortal lineage.

Ptolemy tells us that Alexander travelled directly across the Libyan Desert on his return to Memphis, but Aristobulus is more convincing in his report, in which he states that Alexander retraced his steps.[200] He was greeted in Memphis by a small army of Greek envoys from Europe and Asia Minor bearing gifts and petitions. Astute heralds from Asia Minor quoted their local oracles, which testified to Alexander's birth from Zeus, and predicted more victories in the near future for a man who at 24 was king of Macedon, *hegemon* of the Corinthian League, overlord in Anatolia, and in the Levant, pharaoh and the son of god.

> I mean
> to spoil you
> (*Ba.* 970)

But a discordant note had been sounded. It was reported in Egypt that when he had drunk too much, Philotas, the son of Parmenio (the same Philotas who had played a role in the Pixodarus affair), would boast to his mistress Antigone that he and his father were responsible for the greatest achievements on the expedition. Alexander was a mere stripling who really owed the crown to them. When this story reached Craterus, a member of Alexander's close circle of friends, he secretly escorted the woman to the king. Alexander heard the story and ordered Antigone to continue to listen and report everything she heard directly to him.[201]

> Reckless fool
> you do not know
> the
> consequences
> of your words
> (*Ba.* 358)

## THE BATTLE OF GAUGAMELA (331 BC)

The Nile was bridged at Memphis, and Alexander began retracing his steps to Tyre in the early spring of 331. During the crossing of the river, Hector, a young son of Parmenio and a favorite of Alexander's, boarded a small craft with a number of his friends and attempted to catch up with the king's flagship. The youth's overloaded boat sank, and Hector, who struggled to shore, died from exhaustion. Curtius says that his "[g]rief at losing him struck Alexander deeply; he recovered the body and buried it with a magnificent funeral" (4.8.9).

On the other hand Alexander had little or no sympathy for those who rebelled against him. An example of this can be seen in his dealings with Samaria, where, in the king's absence, insurgents had burned the Macedonian garrison commander alive. All those responsible for the insurrection were relentlessly hunted down by Alexander. Archaeologists found the remains of some of these Samaritans a few decades ago in the desert caves where they had sought refuge. Robin Lane Fox writes, "Alexander's one and only way with rebels was ruthless, and the finds in the Wadi Dalayeh caves are a harsh reminder of what it meant to cross the path of a son of Zeus."[202]

At Tyre, Alexander sacrificed to Heracles, and once again held athletic, musical, and dramatic competitions. A troupe of theatrical artists, members of the guild of Dionysus, arrived from Athens to participate in the affair.[203] Alexander permitted two Cypriot kings, whose navies had been instrumental in the opening up of the eastern Mediterranean, the honor of sponsoring the competitions. Thessalus, who had been arrested by Philip and shackled in chains because of his mission on Alexander's behalf to Pixodarus of Caria six years before, appeared in one production. The king refused to exercise his influence with the judges of the contest, but he was bitterly disappointed when Thessalus failed to win. Alexander claimed that he would have given a portion of his kingdom to see his erstwhile ambassador triumph in the contest.[204]

The victor, Athenodorus, had broken his contract to perform with his guild at the Dionysiac festival in Athens in order to share in the bountiful largesse available at Alexander's court.[205] Back in Athens Athenodorus was fined for his unconscionable absence from an annual event held in honor of Dionysus, the patron deity of the man's own guild. Athenodorus appealed to Alexander for a letter that might explain that he had been summoned to Tyre by royal command and therefore had little choice in the matter. The king, however, who was reluctant to offend the Athenians any further, refused to send the letter, but did supply the money for the fine from his own treasury. This gesture probably did little to conciliate the city, since Athens (and Dionysus) had been deprived of a performance by the accomplished actor who had taken first place at the Dionysia on two occasions.[206]

I warn you
(*Ba.* 789)

Athenian envoys were waiting for Alexander at Tyre, and they requested, once again, that the king release the Athenians captured at the Granicus. One of the Athenians in this delegation, Achilles, had probably been chosen primarily because of the response his name might draw from the king.[207] Alexander, perhaps amused by this, freed the Athenian captives. He was not amused enough, however, to permit the crews of some twenty Athenian vessels in his service to return to Greece. As hostages they served to discourage any impulse that the Athenians might have to join in a movement to undermine Macedonian hegemony in Hellas.

After dealing with this and other concerns, "Alexander dedicated a gold mixing bowl and thirty cups to Hercules of Tyre and then, pressing on against Darius, had orders given for a march to the Euphrates" (C.4.8.16). The king traveled northeast through the Beqaa Valley, emerged on to the plains of northern Syria, and arrived at Thapsacus in late July 331. Across the Euphrates stood Mazaeus, the satrap of Babylonia, accompanied by a small Persian force. Mazaeus, who was there to observe the invaders' movements, retreated, and Alexander was able to cross into Mesopotamia without opposition.

Darius had assumed that the Macedonian king would turn south and march toward Babylon. Because of the difficulties involved in such a march, which were magnified by the oppressive heat of late summer, Alexander headed in the opposite direction and could cross the Tigris unopposed, just north of Mosul. He then proceeded south along the Tigris, and after a few days his scouts made contact with the enemy. A Paeonian commander brought the king the head of an enemy leader he had personally killed in this encounter, and then announced that in his country (up the Axius River north of Macedonia) the bearer of such a gift would have been rewarded with a golden cup. "Yes, but with an empty one. I will drink your health with a cup full of neat wine, and give it [to] you as well" (P.39.2), replied Alexander.

A near-total eclipse of the moon occurred on the night of September 20.[208] The always pious Alexander responded to this awesome phenomenon by sacrificing to the Moon, the Sun, and the Earth.[209] Aristander, whose optimism was irrepressible, welcomed this as a sign that the king would enjoy a resounding victory before the end of the month.

Emotions ran high in anticipation of an epic clash. Plutarch says that camp-followers divided themselves into factions and fought a mock battle under leaders calling themselves Alexander and Darius. When this expression of the mounting tension appeared to get out of hand, Alexander interceded and ordered the leaders to engage in single combat to settle the issue. Alexander armed his namesake, and Philotas invested "Darius" with weapons. The entire camp watched in anxiety and then relief as "Alexander" prevailed.[210]

Victory on the battlefield, however, promised to be more complex. During the intervening two years Darius had assembled some 25,000 horsemen from his eastern satrapies, an untold number of infantry (perhaps 50,000), 200 scythed chariots, and even 15 elephants.[211] He was now encamped on a wide plain near Gaugamela (Tell Gomel), about 70 miles from Arbela. Darius waited, determined to avoid the mistakes that led to the *débâcle* at Issus. Alexander was able to field only 7,000 horsemen and 40,000 footmen. His men were superior in discipline and experience in the field, but he was short in numbers – and well aware of it.

Alexander delayed the attack until he had personally examined the terrain for ditches and stakes planted by the enemy to obstruct his cavalry. He also allowed himself some time to mull over the positioning of his immense and sprawling enemy. This decision to wait, which had been urged by Parmenio, surprised Alexander's officers, and forced Darius to keep his troops prepared for an imminent attack. It was uncharacteristic in formulation and brilliant in effect, and left the Persians in a confused state of exhaustion when the attack finally came on the morning of October 1.[212]

Plutarch tells us that "Alexander allowed his Macedonians to sleep, but himself spent the night in front of his tent in the company of his diviner Aristander, with whom he performed certain mysterious and sacred ceremonies and offered sacrifice to the god Fear [Phobos]" (31.9). It was, as far as we know, the first and last time Alexander sacrificed to Fear. This hideous Greek demon was believed to have the power to unhinge mortals, and supplications in his honor were designed to terrify an enemy. The numerical superiority of the Persians, whose cavalry glaringly outnumbered Alexander's, may have inspired some private fears in the king that he hoped to displace by sacrificing to Fear. On the next day Alexander would even put on a breastplate, something Curtius says was very rare for him. The Roman historian claims that the king resorted to this protection "at the request of his friends rather than through fear of the danger that had to be faced" (4.13.25).

On the eve of the battle Parmenio and some of the older Companions of the king went to observe the enemy from an overlooking ridge left unmanned by Darius. They saw an "entire plain agleam with the watchfires of the barbarians, while from their camp there arose the confused and indistinguishable murmur of myriads of voices, like the distant roar of a vast ocean" (P.31.10).

> A thousand fires
> were burning there in the plain
> and beside each one
> sat fifty men
> in the flare
> of the blazing firelight
> (*Il.* 8.562–3)

Parmenio returned to the royal tent where Alexander was conversing with his friends. Plutarch says that the king's seasoned general tried to persuade him to attack by night because of the imposing disparity in numbers. Alexander is said to have answered with unusual brusqueness, "I will not steal my victory" (31.12).

Arrian, who offers essentially the same account of these events, explains the curtness of the king's remark through others who heard Alexander state categorically that he was determined "to win his victory openly and without stratagem" (3.10.2). Arrian also points out that a night attack might have left the outcome to chance, and that a covert victory would have given Alexander's critics the opportunity to discount or devalue his success.[213]

Plutarch continues,

> When his friends had gone, Alexander lay down in his tent and is said to have passed the rest of the night in a deeper sleep than usual. At any rate when his officers came to him in the early morning, they were astonished to find him not yet awake, and on their own responsibility gave out orders for the soldiers to take breakfast before anything else was done. Then, as time was pressing, Parmenio entered Alexander's tent, stood by his couch and called him two or three times by name: when he had roused him, he asked how he could possibly sleep as if he were already victorious, instead of being about to fight the greatest battle of his life. Alexander smiled and said, "Why not? Do you not see that we have already won the battle, now that we are delivered from roving around these endless devastated plains, and chasing this Darius, who will never stand and fight?"
>
> (32.1–3)[214]

Plutarch implies that Alexander's peculiar deportment on the eve and morning of the battle showed his steadfastness and confidence.[215] He offers evidence elsewhere, however, that supports a simpler explanation for Alexander's behavior: "[A]lthough at other times his society was delightful and his manner full of charm beyond that of any prince of his age, yet when he was drinking he would sometimes become offensively arrogant and descend to the level of a common soldier, and on these occasions he would allow himself not only to give way to boasting but also to be led on by his flatterers . . . . When the drinking was over it was his custom to take a bath and sleep, often until midday, and sometimes for the whole of the following day" (23.7–8).[216] It is clear from this reference that the ordinarily courteous Alexander could be quite rude when under the influence of wine, and that he customarily overslept after drinking a great deal the night before. This, it would seem, may have been one of those occasions, although Plutarch himself apparently never came to that conclusion.

Alexander addressed his officers sometime during the night before the battle. They were reminded that any individual neglect of duty put the entire enterprise at risk. Discipline was of the utmost importance, and a perfect silence was to be maintained by the troops until they issued the collective shout that would rise to a crescendo and strike fear into the heart of the enemy.

> let shame be in your hearts
> and discipline

in the sight
of other men
(*Il.* 15.661–2)

On the morning of the battle, Alexander directed his attention to the Thessalians and allied cavalry. In an exhortation before these troops, Alexander, Callisthenes tells us, prayed to the gods that since he was truly the son of Zeus, they would protect and fortify the Greeks.[217] Aristander, who wore a white robe and a golden crown, accompanied Alexander during the brief interlude before battle. Endowed with the type of vision appropriate for the occasion, Aristander sighted an eagle, the messenger of Zeus, soaring above the head of Alexander and toward the enemy.[218] This omen, when announced to the troops, is said to have filled them with great courage.

Plutarch offers a splendid description of Alexander's appearance before the battle.

> He was already wearing the rest of his armour when he left his tent, a tunic made in Sicily which was belted around his waist and over this a thickly quilted linen corslet, which had been among the spoils captured at Issus. His helmet, the work of Theophilus, was made of steel which gleamed like polished silver, and to this was fitted a steel gorget [throat armor] set with precious stones. His sword, which was a gift from the king of Citium, was a marvel of lightness and tempering, and he had trained himself to use this as his principal weapon in hand-to-hand fighting. He also wore a cloak which was more ornate than the rest of his armour. It had been made by Helicon, an artist of earlier times, and presented to Alexander as a mark of honour by the city of Rhodes, and this too he was in the habit of wearing in battle.
>
> (32.8–11)

Only the barest outline of the battle is recoverable from the surviving accounts. Alexander commanded his Companion Cavalry on the right, and Parmenio led the Thessalians on the left. Darius once again commanded his troops from the center of the Persian line where he stood, visible to all, in his chariot. Alexander's intention, as at Issus, was to create a rift in the center of the enemy's line, and then suddenly to charge to the left toward the Great King's chariot. This tactic was again successful, and Darius fled from Gaugamela as he had fled from Issus.

It is reported that Parmenio experienced such difficulties at his station that Alexander had to abandon his pursuit of the Persian king in order to come to his general's assistance.[219] This claim, based on Callisthenes, is usually interpreted as the use of Parmenio as a scapegoat in order to explain Alexander's inability to capture the Persian king and settle the issue once and for all. Nonetheless, this may very well have been what occurred, especially if Alexander received such an urgent request for assistance before he had begun his pursuit of Darius. It seems unlikely that he would have abandoned the field if the outcome of the battle had still been in question.[220]

Alexander either resumed or began his pursuit of Darius later in the day, but realized that the chase was futile by the time he reached Arbela. Darius had fled to Ecbatana under the assumption, which proved correct, that Alexander would turn south toward Babylon, Susa, and Persepolis, the great prizes of the war. Not long after Gaugamela Alexander was proclaimed king of Asia, which meant Great King.[221] He had claimed Asia through the divine providence of the gods in 334, and he now sacrificed to them in gratitude for his victory at Gaugamela. Special offerings were made to Athena, who had served Alexander well as she had his ancestors.

Soon after Gaugamela Alexander made extravagant gifts of land, titles, and wealth to his senior officers. Merit rather than seniority had become the criterion for promotion, and it was the king who determined whose record deserved recognition and reward. Diodorus tells us that "by giving all the commanders greater prestige he bound them to himself by strong ties of affection [bringing] . . . . the whole force up to an outstanding devotion to its commander and obedience to his commands, and to a high degree of effectiveness, looking toward the battles to come" (17.65.3–4).

## BABYLON AND SUSA (331 BC)

Alexander approached Babylon in battle formation. Mazaeus, who had performed with distinction in the enemy's service at Gaugamela, came out to greet the king as a legitimate successor to Darius III.[222] It was a triumphant entrance into Babylon, not unlike the reception afforded to one of Alexander's models, Cyrus the Great, 200 years earlier. After the reign of Cyrus, however, the Babylonians had revolted against Persian rule and felt the sting of Persian retribution. Xerxes, the despoiler of the Athenian Acropolis, had plundered the E-Sagila, Marduk's temple atop the eight-story ziggurat, and had melted down the colossal gold statue of the Babylonian god for bullion. As in Egypt, Alexander was welcomed as a liberator. He fanned anti-Persian sentiment in Babylon by promising to restore the ziggurat and the temple. His troops were given the opportunity to recuperate from the ordeal at Gaugamela and to luxuriate in the fleshpots of Babylon for more than a month.

In gratitude for an open city and the recognition of his Persian kingship, Alexander retained Mazaeus, a Persian, as satrap of Babylon. The king, in effect, announced a policy that, it was hoped, would attract further support from the Persian nobility. Persians who cooperated with Alexander would be confirmed in their positions and privileges. This move also helped to relieve a problem that had resulted directly from Alexander's unprecedented conquests – the need to find competent and trustworthy administrators who could be spared from expeditionary service in order to govern the conquered territories. Mazaeus was a fine choice. He had shown personal courage and loyalty on the battlefield, and seems to have married a Babylonian woman. Also, despite the regional antipathy toward Persians, Mazaeus seems to have enjoyed considerable popularity in Babylon.

This course of action foreshadowed Alexander's nurturing of harmonious relations between his cadre of executive officers and the Persian ruling class. This would find its most dramatic expression in the Susa marriages of 324 (see Chapter 4). The policy was designed to facilitate Alexander's governing of an immense empire. It was forged out of necessity, rather than any attempt to assimilate the disparate elements into one culture.

Although Mazaeus was left in charge of his province, Alexander appointed a Macedonian to be garrison commander in Babylon. Another of his own officers was chosen to be the chief tax collector. These men served as royal agents, who monitored the satrap's performance in the king's absence. This administrative blending of Macedonians and Iranians established the pattern of governance for the Iranian lands west of India.[223] There is no record of early Macedonian responses to this policy, but later events reveal simmering resentments over such considerate handling of a vanquished people.

After Gaugamela Alexander wrote to the Greeks that all tyrannies were now abolished, and that people could at last live under their own laws.[224] These thoughts were perfectly consonant with the policy that justified the expedition *ab initio*. It would not be long, however, before Alexander was faced with a situation wherein his success outdistanced his propaganda. The Babylonians were the last non-Persians willing to be liberated. After Babylon Alexander would have to claim that he was emancipating the Persians from themselves.

Sustaining his persona of liberator would become virtually impossible once Alexander had occupied Susa, the administrative center of the empire, and Persepolis, its ceremonial hub. The king could, however, begin to emphasize his role as avenger, which he did for the next several months. If, however, he ever wished to be accepted by the Persians as their Great King, such a policy would be contradictory and counterproductive.

At Susa, when Alexander sat on the Persian throne beneath the celebrated golden canopy, he found that his legs were dangling in mid-air above the royal footstool.[225] This was because Darius III was exceptionally tall, while the young conqueror was less than imposing in height. The scene must have been, to say the least, awkward. An alert Macedonian page quickly placed a nearby table underfoot, which evoked lamentations from a Persian eunuch. When questioned by Alexander, the eunuch explained that his former master used to eat from the very table that was now being treated with utter contempt. The king decided to have it removed, but Philotas urged him to leave it where it was, saying, "No, your majesty, don't do that. Take this as an omen, too – the table from which your foe ate his banquets has been made a stool for your feet" (C.5.2.15). Alexander left it where it was.[226]

Another question of protocol involved Sisygambis, Darius' mother. Alexander had received a present of clothes and purple cloth from Macedonia, and he presented this material to the queen mother, along with seamstresses and an offer to teach her granddaughters the techniques of the craft. In Persian society such work was perceived to be demeaning to noblewomen, and the offense left the queen mother in tears. Alexander, thinking that her reaction required his personal attention, sought her out.

> Mother, these clothes I am wearing are not merely a gift from my sisters [sic], but also their handiwork. I was led into error by our own customs. Please do not take offence at my ignorance. I have, I hope, scrupulously observed what I have discovered of your conventions. I know that among you it is not right for a son to sit down in his mother's presence without her permission, so whenever I have come to you I have remained on my feet until you beckoned me to sit. Often you have wanted to show me respect by prostrating yourself before me but I have forbidden it. And the title due to my dear mother Olympias I give to you.
>
> (C.5.2.20–2)

Alexander settled Sisygambis and her grandchildren at Susa, and tutors were left to teach them the Greek language.[227]

Around this time substantial reinforcements, including 6,000 Macedonian foot soldiers, 500 horsemen, and 50 Royal Pages, arrived from Europe.[228] Alexander, concerned about a revolt in Greece that was being spearheaded by the Spartans, had sent 3,000 talents back home to help deal with the problem. The king, who had started his reign in dire financial straits, had recently collected 50,000 silver talents at Susa from the imperial treasury. Fortunately, money was no longer a concern to him. In Greece Antipater had marshaled a force of 40,000 men and had defeated the insurgents outside the walls of Megalopolis. When Alexander learned of Antipater's impressive victory, however, he is said to have remarked that it was merely "a battle of mice."[229]

O
Dionysus
now
action rests with you
And
you are near
Punish this man
But first

distract his wits
bewilder him
with
madness
(*Ba.* 849–51)

# 3   The metamorphosis

## THE SIGNS OF CHANGE

"Here begins Alexander's tragedy; the tragedy of an increasing loneliness, of a growing impatience with those who could not understand," says Tarn, writing of events which occurred during the summer of 330 BC.[1] There is no need, he adds elsewhere, to "deny that the Alexander of 324 was not the Alexander of 334."[2]

Alexander's transformation fascinated and perplexed the ancients. The man whose virtue Plutarch had lauded so fervently came to be "feared by his men for his relentless severity in punishing any dereliction of duty" (P.57.3), and was "increasingly suspicious of his friends" (74.1). In the end, his admirer laments, Alexander became "so much obsessed by his fears of the supernatural and so overwrought and apprehensive in his own mind, that he interpreted every strange or unusual occurrence, no matter how trivial, as a prodigy or a portent, with the result that the palace [at Babylon] was filled with soothsayers, sacrificers, purifiers and prognosticators" (75.1).

Plutarch describes one aspect of the metamorphosis:

> We are also told that when he was [earlier] trying a prisoner on a capital charge, he would place a hand over one of his ears while the prosecutor was speaking, so as to keep it free and impartial for listening to the defendant. But later so many accusations were laid before him that he grew harsh and was inclined to believe even the false charges, because so much that he was told was true. Above all, if anybody spoke ill of him, his judgement was apt to desert him and his mood would become cruel and merciless, since he valued his good name more than his life or his crown.
>
> (42.2–4)

Plutarch calls attention to the roles of fear and anger in this dramatic change, and emphasizes that Alexander was afraid that he would lose the favor of the gods, or that his Macedonians might grow weary of the expedition. For Plutarch, Hamilton tells us, "anger is the chief defect in

Alexander's character."[3] The ancient biographer, who is clearly uncomfortable with this trait in his subject, offers the explanation that it was Alexander's "warmth of temperament which made him fond of drinking, and also prone to outbursts of choleric rage" (4.7).[4]

Curtius, although arguing that Alexander's penchant for adopting oriental customs was the root of his problem, points to the parts played by fear and anger in Alexander's transformation. He also refers to an increase in the frequency and extent of the king's drinking at the time:

> This [orientalization] explains the increase in the plots against his life, the mutiny of his men and the more-public displays of resentment and mutual recrimination among them; it explains why Alexander subsequently oscillated between anger and suspicion which arose from groundless fears, and it explains other similar problems . . . . he was spending his days as well as his nights on these protracted banquets.
>
> (6.2.4–5)

A moralizing Curtius (3.12.18–19) laments that later in life Alexander failed to maintain his earlier moderation. "For then he would surely have overcome the defects he failed to overcome, his pride and his temper" (3.12.19). After praising Alexander's virtues elsewhere, Curtius had come to the conclusion that they were all "marred by his inexcusable fondness for drink" (5.7.1).

Even Arrian felt obliged to acknowledge that in his later years Alexander became "quicker-tempered and, courted as he now was in the barbarian manner, had ceased to be so kindly as in old times to the Macedonians" (7.8.3). When referring to the events of 328, he also associates the king's transformation with wine by stating that "in fact, Alexander had already taken to new and more barbaric ways in drinking" (4.8.2). Justin says bluntly that Alexander, like his father, was simply "too fond of wine" (9.8.15).

Every major account of this period that has survived alludes to Alexander's peculiar relationship with the earthly agent of Dionysus. The ancients had definite opinions about the psychology of drinking. Theognis had claimed that "[b]y fire one tests gold and silver, and by wine one learns the character of a man."[5] Callias of Argos states unequivocally that "wine is the test of character."[6] Philochorus, anticipating the dictum *in vino veritas*, says that drinkers reveal their true natures.[7] Pittacus, the sage of Mytilene, is said to have "advised Periander of Corinth not to get drunk and not to revel . . . [so] that you may not be recognized as the sort of man you happen to be . . . . [f]or . . . wine [is] the mirror of the mind."[8]

Plutarch praises occasional drunkenness in the wise man, for it enables him to relax without having to fear any damaging disclosure or loss of virtue.[9] But strong drink, he believes, intensifies natural tendencies, and those who have difficulty controlling their emotions while sober are likely to be at its mercy while drunk. He contends that wine brings out the best in some and the worst in others: "[I]t shakes out the folds as it were, where duplicity and rancour lurk in the mind, and reveals every trait of character and every secret feeling in transparent language" (*Mor*.715f).

Tolerance for wine, Plutarch observes, varies from one person to the next. He cautions the host at a symposium to be aware of the "change drinking produces in each [guest], into what emotional state he is apt to fall" (*Mor*.620e).[10] Wine not only summons one's character to the surface, he declares, but reshapes it, "just as wine is at first controlled by the character of the drinker . . . as it warms his whole body and becomes mingled therewith, [it] . . . forms the drinker's character and changes him" (*Mor*.799b–c).

During Alexander's reign symposia were social events that included dining, entertainment, and drinking. They were obviously impractical when the army was on the march, so symposia most often took place between campaigns, when the king's men were securely settled behind the walls of a city. They were usually held in a designated part of the royal quarters, and the number of participants varied from a dozen or more close friends to the extravagant wedding celebration at Susa in 324, when the great "Tent of a Hundred Couches" was used and over 10,000 guests received gifts. Ordinarily there would be sixty to seventy symposiasts,[11] including Royal Companions and special guests.

These events served a multitude of purposes for the king, but it is important to note Eugene N. Borza's reminder that the central feature of the symposium, especially the Macedonian variety, was drinking.[12] The sources either directly refer or allude to at least twenty-six (by my count) of Alexander's symposia over an eleven-year period (334–323).[13] Significantly, the majority of these are reported to have occurred during the last three years of his life (325–323).[14] Macedonian symposia commonly "continued until fatigue, boredom, drunken[n]ess, violence or sleep intervened,"[15] and were, it seems, in stark contrast to the convivial atmosphere and lofty colloquies of the Athenians described by Plato and Xenophon.

The Macedonian symposium provided relaxation from the pressures of war. It also, as we shall see, was in its own way a demanding ordeal, marked by social, psychological, and physical tensions.[16] Much of the conversation seems to have revolved around recollections of particularly successful campaigns and on acts of heroism. Both the heroics and foibles of those present could be introduced, but it was prudent to reserve the most flattering superlatives for the king. Toasts were offered to celebrate victories, honor courage, remember fallen comrades, salute the gods, anticipate future conflicts, and express gratitude to the king.[17] All through the toasting, symposiasts shared in the camaraderie by lifting their cups, and drinking huge amounts of undiluted wine. Collective solidarity was expressed through ritualistic drinking, which provided a device for measuring character and loyalty. Refusing to participate in the festivities might cast doubt on one's manliness, amiability, or even allegiance.

Alexander's court historian Callisthenes, who fell from grace, once refused to drink the king's unmixed wine because he knew that he would need the ancient equivalent of a headache tablet the following morning.[18] Later Callisthenes was accused of conspiring in an assassination plot. Although there were more serious allegations regarding the historian's behavior (see below), his refusal to stomach the uncut wine was undoubtedly perceived as an insult by the king, and perhaps as further evidence of his lack of devotion to Alexander.

The young king habitually scrutinized himself and others. The symposium offered an arena in which Alexander could critically measure the usefulness and loyalty of others while eliciting responses that would reassure him of his own worthiness. Competition permeated the environment at the symposium: actors, singers, dancers, musicians, authors, wrestlers, and sycophants vied with one another for royal recognition and largesse.[19] Alexander delighted in bestowing money and gifts upon individuals.

He also enjoyed sponsoring drinking contests at the symposia. On at least one occasion the incentives were lucrative enough to result in fatalities from overindulgence. Alexander does not seem to have competed officially, but he set an exacting pace for his guests, displaying enough stamina to drink until light broke the following morning. At a small drinking party hosted by his Thessalian friend Medius, Alexander reportedly drank to the health of all twenty present, then accepted the same number of toasts in return. He is said to have tried unsuccessfully to match the consumption of Proteas, a Macedonian folk-hero, who "enjoyed a sturdy physique throughout his life, although he was completely devoted to the practice of drinking."[20]

Protectors of Alexander's reputation have made vigorous attempts to deny his heavy drinking. Aristobulus even claimed that the king stayed up all night at drinking parties out of courtesy to his companions.[21] Plutarch repeated a similar rationalization in his life of Alexander, but rejected the notion in a later work.[22] The reality was that by 330 Alexander had begun to rely on the good gift of Dionysus with increasing frequency,[23] and this habit began to contribute to a transformation in his personality. There is only one common thread interwoven throughout the ancient accounts: excessive drinking. More than any other single factor, this helps to explain the metamorphosis in the man.

> god
> has found
> his
> way
> (*Ba.* 1391)

## THE BURNING OF PERSEPOLIS (330 BC)

Remote, and little more than a name to most Greeks, Persepolis was the ceremonial capital of the Achaemenid Empire.[24] Persian kings journeyed to this city annually from Susa or Ecbatana (Hamadan) to undergo a ritual renewal of their office. Held in the spring, when Persians celebrated the New Year, the ceremony was followed by acceptance of homage and tribute from representatives of all parts of their vast domain. Relief carvings of gift bearers in their native attire speak for the ecumenical complexion of the population that was subject to the power of the Persians and their Median partners: Babylonians, Assyrians, Phrygians, Lydians, Cappadocians, Armenians, Indians, and even Scythians were among those who came to offer tribute and place their offerings at the foot of the Great King's throne.

The grand processional staircase of 111 steps was an impressive 50 feet wide. The remains of the Hall of the Hundred Columns and the superb portals of the Apadana suggest that the city, begun by Darius the Great and completed by Xerxes, successfully symbolized the unity of an empire that stretched from the Nile to the Indus and the Jaxartes to the Indian Ocean, and encompassed much of the known world. Persian kings were buried at Persepolis, where the jeweled golden vine, which was symbolic of the Tree of Life, was also housed.[25]

Alexander's men sacked the city shortly after entering it, and wholesale carnage ensued.[26] The last time his troops had been permitted unbridled pillage was at Gaza, where the king had met with fierce opposition and was nearly killed during the siege. Now his troops were again granted license for revenge on an enemy that had recently marshaled an equally spirited defense at the Persian (or Susian) Gates,[27] during which Alexander was forced to abandon his fallen troops on the battlefield – ordinarily an acknowledgment of defeat in antiquity. Persepolis was a city of singular opulence in an empire of unparalleled riches. The troops, constrained at Babylon and Susa, reveled with brutish abandon.

Royal approval of the pillage may have been inspired by an unsettling encounter with mutilated Greeks on the plains outside the city.[28] These recently liberated captives, some without hands, others without ears and noses, furnished evidence that the Persians had cut off any extremities unessential to the work they had been assigned. Alexander wept openly at the *pathos* of this scene and volunteered to arrange their return home. This gallant overture was politely refused because these men, many of whom were old, knew that their own people would see them as grotesque oddities. Furthermore, many of them had married enslaved women by whom they had children. This macabre group realized that it was by remaining among themselves, and apart from the rest of the world, that they would be able to preserve some degree of self-respect.

The king was impressed by the wisdom of their decision. He granted their request for land and made a generous donation of money and provisions, providing yet another example of Alexander's concern for those ignored or persecuted by others. The fact that he alone was able to act as a benefactor to people "without a country" may have pleased Alexander.

While his troops ransacked the city, the king took control of the palace area and the Treasury, which yielded the immense sum of 120,000 talents in uncoined bullion.[29] In total, Alexander had accumulated approximately 180,000 talents in four months, an amount doubtless incomprehensible to Europeans. During Philip's reign the expropriation of the gold mines in the vicinity of Mount Pangaeum had guaranteed the Macedonian king what was then considered to be a staggering annual income of 1,000 talents. Ultimately, Parmenio was ordered to convey the treasure (7,290 tons of gold and silver, by Donald W. Engels' estimate)[30] to Ecbatana, the capital of Media, on the backs of 20,000 mules and 5,000 camels. The king no longer need concern himself over money.[31]

Alexander stayed at Persepolis for about four months, probably from the middle of January through late May of 330. If it had been possible he would probably have resumed the hunt for Darius, but supplies were scarce along the 500-mile route toward Ecbatana and the weather was frigid. This factor had been underscored by a previous expedition against local tribesmen. Curtius offers an instructive description of the conditions presented by the local climate, and Alexander's response to this challenge:

> The desolation of the terrain and the trackless wilderness terrified the exhausted soldiers, who thought they were looking at the limits of the world. They gazed in astonishment at the total desolation with no sign of human cultivation, and they clamoured to go back before daylight and sky also came to an end. The king refrained from reproaching them for their fear. Instead he jumped from his horse and proceeded to make his way on foot through the snow and hard-packed ice. His friends were ashamed not to follow him, and the feeling spread to his generals, and, finally, the men. The king was the first to clear a way for himself, using an axe to break the ice, and then the others followed his example.
>
> (5.6.13–14)

After spending a month in the field, leaving local tribes speechless with his sudden appearances out of a frozen wasteland, Alexander elected to return to Persepolis and join in the ongoing celebration. While drunk at a symposium, he acted in a way he was soon to regret.[32]

Your mind

is

distracted
now
(*Ba*. 332)

The scene is recreated by Diodorus:

> Alexander held games in honour of his victories. He performed costly sacrifices to the gods and entertained his friends bountifully. While they were feasting and the drinking was far advanced, as they began to be drunken a madness took possession of the minds of the intoxicated guests. At this point one of the women present, Thais by name and Attic by origin, said that for Alexander it would be the finest of all his feats in Asia if he joined them in a triumphal procession, set fire to the palaces, and permitted women's hands in a minute to extinguish the famed accomplishments of the Persians. This was said to men who were still young and giddy with wine, and so, as would be expected, someone shouted out to form the comus and to light torches, and urged all to take vengeance for the destruction of the Greek temples. Others took up the cry and said that this was a deed worthy of Alexander alone. When the king had caught fire at their words, all leaped up from their couches and passed the word along to form a victory procession in honour of Dionysus. Promptly many torches were gathered. Female musicians were present at the banquet, so the king led them all out for the comus to the sound of voices and flutes and pipes, Thais the courtesan leading the whole performance. She was the first, after the king, to hurl her blazing torch into the palace. As the others all did the same, immediately the entire palace area was consumed, so great was the conflagration. It was most remarkable that the impious act of Xerxes, king of the Persians, against the acropolis at Athens should have been repaid in kind after many years by one woman, a citizen of the land which had suffered it, and in sport.
>
> (17.72.1–6)

Macedonian soldiers, under the assumption that an accident had occurred, rushed to extinguish the flames. After realizing the actual circumstances, however, they cheerfully joined in the tossing of firebrands.

Plutarch states that "it is agreed [among historians] that Alexander quickly repented and gave orders for the fire to be put out" (38.8). Curtius says: "it is generally agreed that, when sleep had brought him back to his senses after his drunken bout, he regretted his actions and said that the Persians would have suffered a more grievous punishment at the hands of the Greeks had they been forced to see him on Xerxes' throne and in his palace" (5.7.11).

Arrian offers a substantially different version. He recreates a scene in which Parmenio urges the king to preserve the city simply because it makes no sense to destroy one's own property. Devastation of this sort,

Parmenio adds, would serve notice to the Persians that Alexander merely planned to conquer their empire and move on, and this would discourage allegiance. The king, we are told, had a different motive.[33] "Alexander said that he wished to punish the Persians for sacking Athens and burning the temples when they invaded Greece, and to exact retribution for all the other injuries they had done to the Greeks" (3.18.12).[34] Based on Ptolemy, Arrian's account explains that the whole affair was an act of calculated policy, and modern scholars following Arrian have either ignored Thais or simply dismissed her as a romantic invention.

We do know from an inscription, however, that this same Thais who was implicated in the Persepolis scenario in accounts other than Arrian's was (or became) Ptolemy's mistress and had three children by him.[35] Is it surprising that the man who ruled Egypt would ignore her participation when he wrote about this senseless act? His version of the episode as being based on a reasoned decision on the king's part both exculpated Thais through discreet silence and defended Alexander against the charge that he acted in a fit of drunken irresponsibility.

I think
then
you
must have seen
how Bacchus
jostled
the palace
(*Ba.* 605–6)

Arrian's brief treatment of Alexander's stay in Persepolis may reflect the historian's own discomfort with what transpired there. At this point in the *Anabasis*, however, he did feel compelled to record one of his infrequent criticisms of the king: "I too do not think that Alexander showed good sense in this action nor that he could punish Persians of a long past age" (3.18.12). Later in the same work Arrian admits that Alexander himself lamented this colossal vandalism when he returned to Persepolis six years later and observed the magnificent debris through sober eyes.[36] Only 13 of the original 72 columns remained standing.

He razed the palace
to the ground
where it lies
(*Ba.* 633)

An anecdote relayed by Plutarch indicates that Alexander was unsure about his future role in Persia before the city went up in flames. The story tells of a huge statue of Xerxes that was toppled by his soldiers as they forced their way into the palace. The king paused to address the statue as "if it were alive. 'Shall I pass by and leave you lying there because of the expedition you led against Greece, or shall I set you up again because of your magnanimity and your virtues in other respects?' " (37.5). Alexander silently pondered the question in front of the statue before passing it by.

Alexander was at the crossroads of his expedition. The notion of a Hellenic crusade was all but played out, and certainly would have to be abandoned once Darius III was either killed or captured. At that point the king's Greek "volunteers" were to be dismissed, while his Macedonians would need persuasion to continue campaigning zealously across *terra incognita* toward some unknown objective. There was joy in seeing the king in the vanguard of the inebriated incendiaries at Persepolis, because the troops believed it meant that they would soon be returning home. The torching of the royal palace was understood to be a fitting climax to a victorious expedition. They had no idea that their epic journey had just begun, nor were they aware that they were accompanying a leader who was in the process of a personal transformation.

Shall I
lead you there now?
Are you ready
to go?
(*Ba*. 819)

Alexander's prolonged stay in Persepolis was "likely to be the effect of uncertainty and anxiety over what was happening in Greece," Badian tells us.[37] At first glance this seems difficult to understand, especially if one accepts the traditional view that Antipater had triumphed over the Greek insurgents just before the battle of Gaugamela. In that case Alexander would have heard of the victory well before he fired the palaces at Persepolis, and would have had no compelling reason to continue to court Greek opinion in such an extravagant way.

Badian argues that the battle in Greece did not take place until the spring of 330.[38] Therefore, because of regional communications Alexander might not yet have learned of Antipater's victory when he "lit the funeral pyre of the Hellenic crusade."[39] If this is so, Alexander, at the time of the burning, might still have been posturing as a knight errant in the service of Hellenic culture.

Nonetheless, without resorting to ingenious explanations that pervert the actual events, it remains difficult to defend the thesis that Alexander's actions at Persepolis were premeditated. The fact is that Alexander's own men, who were invariably well informed about the king's movements, raced to the scene in order to deal with what appeared to them to be a very serious accident, with coruscating flames and cedar rafters crashing to the floor from 60 feet overhead. Also, the blaze predictably got out of control and became dangerous to both Alexander and his staff. It is inconceivable that the king would have failed to alert his own fire brigade if such a holocaust had been premeditated. Known as a meticulous planner, Alexander would have taken the necessary precautions to minimize the chance of injury to himself and his officers.

The Treasury, no doubt ransacked well before the conflagration, was severely damaged. A mysterious trail of coins unearthed by archaeologists in our own century probably testifies to frantic last-minute efforts to make sure that no monies were left behind. Also, had Alexander decided on such a titanic spectacle in advance, he would undoubtedly have orchestrated the occasion in an appropriate manner, hoping to earn the admiration of Hellas through his flamboyant gesture. It seems clear that this was not the case.[40]

> Flames float out from his trailing wand
>      as he [Dionysus]
>          runs
>       (*Ba*. 146–8)

In any event, Darius was now reported to be at Ecbatana formulating his plans. Alexander marched north to meet him at his earliest opportunity. With only 6,000 footmen and 3,000 horsemen presently at his disposal, the beleaguered Persian king withdrew the 7,000 talents available at Ecbatana and hurried eastward, leaving the city only a week or so before the bulk of Alexander's troops arrived there.

The news of Antipater's victory in Greece, which probably reached Alexander *en route* to Ecbatana, called for a reformulation of the king's objectives. The idea of a crusade had ended, for all practical purposes, with the destruction of Persepolis. Alexander therefore decided to dismiss the Greek troops sent on the expedition by the Corinthian League. Still short of manpower, however, he offered the startling sum of three talents as a bounty to every man who chose to reenlist as a mercenary.[41] Faced with the attractive prospect of becoming rich overnight, many of the Greeks, including a good portion of the Thessalian cavalry, agreed to sign on. Men who chose to go home were given a substantial bonus and became living testimony of the fortunes available to those who campaigned with Alexander. The expenses involved in this episode amounted to either 12 or 13,000 talents,[42] but money seems to have been important to Alexander only in so far as it facilitated his objectives. From his point of view, it was a bargain.

Alexander's Greek troops had thus become professionalized and dependent upon the king through his paymaster. Parmenio had supervised the conveyance of the Treasury to Ecbatana, but Harpalus, Alexander's renegade friend, had been reinstated as the Imperial Treasurer. Parmenio, now 70, was stationed in Ecbatana to guard the Treasury and supervise communications as Alexander moved eastward. The general's function was important, and his assignment could be seen as a reward for his long, distinguished service, but it also removed him from court and the corridors of power.

Alexander, now approaching 26, had come into his own. He no doubt felt that he could manage the campaign quite well without the advice of a marshal who had become a legend while the king was still in swaddling clothes. Alexander appointed Cleander, probably at Parmenio's request, to be the general's second-in-command. Subsequent events would disclose the ephemeral nature of that baron's loyalty to the aging marshal.

## ORIENTALIZATION

The fate of Darius III was ultimately sealed by his own followers rather than by Alexander. Disenchanted with his leadership and alarmed at the possibility that their hapless king might fall into the hands of Alexander while still alive, his own subjects attacked Darius with javelins as the enemy closed in.[43] In August 330 a Macedonian soldier, as he stopped to fetch water, noticed some wounded oxen attached to a covered wagon.[44] He heard a human voice wailing from inside the vehicle and was astonished to discover that it was that of the Great King, in chains and wrapped in a blood-drenched mantle. When Alexander arrived, Darius was already dead. The young king, touched by his foe's pathetic demise, used his own cloak to cover the lifeless body.[45]

> poor fool
> who . . .
> in the pride
> of his horses
> and chariot
> was not destined
> to evade
> the evil spirits
> of
> destruction
> (*Il.* 12.113–14)

The corpse was embalmed and sent back to Persepolis to be placed in the company of the other Achaemenid rulers buried there. The king had intended to capture Darius alive and ceremoniously accept his abdication and submission. This new turn of events forced Alexander to modify his role and immediate aims. He would soon appear as both the legitimate successor to Darius and, ironically, the dead king's avenger.

One of the assassins, Bessus, the satrap of Bactria and a member of the royal house, soon laid claim to the kingship himself and adopted the name Artaxerxes (V). From the safe retreat of his own territory in the northeastern region of the Persian Empire, Bessus, who had acquitted himself well at Gaugamela, intended to press his claim and rid Persia of the foreign invader. Alexander accused Bessus of regicide and announced his intention to bring him to justice for this heinous crime.

Alexander now used the Achaemenid signet while dealing with Asian questions and the Macedonian royal ring when it came to European affairs.[46] He sought the support of aristocratic Persians, some of whom were willing to accept him as the rightful heir to the throne. Oxyathres, the brother of Darius, was appointed one of the king's Companions – the first Asiatic to be so honored.[47] Artabazus, the father of Barsine (who gave birth to Alexander's illegitimate son), who had been in exile at Pella, pledged his support as well as that of seven of his sons.

In exchange for his obeisance, Nabarzanes, the Persian Grand Vizier (or Chiliarch), was pardoned for any role he might have played in Darius' assassination. The Grand Vizier had hoped to ingratiate himself with Alexander by arriving with luxurious presents.

> bringing gifts to Achilleus
> which might soften
> his anger
> (*Il*. 24.119)

Included among these gifts was Bagoas, "an exceptionally good-looking eunuch in the very flower of his youth [with whom] . . . Darius had had a sexual relationship . . . and . . . Alexander . . . too" (C.6.5.23).[48] There is no question that Alexander was also very fond of Bagoas. He was influential in Alexander's acceptance of Nabarzanes, and later instrumental in the discrediting and death of Orsines, a Persian nobleman who had slighted the eunuch. The name Bagoas appears on a roll call of the king's naval officers presented by Nearchus for the year 326 (A.*Ind*.18.1–10), and is also found on a list of residences where Alexander is said to have drunk while carousing in Ecbatana during the last year of his life.[49]

The question of Alexander's sexual involvement with this youth is insoluble, but it is worth noting that Bagoas, too, belonged to a special category of people who posed no real threat to the king and who owed everything they had to him.[50] This seems to have been an optimal relationship from Alexander's point of view. Bagoas benefited as well, and not just as a recipient of Alexander's largesse. The king's good will protected Bagoas from Europeans, many of whom may have found the notion of eunuchism grating, although under the circumstances, they kept any negative thoughts to themselves.

> I give you
> sober warning
> fools
> place
> no chains
> on me
> (*Ba*. 504)

The king's troops probably found Alexander's affection for the eunuch much less interesting than any relationships he may have had with the 365 beautiful Asian women he had inherited from Darius. It is improbable, however, that Alexander ever exercised his royal prerogative to sleep with a different woman every night of the year.[51] It is more likely that his retention of the Great King's harem and public patronage of eunuchs were designed to contribute to a semblance of continuity in the Achaemenid kingship, and thereby help to promote his acceptance among the Persian elite.

To further enhance his chances of being accepted as a legitimate ruler by the Persian nobility, Alexander thought it necessary to make some changes in his appearance and mannerisms. With this in mind, he began to wear a modified version of the Achaemenid royal dress, and to adopt some aspects of Persian protocol at his court.[52] These innovations were introduced gradually in an attempt to mitigate the resistance anticipated on the part of his fellow Macedonians.

At first only a handful of the king's close friends and a few Asiatics witnessed this transformation. Subsequently, this "new" Alexander could be seen riding in public and presiding at court. Discreetly avoiding garments that were likely to elicit ridicule, such as the baggy Persian trousers and the *candys*, a purple or gold upper garment with long wide sleeves, the king settled for a blend of costume that Plutarch calls more modest than the Persian and more stately than the Median varieties.[53] His attire included a purple and white chiton and the royal diadem, and a purple ribbon encircling the *kausia*, a traditional Macedonian hat.[54]

I
feel
as
though
my
mind
were
somehow
changing
(*Ba.* 1269–70)

At the same time that Alexander was modifying his own attire, the Royal Companions were presented with purple hats and white cloaks with a purple border. Within the inner circle, Hephaestion and a few others seem to have adopted the new dress without reluctance. Craterus, however, one of the king's ablest commanders, continued to dress in the customary Macedonian fashion.[55]

Alexander, we are told, often remarked "that Hephaestion was a friend of Alexander's, while Craterus was a friend of the king's" (P.47.10).[56] Both men were extremely useful to him, but each in a different fashion.

Hephaestion served as a liaison with the Asiatics, while Craterus dealt with the Macedonians. In the end Craterus would be sent back to Macedonia to replace Antipater, while Hephaestion remained in Asia, second only to Alexander.

Ancient Greek folklore credits Alexander's mythological ancestor Perseus, who makes no more than a fleeting appearance in our accounts of the king,[57] with providing an early bridge between Greeks and Asians. Also an heroic wanderer, who travelled north of the encircling Ocean to feast with the Hyperboreans and south across Ethiopia to rescue Andromeda, Perseus is best remembered for beheading the evil-eyed Gorgon, Medusa, whose look petrified her beholders. In appreciation for the instructions of Athena and the use of her shield, Perseus dedicated his trophy to the goddess, who wore it on her breast as would her mortal charge, Achilles. The *Alexander Mosaic* portrays the king with a Gorgon on his cuirass (breastplate) in the Achillean tradition, which was actually rooted in the exploits of a paternal ancestor.[58]

> And circled in the midst of all
> was the blank-eyed face of the Gorgon
> with her stare of horror
> and Fear
> was inscribed upon it
> and
> Terror
> (*Il.* 11.36–7)

Perseus, who is described as "pre-eminent among all men" in the *Iliad* (14.320), is also said to have been in Argos when Dionysus arrived from across the sea with Ariadne and an entourage of female devotees.[59] The hero unthinkingly challenged the entire troupe and used Medusa's head to slay the Dionysiac faithful. In one version of this tale, Dionysus himself is said to have been murdered by Perseus and tossed into the icy waters of Lerna, which lead down into the netherworld. Later embellishments have these two sons of Zeus reconciled, but Dionysus would show that he had a long memory when dealing with the heroic descendant of Perseus.

Herodotus tells us that Perseus lent his name to the Persians, who were said to be his offspring.[60] Full of remorse after inadvertently killing Acrisius, his own grandfather, Perseus refused the kingship at Argos and travelled to Asia to live out his final days. There Andromeda bore him a son named Perses, who became the first in a long line of Persian kings. When the Persians invaded Greece during the fifth century, they pointed to Perseus in their family tree as part of the justification for claiming what was theirs. This must have been on Alexander's mind at the time of his invasion in 334. To a number of mythographers "Perseus became the hero of integration between East and West,"[61] and a similar concept may have served as the model for some of the king's later policies.

Alexander's orientalization was bitterly resented by his Macedonians, and a hint of subdued tension began to suffuse his court. Later this would erupt into violent clashes and personal tragedy. At that moment, however, most of the men were more concerned about how long the present (and presumably final) campaign would last. Bessus, the satrap of Bactria, was a blood relative of Darius, and thus a *bona fide* Persian candidate for the throne. He had laid claim to it,[62] but was also well on his way to Bactria. Alexander, instead of taking up the chase, decided to give his army a well-deserved rest at Hecatompylus (Damghan).

A rumor circulated during this period that the expedition was over, and so the elated soldiers began to load their wagons for the long-awaited march home.[63] Alexander, though, had already made the decision to embark on an extensive eastern campaign. He was alarmed at the army's actions, summoned his commanders to the royal tent, "and, with tears in his eyes, complained that he was being brought to a halt in the middle of a brilliant career, to return home more like a defeated man than a conqueror; that the obstacle he faced was not his men's cowardice but the ill-will of the gods who had instilled in soldiers of the highest courage a sudden pining for home – though they would have returned there shortly with increased glory and fame" (C.6.2.18–19). His commanders assured Alexander that they would do anything he asked of them. To prove their point, they openly competed with one another for the most difficult assignments. They did feel, however, that it was necessary for the king to address the troops in person if he wanted them to carry on with the same enthusiasm and determination. Alexander agreed to speak to the entire army after his commanders had had an opportunity "to prepare the crowd to listen to him" (C.6.2.21).

If the speech delivered by Alexander bears any resemblance to that reported in Curtius, it must have been a masterpiece of exhortation. Curtius has the king begin by identifying with the weariness of his men and their longing for peace after so many rugged campaigns. He then announced that he found their desire to go home perfectly legitimate, and claimed that if these victories were secure, he would be the first to turn back. In fact, if that were true, no one, he declared, including themselves – his own soldiers – could prevent him from returning to his mother and sisters to enjoy the fruits of victory that their valor had won.[64]

> But our empire is new and, if we are prepared to admit the truth, unstable; the barbarians still hold their necks stiff beneath the yoke . . . . we are dealing with . . . a pack of wild animals; they are naturally intractable, and even captured and confined they will only be tamed by the passage of time . . . . The moment they see our backs turned they will all be after us [led by Bessus] . . . . a man who committed the most heinous crime by keeping his own king in irons . . . and finally killing him . . . . [this same man might soon be] devastating the cities

of Greece or the Hellespont. What pangs of regret will you feel then that Bessus deprived you of the rewards of your victory? . . . A four days' march remains for us, for men who have trodden so many snows, forded so many rivers, crossed so many mountain ranges. Our progress is not impeded by a sea that covers the road with a surging tide or stopped by the cramping defiles of Cilicia – everything before us is flat and easy. We stand on the threshold of victory.

(6.3.6–16)

We are told that his men were so impressed with Alexander's words that they asked "him to lead them wherever he wished" (6.4.1).

> He spoke
> and led the way
> and the rest of them
> came on after him
> with unearthly clamour
> (*Il.* 12.251–2)

Although the speech related by Curtius is colored by the Roman historian's flair for the rhetorical, it is similar in tone and approach to others recorded in Arrian's work and should not be summarily dismissed as being devoid of veracity or value.[65] Like speeches (also described by Arrian) of Alexander during other times of crisis, it displays a clever oscillation between flattery and reproach, and is designed both to confound the king's soldiers and to induce them to act in a way that would remove any doubts that Alexander might have had about their loyalty and devotion. The king's actual plans for the next campaign were distorted enough to make them sound reasonable. It followed that anyone who elected to shirk his duty at this critical phase of the operation would be burdened with the responsibility for the inevitable catastrophes that might occur. Alexander is credited with saying that their destination was about a "four-day march," but the Bactrian capital was in fact 450 miles away and lay across the snow-laden Hindu Kush. Alexander was fully aware of this, and also knew that even under ideal conditions it would take the army at least one month before it could expect to arrive. When, after some delay, they finally did appear in this region, the Macedonians were treated to two of the most trying years of fighting in the campaign. No significant number of veterans would be released from active service until seven years hence.

Whatever Alexander said saved the day. Thoroughly convinced that this was the end of the campaign, the last conflict, the final thrust, Alexander's men followed their charismatic young king across central Asia just as they would later follow him over the borders of modern Pakistan. Vaguely aware that each "decisive" campaign had a way of transforming itself into the initial stage of yet another operation, the troops sporadically made their dissatisfaction known to him. Alexander, however, was always able to rise to the challenge. In fact, on all but one occasion (as we shall see), he succeeded in convincing his troops that it was in their best interests to follow their king.

Alexander's generosity helped dull their awareness of moving in and out of a monotonous succession of alien worlds.[66] The king's commanders were granted sums of money and fiefdoms beyond their wildest imaginations. Plutarch writes of "Hagnon of Teos, who wore silver nails in his boots; Leonnatus, who had the dust with which he sprinkled his body for wrestling brought by camel-train from Egypt; and Philotas who hunted with nets that could enclose a space of twelve miles" (40.1).

Olympias complained to Alexander that his immoderate benefactions made kings (and hence competitors) out of his friends.[67] But her son still found ostentation amusing in others. He was more troubled by men who refused his gifts than those who requested them – another reflection, it would seem, of his own insecurity.

## THE PHILOTAS AFFAIR (330 BC)

Alexander's pursuit of Bessus into Bactria had to be abandoned when news reached the king that one of his Persian appointees was in open rebellion. Satibarzanes, the satrap of Areia, had submitted to Alexander and been confirmed in office, but shortly after the king's departure Satibarzanes massacred the foreign garrison left to assist him and took Artacoana (probably near modern Herat), the capital of the province. Alexander was rarely so anxious to achieve an objective that he would tolerate disloyalty or allow a deployment of his troops to be jeopardized, and so he raced 70 miles in two days back to Artacoana with a hand-picked force. The astonished Satibarzanes fled to Bactria rather than risk a confrontation, and Alexander subdued any signs of rebellion in the satrapy with brutal determination. The king soon became aware that there were similar difficulties to the south in Drangiana and decided that his presence was needed there in order to secure the province. After suppressing that rebellion, Alexander and his army rested for nine days at Phrada (now Farah), near Lake Seistan in modern Afghanistan.

It was here that a plot to kill Alexander was hatched among some relatively obscure young Macedonian aristocrats.[68] For reasons unknown, Dimnus, a Macedonian youth, and several of his comrades had agreed to assassinate Alexander. Dimnus disclosed the details to his lover Nicomachus, who, in turn, told his brother Cebalinus. Cebalinus then approached Philotas with the information and asked for an audience with the king. Philotas replied that the king was busy, but gave assurances that he would apprise Alexander of the situation. When it became clear during the following day that, for whatever reason, Philotas (who saw the king twice daily) had not yet reported this matter to the king, Cebalinus panicked.

He contacted Metron, a page in charge of the armory, and this young man took the informant directly to Alexander.

The king ordered his men to arrest Dimnus, while he personally interrogated Cebalinus about the plan to assassinate him. When it became evident that Cebalinus had been aware of the plot for two days before approaching Metron, Alexander became suspicious of his loyalty and ordered him put in chains. Cebalinus shouted hysterically that at the very instant he heard about the plan he had rushed to Philotas and had received guarantees that the situation would be reported to the king. Alexander "asked again if he had approached Philotas, if he had insisted that they come to Alexander. When Cebalinus persistently reaffirmed his story, Alexander held his hands up to the sky and, bursting into tears, bemoaned the fact that he had been so repaid by one who had formerly been the dearest of his friends" (C.6.7.28).

Through a self-inflicted wound, or as the result of his resisting arrest, Dimnus was dead before he could be interrogated. Philotas was then summoned to the king's quarters and asked to justify his failure to provide the king with information of such a vital nature. In Curtius' account, Philotas says that he had lent no credence to the information because of its source, and claimed he was reluctant to say anything out of fear that he would be ridiculed for taking a lover's quarrel too seriously. Now, in light of the circumstances of Dimnus' death, it was clear to him that he had made a serious mistake in judgment, and he begged the king's forgiveness.[69] Philotas embraced the king and implored him to remember his past record and see this as an error of omission rather than one of commission. The Roman historian could not "say whether the king believed him or kept his anger concealed deep in his heart. He offered Philotas his right hand as a sign of reconciliation, and said that in his opinion it was a case of information not being taken seriously rather than being deliberately suppressed" (6.7.35).

> You have my promise
> I shall not
> punish you
> (*Ba.* 672)

Later on that day, however, the king called a meeting of his close friends to hear Nicomachus' story in the absence of Philotas. Subsequently his friends' opinions were solicited.

Craterus, who had brought to Alexander's attention certain intemperate remarks made by Parmenio's son when he was in Egypt, and "was not unaware that Philotas' excessively boastful talk about his courage and his services had often grated on the ears of Alexander" (C.6.8.3), spoke at length. He seized the opportunity to discredit Philotas by making a case for his involvement in the plot, and tried to persuade Alexander that absolving Philotas would be a grievous error on the king's part. He went on, "I wish you had also discussed this matter with us in the beginning! If you were set on pardoning Philotas, we would have urged you to keep him ignorant of how much he owed you. Rather that than that he now have cause to think more about his own danger – since he has been taken to the brink of death – than about your generosity. You see, *he* will always be able to plot against you, but you will not always be able to pardon Philotas" (C.6.8.4–5). The accused would also know, Craterus warned, that he had exhausted the king's mercy and would have to make a better job of it next time. He argued that Parmenio, Philotas' father, would be disaffected by this whole affair, no matter what the outcome, and that one day Alexander would be fighting both men if they were not dealt with immediately. Craterus then cleverly placed his admonition in the context of Alexander's overall objectives: "The enemies we are about to pursue are still numerous enough. Protect yourself against enemies within our ranks. Eliminate those and I fear nothing from the foreigner" (C.6.8.9).

Those present seem to have been in agreement with Craterus that Philotas would never have failed to inform the king if he had not been a ringleader or at least an accomplice in the conspiracy. It was suggested that Philotas should be interrogated under torture to determine the full scope of the plot and to force him to disclose the names of all of the conspirators. Alexander imposed an absolute silence concerning all of their discussions, and then ordered a routine march for the following day so that no one would be able to anticipate what was about to happen.

Now
all promises
forgotten
(*Il.* 5.834)

Curtius tells us that Philotas was invited to Alexander's banquet that night and engaged in amicable banter with the king.[70] High anxiety prevailed beneath this charade of conviviality, however, and Alexander, an accomplished actor when the situation called for it, must have given the performance of his life. The gathering ended early because of the fictitious march scheduled for the next day, and Philotas was soon sleeping soundly, relieved that his error had been forgiven and the whole episode forgotten.

The camp was sealed with armed men in order to ensure that no one would be able to escape to Media and tell Parmenio what was about to happen. Craterus, Hephaestion, Perdiccas, Leonnatus, Erigyius (who was banished by Philip at the time of the Pixodarus affair), and Coenus (the jealous brother-in-law of Philotas) were called to the royal quarters. Atarrhias, a loyal veteran, was dispatched with a force of 300 men to Philotas' tent, where the locked door was broken down. The accused was aroused from a deep sleep and arrested.

And when you take him
clap him in chains
and march him here
He shall die
as he deserves
by being
stoned
to
death
(*Ba.* 355–7)

Curtius has Philotas shaking off his drowsiness and, after being shackled, shouting words for Alexander, who was not present: "Your Majesty, the bitter hatred of my enemies has triumphed over your kindness" (6.8.22). Philotas' head was covered so that no one would recognize him as he was shuttled off to the royal tent. On the following day Alexander ordered an assembly at arms, during which Philotas would be tried for treason.

Philotas was no common suspect. He was the Commander of the Companion Cavalry, and a soldier with an outstanding reputation for personal valor. He was also the son of Parmenio, a general whose deeds were legendary among Macedonian soldiers. This was indeed a delicate situation. A mishandling of this prosecution might produce a backlash that could spell disaster for the king. The conviction and execution of Philotas would have to be carried out with the same precision evident in Alexander's most impressive victories on the battlefield.

Hard son of Peleus
Your mother
nursed you
on
gall
(*Il.* 16.203)

The dead body of Dimnus was brought before a jury of 6,000 Macedonian soldiers, but for some time they remained uninformed about the nature of the trial and the identities of those involved. The king, who served as the prosecutor in such cases, appeared before the assembly with a deeply troubled look. He was surrounded by a chorus of close companions, whose grim visages mirrored the gravity of the situation.

Alexander, after standing with his eyes fixed on the floor for some time, finally broke the silence. "Men! I was almost snatched from you by a criminal conspiracy: it is thanks to the gods' providence and mercy that I still live. And the awe-inspiring sight of your gathering has made me feel even more angry with the traitors because my first pleasure in life – no, my only pleasure – is that I am still able to repay all the brave men who have deserved well of me" (C.6.9.2).

He warned his troops to brace themselves for the names of those involved in the plot and proceeded to indict both Philotas and Parmenio. This stunned the audience. Alexander then read an ambiguous letter from Parmenio to his son, with the intention of submitting it as evidence. "First of all take care of yourselves and then of your people – that is how we shall accomplish our purpose" (C.6.9.14). Alexander's interpretation of the text was that it referred to conspiracy in terms comprehensible only to those privy to the plot; the intonation in his reading must have made this point convincingly.

Alexander admitted that Philotas' name was not included among those cited by Dimnus in a list of co-conspirators he gave before his death. He claimed that Dimnus' failure to name Philotas was more a sign of his fear of him than any proof of his innocence, and went on to depict the past record of the accused as evidence of his guilt. Philotas' friendship with Alexander's cousin Amyntas, who was executed for treason, and an indiscreet comment about the king's experience at Siwah were submitted to the jury.

Alexander then converted the trial into a test of allegiance. "Unbridled speech has led to the sword – which, if you believe me, Philotas has sharpened against me or which, if you believe him, he has permitted to be sharpened against me . . . . Men, you keep on asking me to look after myself, and now it is within your power to help me follow your advice. I take refuge in your hands and your weapons. To survive against your will I do not wish; but even in accordance with your will, survival is impossible unless you avenge me" (C.6.9.20–4). Philotas was then brought before the group. In spite of the fact that his haughty nature had made him unpopular in many circles, the stunning reversal of his fortunes apparently aroused their compassion. In an effort to alter this sympathetic environment, a certain Amyntas, who was devoted to the king, launched a vituperative attack on the accused. Philotas had served the barbarian, not us, Amyntas contended. Had he been successful, he argued, the king would have been decapitated, and they would all have been trapped and unable to return home to their loved ones.

Alexander was not particularly keen on this line of argument because it turned his men's thoughts to Macedonia once again, but it was soon followed by an impassioned harangue from Coenus, to which he had no objection whatsoever. Coenus shouted in a voice loud enough to be heard by everyone that his brother-in-law had indeed betrayed the king, his country, and the army. Coenus demonstrated his own conviction in the matter by picking up a stone, which he intended to throw at Philotas. He was restrained by the king himself, who insisted that the accused be given a fair trial and an opportunity to defend himself.

Alexander coolly asked Philotas whether he was going to use his native tongue in his own defense. Philotas, as Alexander knew quite well, was not proficient in the Macedonian dialect. He said that he would use Greek, which the king himself ordinarily employed. Alexander, against whom complaints about orientalization had begun to be heard, and who was fluent in both dialects, commented to the jury, "Do you see how offensive Philotas finds even his native language? He alone feels an aversion to learning it. But let him speak as he pleases – only remember that he is as contemptuous of our way of life as he is of our language" (C.6.9.36). Abruptly, and without explanation, Alexander left the assembly.

Philotas began his defense by noting that the one man who could acquit him had just left the proceedings. Nevertheless, Philotas said, he was determined to present his case, and he did so with some compelling arguments. The accused reminded everyone that none of the conspirators had indicted him, even though those who are about to die usually tell the truth unsparingly. The only real charge against him – and this is confirmed in Arrian's account of his conviction – was that he had failed to report the matter.[71] The king himself, he informed the crowd, had forgiven him for this mistake. This, of course, could not be confirmed because of Alexander's absence. Philotas asked if additional information had been uncovered that had convinced the king to change his mind. Again, the only man who could answer that question was absent.

How could he have been sleeping so soundly when he was arrested, Philotas asked, if he thought that further evidence against him might still come to light? He was certainly guilty of not reporting the incident, but a mere boy had supplied the information, and it sounded more like a lovers' quarrel between adolescents than anything worthy of the king's consideration. He doubted its credibility from the very beginning, and, after all, on more than one occasion he had been laughed at for his naïveté in taking innocuous rumors too seriously.

His most persuasive argument was that Cebalinus remained unharmed and at liberty after divulging this information. Philotas said emphatically that had he been involved in the plot, he most certainly would have murdered the informer before the man had an opportunity to speak to anyone else. In addition, and perhaps unwisely, he reminded the army that his father had once informed the king of a plot that reportedly involved Philip the physician and suffered quite an embarrassment as a result. He wished to point out that sometimes it is extremely difficult to know when to speak or to remain silent.

Throwing himself on the mercy of the court, Philotas pleaded with the crowd to tell him what he might do to exculpate himself. An unsympathetic response shot back, "Don't hatch plots against your benefactors" (C.6.10.36). With this Philotas acknowledged that he was fighting a losing battle. It was his word against that of the king.

this
is a dismal death

> I am doomed
> to be caught in
> (*Il.* 21.281)

Bolon, a crude man but a courageous fighter who had become an officer through a battlefield commission, stepped forward to kindle residual animosity toward Philotas. He recited stories of Philotas' arrogance and ostentation. He followed the lead of the king by reminding the crowd that it was insulting for a native-born Macedonian to need interpreters when he spoke to his own people – namely the Macedonian rank and file – many of whom were ignorant of Greek. The king's bodyguards shouted that Philotas ought to be torn to pieces, but the king returned as abruptly as he had left, just in time to restore order and adjourn the assembly until the following day.

Another meeting between Alexander and his close friends was called. There it was decided, at the urgings of Hephaestion, Craterus, and Coenus, that torture be applied to Philotas so that the whole truth could be known. According to Curtius the king retired to his inner quarters while Philotas was being tortured,[72] but Plutarch states that Alexander listened furtively to everything that went on from behind a stretched tapestry.[73] In any event, Alexander delegated the responsibility for the interrogation to his inner circle and was apparently satisfied with the confession they extracted. This was read before the reassembled crowd the next day in the presence of Philotas, who, unable to walk by this time, was carried in. Philotas and those convicted with him were executed on the spot.

> Never again
> will his proud heart
> stir him up
> to wrangle
> with the princes
> in words
> of
> revilement
> (*Il.* 2.276–7)

It is difficult to say whether Parmenio, who had recently lost another son, Nicanor, through illness,[74] would have stood idly by at the execution of his last son. The old but able general commanded 25,000 men who held him in high regard. He was also in control of the king's communications and supply systems. Faced, he apparently believed, with the prospect of rebellion from within his own ranks while surrounded by an enemy still capable of annihilating the entire invading force, Alexander decided that Parmenio would have to be killed as soon as possible.[75]

> This is no time for hesitation
> You there
> Go down quickly
> (*Ba.* 780–1)

The king recruited Polydamas, who had been an intimate of Parmenio, to deliver orders to several key members of the general's staff that called on them to assassinate their commanding officer. Included among them was Cleander, a brother of Coenus, who, it may be recalled, had been appointed recently by the king himself as Parmenio's second-in-command. Polydamas, disguised as an Arab and traveling in the company of native guides on a racing camel, covered a distance of 800 miles in eleven days. Alexander held both of his younger brothers hostage at Phrada to guarantee that Polydamas would perform his mission as instructed. Even the families of the native guides were held at Phrada to ensure the faithful execution of the plan.[76]

Polydamas arrived at Ecbatana under the cover of darkness and delivered Alexander's instructions to Cleander. On the next day he was scheduled to deliver two letters to Parmenio, an official dispatch from the king and a personal letter written under Philotas' own seal. Polydamas was greeted warmly by the general, who was found in the company of those instructed to kill him. Observing protocol, Parmenio first read the letter that bore the royal seal and probably contained routine information. Shortly after opening the communiqué bearing his son's seal, Parmenio was stabbed in the side and chest by Cleander. The others present also assaulted the general in order to share in the responsibility for the act.

> and none stood beside him
> who did not
> stab
> him
> (*Il.* 22.371)

The plan worked, but predictably it spawned confusion and anger among the general's troops. Order was restored temporarily when the king's instructions were read in public, but many of those who had served under Parmenio for some time were deeply disturbed by this incomprehensible turn of events. Despite the royal sanction for what had been done, several veterans demanded a proper burial for "an eminent man in war and peace . . . [who] performed the duties of a young commander, often even those of a common soldier. He was . . . well-liked by his officers and more popular still with the rank and file" (C.7.2.33). Cleander, uncertain as to whether or not Alexander would approve of the burial, at first did nothing. As the pressure began to mount and discontent began to resemble rebellion, he agreed to the burial, but severed Parmenio's head and sent it back to Alexander as proof that his orders had been carried out.[77]

> For I am
> Achilleus' henchman
> (*Il.* 24.396)

An alternative version of these events is found in Plutarch.[78] He refers to a conspiracy against Philotas, as does Ernst Badian, who has argued that Philotas was the victim of a plot directed by Alexander.[79] This thesis suggests that the king was looking for an opportunity to bring about the fall of the house of Parmenio. However, the conspiracy against Philotas mentioned by Plutarch probably refers to the role played by members of the king's inner circle, who disliked Philotas and ultimately profited from his downfall. Wolfgang Zeev Rubinsohn and Waldemar Heckel offer persuasive arguments along these lines.[80] Helmut Berve, as well as Fritz Schachermeyr, maintains that Alexander simply seized the opportunity to remove a family that he felt was enjoying too much prestige and power. This position is entirely compatible with Plutarch's statement and Badian's assertion.[81]

Parmenio had had good reason to caution Philotas, as he once did, to keep a lower profile.[82] The king had heard of his posturing on several occasions, and although Alexander was often amused at the affectations of his closest friends, they had to be careful to remind him that they knew they owed everything they had to him. Philotas seems to have been more impressed by what he had done for Alexander than what Alexander had done for him. Therefore, with what he clearly felt was justified anger fueling his emotions, and with trusted friends transforming Philotas' error of judgment into a question of his survival, Alexander decided to strike. He did so in a proficient and expedient manner. The decision offered him an opportunity to eliminate the man he felt had belittled him in private, who was, perhaps, as a witness to the Pixodarus affair, the only man alive who had ever seen the king humiliated.

> godlike Achilleus
> I
> made you
> all
> that you are now
> (*Il.* 9.485)

The loss of Parmenio was, on a personal level, less than devastating to the king. Although he was extremely popular among the troops,[83] he frequently offered the king advice that was contrary to Alexander's own plans.[84] Parmenio's assignment at Ecbatana, which had kept him at a distance, brought relief to that situation, and also prevented the general from registering any objections to increasing orientalization at court. Alexander somehow became persuaded that both Parmenio and Philotas saw themselves on the same plateau as the king himself. This situation was both threatening and intolerable to him, and so he dealt with it in the most efficient way possible.

At Phrada the fear that relatives and friends of those convicted might themselves become victims of a general purge created anxiety throughout the camp. Amyntas, the son of Andromenes, and three of his younger brothers were in fact summoned before the assembly. Amyntas was under suspicion partly because of his close relationship with Philotas, and also because Olympias, who had apparently been offended by Amyntas at one time, issued a warning about him.[85] To exacerbate the situation further, Polemon, Amyntas' fourth and youngest brother, had bolted from camp in fear of his life.

> he might even be angry
> with one
> who is
> guiltless
> (*Il.* 11.654)

Amyntas, like Philotas, offered a spirited defense.[86] He declared that it was only natural for him to seek the company of Philotas because of the favor that this man enjoyed with the king.[87] Moreover, it was at the direct order of the king himself, he reminded Alexander, that he had recruited some of the able-bodied men in the service of Olympias in Macedonia and thus incurred her wrath. He showed nothing but contempt for Polemon, whom he may have helped to retrieve. Polemon stood before the assembly and wept uncontrollably because of his belief that he would bear the responsibility for his brothers' deaths.

The pathetic nature of the situation stirred sympathy in the crowd and the king. With tears in their eyes, Alexander's close friends pleaded with the king for compassion, and he responded by declaring that he for one was casting his vote for an acquittal of the entire family. Furthermore, as a peacemaker, he demanded that Amyntas forgive his brother Polemon if he wished to be reconciled to the king. Amyntas complied eagerly. The vindication of these men and others, one of whom was the Attalus who had helped pursue and impale Philip's assassin, alleviated the concern over the prospect of a general purge. It also afforded the king an opportunity to demonstrate his sense of discrimination and ability to mete out justice.

Demetrius, a Royal Bodyguard who may have played a key role in the conspiracy, was also arrested, but he too put up a vigorous defense and was acquitted. However, under circumstances that remain unclear, he was removed from his post shortly after the trials and is never again mentioned in the sources.[88] Despite Arrian's silence about his fate, Demetrius may very well have been executed. His place among the Royal Bodyguards was filled by Ptolemy, the son of Lagus, whose record of the expedition became the foundation for Arrian's account.[89] Curiously, Amyntas was killed in battle soon after the proceedings. By chance or design, almost all of those men whose loyalty was questioned during the expedition eventually disappeared from the historical records before the death of the king himself.

Alexander the Lyncestian, who by now had been in custody for three years or so, was also brought to trial around this time.[90] The charge against him was participation in a plot in 333 that ironically had been called to the king's attention by Parmenio. The Lyncestian, who had probably been rehearsing his defense for some time in captivity, garbled it in front of the assembly. His incoherent mutterings were taken as *prima facie* evidence of his guilt, and he was killed there and then. This conveniently removed any possibility that he might become a rallying point in any future rebellion. Apparently the king was no longer unduly concerned over the reaction of Antipater, his viceroy in Europe, to his son-in-law's treatment. As Bosworth tells us, Alexander was becoming "increasingly autocratic."[91]

Cleitus and 6,000 Macedonian infantrymen were marching to rejoin Alexander while the events of the Philotas affair were unfolding. They arrived in Phrada soon after the Philotas and Parmenio business had been brought to a climax. Alexander, it seems, immediately informed Cleitus that he had been selected, along with Hephaestion, as co-commander of the Companion Cavalry, which had formerly been led by Philotas. Whatever his personal response was to all of the other startling news, Cleitus accepted his promotion without hesitation.

It was an astute move on Alexander's part. Cleitus' appointment helped to stifle the anticipated rumblings among the veterans who accompanied him. These troops were probably astonished at the oriental trappings now in evidence at their king's court, and bewildered by the murder of Parmenio who, like Philip, was a paragon of martial virtue.

In the aftermath of all this Alexander urged his men to write home, and encouraged their cooperation by placing the royal messenger service at their disposal. These letters, earmarked for Macedonia, were collected and seemingly dispatched, but actually were secretly returned to the king for examination. Alexander carefully scrutinized each epistle for criticisms directed toward himself or his policies. Every soldier who included complaints of this sort was reassigned to a special unit, which was separated from the regular army. This "undisciplined" company performed with incredible distinction, most likely because the men felt compelled to demonstrate their loyalty through exceptional gallantry.[92] Once again Alexander had demonstrated his ability to turn a potential liability into an asset.

Unfortunately, Philotas and Parmenio caused Alexander more trouble dead than alive. Soldiers who were discontented over the changes in their king, and in the kingship itself, could point to their compatriots' deaths, particularly the murder of Parmenio, as examples of the decline in the

Macedonian way of life. The number of men who entertained reservations about the king's virtue now multiplied, as did the insecurities of a man said to have valued his reputation more than his life.

There were some unpleasant realities that had to be faced. Perhaps the most distressing of all was the realization that among his own men there were those who thought it would be best for everyone if he were dead. Alexander commemorated his success in avoiding assassination by renaming Phrada Prophthasia ("Anticipation") in honor of the measures he had taken to avoid the fate of his father.[93] Nevertheless, the ghosts of Philotas and Parmenio, like that of Philip, would continue to appear under different guises throughout the expedition.

> Furies
> who
> underground
> avenge
> dead men
> (*Il.* 19.259–60)

## THE DEATH OF CLEITUS (328 BC)

Alexander resumed his pursuit of Bessus during the winter of 330, perhaps reasoning that activity would serve as an antidote to any further reflection on the part of his troops about what had happened at Prophthasia. The king kept his men plodding through deep snow on an exacting northeasterly march toward the mountains of the Hindu Kush and Bactria. In weather far worse than the king had anticipated, he led his army across the mountains between Ghazni and the Kabul Valley. Here a substantial number of soldiers perished, and many of the survivors were frostbitten and snowblinded. The men were then given time to recuperate from this shattering ordeal and to prepare themselves for the further exposure to the elements at even higher altitudes that they would face when climbing the main range of the Hindu Kush.

In late March 329 Alexander crossed the mountains once again, probably through the Khawak pass at 11,000 feet, and led his men to the plains of Bactria below. On the southern face of the mountains a cave in a rock half a mile high was pointed out by natives to be that of the Titan Prometheus,[94] who defied Zeus by stealing fire from heaven and bringing it to earth. Zeus punished Prometheus by having him chained to a rock in the Caucasus and sending an eagle to feast on his liver every day. The organ regenerated nightly, and mankind's benefactor continued to pay this gruesome penalty for thirty years. At last, Alexander's ancestor, Heracles, who was travelling in the region, ended the bird's predatory activity with a shot from his bow. Heracles was forgiven by his father for this transgression because of the contribution it made to his son's reputation. Alexander's staff, utilizing the widespread but erroneous belief that the Hindu Kush was an easterly extension of the Caucasus mountains, proclaimed that his expedition had located the cave of Prometheus. The king, once again, was walking in the footsteps of a famous ancestor.

Herakles
the high-hearted
son of Zeus
(*Il.* 14.250)

Alexander's appearance in the early spring caught his quarry unprepared. Bessus retreated north across the Oxus (Amu Darya) River into Sogdiana, and his fellow Bactrians, angered by the ravaging of Bactrian land and dispirited by their leader's hasty flight, deserted him and his cause. Alexander's troops crossed the Oxus on straw-filled skins as they had crossed the Danube. The king soon received word that Bessus, like Darius, had been arrested by his own followers. Spitamenes, a Sogdian leader, informed Alexander that Bessus could be taken without resistance if a small force was sent. Ptolemy was delegated to collect Alexander's only rival to the Persian throne. Spitamenes, the informant, who would be heard from again, disappeared as he approached.

Once Bessus was taken into custody, Ptolemy asked for instructions as to what to do next. Alexander ordered him bound, stripped naked, and collared in a wooden yoke, the mark of a slave. The captive was to be tied to a post and stationed on the right side of the road where the king and his army would pass. When Alexander approached Bessus, he stepped down from his chariot and asked why he had betrayed Darius, his king, kinsman, and benefactor. Bessus replied that he, like the others, had aligned himself against Darius because it was hoped that this action might encourage Alexander to grant them immunity.

The king ordered Bessus flogged while a herald paraded in front of him, declaiming his crimes to every passer-by. Alexander then, according to Arrian, "summoned a council of those present, brought Bessus before them, and accusing him of treachery towards Darius, commanded that his nose and ear-laps should be cut off, and that he should be taken to Ecbatana, to be put to death there in the assembly of Medes and Persians" (4.7.3). The historian registers his personal regret over the excessiveness of the punishment and describes the mutilation of Bessus "as barbaric."[95]

Alexander's massacre of the Branchidae occurred during this period.[96] The ancestors of this group had at one time been in control of the oracle of Apollo at Didyma outside of Miletus. They were accused, perhaps unjustly, of pilfering the temple and handing its treasures over to Xerxes. The Branchidae, it was said, were then relocated to a distant part of the Persian Empire out of fear of reprisal on the part of the incensed local population. Strabo, following Callisthenes, utilizes this story as an explanation for the slaughter: it was an act of retribution for the sacrilegious behavior of their ancestors.[97] The testimony in Herodotus[98] does not seem to support these allegations against the family, but Alexander may have used these charges, whether he believed them or not, as justification for the massacre.

The action, as H. W. Parke has recently suggested, may have been prompted either by those among Alexander's advisers who still thought it useful to echo the theme of Panhellenic retribution, or by Milesians accompanying the king, who had feared that the oracle would be returned to the Branchidae.[99] Nonetheless, this mass murder amounted to a punishment for something that had taken place a century and a half before. Parke places this event within the context of other tragic episodes, such as the murder of Parmenio. He sees these as "symptomatic of the breakdown of the moral purpose behind the expedition, which resulted from its overwhelming success in . . . the capture of the Persian capitals of Susa, Persepolis and Ecbatana. Nothing like these grim events had disfigured the earlier campaigns. Tarn found a physical explanation – that the high altitudes and dry air drove the Macedonian commanders to excessive drinking. This had from his viewpoint the advantage that it could explain, if not justify, lapses from the lofty standard which he expected of Alexander."[100]

After resting at Maracanda (Samarkand), Alexander went north to the Jaxartes. While planning a new city on the banks of the river, Alexander turned his attention toward the problems which were proliferating in Sogdiana. Cities such as Cyropolis (Ura-Tyube), which had surrendered to him, were soon swept up in what emerged as a patriotic reaction to the king's invasion. The cities were retaken at considerable cost, including head and throat wounds to Alexander. The latter left his vision clouded and voice impaired. A furious Alexander ordered Cyropolis to be sacked, even though it was a city associated with a man he held in the highest esteem.[101]

> It does not become me
> unrelentingly
> to rage on
> (*Il.* 19.67–8)

The king completed Alexandria Eschate (the farthest), and settled it with Greek mercenaries and Macedonians no longer fit for active soldiering. Natives were impressed into slavery for the settlers, and the city was designed to be a showcase that would supersede Cyropolis as the premier outpost on the northeastern frontier of the Persian Empire. Alexandria Eschate could also, in the future, serve as a point of departure for an all-out war against the Scythians, but for the present it functioned as a regional defensive center. Recovering from his wounds and still a bit shaky, Alexander personally supervised the construction of the walls of yet another city bearing his name.[102]

The king's concentration was disturbed, however, by some Scythians on the opposite bank of the river, who continually harassed his workers and stung him with personal insults. Alexander bristled and resolved to cross the river and teach his hecklers a lesson, but Aristander reported that the sacrifices were clearly unfavorable for such a course of action.[103]

> Do not hold me back
> when I would be going
> neither yourself
> be a bird of bad omen
> . . . You will not
> persuade me
> (*Il.* 24.218–19)

Nevertheless, Alexander summoned his close friends and argued in favor of the crossing. Erigyius, who through a chance encounter with Aristander had learned of the bad omens (which Alexander had apparently kept to himself), used this information in his argument against the venture. A surprised and embarrassed Alexander became indignant.

Aristander was summoned to the royal tent and reprimanded for divulging a personal (rather than official) request on the king's part. Pale and speechless, Aristander was forced to repeat his warnings for all to hear. He meekly explained that he was concerned over Alexander's health and feared that the king might not be up to such a task.

> now
> I
> terribly dread
> the swift-footed
> son of Peleus
> (*Il.* 18.261)

Aristander was dismissed, but reappeared while the same matter was still under discussion with the propitious news that he had just engaged in another sacrifice, which had produced entrails more favorable than any he had yet seen during his entire career.[104] This revelation silenced the pious reservations of Erigyius, as well as any other objections that might have been raised.

The king again used straw-filled skins to cross the Jaxartes. On the opposite shore he confounded the Scythians and their encircling tactics, killing over one thousand men and routing the rest.[105] During the pursuit, however, Alexander drank some contaminated water and came down with a serious case of diarrhea.[106] He collapsed and had to be carried to camp. The king was disappointed at failing to overtake the elusive Scythians, but mollified by devout courtiers who calculated that during the chase their king had passed beyond the northeastern limits reached by the god Dionysus.[107]

Why
son of Peleus
do you keep after me
in the speed of your feet
being mortal
while I
am
an immortal god?
(*Il.* 22.8–9)

A serious setback was experienced, however, in some of the newly
acquired territories. Spitamenes led Bactrian and Sogdian troops and other
Scythians in a concerted effort to undo all of these recent conquests.
Maracanda itself was besieged. Alexander dispatched two Macedonian
officers and Pharnuches, a Lycian interpreter, to reinforce the garrison.
The entire contingent was lured into a trap, and, confused over who
should command, they all retreated to an island where only 340 out of
2,360 men managed to survive.[108]

Alexander was stunned. He gathered a striking force and travelled more
than 160 miles in three days to redress the grievance, but Spitamenes
managed to disappear. The king had to be content with burying his dead
and devastating the entire region to discourage the enemy's return. Now
aware that the relief force he had originally sent was totally inadequate,
and that the confusion in command was ultimately his responsibility,
Alexander threatened the life of any survivor who breathed a word of
what had taken place.[109]

Let every mouth be hushed
(*Ba.* 69–70)

The king was forced to spend the next two years in Bactria and Sogdiana
fighting an elusive but seemingly ubiquitous enemy, at whose hands his
troops experienced a number of serious setbacks.

Cunningly
cleverly
Bacchus
the
hunter
lashed

. . .

against
his
prey
(*Ba.* 1190–1)

For the time being, Alexander wintered at Bactra. Cutting short his stay, he left at the first sign of suitable weather and went east by way of the Oxus Valley, crossed the Oxus River, and divided his forces. Following a further division of the army, he undertook the siege of a seemingly inaccessible enemy outpost atop a rock fortress commanded by Ariamazes.[110] The king was told by its defenders that he would have to produce soldiers with wings if he hoped to mount the walls, which were sheer on all sides. Aroused by their haughtiness and faced with the "impossible," Alexander sent out a call for volunteers trained in mountain warfare. He offered the incredible sum of 12 talents to the first man who reached the summit, and other handsome emoluments for all those who scaled the cliffs. Three hundred mountaineers, equipped with ropes and iron pegs, made an overnight attempt. Thirty fell to their deaths and were buried in the huge snow drifts. The rest made it to the top and signaled the king with flags from the peak. Alexander asked the smug defenders to turn around and view his airborne troops. Startled at what they saw, they surrendered.

Returning to the base at Maracanda in mid-to-late summer 328, the extraordinary pressures of this type of warfare would soon give way to the welcome relief of the symposium. At one such gathering, what should have been a relaxing event turned out to be a tense drunken scene that mushroomed into a personal tragedy.

> The deity
> the son of Zeus
> [Dionysus]
> in feast in festival delights . . .
> But him who scoffs
> he hates
> and him
> who mocks
> his life
> (*Ba.* 417–24)

This incident took place amidst the frustration over unanticipated delays in his planned march toward India, and the bewildering effects of the first major defeats experienced by Macedonians in nearly a quarter of a century. Plutarch's account of the drunken brawl is probably based on the recollections of Chares, an eyewitness to the events.[111]

On this occasion Alexander invited Cleitus, the co-commander of the Companion Cavalry, to share in the enjoyment of some attractive Greek fruit that had just arrived from the coast.[112] Cleitus was sacrificing at the time, and three of the sheep upon which he had already poured libations trotted after him as he walked hurriedly toward the royal quarters. Alexander, it is said, had just a few days previously dreamed of Cleitus dressed in black among the dead sons of Parmenio. He was alarmed at this specter, and consulted his soothsayers, who agreed with the king that this was not a good sign. Alexander ordered burnt offerings in the interest of Cleitus' safety, but his guest arrived before these orders could be carried out.

Alexander had also been negligent in his official religious obligations that day.[113] The Macedonian calendar called for an annual sacrifice to Dionysus, but the king had decided to honor Castor and Polydeuces (Pollux), two heroes who had become gods, instead.

> who now
> revolts against
> divinity in me
> thrusts me
> from his
> offerings
> forgets
> my
> name
> in
> his
> prayers
> (*Ba.* 45–6)

The Dioscuri, it may be recalled, had been mentioned by Aristotle in the same breath as Achilles and Heracles, and had also appeared with Alexander and Nike in a painting by Apelles.[114] Perhaps because Alexander's flatterers had informed him that he had passed the outer limits of Dionysus' travels while chasing the Scythians, the king thought he could neglect the god he had outdistanced, and elect instead to honor divinities more in keeping with his heroic image.

> Do you hear his blasphemy
> against the prince of the blessed
> the god of garlands
> and
> banquets
> (*Ba.* 374–8)

A great deal of wine was drunk on this occasion and, in the midst of the entertainments, some verses were recited that satirized the Macedonian officers involved in the *débâcle* at the hands of Spitamenes during the preceding year.[115] Considering the audience, it is highly unlikely that any poet would have risked the reprisal of those in attendance without first receiving royal approval for such a reading. It may well be that within the king's entourage it had become commonplace to assign culpability for the defeat to the commanders involved, thus absolving the king of responsibility.[116] These verses might also have been a type of rehearsal of the official policy that was about to be adopted in regard to the setback. Nevertheless, a number of Macedonian guests were embarrassed and offended by what was said in the presence of Persians, and voiced their anger to the singer, "but Alexander and those sitting near him listened with obvious pleasure and told the man to continue" (P.50.9).

This is the point at which Cleitus made his presence known. He was an important figure, and his family enjoyed close ties with the royal family. Lanice, his sister, had been Alexander's wet-nurse, and the king, we are told, thought of her as his mother.[117]

> I had set you on my knees and cut little pieces from the meat
> and given you all you wished
> and held the wine for you
> And many times you soaked the shirt that was on my body
> with wine you would spit up
> in the
> troublesomeness
> of
> your
> childhood
> (*Il.* 9.488–91)

Two of Lanice's sons had already given their lives during the expedition, and a third son, Proteas, was an officer and drinking companion of the king. Cleitus had led the Royal Squadron of the Companion Cavalry under Philip as under Alexander and, it may be recalled, was appointed as co-commander of the entire brigade after the Philotas affair.

Probably Alexander's senior by twenty or so years, Cleitus had saved the king's life at the Granicus and was more fond of telling the story than his commanding officer was of hearing it.[118] His eleventh-hour invitation to the symposium implies that Cleitus was not regularly present at these affairs, and his recent appointment as satrap of Bactria[119] may have been made with the intention of removing an uninhibited and independent voice from court. Furthermore, as an old-guard Macedonian he may have been less than gratified by a promotion that separated him from his comrades and left him among hordes of faceless barbarians.

Drunk and angry, Cleitus exclaimed "that it was not right for Macedonians to be insulted in the presence of barbarians and enemies, even if they had met with misfortune, for they were better men than those who were laughing at them" (P.50.9). Alexander, equally drunk, reacted by charging that "if Cleitus was trying to disguise cowardice as misfortune, he must be pleading his own case" (P.50.10). Cleitus jumped up and shouted "Yes, it was my cowardice that saved your life, you who call yourself the son of the gods, when you were turning your back to Spithridates' sword. And it is the blood of these Macedonians and their wounds which have made you so great that you disown your father Philip and claim to be the son of Ammon!" (P.50.11).

They are liars
who call you
issue of Zeus
. . . since you fall
far short
in truth
of the others
who were begotten
of
Zeus
(*Il.* 5.635–7)

Alexander was outraged and screamed, "You scum . . . do you think that you can keep on speaking of me like this, and stir up trouble among the Macedonians and not pay for it?" (P.51.1). Cleitus responded that he, like other Macedonians, was already paying for the king's efforts. "It's the dead ones who are happy, because they never lived to see Macedonians being beaten with Median rods, or begging the Persians for an audience with our own king" (P.51.2).

Alexander's friends jumped to their feet and berated Cleitus, while some older men tried to calm both of them. The king then turned to some Greek courtiers and in a barely audible voice asked them if Greeks did not look like demi-gods and Macedonians like wild animals when they were in mixed company. Cleitus, who could not hear the remark, continued his attack by challenging the king "to speak out whatever he wished to say in front of the company, or else not invite to his table free-born men who spoke their minds: it would be better for him to spend his time among barbarians and slaves, who would prostrate themselves before his white tunic and his Persian girdle" (P.51.5).

Alexander lost control of himself and threw an apple at Cleitus that hit the outspoken courtier. He then frantically searched for his dagger, which one of the Royal Bodyguards had hidden (apparently to protect the king from himself while he was drinking). Although a crowd attempted to pacify him, "Alexander leaped to his feet and shouted out in the Macedonian tongue for his bodyguard to turn out, a signal that this was an extreme emergency; then he ordered his trumpeter to sound the alarm, and because the man was unwilling to obey, he struck him with his fist. Afterwards the trumpeter was highly praised for his conduct, because it was chiefly thanks to him that the whole camp was not thrown into a turmoil" (P.51.6–7).

Cleitus was ushered out of the tent, but managed to return to taunt Alexander with a line from Euripides' *Andromache*: "Alas, what evil customs reign in Greece" (683).[120] Euripides' plays were favorites of Alexander's, and as the play featured an ancestor of his mother's (Andromache), it is certain that the king knew the lines of Peleus that followed, which proclaim it a pity that only one man wielding a sword among ten thousand others received the credit for a victory on the battlefield. Alexander wrenched a spear from one of his bodyguards and killed Cleitus on the spot. He sobered up immediately and, seeing "his friends standing around him speechless, he snatched the weapon out of the dead body and would have plunged it into his own throat if the guards had not forestalled him by seizing his hands and carrying him by force into his chamber" (P.51.11).

> When you realize
> the horror you have done
> you shall suffer
> terribly
> (*Ba.* 1259–60)

Remorseful over the tragic consequences of his ungovernable anger, and probably mindful of the striking similarity between his own drunken behavior and that of Philip nine years before at the wedding feast, Alexander shut himself up in the royal tent for three days and continued sobbing in isolation until concerned parties forced their way into his apartments.[121] In an attempt to console the king, Aristander reminded him about the dream in which Cleitus had appeared dressed in black. He assured Alexander that even he was powerless over events ordained by fate.[122] This provided some solace. Callisthenes, Alexander's historian, also made an attempt at consolation by offering conventional sympathies and reassurances.[123] It was the idiosyncratic approach of Anaxarchus the philosopher, however, that elicited an effective response. The philosopher exclaimed,

> Here is this Alexander whom the whole world now looks to for an example, and he is lying on the floor weeping like a slave, terrified of the law and of what men will say of him. And yet all the time it should be he who represents the law and sets up the criterion of justice. Why else did he conquer, unless it was to govern and command? It was certainly not to allow himself to submit like a slave to the foolish opinions of others. Do you not know that Zeus has Justice and Law seated by his side to prove that everything that is done by the ruler of the world is lawful and just?
>
> (P.52.5–6)[124]

The shock resulting from this approach, coupled with the seductiveness of the analogy, was powerful enough to end Alexander's flirtation with the only Homeric solution for a hero incurring such shameful disrepute: suicide. This course had been taken by Ajax, another of Alexander's mythological ancestors.[125] The philosopher's prescription not only provided relief from the guilt that Alexander was experiencing, but also offered a rationale for claiming divine right should he be confronted with other unpalatable realities of this type in the future. This principle provided a panacea for the anxiety that Alexander felt when his mistakes revealed his flawed nature. It is not surprising that it helped to make Alexander "in many ways more proud and autocratic than before" (P.52.7).

Do not be

so

certain

that

power

is

what

matters

(*Ba.* 310)

Arrian maintains that Cleitus had for some time been discontented with Alexander because of the king's orientalization. At the symposium he had become even more disturbed by blasphemous sycophants who compared Alexander favorably to the Dioscuri and Heracles. During the fracas Arrian claims that Cleitus "spoke up in favour of Philip's achievements, making little of Alexander and his" (4.8.6). Arrian's version also records that after the deed, Alexander "kept again and again calling himself the murderer of his friends, refused firmly all food or drink for three days, and neglected all other bodily needs" (4.9.4).

Arrian blames Cleitus for what happened and pities Alexander "for his misfortune, since he then showed himself the slave of two vices, by neither of which is it fitting for a man of sense to be overcome, namely, anger and drunkenness" (4.9.1). Nevertheless, the ancient historian commends his hero because "he admitted that he had erred, as a man may" (4.9.6).

But had he? Arrian clearly indicates that the official explanation pointed to Dionysus as the culprit.[126] Alexander's failure to pay tribute to the god on the appointed day, everyone was told, was the only explanation for this incomprehensible turn of events. The murder of Cleitus was the work of an angry god.

If I were you

I would offer him a sacrifice

not rage and kick

against necessity

a

man

defying

god

(*Ba.* 794–5)

Arrian candidly remarks that the king compensated for his indiscretion by offering a belated "sacrifice to Dionysus, since it was not uncongenial to him that the disaster should be referred to divine wrath rather than to his own evil nature" (4.9.5).

> Dionysus
> . . . has power
> over
> me
> (*Ba.* 1037–8)

Alexander was still guilt-ridden, and his actions hinted at self-destruction. The king's soldiers were fearful of finding themselves leaderless at the earth's end and surrounded by hostile forces. His troops declared Cleitus guilty of treason, and therefore solely responsible for the entire brutal affair.[127] Alexander was thereby relieved of any culpability in the matter. The posthumous conviction of Cleitus would ordinarily have required that his corpse be left uninterred, but the king insisted on proper burial rites. Alexander emerged as the victim of the man he had murdered.

It may be recalled that during the conflict that erupted at Philip's last wedding Alexander had ridiculed his father's drunken comportment. Alexander was then 18, an impeccable physical specimen, and an ascetic of sorts, who found Philip's demeanor appalling. Nine years later, under strikingly similar circumstances, his own behavior proved to be virtually indistinguishable from that of his father.

Alexander's anger is conspicuous in this episode. The king's tutor, Aristotle, was curious about this emotion and the circumstances under which it becomes activated in people. He may provide some help in understanding his pupil's behavior. We get angry, he says, at

> those who speak ill of us, and show contempt for us, in connexion with the things we ourselves most care about: thus those who are eager to win fame as philosophers get angry with those who show contempt for their philosophy . . . and so on in other cases. We feel particularly angry on this account if we suspect that we are in fact, or that people think we are, lacking completely or to any effective extent in the qualities in question. For when we are convinced that we excel in the qualities for which we are jeered at, we can ignore the jeering.[128]

In his fatal confrontation with the king, Cleitus was unfortunate enough to identify publicly areas in which Alexander was less than secure: the memory of his father; his "divine paternity"; the opinions of others; his military judgment; his courage; his orientalization; and his increasingly visible megalomaniacal streak.

> gall
> which makes a man grow angry
> for all his great mind
> that gall of anger

that swarms like smoke
inside of a man's heart
and becomes a thing
sweeter to him by far
than
the
dripping
of
honey
(*Il.* 18.108–10)

The death of Cleitus made it clear that it was perilous for anyone to disagree with the king in public, and Curtius may be accurate in his assertion that this scene spelled an end to liberty at the Macedonian court.[129] Public criticism of Alexander appears rarely in the extant sources from this point on.

There was, as always, the business of war. Spitamenes showed himself to be an astute general, who plagued Alexander with his guerrilla tactics. Like Alexander he seemed to have the ability to appear out of nowhere and then vanish as quickly as he had come. This threat required concentration. Alexander reorganized his cavalry into five units which could operate independently. He chose to lead one himself, and selected the following individuals to be the commanders of the other four units: the steadfast Hephaestion, who had shared command with Cleitus; Ptolemy, who had been exiled by Philip and appointed as a Royal Bodyguard in the wake of the Philotas affair; Perdiccas, who had not only helped to pursue and kill Philip's assassin, but had also played an important role in the downfall of Philotas; and Coenus, who was also instrumental in this affair.[130]

Alexander directed Hephaestion to herd the natives and all available supplies into cities in Sogdiana, setting up winter quarters at Nautaca. Spitamenes, who soon became desperately short of essentials, was forced to risk open conflict with the Macedonians. After suffering a crushing defeat, Spitamenes fled into the wilderness with the Massagetae, a wild Scythian tribe. When the tribesmen learned that Alexander himself was approaching, they decapitated Spitamenes and sent his head to the Macedonian king.[131]

It was in the early spring of 327, with large parts of Sogdiana still up in arms, that the 27-year-old king took his first wife.[132] Her father Oxyartes was a captured Bactrian baron who had been treated well by Alexander. His daughter, Roxane ("Little Star"), reputed to be one of the most beautiful young women in Asia, became Alexander's captive. Plutarch tells us, in a manner reminiscent of his description of the first meeting between Philip and Olympias, of their love at first sight.[133] They were soon married in the presence of Oxyartes, who became a staunch supporter and invaluable ally of his new son-in-law. In the Macedonian (and Iranian) tradition, Alexander and Roxane were united through the joint slicing of a loaf of bread.[134] This was accomplished, it was said, like the opening of the Gordian knot – with a sword. The two remained married until the king's death, after which Roxane gave birth to a boy she called Alexander.[135]

> he who tracks
> some boundless
> superhuman dream
> may lose
> his harvest
> here
> and
> now
> (*Ba.* 398–9)

Love aside, this match, like those of Philip, had obvious practical advantages. Plutarch admits that politics "played a great part in furthering his [Alexander's] policy of reconciliation" (47.7). The marriage was critical to Alexander's success in securing the subjugation of Sogdiana. Despite Plutarch's romanticizing, however, it seems unlikely that Alexander went into this marriage with the same libidinal gusto his father would have had. Neither the bride nor the groom seems to have spoken the other's language. In fact, this may have been the most demanding of the many sacrifices Alexander had to make in the interest of his career.

> and
> I
> had to endure
> mortal marriage
> (*Il.* 18.433)

Alexander ordered Peucestas, a Companion who did speak Roxane's language, to recruit and train 30,000 native youths to learn the Greek language and the Macedonian style of fighting. Alexander later called these boys *Epigoni* ("Successors"). They were thoroughly trained over a period of several years and made a spectacular début at Susa in 324. In one sense they served as hostages, but they also testified to a realization on the king's part that he would soon need additional manpower if he were to retain, let alone expand, an empire now sprawling over two continents. He had already begun to incorporate Asiatics into each of his squadrons, which was an alarming development to some of his Macedonian veterans.

## PROSKYNESIS

Blending the role of a Macedonian king with that of a Persian monarch was a formidable task, even for someone with Alexander's political acumen. Maintaining separate courts and employing separate rings for business conducted in each capacity seemed novel at first, but the king knew that it would become necessary to bring uniformity to these procedures. If some measure of integration could be accomplished among the noblemen at court, he reasoned, it might help to facilitate the governance of both factions.

Alexander elected to use the symposium as a vehicle through which he could address the discomforting situation at court.[136] There was a mixed audience of Macedonians, Greeks, and Persians, and each group had its own rituals and traditions. Alexander's solution seems to have involved ritualistic homage as it was performed by subjects in the presence of the Persian king. This practice the Greeks called *proskynesis*.[137] It had been inaugurated by Cyrus the Great, and had come to be expected of the Great King's subjects. Alexander wanted to retain this ritual among the Persians, and to streamline protocol he intended to have the custom adopted by his Greek and Macedonian courtiers as well.

There was a fundamental problem, however. In the Greek-speaking world obeisance (which could involve prostration) was reserved exclusively for honoring the gods, and prostration implied worship. Thus, among Greeks and Macedonians, it was believed erroneously that through this act, the Persians worshipped their king as a god. Alexander realized that this was a sensitive and potentially divisive issue, and that he would have to treat the matter with care. It was decided to introduce *proskynesis* on an experimental basis by encouraging a select few Greeks and Macedonians to set the example.[138] Hephaestion staged the scene and coached the participants in their roles. He undoubtedly emphasized to them the practical advantages of this ritual to the king, and explained that it was not at all what the untutored believed it to be. Those involved were expected to accept a cup of wine from the king, offer a libation at the altar, perform *proskynesis* before Alexander, and then receive a kiss from him. In the Persian tradition, the royal kiss was a social distinction reserved for kinsmen of the Great King, but here it was employed to signify an equality of sorts and to compensate for the servility of the gesture that preceded it.[139]

Everything went according to plan until Callisthenes (later reported by Hephaestion to have agreed to this procedure in advance)[140] omitted the *proskynesis* in his approach. This was noticed by Demetrius, one of the Companions. Alexander, who was conversing with Hephaestion at the time, refused to kiss Callisthenes when informed of the omission. Callisthenes was embarrassed by the circumstances, but made no effort to retrace his steps and include obeisance in his routine. Instead, he announced in a voice loud enough to be heard by everyone present: "Very well then, I shall go away the poorer by a kiss" (P.54.6).[141]

Further difficulties followed on the heels of this display. It soon became clear that a number of Macedonians were unlikely to engage willingly in this ritual. To avoid polarization, perhaps even open defiance at court, Alexander was forced to abandon temporarily the idea of persuading Europeans to perform *proskynesis*. The experiment had turned into an embarrassment, and the king, although incensed, could do little but call a halt to it.

the
anger
came on
Peleus'
son
(*Il.* 1.188)

## CALLISTHENES

While the expedition was still ostensibly a war of retribution, Callisthenes continued to perform an indispensable function for the king. His panegyric account of Alexander's conquests described the king in heroic terms for a Greek audience. He formulated the image of a man favored by the gods, and even alluded to the notion that Alexander was a son of Zeus.[142] Callisthenes apparently felt, however, that writing elegant propaganda in the service of the king was quite different from appearing to acknowledge his patron's divinity in public. The historian's sense of propriety had been affected, and it prompted Callisthenes to act in a manner that turned him into an opponent in the king's eyes.[143]

Aristotle is said to have remarked that his cousin's son was an accomplished speaker but devoid of common sense.[144] This is certainly an accurate observation if we recall the comment attributed to Callisthenes that it was through his description of Alexander's exploits that the king shared in divinity, and not through Olympias' fanciful tale about her son's conception.

you will give glory to me
and
your life
to
Hades
(*Il.* 11.445)

Callisthenes, it was believed, had joined the expedition to ensure that Olynthus, his native city, would be restored, in the same fashion as Philip had agreed to restore Stagira for Aristotle.[145] Pompous and antisocial, the antiquarian refused dinner invitations and remained aloof at the gatherings he did attend.[146] He may have been uncomfortable at Macedonian symposia, where unmixed wine was consumed in epic proportions and a colloquium could develop into a drunken circus.

Callisthenes' pedantry and parochialism seem to have worn thin with the king by this time. The historian probably shared Aristotle's view of the barbarian as a subhuman species, which should be used by Greeks like plants and animals.[147] He may also have disapproved of Alexander's integration of barbarian troops into the army, been less than ecstatic over the king's marriage to Roxane, and begun, perhaps, to experience pangs of conscience over his role in helping to create (through his writing) a climate of blasphemous praise for the king at court. An emerging theme at symposia had become a comparison of Alexander's exploits with those of Heracles and Dionysus.[148]

> You have done me wrong
> . . . I warn you
> once again
> (*Ba.* 788–9)

Despite the gruesome example of Cleitus, Callisthenes had chosen to draw the line at *proskynesis*, and the historian's heroics earned admiration and support from unlikely quarters. Macedonians felt just as offended as Callisthenes at the prospect of demeaning themselves by obeisance, and looked toward this intellectual as a symbol of their own resistance. For the moment, Callisthenes, to his own astonishment, actually enjoyed some popularity. To Alexander, however, he had become an obstructionist responsible for the abandonment of a royal project of critical importance.

> By god
> I'll make
> him pay
> (*Ba.* 345–6)

Alexander could not deal with Callisthenes in the same fashion as he had dealt with Cleitus, but there were other weapons in the king's arsenal. At one of the symposia Callisthenes was encouraged to speak on the virtues of Macedonians. He was so eloquent in discussing this subject that those present applauded him and threw garlands.[149] At this point the king cited a modified passage from the *Bacchae* in which Euripides said, "Give a wise man an honest brief to plead and his eloquence is no remarkable achievement" (*Ba.* 266–7).[150] He then went on to challenge Callisthenes to exhibit his prowess by being equally persuasive in his criticisms of Macedonians. This exercise would also enable the Macedonians to identify their own shortcomings and improve upon them, the king asserted.

Speak freely
(*Ba.* 672)

Callisthenes fell into the trap and expounded upon those defects conspicuous in Macedonians. He even noted that Philip's rise to power was made possible through the failure of the Greeks to cooperate with one another, and quoted a proverb to underscore his point: "Once civil strife has begun, even scoundrels may find themselves honoured" (P.53.5). The Macedonians were outraged at his accusations. The king, now in command of the situation, declared that instead of demonstrating his eloquence, Callisthenes had revealed his animosity toward Macedonians.

I
detest
that man
who
hides one thing
in the depths of his heart
and speaks forth
another
(*Il.* 9.312–13)

By luring Callisthenes into this further display of his oratorical skills, Alexander had (in a manner suggestive of Philip) manipulated the historian into relinquishing his own support. The result was a loss of the ephemeral support that Callisthenes had enjoyed at court.

A tongue
without reins
defiance
unwisdom
their
end
is
disaster
(*Ba.* 386–8)

## THE PAGES' CONSPIRACY (327 BC)

During the late spring of 327 Callisthenes was still tutoring Macedonian Royal Pages on the expedition. At that time, in Bactria, one of his most zealous pupils became involved in an incident that culminated in another plot on Alexander's life. The student was Hermolaus, a spirited young man who, on one occasion, let his natural enthusiasm carry him beyond acceptable limits.[151]

The pages, as tradition dictated, were attending the king on a boar hunt when Hermolaus pre-empted the king's first shot and slew the boar himself. A furious Alexander had Hermolaus flogged in the presence of the other pages, and deprived the boy of the use of his horse. This penalty may have been customary for such an offense, but it was a source of utter humiliation to Hermolaus. The young man brooded over what he considered to be excessive punishment and resolved to assassinate the king.

The extreme reaction of Hermolaus to the discipline imposed is less surprising than the fact that he was able to convince at least five and perhaps as many as eight other Royal Pages to join in the conspiracy. Alexander was still relatively young at 29, superbly courageous, incomparable as a military leader, passionately concerned about the health and welfare of his troops, and, in general, a uniquely successful individual. One might presume that he would be the idol of young Macedonians in their middle to late teenage years who were training to be warriors themselves. Yet, it is obvious that these noble youths, like those involved in the Philotas affair, were not mesmerized by their king.

Curiously, the pages involved in the conspiracy of 327 seem to have had more in common with old-guard Macedonians like Cleitus than with the rising young stars in the royal entourage, such as Hephaestion and Perdiccas. As we shall see, their resentment centered on the transformation of the Macedonian kingship under Alexander. They may have adopted this attitude from their fathers who, after the slaying of Cleitus, would only dare to utter such thoughts within the confines of the family circle. It is also possible that these young men may have arrived from Macedonia after the manifest changes in the kingship made by Alexander were already evident, and they neither understood nor liked what they saw. Pages who had joined the host during an earlier period would have had time to adjust more readily to the transformations on a day-to-day basis, just as their fathers had done. More recent arrivals[133] may have interpreted what they saw as the justification for a noble but perhaps suicidal act.

Tyrannicide was perceived as a virtuous deed in the ancient Greek world. Harmodius and Aristogeiton, for example, the Athenian assassins of Hipparchus, were viewed as heroes by their fellow citizens.[153] In fact, their deed may have been lauded by Callisthenes in his tutorials on the expedition. Even if that were so, however, it is unlikely that the historian ever imagined that the young men who listened to him might choose to replicate the act themselves.

Methodical planning was necessary. The youths waited thirty-two days until through assignment switching, all of the pages involved in the conspiracy were on duty guarding the royal bedchamber. The intention was to murder the king in his sleep, but Tyche intervened. Aristobulus tells us that Alexander, on his way from a symposium to his sleeping quarters, was intercepted by an older woman who had become important to the king during this particular period in his life.[154] She was a Syrian prophetess, who was initially permitted to travel with the court as an amusing oddity, but turned out, at least in Alexander's eyes, to possess a remarkable ability to predict the future. Alexander was so impressed by this woman (another "surrogate mother" of sorts) that he "gave her access to his person day and night and she now often watched over him as he slept" (A.4.13.5).

We are told that on the night agreed upon by the pages for the assassination, the prophetess was visited by a divine spirit. She accosted Alexander and begged him to go back to the drinking party and remain there. Alexander thought her advice "divine" and returned to the symposium. Whether either this version, which is favored by Arrian, or another he cites, which describes Alexander as "drinking unprompted till daybreak" (4.13.5), is authentic, the point is that the king did not return to the royal apartments until dawn, when the conspirators' replacements arrived to assume their watch. Alexander actually tipped the departing pages, and commended them for staying past their watch.[155] The young plotters were probably in a state of confusion, and praying for some miracle that would permit them to implement the plan. Nothing miraculous occurred, however, and the assassination had to be rescheduled.

Within hours this delay had led to a security leak in the conspirators' ranks, and Ptolemy was told of the enterprise. Unlike Philotas, whose procrastination proved fatal, Ptolemy immediately (although with some difficulty) roused Alexander from his drunken sleep and informed him of the plot. The king ordered the arrest and shackling of all those implicated, and then resumed his attempt to sleep off the effects of his drinking.

On the following day, Alexander, having composed himself, summoned a general assembly to try the would-be assassins. During the trial Alexander was, once again, intensely curious as to why these young men were determined to take his life. Hermolaus spoke on behalf of the pages. Arrian informs us of one version that attributes the following words to Hermolaus:[156]

> no free man could longer endure Alexander's arrogance . . . the unjust end of Philotas, and the still more illegal death of Parmenio and of the others who perished at that time, the drunken murder of Clitus, the Median dress, the plan not yet abandoned to introduce obeisance, and Alexander's drinking and sleeping habits; it was all this he would bear no longer and sought to liberate himself and the other Macedonians.
>
> (4.14.1–2)

Curtius says that they were then turned over to the units to which they had been attached and were tortured to death by them.[157] Each unit, it seems, attempted to outdo the other in the intensity of the pain inflicted as proof of their own loyalty to the king.

The association between Hermolaus and Callisthenes afforded Alexander an opportunity to implicate the historian in the conspiracy, and thereby remove his contaminating influence from court. When and how this occurred is problematic.[158] Ptolemy says that Callisthenes was tortured and hanged when the conspiracy came to light, while Aristobulus maintains that he was fettered and carried around with the army until he died of some illness.[159]

Chares, the court chamberlain, claimed that Callisthenes was arrested and imprisoned with the intention of eventually having him tried by the council (*synedrion*) of the Corinthian League in Aristotle's presence.[160] Since Callisthenes was a notable historian and a kinsman of Aristotle, this may have been the most prudent solution to the problem. It would technically relieve Alexander of any responsibility for the man's death. Chares reported that a bloated and lice-ridden Callisthenes died in captivity seven months after his arrest. Thus, the proposed trial never materialized.

With the contemporary eyewitnesses offering conflicting accounts of Callisthenes' demise no firm conclusion can be drawn. Nonetheless, there is little doubt concerning the irony of his fate. Callisthenes became a victim of the man whose virtue he extolled.

> to speak the words
> of freedom
> before
> the
> tyrant
> (*Ba.* 775–6)

## NYSA AND AORNUS (327 BC)

Plutarch tells us that early one morning in the summer of 327, when Alexander was about to invade "India," he set fire to his own baggage wagons and those of his Companions.[161] Concerned that the amount of booty accumulated would affect the army's mobility in a campaign, he then ordered the burning of his soldiers' wagons. The response of his troops was just as surprising as the king's order. A vast majority of the soldiers cheered, raised a battle-cry, shared military essentials with their comrades, and even assisted in the disposal of superfluous items. He further informs us that "Alexander was filled with enthusiasm at their spirit and his hopes rose to their highest pitch" (57.2). He adds, however, that by this time the king "was already feared by his men for his relentless severity in punishing any dereliction of duty" (57.3).

When Alexander finally descended into the Kabul Valley to embark on this next campaign, he had to deal with a significant manpower shortage. His fighting force had been substantially depleted over the years by combat and illness. Troubles in Bactria and Sogdiana had required him to leave 10,000 infantry and 3,500 cavalry (probably, for the most part, mercenaries) in those areas, which further complicated his situation. Although some authorities cite a figure of 120,000 men being led into "India" by Alexander, this count (perhaps inclusive of Asiatic troops and the various and sundry camp followers who accompanied him) appears inflated.[162] Despite periodic replacements from Macedonia and the supplementation of his forces by Iranian troops, the king probably began this invasion with some 35,000 European fighting men[163] – a figure which was almost identical to the number of soldiers (cited by Arrian 1.11.3) who had crossed the Hellespont with him seven years before.

> Far behind me lie those golden-rivered lands
> Lydia and Phrygia where my journeying began
> (*Ba.* 13–14)

At the time he had crossed into Asia Alexander had known little about "India." The Greek historian Herodotus, Ctesias, a Greek physician at the Persian court, and Scylax, a Greek in the service of Darius I, who had sailed down the Indus River and up to the Gulf of Suez, had all written about it,[164] and Alexander was no doubt familiar with what they had reported. This information, however, was at best fragmentary and speculative. Aristotle, for example, thought that Ocean, a river (and deity) which was believed to encircle the earth, could be seen from the summit of the Hindu Kush, but Alexander knew by 327 that this was nonsense. To some India began across the Hindu Kush in modern Pakistan, while to others it was the territory east of the Indus River. Unaware of the length of the great subcontinent and the width of the Ganges plain, Alexander may have believed at the outset that Ocean was within striking distance of the eastern bank of the Indus.[165] One of his goals, most certainly, would have been inclusion among the mythical figures who were said to have reached it.

Inevitably, India had become the backdrop for the mythological adventures of some of the more itinerant Hellenic deities. Heracles and Dionysus were said to have wandered about there, and Arrian's account, which comes closest to the official version of the expedition, places a special emphasis on the past presence of these meandering divinities in his discussion of the Indian campaign.[166] Dionysus, it was claimed, led his throng to India, and introduced the vine and other aspects of civilization.[167] Heracles was believed to have passed that way fifteen generations later. Both were ancestors of Alexander and sons of Zeus by mortal women who became recognized as goddesses.

> Alkmene bore me a son
> Herakles the strong-hearted
> while Semele's son
> was Dionysos

the pleasure
of
mortals
(*Il.* 14.324–5)

Carpeted with exotic flora and swarmed over by marvelous fauna, "India" was inhabited by an exotic race "darker-skinned than all other men except the Ethiopians" (A.5.4.4). This alluring land issued a Siren's call to a man of such irrepressible curiosity. Alexander was to discover that this was one of those rare instances when his experience matched his imagination. Teeming rivers, crocodiles, warrior elephants, fakirs, and naked philosophers awaited him. But India also housed some of the toughest fighting men he was ever to face, and unseen dangers against which genius and perseverance proved to be of no avail.

Persian influence in the Punjab reached back to the reign of Cyrus the Great and Darius I, who had conquered the Persian satrapy of Hindu (modern Sind). The Achaemenids had lost much of their Indian territory during the intervening period, but the presence at Gaugamela of troops from Gandhara, an area just south of the Hindu Kush, gives evidence of Persian suzerainty in that region in 331. Alexander's conquest of "India" (geographically, for the most part, contemporary Pakistan) may, in part, be seen as a reassertion of the authority enjoyed there by his Persian predecessors.[168]

As soon as Alexander's claim to the Persian kingship became earnest, he was sought out by Indian chieftains who were willing to honor him as the Great King in exchange for his support against their local enemies. After crossing the Hindu Kush, Alexander summoned Taxiles (Omphis) of Taxila and all rajahs west of the Indus to submit to him, and to offer more detailed information about what lay ahead. Taxiles brought an impressive variety of gifts, including twenty-five war elephants, which were of particular interest to Alexander.[169] Hephaestion and Perdiccas were ordered to march ahead to the Indus with half of Alexander's army and told to accept the surrender of, or take by storm, every town in their path.

The king undertook the somewhat more demanding task of subduing the tribes of Bajaur and Swat north of the Cophen (Kabul) River. In Swat the king attacked Massaga,[170] the greatest city in the region, whose defense had been bolstered by the hiring of 7,000 Indian mercenaries. Outside the walls Alexander executed a successful feigned retreat, similar to that of Philip at Chaeronea, but most of his adversaries were able to flee inside the walls of the city before his counterattack. In addition to his manpower losses and personal embarrassment, Alexander was wounded (although not severely) during the siege when his bridge over a breach in the wall collapsed. The Indians, however, were severely battered in the three-day siege. The garrison surrendered on the fourth day after their commander was killed by a missile from a catapult.

Alexander had hoped to employ the Indian mercenaries in his future operations, but they had no wish to fight against other Indians on his behalf. Arrian says that they planned to slip away from their encampment outside the city under the cover of darkness.[171] Informed of this, Alexander surrounded the hill on which they were encamped and massacred them all. Diodorus asserts that Alexander guaranteed the Indians safe conduct, but withdrew it without warning and slaughtered them.[172] Plutarch, following the version recited by Diodorus, says that Alexander's "action [at Massaga] remains a blot on his career as a soldier" (59.7). Tarn speculates that this butchery "may have been some horrible mistake due perhaps to defective interpreting and to Alexander's growing impatience."[173]

Although it occurred before the Massaga affair, the story of Nysa is related here to underscore Alexander's changing perceptions at the time. Envoys from the city of Nysa found the king in his tent, still wearing his armor and helmet, carrying a spear, and covered with dust from his riding that day. Amazed to see a king of such repute in this mundane posture, they fell to the ground and remained silent. This was a good start, and Alexander was quick to set them at ease. Acuphis, their chief representative, was there to reveal to the king that their city had been founded by a deity identified by Alexander's entourage as the Greek god Dionysus.[174] Acuphis begged Alexander to leave the city of Nysa as he had found it – aristocratic, orderly, and free from external governance. He offered local ivy, which did not grow anywhere else in India and was a special Dionysiac attribute, as proof that the city had indeed been founded by the god.

All of this "was congenial to Alexander and he wanted to believe the tale about the wandering of Dionysus; he also wanted Nysa to be founded by Dionysus, in which case he had already reached the point Dionysus reached, and would go even farther. He also thought that the Macedonians would not refuse to join him in still further efforts, in emulation of Dionysus' achievements" (A.5.2.1). Alexander granted the request for freedom and independence to Nysa, but demanded that its inhabitants send him 300 horsemen and 100 of their leaders. Acuphis smiled at this request.[175]

This prompted the king to inquire why his demand had provoked amusement. Acuphis wanted to know how a city deprived of a hundred of its best citizens could remain well governed. Take twice the number of our inferior citizens instead, he urged, and when you return, you will find the same civic order characterizing the city. Alexander saw wisdom in this logic and agreed to the request without even asking for substitutions. He did, however, require that Acuphis' own son and grandson accompany him on the campaign.

"Alexander was seized with a yearning [*pothos*] to see the place where the Nysaeans proudly displayed certain memorials of Dionysus" (A.5.2.5). The king took his Companion Cavalry and the Royal Squadron of the infantry to what his officers called Mount Merus (after Zeus' thigh [*meros*], in which Dionysus was hidden before birth to protect him from the wrath of Hera). It was indeed full of ivy, which the Macedonians had not seen for some time, even in the regions where Dionysus' other familiar attribute, the vine, was evident. Dionysus also symbolized all forms of moisture, and ivy grew in shady glades where the earth was cool and moist.

> [T]hey eagerly made wreaths of it and crowned themselves there and then, singing hymns to Dionysus and calling on the various names of the god. Then Alexander sacrificed there to Dionysus, and feasted with his Companions. Some have also related (if anyone can believe this story) that many Macedonians of distinction in his company, after crowning themselves with the ivy and invoking the god, were possessed by Dionysus, raised the Dionysiac cry, and were transported with Bacchic frenzy.
>
> (5.2.6–7)

Alexander could not resist the call to a mountain lair of the god. Once there he celebrated with his Companions, and led them, no doubt, in Bacchic hymn-singing and an enthusiastic recitation of Dionysiac epithets. Ivy would surely have been included among the qualities recalled. Like the vine and the serpent, this sacred plant evinced a metamorphic quality. Other Bacchic names were probably echoing through the Swat highlands as well – relaxer of the mind, healer of sorrow, dispeller of care, provider of joy, merrymaker, lover of laughter, disturber of the soul, mind-breaker, bestower of envy, liar, dispenser of anger, noisemaker, chaser of sleep, slayer of men.[176]

It was profitable for Alexander to find the claims of Acuphis persuasive at this juncture. After a grim period of slaughter, Dionysiac revelry provided a legitimate retreat into an altered reality from which his men would emerge with a sense of renewal. What's more, such royal acceptance of local folklore confirmed the fact that Alexander had duplicated the god's presence in this vicinity. Through his own efforts and with the help of his troops, the king hoped, in the near future, to advance beyond the limits reached by Dionysus.[177]

I

raised

my

sight

to

higher

things

(*Ba.* 1237)

Sacrificing to Dionysus at Nysa also offered supplemental expiation for Alexander's tragic indiscretion at Maracanda, and reassured his troops that the king did in fact worship Dionysus, the most popular of divinities among Alexander's rank and file soldiers. Once again, when it suited his own purpose, the king had decided to draw upon the power of Dionysus.

> you do not hear
> or else
> you disregard
> my words
> of
> warning
> (*Ba.* 787)

Scholarly controversy still dominates the study of ancient Greek perceptions of Dionysus in India.[178] The issues are made more confusing by the fact that Alexander's triumphant march through the Punjab and Sind contributed significantly to the way in which the god would be remembered in relation to that remote land. Some would make Dionysus' presence there nothing but a postscript to Alexander's invasion. It should be recalled, however, that Euripides had already placed Dionysus as far east as Bactria. Alexander had no reason to doubt, especially after observing the unique signature at Nysa, that he was following in the veiled footsteps of his enigmatic ancestor. As Bosworth has suggested, "there was probably a tradition that Dionysus had begun his triumphal progress west from the Indian lands."[179]

Paraphrasing one of his sources in a discussion about Dionysus in India, Arrian tells us that the deity "taught them [the natives] to reverence various gods, but especially of course himself, with clashings of cymbals and beating of drums . . . so that even against Alexander the Indians came to battle to the sound of cymbals and drums" (*Ind.*7.8–9). Such implausible tales of Dionysus in India troubled Arrian, but he was wary of becoming excessively analytical when it came to religion, "[f]or things which are incredible if you consider them on the basis of probability appear not wholly incredible, when one adds the divine element to the story" (5.1.2).

Members of Alexander's entourage had a talent for identifying Greek deities in the guise of alien counterparts, and, early in 326, this proclivity played a role in the king's assault upon the "rock" of Aornus.[180] The "rock" was a 7,000 foot-high massif with precipitous cliffs that loomed 5,000 feet above a bend in the Indus River. The native population sought refuge from the invaders in this mountain retreat (Pir-Sar), and a rumor circulated, based on a tale about a local god, that Heracles (Krishna) himself had failed in an effort to storm the fortress.[181] "As soon as Alexander heard this, he was seized with a longing [*pothos*] to capture this mountain too, not least because of the legend about Heracles" (A.4.28.4).

Utilizing local intelligence, Alexander learned that the best approach was from Una-Sar, a nearby ridge of even greater altitude. After experiencing considerable difficulty, he finally succeeded in placing the main body of his troops on the adjacent peak, only to discover that it was separated from Aornus by a deep and wide ravine. Not to be denied, Alexander had his men build a causeway across the ravine. All along they were under a vicious attack from the Indian defenders, but as soon as his skirmishers and siege engines could be activated, the king was able to ward off these attacks, and in three days the causeway was completed. The astonished Indians asked for a truce, and the king willingly granted it. In a manner reminiscent of the events at Massaga, however, the king, when he learned of their intention to escape that night, personally led a charge that left the Indians at his mercy. Alexander's incredible victory at Aornus made it clear to the local inhabitants that it was futile to resist this undauntable intruder.

Against
the unassailable
he runs
with rage
obsessed
(*Ba.* 1000–1)

On the "rock" Alexander erected altars to the gods. Undoubtedly he held a special dedication to Heracles, whom he had just outdone, but the highest honors were reserved for Athena, a divinity special to both Heracles and Alexander. The king had sacrificed to her on the eve of his advance into India, and now, after a successful conclusion to the first phase of this campaign, he erected an altar to Athena Nike on a site that towered over the Indus River below.[182]

On his march to the bridge that Hephaestion had erected over the Indus, Alexander learned that a number of Indians in the district had fled to Abisares of Kashmir and, in their haste, had left elephants grazing near the river. Alexander was intrigued by these animals. He was well aware that they were likely to play a prominent role in the conflicts ahead. The king added elephant hunters to his staff, and, under their direction, he engaged in an elephant hunt that reached a climax when two of the beasts thundered off a cliff. For Alexander it was an exhilarating experience. All thirteen surviving beasts were incorporated into his army,[183] and he was ready to advance into the territory beyond the Indus River, which he considered to be India proper.

We have him
in our net
He
may be quick
but he cannot
escape us
now
(*Ba.* 451–2)

# 4  The ambivalent victor

## INTO "INDIA" (326 BC)

During Alexander's day the boundaries of "India" were amorphous, but to the king the region was well defined. "India" referred to those lands east of the Indus River.[1] Crossing over Hephaestion's bridge at Ohind (Udabhandapura), just north of Attock, in May 326, was therefore a momentous achievement. Alexander held athletic and equestrian games, while sacrificing to the gods and seeking their approval of his intention. The sacrifices proved favorable, and the king crossed the river at dawn, "so entering the land of the Indians" (A.5.4.3).

Alexander marched consecutively to the Hydaspes (Jhelum), Acesines (Chenab), Hydraotes (Ravi), and Hyphasis (Beas) rivers in the Punjab region of present-day northeastern Pakistan and northwestern India. His success in this area was contingent upon setting one rajah against another, and forcing the submission *seriatim* of all others who resisted him. At Ohind Alexander was presented with exquisite gifts from Taxiles, who sought Alexander's support against Abisares of Kashmir and Porus of Paurava, his formidable enemies. This time Taxiles sent the king 200 silver talents, 3,000 bulls, and 10,000 sheep for sacrificial purposes. In addition, he included 700 Indian cavalry, 30 elephants, and Taxila itself, the most important city between the Indus and the Jhelum, lying 20 miles northwest of modern Rawalpindi.[2]

The king advanced toward Taxila, which had been the capital city of a former Persian satrapy, and was greeted on the way by Taxiles. This Indian potentate had been so lavish in his blandishments that it made Alexander ill at ease, until it became clear that the man was just as eager to receive gifts as to bestow them. Plutarch relates a dialogue said to have taken place between the two rulers:

"[I]f I [Taxiles] possess more than you, I am ready to be generous towards you, and if I have less, I shall not refuse any benefits you may offer." Alexander was delighted at this, took his hand and said,"Perhaps you think that after your kind words and courtesy our meeting will pass off without a contest. No, you shall not get the better of me in this way: I shall fight with you to the last, but only in the services I offer you, for I will not have you outdo me in generosity." Alexander received many gifts from him, but returned even more, and finally presented him with a thousand talents in coin.

(59.3–5)[3]

> and always
> he gives gifts
> (*Il.* 20.298–9)

Some of Alexander's friends were annoyed at the extravagant turn the king's spirited competition with Taxiles had taken. At a symposium on the following night, Meleager, a battalion commander who had been drinking heavily, sarcastically congratulated the king on discovering in "India" a man who was worth that much money. Alexander responded by saying that envious men only torment themselves, a retort suggestive of the king's exchange with Cleitus in Maracanda.[4] The matter was left at that, but Meleager, as far as we know, was never promoted above the rank of battalion commander.

Taxila was not only a trading center that attracted merchants from the Ganges Valley, Kashmir, and Bactria, but also a seat of higher learning in "India." It was here that Alexander heard of a group of ascetics who lived naked just outside the city. Onesicritus, the royal helmsman, was sent to inquire about the beliefs of these men, who were referred to by the king's courtiers as Gymnosophists or "naked philosophers."[5] He was also instructed to persuade their leader, Dandamis, to join Alexander's host. Onesicritus, a student of Diogenes of Sinope, the founder of the Cynic school of philosophy, was a natural choice to be the envoy, but it is difficult to determine exactly what transpired on his mission. Some of the confusion may be traced to Onesicritus himself, who wrote his recollections of the expedition in the form of a historical romance.[6] His tales of the king's encounters with Indian philosophers are colored by his Cynic training and convictions. He is responsible for creating imaginary dialogues between Alexander and the ascetics, as well as the romantic image of Alexander as a philosopher in arms.[7]

Arrian, who follows a source other than Onesicritus in describing this episode, tells us that a longing (*pothos*) came over Alexander to add one of these men of incredible endurance to his entourage. Dandamis, the oldest of the Gymnosophists, "said he would not join Alexander nor let any of the others do so; in fact he is said to have replied that he himself was just as much a son of Zeus as Alexander, and that he had no need of anything Alexander could give, since he was contented with what he had; he saw, moreover, that Alexander's companions were wandering about over all that land and sea to no profit, and that there was no limit to their many wanderings" (7.2.2–3). Arrian had introduced his remarks about the king's experiences with Indian ascetics by commenting that "while Alexander was not wholly beyond comprehension of better courses, he was fearfully mastered by love of fame" (7.2.2).

Elsewhere, Arrian recounts the story that Alexander once came upon the Gymnosophists in an open meadow where they were engaged in disputations. Upon seeing the king and his army, they began to stomp the ground with their feet. Alexander asked what was meant by this display, and was told, "King Alexander, each man possesses no more of this earth than the patch we stand on; yet you, though a man like other men, except of course that you are restless and presumptuous, are roaming over so wide an area away from what is your own, giving no rest to yourself or others. And very soon you too will die, and will possess no more of the earth than suffices for the burial of your body" (7.1.6). Arrian tells us that Alexander responded to these remarks by praising the speakers for what they said. The historian also comments that the king did the opposite of what they recommended, and draws his telling conclusion that Alexander "would always have searched far beyond for something unknown, in competition with himself in default of any other rival" (7.1.4).

A renegade Indian Gymnosophist named Calanus joined Alexander's expedition, despite the censure his action drew from his own group. He instructed some of Alexander's officers in his way of life, and the king became quite attached to him. By the time he reached Persis, however, Calanus, who had previously enjoyed perfect health, became severely ill. Ignoring the king's entreaties, the sage refused to adopt any regimen that would alter his traditional way of life. In Persis, as we shall see, Calanus insisted on burning himself to death.

## THE BATTLE OF THE HYDASPES (JHELUM) RIVER (326 BC)

In the spring of 326 the king marched toward the Jhelum with 5,000 additional Indian troops under the leadership of Taxiles. Alexander pitched camp near modern Haranpur, and met with a swift and turbulent river, swollen by melted snow from the Himalayas, and rain, heralding the onset of the monsoon season. Porus, the rajah of the Paurava, a longstanding enemy of Taxiles, stood waiting to confront Alexander with an army of some 20,000 infantrymen, 3,000 horsemen, 300 chariots, and 85 elephants.[8]

> He would not make way for Achilleus
> who
> breaks men
> in battle
> (*Il.* 13.324)

Alexander also heard that Abisares of Kashmir was on his way to join forces with Porus, although that rajah had given signs of submission through emissaries in Taxila.

The king hoped to cross the Jhelum as soon as possible, but his horses, lacking the necessary specialized training, were certain to panic and bolt from their rafts once they had picked up the elephants' scent. This would throw the entire army into disarray. Well aware of his advantage, Porus concentrated his elephants directly across the shore from the invaders, while blanketing the shore with scouts who would report any attempt at a crossing.[9]

The challenge stimulated Alexander's imagination. He dazzled Porus with a kaleidoscopic display of motion and illusion from his side of the Jhelum. During the day his troops would suddenly place their boats and rafts on to the river and simulate the first stages of a crossing until Porus put his army on full alert and strategically relocated his elephants. At night Alexander led his cavalry up and down the western bank in a chorus of battle cries and trumpets, which could also be taken as a prelude to invasion.

Alexander even announced publicly (for Porus to hear) that he intended to wait out the summer season and attack in the autumn, when conditions were less prohibitive. A huge volume of provisions was ostentatiously imported into camp to lend credence to this spurious assertion. The ultimate objective of all this was to convince Porus that he was expending far too much energy in responding to each of Alexander's many ruses. Then, it was hoped, he would stop sending out the beasts.

Aware that his troops were becoming frustrated and exhausted, Porus posted a permanent guard and ordered the rest of his men to remain at ease until the real crossing had begun. Alexander, who had been offended by Parmenio's suggestion of the same approach at Gaugamela, decided on a night attack. The crossing would take place near modern Jalalpur, at a thickly wooded bend in the river about 17 miles upstream. Here there was a deep ravine close to the bank where Alexander could conceal his cavalry, and an island between the two mainlands that would serve as a screen for his movements. A strong detachment of troops left back at the main camp under Craterus continued to prepare openly for their role in the invasion, which would occur when the elephants facing them were withdrawn or the enemy was routed.

In a veritable *coup de théâtre*, Alexander had a man who resembled him in age, features, and build dress in royal attire and parade in and out of his tent surrounded by the traditional guard.[10] At a distance the double offered a convincing impersonation of the king, while elsewhere the real Alexander imperceptibly tended to the details of his strike.

> Now
> for the night
> we shall keep watch on ourselves
> and tomorrow
> early

before dawn shows
shall arm ourselves
in our weapons
and . . .
waken
the
bitter
war
god
(*Il.* 8.529–31)

When the time came the king and his assault force moved toward the crossing in silence, enjoying relative invisibility because of their discreet distance from the bank. The surprise attack was complicated by a heavy downpour and a severe thunderstorm, during which a number of Alexander's men were struck and killed by lightning. The crossing occurred at first light, but was detected almost immediately after Alexander, in a thirty-oar ship, passed the island.

As Porus' scouts galloped to inform their king, Alexander became the first to set foot on what was assumed to be the mainland. To his astonishment and dismay, however, he discovered that it was yet another island, and that a narrow but deep stream still separated his force from its destination. A frantic search began for a ford. One was discovered that would barely suffice, and "Alexander led them across it, though with difficulty, for the water at its deepest was above the breasts of the foot-soldiers, while the horses kept only their heads above the river" (A.5.13.3). If the king, who was less than imposing in height, could make it, the rest could as well.

Porus ordered his son to take 60 chariots, along with 1,000 horsemen, and attempt to prevent the invaders from landing. They were too late. Alexander's crack cavalry proved too accomplished for the outnumbered Indian horsemen, and heavy casualties were inflicted, among them Porus' son. Driven off course by Alexander's mounted archers, the four-horsed chariots of the Indians became mired in the rain-sodden soil and proved to be as ineffective as they had been for the Persians at Gaugamela. Porus, leaving some elephants behind to deter a crossing from the invader's main camp, moved north with the bulk of his army to await a decisive confrontation with Alexander.

The use of elephants by the enemy provided a new challenge for Alexander, but he devised a technique that transformed them into a hazard to their own masters. Faced with the mammoth brutes, which may have been stationed 50 feet apart at the front of the Indian line, Alexander decided to launch a two-phase cavalry charge against the horsemen and chariots on Porus' wings first. After Porus had committed horsemen from both wings to an attack against what he thought was the enemy's entire cavalry,

Coenus, in hiding, would suddenly appear with his horsemen and trap the Indians in a pincer movement. If successful, these tactics would enable Alexander's infantry, who had been specially trained for the purpose, to deal with the elephants, but this could not occur until the enemy had been thrown into a state of confusion.

Arrows and javelins would then be directed at the mahouts who piloted these intimidating creatures, and they would be dismounted by the long Macedonian pikes. In their initial encounter against these beasts, however, the formation of the "invincible" phalanx was broken, and many of the king's infantrymen were trodden under hoof. Nevertheless, they were able to regroup before the advancing Indian troops reached them and, eventually, the king's inventive tactics began to pay off.

Alexander's men struck viciously at the tender parts of each elephant's body with a double-headed axe, leaving many of the animals in such excruciating pain that they rushed about trampling friend and foe indiscriminately. Following their plan, the phalanx now generally managed to evade the elephants' charges, and then shot at them from behind as the beasts wheeled about. As a result, the Indians were soon suffering more from these bewildered brutes than were the Macedonians. In the end, too weary to sustain a charge, the riderless elephants retreated in unison, trumpeting their bone-chilling sirens of distress. By now Porus' troops were surrounded and had begun to panic. Craterus crossed from the main camp and set his fresh troops after the retreating enemy in what turned out to be a bloody rout.

Even though victory was no longer possible, Porus, who was no Darius, appeared determined to see it through to its grim conclusion, until he suffered an incapacitating shoulder wound. Then this stately rajah, who was, like Darius, about six-and-a-half feet tall, began to back his immense elephant away from the field with methodical dignity. Alexander was impressed with his bearing and deportment, and sent Taxiles off to persuade this remarkable adversary to surrender. Porus responded by attacking his longstanding enemy. Taxiles, on horseback, managed to distance himself in the nick of time. Nevertheless, "Alexander did not show anger against Porus" (A.5.18.7), but continued to extend the olive branch through a succession of messengers. Finally, exhausted and dehydrated after a battle reportedly lasting eight hours, the vanquished monarch dismounted and surrendered after being beseeched to do so only by a trusted friend.

After quenching his thirst and regaining his breath, Porus asked to be brought to the victor. Alexander, together with a few Companions, rode out to meet him and asked how he thought he should be treated. His celebrated reply was, "Treat me, Alexander, like a king" (A.5.19.2).[11] Delighted by this response, Alexander wanted to know what else he might do that would please him. Porus answered laconically that everything he desired was embodied in that request. Arrian tells us that "Alexander was all the more pleased with this reply" (5.19.3).

Aristotle had written that noble men should desire the recognition of other noble men because it validated their own virtue.[12] This, and the fact that Porus was needed as an ally if the Punjab were to be held, probably influenced Alexander's notable encounter with such a chivalric peer. In recognition of the rajah's gallantry, and because he could scarcely hope to control this region himself, Alexander restored the Paurava to Porus. He eventually invested him with all of the territory east of the Jhelum and west of the Beas.[13] The rajah remained a loyal and valuable supporter throughout Alexander's life.

> These two fought each other
> in heart-consuming hate
> then joined with each other
> in close friendship
> before they were parted
> (*Il.* 7.301–2)

Porus was prevailed upon to reconcile with his old enemy Taxiles, who had also been given additional territory. The Indian rulers balanced one another east and west of the Jhelum, but both remained under the aegis of Alexander.

Bucephalas, Alexander's famous steed, died of the wounds he suffered during the battle.[14] He was 30 years old, but it was still said that no one but Alexander could mount this large and noble horse. The two had been together through crisis and triumph for most of their lives. Plutarch tells us that the king "was plunged into grief at his death, and felt that he had lost nothing less than a friend and a comrade" (61.2). A city, Bucephala, was founded in the horse's name on the west bank of the Jhelum.[15]

Alexander was exceptionally fond of animals. There is a story that he loved a dog called Peritas (after the Macedonian month of January), which he had raised from a puppy. He honored this faithful creature by naming a city after him as well.[16] Furthermore, a shrine dedicated to Helios (the Sun) in Taxila is said to have housed Porus' retired elephant, dubbed Ajax by Alexander after the beast's Homeric performance at the Jhelum.[17] It is clear from the sources that the king found animals to be more loyal and less troublesome than human beings, whose allegiance often carried qualifications.

Abisares of Kashmir, who never appeared at the Jhelum, subsequently sent his brother to Alexander with rich gifts, including forty elephants. He agreed to do anything that the king wished him to do, short of relinquishing his own title. Abisares' brother claimed that the rajah was ill, or he would have appeared in person. A suspicious Alexander demanded his presence, but seems to have withdrawn his ultimatum when the illness was authenticated. A city of Victory, Nicaea was founded (with Athena in mind) on the east bank of the Jhelum.[18] The king made his customary sacrifices to the gods in thanksgiving for his resounding triumph. Athletic and equestrian competitions in honor of the gods were held where the crossing had taken place, and the troops were given a month's rest. When the march was resumed, Craterus was left behind to fortify the new cities. He was also ordered to construct a fleet. Upon the king's return, this fleet would sail down the Jhelum, into the Indus, and then out to the open sea.

Some scholars report that for a time Alexander's geographical misconceptions led him to believe that the rivers he encountered were really sources of the Nile River. He perhaps reasoned that the whole expedition would be able to sail on the Indus – which would become the Nile – into his Egyptian Alexandria.[19] Considering Alexander's excellent intelligence system,[20] however, this assertion, as Peter Green points out,[21] is as unlikely as the contention that he still believed that the end of the land was within a short march. Alexander personally interviewed those best informed about the region in which he traveled, and passed on only cursory information to those accompanying him. The troops could thus be persuaded to advance from one river to the next with the deceptive promise that they would soon be treated to a glimpse of the Eastern Ocean.

Alexander moved eastward across the lands bordering Porus' kingdom, accepting the surrender of dozens of independent cities along the way. The inhabitants of these cities apparently decided against offering any opposition to the man who had defeated Porus so convincingly. All did not go smoothly, however. The crossing of the Chenab was so rough that many of the king's boats and men were lost. It was also necessary for Hephaestion to deal with Porus' rebellious cousin (also called Porus). Alexander continued on to the Ravi, where, after the crossing, he learned of the planned resistance on the part of the warlike Cathaeans, who lived between the Ravi and the Beas.

The Macedonians besieged the Cathaean capital at Sangala with the assistance of 5,000 Indian troops under Porus. Although they were finally able to overcome its defenders after several days of intensive fighting, the fierce resistance forced Alexander at one point to step down from his horse and inspire his phalanx by leading it on foot.[22] Ptolemy claims that 17,000 Indians were killed and 70,000 captured.[23] This may be an exaggeration. He also records that some 1,200 Macedonians were seriously wounded, with 100 reported killed. This is the largest number of casualties suffered by Alexander's army that is acknowledged by the "official" sources. Alexander sent word to the other hostile cities in the vicinity that he "would not treat them harshly if they stayed where they were and received him in a friendly way, just as he had shown no harshness to any of the other self-governing Indians who had voluntarily surrendered" (A.5.24.6).

Nevertheless, thousands of terrified Indians fled from these cities, with

Alexander, once he had learned of their dispersal, in pursuit. Most of those refugees who enjoyed a head start managed to escape, but those "left behind in the retreat through infirmity were captured and put to death by the army, to the number of about five hundred" (A.5.24.7). Alexander returned to Sangala, leveled the city, and distributed the territories formerly controlled by the Cathaeans among tribes who had made their submission. Schachermeyr observes that Alexander was "a Titanic son" who had no foreign policy other than a request for submission and loved all people in so far as they obeyed him and him alone.[24]

Curtius relates a story regarding Sophithes, a local king in this area, who emerged from one of his cities and turned over his golden scepter, himself, his children, and his people to Alexander.[25] He treated the king to an exhibition of several powerful and courageous hunting dogs that, it was said, must have had some tiger blood in them. Four of these dogs, the story goes, were pitted against a huge lion. A man who worked with these animals tugged at the legs of one of the dogs that had its teeth embedded in the lion, but the trainer could not distract the hound from its prey. The man then began to hack away at the dog's leg with a scimitar. This drew indignant protests from Alexander, who was silenced by Sophithes' promise to give the king three other dogs of the same type. The handler then proceeded to slowly sever the dog's leg without so much as a yelp or whimper from the animal. It bled to death with its teeth still implanted in its quarry. This display of determination and tenacity obviously impressed Alexander.

After the Battle of the Jhelum Alexander sacrificed to Helios, "who had given him the eastern regions to conquer" (D.17.89.3).[26] As he advanced to the Beas River, he may well have wondered what mistake had been made in the sacrifice. It was the monsoon season, and rain fell incessantly on his men, accompanied by an oppressive humidity and continual lightning and thunder.

The rain continued for seventy days, leaving uniforms unwearable, corroding armor and weapons, and miring carts in what had begun to resemble an endless bog.[27] Moisture was everywhere, the food was moldy, and mildew and rot soon became a most familiar odor. Illnesses began to spread through the camp. What was worse, however, was that the inundation had flushed out a legion of snakes of every size and variety imaginable, and they were everywhere. Strabo quotes one of Alexander's trusted friends on the subject:

Nearchus wonders at the number of the reptiles and their viciousness, for he says that at the time of the inundations they flee up from the plains into the settlements that escape the inundations, and fill the houses; and . . . the inhabitants not only make their beds high, but sometimes even move out of their houses when infested by too many of them; and that if the greater part of the multitude of reptiles were not destroyed by the waters, the country would be depopulated; and that the smallness of some of them is troublesome as well as the huge size of others.

(15.1.45)

Alexander's men found deadly krait (venomous Asian snakes) in their boots and shuddered at the sight of enormous boa constrictors.[28] They slept in hammocks tied between trees in order to avoid a snakebite that might result in their bleeding to death or being poisoned. Alexander, Nearchus tells us through Arrian, "collected and kept by him all the Indians most skilled in medicine, and had it announced in camp that anyone bitten by a snake was to go to the royal tent" (A.*Ind*.15.11). This was one privilege that none of his soldiers was anxious to exercise.

O
Dionysus
. . .
Be
manifest
a
snake
with
darting
heads
(*Ba*. 1017–18)

## "MUTINY" AT THE HYPHASIS (BEAS) RIVER (326 BC)

The king, now just inside modern India, had every intention of crossing the Beas River.[29] It soon became clear, however, that the greatest obstacle to this objective came from within his own ranks. Veterans who had crossed the Hellespont with him eight years before, and had marched over 17,000 miles, were having no more of it. Rumors circulated about the Ganges River, and about a kingdom ahead with 80,000 horsemen, 200,000 foot soldiers, 8,000 chariots, and, worse yet, 6,000 elephants. Alexander's soldiers had survived every conceivable ordeal until now. They had been motivated by Alexander's example, and his clever use of reward and punishment. They had also, occasionally, felt the shame of disappointing this extraordinary leader. But as they looked across the Beas at yet another desolate plain, it became apparent to his soldiers that perhaps the king would simply keep going. Arrian himself states that for Alexander "there could be no end of the war as long as any enemy was left" (5.24.8).

Forever quarrelling
is dear to your heart

and wars
and battles
(*Il.* 1.177)

Hoping to please his troops, Alexander authorized a ravaging of the Indian countryside.[30] It was not Persepolis, but there was plenty to be had. The troops wreaked havoc on the natives, most of whom had voluntarily surrendered to the king. While his men were away, Alexander courted whatever family they had accumulated on the expedition.[31] It was announced that a monthly ration was to be distributed to their women, and a bonus, based upon their fathers' records, given to the soldiers' children. This attention and consideration, though flattering to all of the parties concerned, was especially gratifying to the young boys who might someday serve under Alexander.

Unfortunately for the king, however, all of this counted for naught as far as his troops were concerned. His men gathered in small groups, commiserating over their plight and lamenting the fact that Alexander was "taking on one hard and dangerous task after another" (A.5.25.2). Some soldiers were so disgusted that they were openly proclaiming their refusal to follow Alexander any further. As despair grew and discipline evaporated, the threat of outright mutiny loomed. The king called a meeting of his regimental commanders and spoke to them in an impassioned voice. Arrian, relying on Ptolemy, who was present on this occasion, provides us with a speech that, although flawed in regard to some particulars, is convincing in tone and consonant with past examples:[32]

I observe that you, Macedonians and allies [Greek officers], are not following me into dangers any longer with your old spirit. I have summoned you together, either to persuade you to go forward, or to be persuaded by you to turn back. If indeed you have any fault to find with the exertions you have hitherto endured, and with me as your leader, there is no object in my speaking further. If, however, it is through these exertions that Ionia is now in our hands, and [a summary of their conquests] . . . why do you hesitate to add the Hyphasis and the peoples beyond the Hyphasis to this Macedonian empire of ours? Do you fear lest other barbarians may yet withstand your approach? . . .

For my part, I set no limit to exertions for a man of noble spirit, save that the exertions themselves should lead to deeds of prowess. Yet if any one longs to hear what will be the limit of the actual fighting, he should understand that there remains no great stretch of land before us up to the river Ganges and the eastern sea . . . . if we flinch now, there will be many warlike races left behind on the far side of the Hyphasis . . . . Then our numerous exertions will indeed be profitless, or we shall have to start again with fresh exertions and dangers. But you must persevere . . . . Exertions and dangers are the price of deeds of prowess, and it is sweet for men to live bravely, and die leaving behind them immortal renown. Or do you not know that it was not by remaining in [Greece] . . . that our ancestor [Heracles] attained such renown that from a man he became, or was held, a god? Even Dionysus, a more delicate god than Heracles, had not a few labours to perform. And yet we have actually passed beyond Nysa and taken the rock Aornos, which Heracles could not take. Let it be your task to add what yet remains of Asia to the possessions already won, a small conquest in comparison.

(5.25.3–26.6)

and I see no good thing's accomplishment
for us in the end
unless
we do
this
(*Il.* 7.352–3)

Alexander then reminded his troops that he shared in all of their labor and risks, not for himself, but for them, and promised that in seeing this campaign through, all would be rewarded beyond their wildest dreams. After their work was completed he would allow anyone who wished to return home to do so, and perhaps lead them back himself, while making it unimaginably profitable for those who chose to remain in Asia.

Alexander's words were greeted with an unsettling silence, since "no one either dared to oppose the King on the spur of the moment, or was yet willing to agree" (A.5.27.1). Alexander then invited anyone who disagreed with him to voice his views, but silence continued to reign. Finally, Coenus, a senior officer who had recently acquitted himself well in the battle against Porus, spoke up. His recorded words, even if they belong more to Arrian than to Coenus, offer some insight into how it was thought best to approach the king on a subject that was likely to trigger his anger.

Coenus made it clear that he was not speaking for his fellow officers, who "are zealous to serve you in every way, but on behalf of the majority in the army" (5.27.2). Not, he emphasized, to curry favor with them, but in order to be "useful to yourself in present circumstances and most conducive to safety for the future" (5.27.3). To justify his earnest response to the king's rhetorical request for opposing arguments Coenus cited his age, "the superior rank you have granted me, and the unhesitating daring I have shown up to now in exertions and dangers" (5.27.3). The words passed on by Arrian portray a man who seems to be walking on, and occasionally cracking, egg shells.

The successes achieved by you as our leader and by those who set out with you from our homes have been so numerous and splendid that for that very reason I think it more in our interest to set some limit to exertions and dangers. Surely you see yourself how many Macedonians and Greeks we were when we set forth with you, and how many survive. The Thessalians you sent straight home from Bactria, observing that they had little heart left for further exertions, and you were right. As for the other Greeks, some have been settled in the cities you have founded, and even they do not remain there entirely of their own free will . . . others have been invalided from wounds, and have been left behind in different parts of Asia; but most have died of sickness, and of all that host few survive, and even they no longer enjoy their bodily strength, while their spirit is far more wearied out. One and all, they long to see their parents . . . wives . . . children . . . homeland . . . for with the honour of the provision you have made for them, they will return great and wealthy . . . . It is not for you now to be a leader of unwilling troops. For you will no longer find men meeting dangers as they once did . . . . But if it please you, return in person to your own country, look on your own mother, settle the affairs of the Greeks and, after bringing these victories, numerous and splendid, to your father's house, then indeed begin again and fit out another expedition . . . . but your followers will be other Macedonians, other Greeks, young men in place of old, men who are fresh and . . . have no immediate fear of war, having no experience of it . . . they [will] see the partners in your earlier exertions and dangers returned to their own lands and raised from poverty to riches and from obscurity to high renown. Nothing, Sire, is so unquestionably good as a sound mind in good fortune and, though with you as commander and such an army to lead our enemies can inspire no fear, the strokes of divine power are beyond the foresight and therefore beyond the precautions of human beings.

(5.27.4–9)

The aging commander apparently felt that someone had to apprise the king of the gravity of the situation. That responsibility had fallen on him by default. If Alexander would have become upset over a speech of this sort within his intimate circle of friends, he was outraged at such candor in front of his officer corps. To aggravate the situation further, the speech met with general approval. Many a seasoned officer was moved to tears.[33]

Alexander was "irritated at Coenus' freedom of language and at the timidity of the other officers" (A.5.28.1), and summarily dismissed the entire group. He reconvened them the very next day, only to announce that he, for one, was going on ahead, but would not force any Macedonian to accompany him against his will. He would be joined exclusively by those who followed their king on a voluntary basis. Others who wished to turn back could do so, but would have to let their fellow countrymen know that they had left their king surrounded by enemies.

Run away
by all means
if your heart drives you
I will not entreat you
to stay here
for my sake
There are others
with me
who will do me
honour
and above all
Zeus
(*Il.* 1.173–5)

Still angry, Alexander withdrew to his tent for two days, refusing to see any of his Companions, and hoping for a miraculous change in the prevailing mood.[34]

The king had used every technique in his repertoire. He knew full well that it would be impossible to carry on without his Macedonians, for although they now constituted a numerical minority in his army, they remained indispensable to his command structure, battle plans, communications, and logistics; and so to proceed without them guaranteed disaster. The problem was that his troops were equally aware of this. At that particular juncture it was still quite possible for them to retrace their steps back to the Hellespont through territory already subjugated, even, if necessary, without their king.

as if I were some dishonoured vagabond
(*Il.* 16.59)

The Macedonians responded to Alexander's Achillean posturing with their own sullen comportment. When it became clear that neither his officers nor the common soldiers would accept him in the role of a victim of circumstances, which had worked so well at Maracanda, Alexander was under pressure to come up with a device that would save him from a humiliating reversal. He rose to the challenge by solemnly ordering sacrifices to determine divine opinion regarding the crossing. To everyone's relief, the sacrifices proved unfavorable.[35]

Can you not see
that the power
of Zeus
no longer
is
with you
(*Il.* 8.140)

The king then called in some of his older Companions and close friends to share this inauspicious but useful information. He came to the conclusion, he said, that all things considered, it was best to turn back. He then proceeded to announce this decision to the entire camp. The army was beside itself with joy. Throngs flocked to the royal tent, weeping openly, and imploring the gods to bless their king.

> you will eat out
> the heart within you . . .
> that you did no honour
> to the best
> of the Achaians
> (*Il.* 1.243–4)

N. G. L. Hammond sheds some light on Alexander's handling of the situation:

> He convened not a meeting of the Assembly but a meeting of the leading officers, among whom were non-Macedonians. Such groups gave advice only. The decision rested with the Commander. When the standstill continued, he called a meeting of Macedonian leading officers only. He conveyed through them his military decision to turn back. He had avoided the constitutional issue, except insofar as the sacrifice was made and the omens were respected by him as king of Macedon. He emerged unscathed in this role, and even as commander of the army he earned his soldiers' gratitude.[36]

Alexander divided the army into 12 units and ordered each of them to erect altars as high as and wider than the largest of the siege towers. These monuments would serve as a thanksgiving "to the gods who had brought him so far as a conqueror, and as memorials of his own exertions" (A.5.29.1). When the altars were finished, Alexander performed sacrifices atop these edifices in a scene of exemplary piety rivaling any mythological tale. Alexander's altars at the Beas were to symbolize in the East an analogy to the 12 altars erected by his forefather Heracles at the other end of the world. They were also emulative of Dionysus.[37]

Some historians argue that Alexander ordered traces to be left that would suggest that his camp and its inhabitants were three times their actual size.[38] Armor of superhuman proportion, Cyclopean beds and couches, and outsized equestrian equipment were scattered about, it is said, to inspire the notion that giants, not men, had passed that way. While most modern historians refuse to take any of this seriously, such thinking may not have been all that alien to a king with Alexander's theatrical tendencies and flair. Swept up in the elation of finally looking toward home, the army blissfully indulged their king in the creation of a grand illusion to bemuse posterity.

> my glory
> will not
> be
> forgotten
> (*Il.* 7.91)

Alexander's soldiers playfully suggested to him that they were responsible for the only defeat he had ever sustained. He understood the irony in this "family" joke all too well. It was the humor that eluded him. What could have been mutiny had blossomed into a tearful reconciliation, but the fact that his own troops would not follow him, even if ordered to do so, was a reality that Alexander found difficult to accept. Perhaps by design, the troops blamed themselves for the embarrassing state of affairs that had developed, thereby relieving their king of any responsibility in the matter. While willing to accept the implication that the fault lay elsewhere, Alexander was uncomfortable with the vocabulary of defeat, and resentful over a lost opportunity to see one of the most extravagant of his wishes fulfilled. Publicly he bowed to the will of the gods and accepted the gratitude of his troops. In private he fumed.[39]

> the heart
> within him
> . . . its
> wearisome
> anger
> (*Il.* 10.107)

Of late Alexander had been the victim of an unlikely coalition of forces against which even his brilliance and tenaciousness proved to be inadequate. Insufferable damp, the ubiquitous snakes, even his own followers may have appeared to him to be in a sinister conspiracy against his destiny. Alexander would count his experience at the Beas among the most bitter in his career, and ascribe his humiliation there to the only god toward whom he had displayed a pattern of disrespect, Dionysus.[40]

## OCEAN (325 BC)

Alexander's men returned to Babylon, but not by retracing their steps. After marching back to the Jhelum and repairing the damage done to Nicaea and Bucephala by the rains, Alexander inspected the ships prepared by Craterus, and then mapped out his plans to subdue the Malli and Oxydracae, two fierce, independent tribes in the lower Punjab and Sind. He was determined to overcome all opposition on both sides of the river system in this vicinity, down to the mouth of the Indus itself.

In one sense, by turning south and conquering this region, Alexander was simply restoring Persian control over the southeastern portion of the kingdom and reestablishing a secure eastern frontier. On the other hand, this exacting journey enabled him to get to Ocean while simultaneously making it clear to his men that the alternative to crossing the Beas was less attractive than they might have imagined.

> I go now to the ends of the generous earth
> on a visit to Okeanos
> whence the gods
> have risen
> (*Il.* 14.200–1)

Coenus died at the Jhelum of an unspecified illness and was given an elaborate funeral. There is no hard evidence to suggest a sinister explanation, but among soldiers who had witnessed the disappearance of more than one man who had fallen from grace, there must have been a few questions raised at this coincidental end to an officer who had the temerity to champion their cause publicly before the king.[41]

Early in November 326 a great armada set sail from Jalalabad under Alexander, with Onesicritus as his chief steersman and Nearchus as his admiral.[42] The king's sailors were from Phoenicia, the Greek islands, the Hellespont, Asia Minor, and Egypt. Thirty-two sponsors were given the distinction of contributing to this enterprise, in the same manner that wealthy Athenians financed vessels for their city's navy. Arrian's list of the honorary captains of these warships (trierarchs), drawn from Nearchus' account, includes Hephaestion, Leonnatus, Lysimachus (a Royal Bodyguard who tried to restrain Alexander during his brawl with Cleitus), and Bagoas, the son of Pharnuches.[43] Some of the other names listed belong to men who were important both during and after the expedition: Craterus, Perdiccas, Peucestas (soon to help save the king's life), Ptolemy, Medius of Larisa (a drinking companion of the king), and Eumenes of Cardia, the Royal Secretary under both Philip and Alexander.

At the Jhelum Alexander made his customary sacrifices, as well as those ordered by Ammon to Poseidon, Amphitrite (the daughter of Ocean and wife of Poseidon), the Nereids, Ocean, Jhelum, Chenab, and Indus. Competitions were held in honor of the gods, and the king's troops were treated to a sumptuous feast. At dawn on the day of departure Alexander stood on the prow of his ship and poured a libation from a golden bowl into the Jhelum. He called upon that river, the Chenab, and the Indus and prayed for their good graces. He also poured a libation to Heracles Propator (Forefather), and one to Ammon, his only public sacrifice to the latter deity on record.[44]

Trumpets blared and a flotilla of 2,080 ships of diverse size and description, with their sails dyed purple, set out on its voyage southward.[45] The number of fighting men in Alexander's host may actually have approximated the 120,000 claimed by Nearchus.[46] It was a splendid pageant, enhanced by a chorus of spontaneous singing from the local population, who were drawn to the shore to witness such a strange sight. Alexander's strike force sailed with him. Craterus led an infantry battalion and the cavalry along the western bank, while Hephaestion paraded down the eastern side with the remainder of the troops and all of the elephants in what must have been a majestic spectacle.

> Bear on the god
> son of god
> escort
> your
> Dionysus
> home
> (*Ba.* 84–7)

Traces of tension and internal conflict, however, were detectable beneath the euphoric pageantry. It was out of necessity that Craterus and Hephaestion marched down the Jhelum on opposite sides of the river. Their rivalry for the king's approbation had blossomed into a reciprocal hatred, which ultimately became unsettling to others beside themselves. While Craterus could not match Hephaestion's enthusiasm when it came to some of Alexander's policies, the general was loyal, extremely able, and very useful. In the following incident, it is interesting to note the way in which each of the individuals was rebuked by Alexander. It may shed some light on Alexander's feelings toward the two men, as well as how he saw them in relation to his power.

At one point the two rivals drew swords and went at one another, with their friends and supporters joining in the fracas. The king rode up and berated Hephaestion there and then, reminding him "that he must be a fool and a madman if he did not understand that without Alexander's favour he was nothing" (P.47.11).[47]

> So he spoke
> and Patroklos obeyed
> (*Il.* 1.345)

Later Craterus was sharply reprimanded in private, and the two were forced to effect a reconciliation. Alexander "swore by [Ammon] and the rest of the gods that these were the two men he loved best in the world, but that if he ever heard them quarrelling again, he would kill them both, or at least the one who began the quarrel. After this, it is said, neither of them ever did or said anything to offend the other even in jest" (P.47.12).

Alexander's actions can perhaps best be understood in terms of Aristotle's discussion of friendship. The philosopher maintains that relationships with other people seem to proceed from one's relationship with oneself.[48] In the noblest of friendships, he says, a virtuous person not only treats a friend as if he were a second self, but is willing to sacrifice his own personal interests for those of his friend. While Alexander's behavior with Hephaestion often lived up to some of Aristotle's loftiest requirements for true friendship, when it came to a clash of interests there can be little doubt as to who was uppermost in the king's mind.

*En route*, at the confluence of the Jhelum and the Chenab, the king's own ship was put in extreme danger by the swift and violent current.[49] Diodorus tells us that Alexander, with death staring him in the face, plummeted into the river where his friends were swimming alongside the ship in case it should capsize.[50] Both the king and his ship managed to make it ashore. This terrifying experience is reminiscent of a Homeric encounter wherein Alexander, like Achilles (*Il*. 21.228–382), struggles with a river and triumphs over it.

The Malli (Malavas), who provided Alexander's most formidable challenge in his trek toward Ocean, inhabited the region between the Chenab and the Ravi. They lived up to their reputation as ferocious warriors. Despite this, Alexander viciously suppressed any resistance and moved through the territory like a tornado. One of the cities east of the Ravi housed Brahmans, the priestly aristocratic class that provided much of the inspiration for the stiff opposition to the invaders, and against whom Alexander sometimes adopted a policy of extermination.[51]

In some instances the defenders burned their houses from the inside as their city was razed. This was typical of the type of uncompromising resistance that Alexander's men could expect to find throughout the remainder of this campaign. The enthusiasm of the troops was soon flagging again. During the assault on one Brahman town, it was Alexander himself who mounted the wall first, in order to shame his men into a more spirited attack.[52]

> may that man
> who this day
> wilfully hangs back
> from the fighting
> never win home again . . .
> but stay here
> and be made dogs' delight
> for their feasting
> (*Il*. 13.232–4)

Soon after, in Arrian's account of a famous and near-fatal episode, Alexander took it upon himself once again to provide the incentive against a besieged citadel.[53] Impatient at the perfunctory efforts of his soldiers, he seized one of the scaling ladders during a siege and, with his shield over his head, proceeded to lead the assault. With only a handful of alert attendants scurrying up the ladder after him, the king began to engage the enemy in intense fighting on top of the wall. Once they realized that their king was in jeopardy, his men rushed up the other two available ladders, only to overload and break them. Astride the battlements in his conspicuous panoply, and vulnerable to archers from several directions, Alexander jumped down inside the wall.

> Could not a god
> hurdle
> your city walls?
> (*Ba.* 654)

Three of the men who had made it to the top of the wall before the ladders collapsed jumped down inside with Alexander. They were Peucestas (a native of Mieza), Leonnatus, and a certain Abreas, a corporal in the infantry. Alexander fought furiously, killing several of the enemy, until the Brahmans attacked the intruders with every missile available. Abreas was killed almost instantly. Then Alexander was struck by a long, heavy Indian arrow with such force that it went through his cuirass and pierced his lung. With blood pouring out around the shaft, the king became faint and gradually collapsed behind his shield.

> Disaster caught his wits
> and his shining body
> went
> nerveless
> (*Il.* 16.805)

Peucestas raised the sacred shield of Troy over the king on one side while Leonnatus defended him on the other. Once it became clear that the king was inside the enemy's walls, his men desperately hammered makeshift pegs into the mud wall and climbed on top of one another to gain access to the top. When their fallen king was spotted, groans were mingled with a battle cry. The brute strength that makes its fleeting appearance in these times of crisis enabled them to bring down a big enough portion of the wall to permit their comrades to pour into the city. Every native man, woman, and child was slaughtered.[54]

Meanwhile, Alexander, perhaps closer to death than to life, was carried out on his shield. The shaft of the arrow was cut off with difficulty and his cuirass was removed. The arrowhead – 4 by 3 inches – had embedded itself above the nipple. Alexander ordered it cut out. Perdiccas operated with his sword, the blood gushed forth, and Alexander fell into a dead faint. This served to arrest the bleeding and probably saved his life. Critobulus, a physician from Cos who had treated Alexander's father and is mentioned as one of the trierarchs at the Jhelum,[55] tended to him for the next few days. It seemed unlikely that the king would survive.

> and the mist mantled over his eyes
> and the life left him

> but he got his breath
> back again
> (*Il.* 5.696–7)

Slowly, Alexander began to respond, but when news of the severity of the king's wound, and even rumors of his death,[56] reached his other troops – he customarily divided his forces when marching into hostile territory – an atmosphere of gloom and despair began to permeate the camp. Despite their bitter complaints about the king, they loved him and his indomitable spirit. It was an ambiguous, intense, family-like relationship, and with Alexander apparently on the verge of death, their love rose to the surface.

His men were also concerned about themselves. The king did not (nor would he ever) designate a successor, and once again they were surrounded by a fierce and able enemy. Past history, and an awareness that a tempest was brewing just below the royal level, led his men to believe that without Alexander there was a good chance that they would perish in the midst of the barbarian. Panic spread.

> you see an army mustered under arms
> stricken with panic
> before it lifts a spear
> This panic
> comes
> from
> Dionysus
> (*Ba.* 303–5)

Word that the king's condition had improved was met with disbelief, and even a letter of reassurance from the king himself was thought to have been forged by his top officers. This was a telling comment on the credibility that the rank and file now associated with information emanating from the highest circles.

Of necessity, and despite his still critical condition, Alexander insisted that he be transported downstream to the main camp so that his troops could bear witness to the fact that he was still alive. He was in such a fragile state, this being just seven days after the injury, that the vessels following his ship remained at a distance so that their oars would not interrupt the sleep necessary for his recuperation. With the deck cleared so that his troops might have an unobstructed view of him, Alexander appeared at camp where the Chenab and the Ravi meet. A crowd gathered on the shore and began to stare at the ship. Since he was motionless, the troops thought that they might be watching a corpse, until the king raised his hand and waved to them. The cheering crowd extended their hands toward heaven and Alexander.

> this man
> is out
> of
> another
> age
> than ours
> and
> one
> of
> the
> ancients
> (*Il.* 23.790)

Extremely weak from his massive blood loss, the king was carried to the shore on a stretcher and, at his own insistence, hoisted on to a horse. He rode to his tent, dismounted, and managed to stumble into his quarters. It was an incredible display of will power, which earned spontaneous applause and a garland of flowers from his troops. If any of the king's men still harbored reservations about Alexander's invincible nature, this performance must have removed those doubts.

> And yet the day of your death is near
> but it is not we
> who are to blame
> but
> a great god
> and
> powerful
> Destiny
> (*Il.* 19.409–10)

Among his friends, however, the prospect of Alexander's death brought home the precariousness of their own situation, and drew complaints about a king who was acting more like a soldier than a general. These remarks stung Alexander, who "was irritated . . . because he knew that they were true and that he had laid himself open to this censure. And yet his rage in battle and passion for glory made him like men overcome by any other form of pleasure, and he was not strong-minded enough to keep out of dangers" (A.6.13.4).

> Cursed courage
> (*Il.* 16.31)

Once again, Alexander's tutor Aristotle provides a yardstick by which we can measure the king. The philosopher says that true courage lies between rashness and fear.[57] Cowardice and disgrace should be avoided, but so should excessive fearlessness. The rash man "would be a sort of madman or insensible person if he feared nothing [and] . . . is also thought to be boastful and only a pretender to courage . . . the brave man *is* . . . the rash man wishes to *appear*; and so he imitates [the brave man] . . . in situations where he can."[58]

The virtuous man, Aristotle claims, "is his own best friend and therefore ought to love himself best."[59] He therefore "wishes to live with himself; for he does so with pleasure, since the memories of his past acts are delightful and his hopes for the future are good, and therefore pleasant."[60] Happy, he will find wounds and the prospect of death in war painful and contrary to his nature, but he will face them because it is virtuous to do so and ignoble not to. Someone lacking in nobility "does not seem to be amicably disposed even to himself, because there is nothing in him to love,"[61] and he might, perhaps, find death more welcome than life.

Alexander was infuriated at the charges of recklessness, but an older Boeotian on the expedition learned of the king's anger over these remonstrances and approached him on the subject. In his regional dialect, the man told the king: "Alexander, deeds are men's work" (A.6.13.5). He elaborated on his point by quoting a verse from Aeschylus to the effect that suffering was the price a man of accomplishment inevitably paid.[62] This line of thinking, which implied that lesser men would never understand his heroic nature, appealed to Alexander. He showed immediate approval of the sentiment and developed a close tie with the man who expressed it.

> For us there can be no design no purpose
> better than this one
> to close in
> and fight with the strength of our hands
> at close quarters
> (*Il.* 15.509–10)

As the king slowly recovered, he worked his way southward. Other Mallian tribes submitted to him, as did the Oxydracae, who lived south of the Malli. These people excused themselves for not capitulating sooner by explaining that they cherished freedom and self-government even more than the others, a "freedom they had preserved intact from the days when Dionysus came into 'India' until Alexander's time, but, if it so pleased Alexander, since the story prevailed that Alexander too was born to a god, they would accept a satrap whom Alexander might appoint, pay tribute determined by him, and also give as many hostages as he might require" (A.6.14.2).

The invading army encountered sporadic resistance in the winter of 326/ 325. In one of these attacks Ptolemy was hit by a poisoned arrow and came close to death himself. Alexander, it is reported, had a dream in which a snake directed him toward a plant that contained a cure.[63] Men were sent foraging about with a description of the plant in Alexander's dream. When it was discovered and used, Ptolemy showed signs of recovery. John W. Snyder reports that such a plant exists and contains *Rauwolfia serpentina*, a tranquilizer that has been used for thousands of years in the treatment of poisonous snakebite.[64]

It is reasonable to assume that Alexander and his men availed themselves of every opportunity to drink heavily during this arduous campaign. At one symposium a drunken Macedonian named Corragus challenged Dioxippus, an accomplished Athenian boxer, to single combat.[65] Dioxippus, who was well liked by the king but resented by some Macedonians because he was not a soldier, scoffed at the bravado but accepted the challenge. On the following day Corragus, fully armed, faced Dioxippus, who was smeared with oil, carried a club in his right hand and a purple cloth in his left, and wore a garland on his head. The deft athlete was able to disarm Corragus and would have beaten the man to death if it had not been for the intervention of the king.

Alexander was dismayed at the outcome, "for he feared that a mockery had been made of the celebrated Macedonian valour" (C.9.7.23). Courtiers attempting to please the king planted a golden cup in the boxer's room and publicly accused him of stealing it at another symposium. This affront was too much for the famous boxer to bear and he committed suicide, but not before writing a letter to the king. "Alexander was pained by his death, which he thought indicated resentment rather than remorse on Dioxippus' part, especially when the excessive jubilation of the men jealous of him revealed the falseness of the accusation against him" (C.9.7.26).[66]

Alexander continued his descent down the Indus until he reached its delta at Pattala (near Bahmanabad) in July 325. Nine months had elapsed since he departed from Nicaea on the Jhelum. At Pattala he began construction of a harbor and docks, although he initially lacked laborers because the local ruler, who had already submitted to Alexander, had evacuated the region in fear over the king's intentions. It was known that any sort of resistance to Alexander would be met with vicious repression, and fear of the invader soon spread throughout the region.

> You on the streets
> You on the roads
> Make way
> (*Ba.* 68–9)

When the king made it clear that everyone would be able to return safely, the vast majority of people in the area resumed a normal existence. The Indian campaign, however, was, as Tarn says, "unique in its dreadful record of mere slaughter."[67]

Alexander sailed down both branches of the Indus in order to determine which would be the safer outlet for the fleet, and ultimately used the western arm to reach the Arabian Sea. His ships, however, were badly damaged when they encountered severe storms during his first venture. After securing some Indian guides, and building new ships, they were faced with a previously unknown phenomenon – tidal changes. His naval officers, accustomed to the minimal fluctuation of the Mediterranean, experienced considerable embarrassment while attempting to contend with this problem. At one point the fleet was left stranded as the tide receded; when it returned many of the ships were wrecked or damaged.[68]

After putting in at a river island, Cilluta, Alexander sailed to an outlet into the sea to determine if the passageway could be used safely.[69] Another island farther out was sighted, and Alexander decided to continue on to it. For most other adventurers, reaching the world's edge would have been a source of joy, but for Alexander it was more like a hollow triumph. This was Ocean, but not at its easternmost point, which had been his aim.

Nevertheless, Alexander carried out the sacrifices mandated by Ammon for this special occasion.[70] He sailed out from the second island into the open sea to observe whether any country stood out nearby. None was visible, so Alexander slaughtered two bellowing bulls in honor of Poseidon and cast them into the sea. He then poured libations, threw the golden cup along with the golden bowls in which the wine was mixed out on to the waves, and prayed "that no man after him might ever pass beyond the bounds of his expedition" (P.66.2).

> and another man
> may shrink back
> from likening himself to me
> and contending
> against me
> (*Il.* 1.186–7)

Looking out across the Arabian Sea he may have pondered how striking and memorable his death would have been in that Malli town, and why he had been deprived of such a glorious and heroic exit.

> Because
> you
> cannot
> see
> (*Ba.* 210)

## THE GEDROSIAN DESERT (325 BC)

Disturbed by the multiplying problems in his intelligence system, increasing difficulties in communication, and rumors of the mismanagement and corruption of the satraps, the king began to sense some loss of control over his immense empire. During a conversation with Calanus, the Indian wise man reached for a dry and shrunken oxhide and placed it on the ground. When he stepped on or near its borders the hide would immediately rise up in some other area, but when he placed his full weight in the middle, the entire piece flattened out.[71] The moral of the exercise was to show Alexander that he would gain greater control over his empire by concentrating his authority at its center rather than at its edges. Prevented from continuing eastward by the refusal of his troops, and fearful of losing what he had already gained, the king decided to return to the west.

Before Alexander arrived at Pattala, Craterus was ordered to lead approximately half of the troops, including those unfit for combat, through the Bolan pass and westward to Carmania, subjugating any pockets of resistance along the way.[72] Instead of taking this route himself, the king had decided to lead his sturdiest men to Carmania across the harsh sands of the desert in southern Gedrosia (Baluchistan). This route would enable the king to establish dumps of food and supply fresh water to his fleet, which would sail from the mouth of the Indus to the Euphrates, thereby linking "India" and Babylonia. Alexander's sacrifices out in the open sea were an appeal to the gods for the safe voyage of this fleet.

Although he asked for divine help, Alexander took no chances. The king personally "sailed down again by the other [eastern] mouth . . . and discovered . . . that . . . [this] side was easier to navigate" (A.6.20.2–4). He made arrangements for the construction of another harbor on the lake which was on the eastern arm, and provided a garrison for the protection of the fleet. He then returned to Pattala.

Arrian's *Indica* (chapter 20) states that Alexander was preoccupied with the fate of his fleet from the time that this idea was conceived. The author cites Nearchus as saying "Alexander had a longing [*pothos*] to sail out into the sea and round from India to Persia, but was apprehensive of the length of the voyage and the risk that they would find a land uninhabited or destitute of roadsteads or inadequately provided with useful products, so that his whole fleet might be actually destroyed; such a sequel to his great achievements would be a serious stain on them and would obliterate his good fortune. Yet his perpetual desire to do something new and extraordinary won the day" (20.1–2). Despite the successful example provided by Scylax, which Alexander surely knew through Herodotus, it was still a perilous enterprise.[73]

he will learn his own strength
(*Il.* 8.535)

The king was also in a quandary over who would be in command of the voyage. There were considerable risks involved, and he needed an admiral whose presence would convince the sailors that they were not "being sent off without due thought into manifest danger" (20.3). Alexander and Nearchus discussed the candidates, but each, in turn, was rejected by Alexander either because "they were not willing to risk themselves for his sake, or as chickenhearted, or as mastered by a yearning [*pothos*] for

home, and [he] accused each of them of different faults" (20.4). Nearchus
then made his offer to lead the fleet himself, but Alexander protested
"that he would not allow one of his own friends to endure such hardships
and incur such danger" (20.6). Nearchus, we are told, "did not give up
for that reason but pressed more urgently, and so Alexander, well pleased
with his eagerness, appointed him admiral of the entire fleet" (20.6–7).
Alexander knew that those assigned to the fleet would be more optimistic
about their detail once it became clear that they were to be led by "the
last person Alexander would have exposed to an obvious danger unless
they were likely to come through safe" (20.8). His troops, placing their
faith "in Alexander's incalculable good fortune in other ventures . . .
thought that there was nothing that he might not both dare and carry
through" (20.11).

Arrian tells us that the prospect of leading a large force intact through
a territory that had devastated troops of illustrious predecessors offered
an irresistible lure to Alexander that far overshadowed any reservations.
His account is lent credence by that of Strabo, who tells us, on Nearchus'
authority, "that Alexander conceived an ambition to lead his army through
Gedrosia when he learned that both Semiramis and Cyrus had made an
expedition against the Indians, and that Semiramis had turned back in
flight with only twenty people and Cyrus with seven; and that Alexander
thought how grand it would be, when those had met with such reverses,
if he himself should lead a whole victorious army safely through the same
tribes and regions" (S.15.1.5). It was reminiscent of Alexander following
the traces of Perseus and Heracles into the Libyan Desert.

Leaving from the vicinity of modern Karachi and travelling westward,
Alexander crossed the boundary between "India" and Iran and, in a
murderous campaign, subdued the Oreitae, who had refused to submit to
him.[74] He appointed Apollophanes, a Macedonian, governor of the Orei-
tan territory and of Gedrosia, the satrapy he was about to enter. Leonnatus was assigned the dual tasks of maintaining security among the Oreitae
and completing the establishment of another Alexandria. Alexander then
marched south into Gedrosia and prepared himself for the fateful trek
across the region now known as the Makran.

The southwest monsoon delayed his fleet's sailing, and while Alexander
began his march from Pattala in mid-July, his ships did not get under way
until late October. When it became clear that there would be no rendezvous with Nearchus along the coast of the Makran, Alexander could only
speculate about what had happened to the vessels. He did not tarry for
long once an area had been stripped of all available provisions. Never
dilatory, Alexander elected to lead his troops from Jhau to Turbat, a 150-
mile march through treacherous territory that was lean in supplies and
virtually waterless. This leg was further complicated by the unbearable
heat.

Predictably, the march turned out to be a nightmare. Arrian describes it:

> [T]he scorching heat and want of water destroyed a great part of the army . . . the depth of the sand and its heat, burning as it was, and in most cases thirst as well brought about their destruction, as they even came across high hills of deep sand, not beaten down, but letting them sink in as they stepped on it, like liquid mud or . . . untrodden snow . . . . the lengths of the marches . . . did most to distress the army . . . . if the [night] march was prolonged by its length into the day, and they were caught still marching, then they were tormented in the grip of heat combined with ceaseless thirst . . . . Nor was it easy any longer to bring along the troops who were suffering . . . . some were left behind on the roads from sickness, others from weariness or heat or . . . thirst . . . . few out of many were saved: most of them were lost in the sand, like men who fall overboard at sea.
>
> (6.24.4–25.3)

Mules, creatures dear to Dionysus, and horses were killed and eaten without authorization by soldiers who falsely claimed that the beasts had perished from thirst or fatigue. Alexander was aware of this, but decided it was prudent to ignore it under the circumstances. The royal seals on supplies sent to the coast were broken open by "the guards themselves . . . [who] used the food, sharing it out among those suffering most from hunger" (A.6.23.4). Alexander chose to ignore this as well. Poisonous snakes presented a constant threat "for herbs grew on the sand-hills, and beneath these herbs the snakes had crept unnoticed; and they killed every person they struck" (S.15.2.7).

without
being seen
(*Ba.* 840)

A tragic scene was played out when the army rested in the vicinity of a torrent bed, which still contained a trace of water that had trickled down from the hills. The army, forced inland by the terrain, remained unaware of the rain that beat against the coastal side of the hills, unseen and unheard. The resultant flash flood carried away a sizable number of women and children, pack animals, wagons, and the king's personal gear. Soldiers grabbed what weapons they could lay their hands on and escaped with great difficulty.

When water was found, Alexander would keep his troops at a discreet distance so that they would not kill themselves through overindulgence (as some had), or pollute the water by rushing into it in full dress. The common problem was a parched palate, and here Arrian recounts a story concerning the king that he considers to be among the noblest tales told about his hero:[75]

Alexander himself was in the grip of thirst, and it was with much difficulty that he persisted in leading the way on foot, so that the rest of the troops should . . . bear their sufferings more easily, with all sharing the distress equally. At this moment some [men] . . . collected [a little water] . . . and hurried to Alexander, feeling that they were bringing something of great value, and, when they came near, poured the water into a helmet and offered it to the king. He took it and thanked them, but then poured it out in the sight of every one; and at this action the army was so much heartened that you would have guessed that all had drunk what Alexander had poured away.

(6.26.1–3)

The army wended its way through the Gedrosian Desert for 60 days.[76] At one point a sandstorm erased any recognizable landmarks, and the guides began to lead everyone farther inland. Alexander himself seized the initiative and, with a small detachment of horsemen, was able to locate the coastline. They found some fresh water as well, and for a week the army was able to travel along the coast, digging wells and enjoying an ample supply of water. The guides then picked up the trail to the Gedrosian capital, Pura. The bedraggled survivors of this horrible ordeal finally groped their way toward an inhabited land and relief.

The losses were staggering. Arrian comments that Alexander and his army "suffered more here than during all the rest of his expedition" (*Ind*.26.1). It has been reasonably estimated that Alexander began this journey with 60,000–70,000 soldiers, of whom 15,000 survived.[77] The Companion Cavalry, the king's *corps d'élite*, was reduced from 1,700 to 1,000 men. When one also takes into consideration the substantial number of non-combatant casualties, this was, without question, a *débâcle* of major proportion and without parallel in Alexander's career.[78] How can this tragic mistake be explained?

Badian has demolished the arguments of apologists who depict Alexander as the victim of unforeseen circumstances in a feasible operation. It is his assertion that Alexander was well aware of what he was getting himself into, but nevertheless remained determined to outdo the semi-mythical Babylonian queen, Semiramis, and Cyrus. Badian writes:

Imitation of heroes – Achilles, Heracles, Dionysus – had always been part of Alexander's personality. However rational and calculating in his methods, he was a mystic in his ultimate motivation. But this time there may be more to be added. His defeat by his own men had shaken his supernatural standing among men, and (worse still) his own belief in himself and his divine protection. What had happened since – the all but fatal wound that had restored his soldiers' love and loyalty; the conquest of southern India, which . . . was . . . [an] outstanding . . . achievement . . . had helped him recover. But something more striking was needed; a countervailing triumph to erase the memory. Nature and myth provided the challenge.[79]

The king emerged from the Gedrosian Desert without learning whether or not his fleet had survived its journey. By this time he was willing to believe the worst. Just as troubled about the fleet as he was about his debilitated land forces, Alexander was beginning to believe that his latest efforts were turning into an epic folly. Instead of erasing his humiliation at the Beas, this ill-conceived *pothos* could permanently sully his reputation.[80] Nearchus remained incommunicado, and the silence galvanized Alexander's insecurities.

In reality, there were times during the fleet's voyage when the king's anxiety might have proved to be prophetic. At one point Onesicritus attempted to persuade Nearchus to take a short cut across a "bay" in order to save time.[81] Nearchus rejected the suggestion on the grounds that they were under explicit orders to explore the coast. This "bay" turned out to be the Persian Gulf, and if the admiral had followed the royal steersman's advice, the fleet might have ended up hopelessly lost while unknowingly following the coast of the Arabian peninsula.

Although he too was plagued by grave problems, Nearchus managed to succeed in his mission and survive to write his recollections of it.[82] In Herodotean fashion he wrote of aboriginal men who ate ground fish and lived in huts constructed of whalebone. He also told of his encounter with a convoy of whales, which submerged when Nearchus and his men turned their ships toward them, splashed with their oars, and let out a loud battle cry. Nearchus reported that his men applauded the maneuver and praised their leader's courage and inventiveness.[83]

## CARMANIA (325–324 BC)

As soon as he reached Pura, the Gedrosian capital, Alexander planned to discharge Apollophanes, the province's recently appointed satrap, for failing to follow his order to supply the provisions that never arrived in the desert. This intention on the part of the king ignored the fact that Apollophanes' men would have found it next to impossible to ferret out Alexander and his troops during their journey. Alexander was obviously anxious to fix the responsibility for his own calamity on someone else. The king soon learned, however, that the Oreitae had revolted and that Apollophanes had been killed while attempting to suppress the insurrection. It was Leonnatus who sent Alexander news of both Apollophanes' death and of his own success against the enemy in the very same battle during which the satrap had fallen.[84]

The king was still disturbed by the events in the desert. Plutarch tells us that Abulites and Oxathres (father and son), the satraps of Susiana and Pareitacene, were among those who eventually faced the king's wrath.[85]

Abulites brought Alexander 3,000 talents in coin instead of supplies, apparently assuming that whatever he could supply otherwise would be of little use to the king. Alexander had the money thrown to some horses, which ignored it, and asked the satrap if he now understood what good money was to him and his men. Abulites was imprisoned and executed. His son was killed by the king himself. Presumably sober, but infuriated, the king grabbed a Macedonian pike and ran Oxathres through, just as he had slain Cleitus.

J. R. Hamilton cautions against rejecting this account and relying exclusively upon Arrian, who offers a terse rendition of these events. Hamilton concludes that "the suspicion must remain that Alexander was still [later], in Susa, seeking a scapegoat for a disaster for which he was largely responsible and which seriously damaged his reputation for invincibility."[86]

In Carmania Alexander was greeted by Stasanor and the Persian Pharasmanes. They brought pack animals and camels, which could have made a critical difference in the desert. Alexander and Craterus were also reunited. His general brought the other half of the army through virtually intact, and recounted the details of an uprising in Drangiana with which he had successfully dealt.

News from elsewhere was far more disturbing. Charges of large-scale extortion, the mistreatment of subjects, and even the plundering of tombs by his own officials came to the king's attention. It had been more than two years since Alexander had crossed the Hindu Kush into "India," and those who knew his intrepid nature might have assumed that he had perished – or would soon perish – heroically against some obscure and remote enemy. Flagrant abuses were widespread, and some of the king's highest officials were accused of insubordination and embezzlement.

Harpalus, the Royal Treasurer, maintained a private army and drew freely from Alexander's monies.[87] Idiosyncratic in many respects, he imported Pythonice, an attractive Athenian courtesan, and kept her in regal splendor at Babylon. When she died, Harpalus dedicated a temple to her in the name of Pythonice Aphrodite that was said to have cost him (or rather, the king) 200 talents. Glycera ("Sugar"), Pythonice's successor, was ensconced at Tarsus, where the Treasurer spent most of his time, and visitors were required to perform *proskynesis* in her presence. Harpalus did provide grain for Athens during several years of severe famine (330–326), and was granted Athenian citizenship as a gesture of the city's gratitude. At Alexander's suggestion, Harpalus transplanted Greek flora into Babylon's Hanging Gardens. The plants and shrubs flourished in the royal gardens with one notable exception – ivy![88]

Rumors of Harpalus' behavior reached Alexander in "India," but there was little he could do about it until his return to the West.[89] Before the end of 324, a satyr play, Python's *Agen*, was put on at Alexander's court. It portrayed Harpalus using the Magi to conjure up the spirit of Pythonice.[90] Some time would elapse before the king would learn the full scope of his Treasurer's activities, and by then it would be impossible to grant his friend yet another pardon.

Reports of misconduct were rampant. Alexander, Arrian tells us, "is said at this time to have grown quicker to give credit to accusations, as if they were reliable in all circumstances, and to punish severely those who were convicted even of slight faults on the ground that in the same frame of mind they might commit grave crimes" (7.4.3).

> Bacchic violence
> spreads
> (*Ba.* 778–79)

During the next few months six satraps were deposed. All but one (Apollophanes, who had already died in battle) were executed. Several high-ranking officers were summoned to the king's court, only to meet the same fate in what has been described by Badian as a "reign of terror."[91] According to Arrian the king had become *oxyteros* ("harsher").[92] He was now capable of the same kind of dissimulation as his father. He masked his anger against Astaspes, the satrap of Carmania, who was suspected of entertaining notions of revolt. When the conditions were favorable, however, Alexander executed him.[93]

> Descend from Olympus lord
> Come whirl your wand of gold
> and quell with death
> this beast of blood
> whose violence
> abuses man
> and
> god
> (*Ba.* 553–5)

He summoned officers from Media. Among them were the same men who had been involved in the assassination of Parmenio.[94] The most prominent commanders were the Thracian Sitalces and Cleander, the brother of the same Coenus who had opposed Alexander at the Beas. They were ordered to have most of their troops accompany them. The Medians, following close behind, indicted these generals with charges that were subsequently corroborated by Macedonian soldiers (many of whom still resented the way in which Parmenio met his fate). The question was whether the king would, under the present circumstances, grant immunity to men who had done him such a special service in disposing of Parmenio. Sitalces and Cleander, however, were executed "to make the other[s] . . . fear that if they committed the like crimes they would suffer the like fate" (A.6.27.4).[95]

> his purposes are fierce
> like a lion
> who when he has given way
> to his own great strength
> and his haughty spirit
> goes among the flocks of men
> to devour them
> (*Il.* 24.40–3)

A certain Heracon was among the generals from Media who stood accused. He was initially, we are told, cleared of charges that he had abused the Median populace. He would not, however, like many others previously accused and acquitted of serious crimes on the expedition, survive Alexander. Heracon was later arrested for pillaging the temple at Susa, convicted of that charge, and killed. If the allegation concerning the desecration of the temple was valid, it meant that this man had learned nothing at all from the fate of those recently convicted of the very same crime and executed. Ignorance of this magnitude would make him a dense man indeed.

> Achilleus
> has destroyed pity
> and there is not
> in him
> any
> shame
> (*Il.* 24.44–5)

Curtius, who says that the fourth of the generals from Media was named Agathon, also tells us that 600 of the 6,000 troops accompanying the officers were executed as accessories in a literal decimation.[96] He adds that after examining the evidence (which included the rape by Cleander of a virgin from an aristocratic family), Alexander pointed out that the prosecutors had overlooked the most important of all charges, "namely the defendants' assumption that he [Alexander] would not survive. For, he said, men wishing or believing that he would safely return from India would never have ventured upon such crimes" (10.1.7).

A number of the prominent officials killed during this cycle of brutal punishments clearly served as scapegoats for the king's *débâcle* in the desert. Another motivation for the purge, Badian suggests, may have been fear.[97] The events at the Beas River had conjured up an ominous specter in Alexander's mind, that of his own officers and men finding common ground against him. Could it have been merely coincidental, regardless of the nature and validity of the charges against Cleander, that once the king set foot in habitable Iran, Coenus' brother was called to court, subsequently declared guilty, and executed? The conduct of his

Imperial Treasurer may also have led Alexander to suspect that there was a much larger plot afoot, since Coenus, Cleander, and Harpalus all belonged to a royal family originating in the Macedonian "out-kingdom" of Elimiotis.[98]

Some of the king's concerns, however, were more real than imagined. During Alexander's absence several of his satraps, perhaps looking to protect themselves from one another should the king die, had been enlarging the ranks of the mercenary soldiers at their disposal. Another threat posed by hired soldiers had recently become clear to the king when the report reached him that Philip, his satrap for the northwestern portion of his Indian conquests, had been killed by his own mercenaries.[99] While still in Carmania and reflecting over the implications of all this, he decided to order his satraps to dismiss all of their mercenaries.[100] This action, which removed any immediate threat to the king, inevitably caused grievous problems throughout the empire.[101]

Every major source refers to a spectacular Dionysiac festival in Carmania,[102] a land producing vines "thick with large grapes" (S.15.2.14), to celebrate the survival of those who emerged from the desert. Plutarch says that the whole army participated in what is described as:

> [A] kind of Bacchanalian procession. Alexander himself feasted continually, day and night, reclining with his Companions on a dais built upon a high and conspicuous rectangular platform [*thymele* = an altar, for example one of Dionysus in the theater], the whole structure being slowly drawn along by eight horses. Innumerable waggons followed the royal table, some of them covered with purple or embroidered canopies, others shaded by the boughs of trees, which were constantly kept fresh and green: these vehicles carried the rest of Alexander's officers, all of them crowned with flowers and drinking wine. Not a single helmet, shield or spear was to be seen, but along the whole line of the march the soldiers kept dipping their cups, drinking-horns or earthenware goblets into huge casks and mixing-bowls and toasting one another, some drinking as they marched, others sprawled by the wayside, while the whole landscape resounded with the music of pipes and flutes, with harping and singing and the cries of women rapt with the divine frenzy. Not only drinking but all the other forms of bacchanalian license attended this straggling and disorderly march, as though the god [Dionysus] himself were present to lead the revels.

(67.2–6)

Breaking off
a tiny fragment
of that ether
which surrounds
the world
he molded

from it

a

dummy

Dionysus

(*Ba.* 292–4)

Arrian believed this less-than-flattering story to be unreliable;[103] Curtius thought it quite credible but reprehensible. A thousand sober men, he conjectured, "could have captured this group on its triumphal march, weighed down as it was from seven days of drinking" (9.10.27). The somber Roman historian moralizes that fortune "allots fame and a price to things, and she turned even this piece of disgraceful soldiering into a glorious achievement!" (9.10.28). A Roman army, he seems to imply, would never have been guilty of such a lack of discipline. In discussing Curtius' account, Badian acknowledges his embellishments, but says that "the facts should be accepted, especially in view of Alexander's life-long love–hate relationship with Dionysus."[104]

Arrian will admit only that Alexander sacrificed in gratitude "for his conquest of India and his army's safe transit through Gadrosia [*sic*], that he conducted musical and athletic games, and that he enrolled Peucestas as an additional bodyguard" (6.28.3). Peucestas was honored for his valor against the Mallians on Alexander's behalf. The king was so grateful that he increased the traditional number of bodyguards from seven to eight to accommodate him.[105] In this way Peucestas joined the ranks of some of the king's favorites, which included Leonnatus, Hephaestion, Lysimachus, Perdiccas, and Ptolemy.

When Alexander had all but despaired of the fleet, his admiral finally appeared on the scene, but under circumstances of mistaken identity and recognition that read like a Homeric epic with Nearchus as the hero.[106] Nearchus reached the area of the Persian Gulf near the Strait of Hormuz around December 325, beached his ships, and set out on foot to find his king. Understandably pessimistic after his experience in the Makran, Alexander at first thought that the news of Nearchus' appearance was a false rumor and arrested the satrap responsible for circulating fallacious reports. The king's scouts actually passed right by Nearchus and his travelling companions. They assumed that these men, all of whom were bearded, wizened, and briny, were vagrants.

When Nearchus and Alexander were reunited, the king initially failed to recognize his admiral.[107] Once Nearchus' identity had been established, Alexander jumped to the conclusion that these ragamuffins were the sole survivors of the journey, and that the rest of his naval expedition had been lost. Alexander "did not feel so much pleasure at the safe arrival of Nearchus . . . as pain at the loss of all his force" (A.*Ind.*35.2). He wept for what appeared to be an "utter disaster," gave Nearchus his right hand, and led him outside, out of earshot of the others, to hear the grim details.

When Nearchus revealed that the fleet was virtually intact and being repaired at that very moment, the king wept again, this time for joy. As mentioned earlier, Alexander's fear, according to Arrian (based on Nearchus), was that "such a sequel [as the destruction of an entire fleet] to his great achievements would be a serious stain on them [him] and would obliterate his good fortune" (A.*Ind*.20.2).

It seemed too good to be true. Alexander swore "by Zeus of the Greeks and the Libyan Ammon that he really rejoiced more at the news than at having come as a conqueror through all Asia, since the distress he had felt at the supposed loss of the fleet actually balanced all his other good fortune" (A.*Ind*.35.8). Sacrifices in gratitude for the safe return of the expedition were offered in honor of Zeus the Saviour, Heracles, Apollo the Averter of Evil, Poseidon, and all of the other sea gods.[108]

He is mocking me
(*Ba*. 503)

The admiral was showered with flowers and ribbons in a festive procession, and afterward Alexander informed him that someone else would have to take the fleet to Susa, since he refused to let his friend run such risks again. Nearchus responded by saying that he would, of course, obey any orders from Alexander, but that if the king was inclined to grant him a favor, he could do so by permitting him to complete his mission in guiding the fleet to Susa. "Let it not be said that you entrusted me with the difficult and desperate work, but that the easy task, with fame sure to follow, was taken away and put into another's hands" (A.*Ind*.36.6). The king appreciated his argument and reluctantly complied with the request. Nearchus was escorted to the coast and set sail once again.

During a celebration held at this time, after Alexander "had drunk well" (P.67.8), he went to watch some singing and dancing competitions.[109] The eunuch Bagoas, a favorite of the king's as he had been of Darius III, was awarded first prize in the dance segment. Garlanded, and wearing his victor's crown as well as his costume, Bagoas took a seat of honor next to the king. The Macedonians erupted into spontaneous applause and urged the king to bestow a kiss upon the winner. Alexander wrapped his arms around Bagoas and kissed him, to the utter delight of his fellow celebrants. In the midst of the revelry everyone was able for the moment to escape the memory of those thousands of men left in the desert. The gift of Dionysus had the power to transform the past into a tolerable recollection.

the gladness
of
the
grape
(*Ba*. 423)

The Makran had taken its toll on Alexander. While he was able to create the illusion that this disaster was a victory, the reality of the experience had been burned indelibly into him and now contributed to the way in which he saw himself. Too grim to be faced squarely, the anxiety it engendered surfaced in other ways. Peter Green offers a subtle analysis of the nature of the change that had taken place in Alexander:

> [T]he man who burnt Persepolis was also the boy who had destroyed Thebes. From the very beginning his ambition had been insatiable, and murderous when thwarted. But in any consideration of his later years, the combined effects of unbroken victories, unparalleled wealth, power absolute and unchallenged, continual heavy physical stress, and incipient alcoholism cannot be lightly set aside. Abstemious as a boy, he now regularly drank to excess. Nor was it political pressure alone which now dictated the king's actions, but his own increasingly dominant and uncontrollable megalomania.[110]

Neglectful of Dionysus in his earlier years and intermittently irreverent toward him later on, Alexander had come to appreciate the way in which the god might be used to underscore the magnitude of his own accomplishments. This is not to support the claims of some modern scholars that the king saw himself as a new Dionysus.[111] Such contentions defy both the sources and the man's self-conception. Alexander seems to have treated the god in very much the same fashion as he treated any of his underlings, as a useful pawn in the achievement of his own objectives. It was no concern of his that the youngest of the Olympians, conceived by a mortal and insecure in his divinity, could be unspeakably vicious to mortals who resisted him. Yet, heroes had been known to feel the sting of this invisible enemy against whom courage and will of the sort Alexander had displayed were of little avail.

> Slow
> but unmistakable
> the might of the gods
> moves on
> It punishes
> that man
> infatuate of soul
> and
> hardened in
> his
> pride
> who
> disregards
> the
> gods
> (*Ba.* 882–7)

Even Bagoas was ultimately involved in the king's satrapal purge. Orsines, who was said to be a descendant of Cyrus, had assumed the satrapy of Persis while Alexander was in "India" "not by appointment of Alexander, but because he felt that he was the right person, in the absence of any other governor, to keep the Persians in order for Alexander" (A.6.29.2). Curtius tells us that Orsines honored the king and his entourage with handsome gifts including "herds of horses . . . chariots trimmed with silver and gold . . . fine jewels, heavy gold vessels, purple garments and 3,000 talents of silver coin" (10.1.24), but that he neglected to include Bagoas in his presentations. When this was pointed out to the self-made satrap, he answered "that he paid his respects to the king's friends, not his whores, and that it was not the Persian custom to regard as men those who allowed themselves to be sexually used as women" (10.1.26). Bagoas responded by maligning Orsines whenever the opportunity presented itself. He even claimed that his denigrator had removed 3,000 golden talents from the tomb of Cyrus.

Arrian states that Orsines was accused of plundering temples, rifling ancient tombs, and putting Persians to death unjustly,[112] a familiar litany of charges by this time. We can never be sure whether his own wrongdoings, calumny on the part of Bagoas, or the king's alarm at Orsines' self-confidence caused the man to be hanged. Perhaps all three elements contributed.

the

terror

was

on

them

all

(*Il.* 18.247)

Aristobulus tells us that even before he had entered the satrapy of Persis, the king had decided to turn it over to Peucestas.[113] Peucestas was not promoted to satrap just because he had saved the king's life. It was also in recognition of the enthusiasm with which he had adopted Persian customs. In his new role Peucestas wore Persian dress and communicated in the native language, something that even the king himself was apparently unable to do. His willingness to adapt so completely was compatible with the king's intentions, and may have also made him more palatable to the Persians. It did not, we may surmise, sit all that well with other Macedonians.

## PERSIS (324 BC)

Alexander arrived in Persis early in 324. As he entered, he observed the royal custom of distributing money to the women of the province.[114]

Through this act he honored the role that women were said to have played in the consolidation of Cyrus the Great's monarchy, and served notice that he intended to reinforce his image as the legitimate Persian monarch. The king's disappearance into "India" and protracted absence had encouraged rebellion and dereliction of duty. Now, more than ever, it was necessary to convince his Iranian subjects that their Greek-speaking king was not an ephemeral phenomenon.

The Asiatic flavor of Alexander's court became more distinct as he travelled between the ancestral capitals of the empire during the next year and a half. Persian ostentation, which was perverse by Greek standards and earlier had been the object of the king's own sarcasm, became commonplace.[115] Alexander, to the dismay of his soldiers, routinely wore a Persian white-striped tunic and diadem to complement the traditional Macedonian dress. His grand entertainments, which were in keeping with the image he wished to project, seem to have fed his megalomaniacal tendencies.

The accomplishments of the king's Indian expedition were now celebrated as superior to those of Dionysus. Alexander enjoyed this favorable comparison to the god. He also apparently delighted in appearing as one of the gods. Ephippus, an eyewitness, says that the king had taken to dressing in the characteristic costumes of various divinities and then playing the appropriate role. He writes:

> Alexander also wore the sacred vestments at his dinner-parties, at one time putting on the purple robe of Ammon, and thin slippers and horns just like the god's, at another time the costume of Artemis, which he often wore even in his chariot, wearing the Persian garb and showing above the shoulders the bow and hunting-spear of the goddess, while at still other times he was garbed in the costume of Hermes . . . on social occasions he wore the winged sandals and broad-brimmed hat on his head, and carried the caduceus in his hand; yet often, again, he bore the lion's skin and club in imitation of Heracles.[116]

Alexander's thoughts were never far from the slopes of Olympus, and he seems to have welcomed this type of retreat from the tedium of administration. At play, he could masquerade as his own divine father, or flaunt the attributes of an intrepid ancestor, or even, if he chose to, parade in the sacred attire of Apollo's sister Artemis.[117]

First

. . .

you must
dress yourself
in women's clothes
(*Ba.* 821)

He could imagine himself as Hermes, the messenger of the gods, who

was swifter than all of the others and, if the situation required it, invisible.
It was, of course, this very same deity who had shepherded young Dionysus to safety and, as Psychopompus, escorted dead souls down to the
netherworld.

here I am
dressed in the costume
of the god
prepared
to
go
(*Ba.* 180)

Unintentionally, the king now bore a greater resemblance to Dionysus
than to any of the other Olympians he had elected to imitate.[118] In Iran
Alexander was an exotic foreigner who had appeared out of a distant land
and established his ascendancy through might and magic. He came and
went with startling rapidity, leaving countless victims strewn in his path.
Loyal subjects were rewarded extravagantly, and enemies punished with
merciless severity. Attentive and courteous toward women, Alexander
earned their devotion through his consideration and benevolence. Like
Dionysus, he too seems to have made plans for his own mother's apotheosis.

You do not know
the limits of your strength
You do not know what you do
You do not know
who you are
(*Ba.* 506)

The king moved in and out of his roles with mercurial aloofness, exhibiting
a metamorphic quality that was distinctly Dionysiac. Furthermore, in his
last few years, he could be seen garlanded and flushed with wine more
frequently than in earlier days of glory.

possessed
by
Dionysus
(*Ba.* 119)

## CYRUS' TOMB (324 BC)

Early in 324 the king discovered firsthand that the tomb of Cyrus the
Great at Pasargadae had been ransacked and resealed by its violators.[119]
Cyrus' corpse was dislodged during what turned out to be futile attempts

to remove his golden sarcophagus from the tomb. The dead king's bones were left unceremoniously scattered about the floor.

Alexander, who held Cyrus in high esteem, was shaken by the discovery of this spoliation. Aristobulus was ordered to return the salvageable parts of the body to the sarcophagus, restore the tomb, wall it up, and set the royal seal in clay at the entrance. Alexander had the Persian inscription on the tomb copied in Greek letters below the original. It read, " 'O man, whoever you are and wherever you come from, for I know you will come, I am Cyrus who won the Persians their empire. Do not therefore grudge me this little earth that covers my body.' These words made a deep impression on Alexander, since they reminded him of the uncertainty and mutability of mortal life" (P.69.4–5).

> They humble us with death
> that we remember
> what we are
> who are not god
> but men
> (*Ba.* 1002–3)

The king was determined to punish those involved in this outrage, but the interrogation and torture of the Magi (who were responsible for safeguarding the tomb) failed to produce any reliable information. It was at this point that Bagoas seized the opportunity to undo the man who had treated him with contempt. According to Curtius, he bribed witnesses to swear that Orsines had played a role in the desecration.[120] Alexander believed the accusations and had the self-appointed satrap, together with Polymachus, a Macedonian from Pella,[121] executed for plundering the tomb. Curtius remarks in this context that "Alexander had begun to be quick to order summary execution and also to believe the worst of people" (10.1.39).

Harpalus, who had heard of the ruthless way in which Alexander was now meting out justice to anyone suspected of insubordination or graft, decided to flee to Europe.[122] He left with 5,000 talents, 6,000 mercenaries, and his consort, "Sugar." Harpalus headed for Athens, which had granted him citizenship, where he hoped to find allies to defend him against the king. However, his "fellow Athenians" refused to allow him to enter the city until he had deposited his mercenaries elsewhere. Harpalus complied with their request and brought 700 talents into Athens, only to find himself imprisoned while envoys were sent to Alexander to ask what should be done with him. Harpalus managed to escape to Crete, where he was ultimately assassinated by one of his underlings.

Death was in the air. Calanus, the Indian philosopher who had joined the expedition in the Punjab, fell ill in Persis. Ignoring the king's entreaties, Calanus, who was 73 years of age, informed Alexander that he intended to cremate himself rather than witness the deterioration of his corporeal envelope.[123] The king's vigorous protestations fell on deaf ears, and Ptolemy was ordered to build a funeral pyre for the philosopher's self-immolation. Calanus rode on horseback up to the structure, said a prayer, poured a libation, and cut off a lock of his own hair to throw on the pyre. He urged the Macedonians present "to make this a day of gaiety and celebration and to drink deep with the king, whom, he said, he would soon see in Babylon" (P.69.7).[124] Calanus then reclined, covered himself, and waited unflinchingly for the approaching flames to consume him.

Alexander commemorated his friend's demise at the funeral pyre. Chares, the king's chamberlain, who was probably an eyewitness, said that Alexander then proposed a drinking contest, whereby the winner would receive a talent, the second best half a talent, and so forth.[125] Thirty-five participants are reported to have died as an immediate by-product of their excessive consumption of uncut wine, and six more died in the aftermath. The victor is said to have drunk 12 quarts, received his talent, and died four days later.

> Do not let
> his fate
> be
> yours
> (*Ba.* 341)

Shortly thereafter the king was reminded of the grave consequences of his own drinking six years before. Arrian tells us that on his way to Susa the king passed through Persepolis and saw the remains of "the Persian palace to which he himself had formerly set fire, as I related while expressing my condemnation of his act. In fact Alexander himself did not approve [of] it on his return" (6.30.1). He did not tarry in the rubble. This was not to be the sole occasion upon which Alexander experienced remorse as a result of his drinking.

> He walks among
> the ruins
> he
> has made
> (*Ba.* 602–3)

Nevertheless, as Bosworth tells us, "The intemperance of the court was now assuming legendary proportions, and the excesses of the transit of Carmania were to recur periodically throughout Alexander's last months of life."[126]

In March 324, as the king approached Susa, he was joined by Nearchus, who had succeeded in exploring the Persian Gulf as far north as the Euphrates, and had then sailed up the Pasitigris for his rendezvous with Alexander.[127] The arrival of the fleet and success of his admiral's mission relieved the king's anxiety and warranted yet another joyous celebration.

Leonnatus also appeared, and Alexander held ceremonies signaling an official end to the Indian expedition. Hephaestion and all of the body-guards were presented with golden crowns, and Peucestas and Leonnatus were singled out for their heroism in saving the king's life in "India." Nearchus and Onesicritus each received a similar distinction for leading the fleet on its epochal voyage.

## SUSA (324 BC)

A festive spirit suffused the atmosphere at Susa. The most extraordinary of the events that occurred in the early spring of 324 involved a five-day celebration. It featured the marriage of more than ninety of the most prominent Macedonians and Greeks, including Alexander and Hephaestion, to Iranian women of royal and aristocratic blood.[128] While remaining married to Roxane, Alexander took two other wives: Stateira, the late Persian king's eldest daughter, and Parysatis, the daughter of Artaxerxes III (Ochus). The king thus associated himself with both of the royal houses from which the last two Achaemenid rulers had emerged, and echoed his father's polygamous diplomacy. On the personal side, Hephaestion was married to Drypetis, the sister of Alexander's bride Stateira, so that, we are told, their children would be related to one another.[129]

> In the other corner
> Patroklos went to bed
> with him also was a girl . . .
> whom brilliant Achilleus
> gave him
> (*Il.* 9.666–7)

Alexander arranged all of the other matches as well. The list of bride-grooms reads like a roll call of those men who were closest to the king during the year before his death. Craterus married the niece of Darius III; Perdiccas, the daughter of the satrap of Media; and Ptolemy and Eumenes each married a daughter of Artabazus. Nearchus married a daughter (by Mentor) of Barsine, who had been Alexander's first mistress. The king endowed each of the brides with a handsome dowry, and the ceremonies were conducted according to Persian tradition.

An account based on Chares, who may have attended personally to the details, describes the scene:

[H]e concluded marriages of himself and of his friends besides, con-structing ninety-two bridal chambers in the same place. The structure was large enough for a hundred couches,[130] and in it every couch was adorned with nuptial coverings, and was made of silver . . . but his own couch had supports of gold. He also included in his invitation to the banquet all his personal friends and placed them on couches opposite himself and the other bridegrooms, while the rest of his forces, both land and naval, he entertained in the courtyard with the foreign embassies and tourists . . . . the structure was decorated sumptuously and magnificently with expensive draperies and fine linens, and underfoot with purple and crimson rugs interwoven with gold . . . . there were columns thirty feet high, gilded and silvered and studded with jewels. The entire enclosure was surrounded with rich curtains having animal patterns interwoven in gold, their rods being overlaid with gold and silver. The perimeter of the courtyard measured four stadia. The call to dinner was sounded on the trumpet, not only at the time of the nuptial banquets, but always when on other occasions he chanced to be making libation, so that the entire army knew what was going on . . . . [V]ery many persons . . . contributed their services . . . the jugglers from India . . . . [harpists, flutists, singers, dancers] . . . . And from that day forth the people who had previously been called "Dionysus-flatterers" were called "Alexander-flatterers" because of the extravagant presents in which Alexander took such delight.[131]

Tragedies and comedies were performed by some of the best actors available, including the inveterate Thessalus. Every guest at the symposium received a gold cup as a memento of the affair.

W. W. Tarn saw the mass marriages as a noble and prescient gesture on Alexander's part to cultivate a vision of the brotherhood of humanity,[132] but Badian's analysis of the evidence concludes that such an assertion is untenable.[133] A number of other modern scholars have interpreted these marriages as a dramatic illustration of Alexander's policy of fusion.[134] The most convincing of these interpretations, that of J. R. Hamilton, sees Alexander commingling the European and Asian elite in order to administer his pluralistic state more effectively.[135] This view enjoys some support from the sources, and speaks of a more pragmatic than ideological Alexander when it came to dealing with the problems of governance.

A. B. Bosworth, however, has raised serious objections to the assumption that a policy of fusion in any form ever existed.[136] He points out that the general rule was to keep Macedonians and Persians separated from one another. Alexander himself waited until 324 to connect himself to the Achaemenid dynasty through marriage. Furthermore, if a process of fusion was, in fact, envisioned, why were there no unions between Asiatic men and European women? All indications, Bosworth claims, suggest that Alexander fully intended to rule the Persian Empire through his Macedonian marshals. The Susa marriages merely served to authenticate their position in the eyes of Iranians, just as Alexander's marriage to Stateira and Parysatis helped to make his regime appear legitimate.[137]

Admittedly, the king was anything but discriminatory in dispensing royal largesse. Moreover, he had by this time integrated Persians into his army, from the squadron level up to and including his command structure.

Alexander's willingness to assimilate Asiatics, however, is better explained, Bosworth suggests, by practical necessity than by any application of humanitarian principles. Bosworth asserts that Alexander would have willingly replaced the Iranian rank and file in his key units with compatriots trained in his own system had enough Macedonians been available. But a manpower shortage dictated the utilization of Asiatic subjects. Alexander played his Iranians off against his Macedonians, and attempted to integrate those conquered while simultaneously fostering a division that encouraged a climate of competition. In the end, everyone's best efforts would be used to further royal intentions.

Alexander continued to underestimate the intensity of Macedonian contempt for the whole process of orientalization. His incorporation of Asiatics into the army offended the Macedonians, who "thought that Alexander was going utterly barbarian at heart, and treating Macedonian customs and Macedonians themselves without respect" (A.7.6.5). They were, it seems, "greatly pained to see Alexander wearing the Median dress, while the marriages celebrated in the Persian style did not correspond to the desires of most of them, including even some of the bridegrooms, despite the great honour of being raised to equality with the king" (A.7.6.2).

The Susa marriages may have had a significance that the king thought best to keep to himself. The offspring of these unions could never hope to be fully accepted in either Europe or Asia. If Alexander, who had, in a sense, engineered their births, had survived, he would have been seen as a patriarchal godfather of sorts, a benevolent patron toward whom they had to look for any recognition and encouragement. This next generation of leaders, who would have been seen as a race apart, would have no choice but to feel indebted to the king and obliged to display exceptional interest in his success and well being.[138]

Alexander also publicly acknowledged the marriages of his common soldiers at Susa and rewarded them with gifts. The gifts they received, however, were contingent upon registration,[139] which probably included identifying the gender, name, and number of their offspring. Like Philip, Alexander had become accustomed to harboring a private agenda when it came to public action.

Whatever Alexander's intentions, his marshals did not dare to raise objections to their matches while the king was alive. Once he was dead, however, they were able to reveal their true feelings toward this idea, and it seems that all of them, with the exception of Seleucus, discarded their Asiatic wives. Seleucus had married Spitamenes' daughter, and possibly stayed with his bride because he found that she was extremely useful in consolidating a troublesome portion of the empire he had carved out for himself.

At Susa the king offered to settle the outstanding debts of all of his troops,[140] presumably to cultivate a better rapport with his men. But a general suspicion spread throughout the ranks that this was a ruse, and that the king merely wanted to identify those who were in debt. Thus, only a handful of men stepped forward to take advantage of the king's generosity. An embarrassed and angry Alexander chided them for a lack of faith in him. Arrian quotes him as exclaiming that "the king . . . must always speak the truth to his subjects, and none of the subjects must ever suppose that the king speaks anything but the truth" (7.5.2).

Seasoned veterans must have exchanged astonished looks of disbelief. It was not until Alexander announced that he no longer required their names, but merely an IOU for reimbursement, that the soldiers surged forward to have their debts liquidated. Arrian informs us that "they were more gratified by the concealment of their names than by the extinction of the debts" (7.5.3). This whole business cost the king at least 9,870 talents.[141]

Whatever popularity Alexander may have gained through this magnanimous gesture was soon lost when 30,000 young Iranian men appeared.[142] Recruited in the northeastern provinces six years before, they had been put through a rigorous apprenticeship that included Macedonian military training and the Greek language. Dressed in Macedonian clothing and wielding their own *sarissae* (pikes), these young men put on a display of precision marching. Their enthusiasm, agility, and proficiency earned effusive praise from the king. He referred to them as *Epigoni* ("Successors"). This was no doubt taken as a warning by his Macedonians that they were no longer irreplaceable.

The shocked and furious Macedonians referred contemptuously to their Asiatic counterparts as "war-dancers." They were obviously concerned about whether the king would actually contemplate replacing them with barbarians. As we have seen, Asiatic troops had been incorporated into the army for some time, and the process of "barbarization" had perplexed and disturbed the Macedonians. The king's primary concern, however, seems to have been, as Bosworth suggests, to maintain adequate manpower to execute his plans.[143] To accomplish this he had to draw on the Asian population. Otherwise he would have drained Macedonia of its fighting force, and his homeland, unable to defend itself, would have recalled him to Europe. This eventuality would have spelled doom for Alexander's Asian Empire.

The "Successors" helped to safeguard against that prospect. They also served as hostages from a distant region and from people likely to cause Alexander trouble. Furthermore, like Macedonian Royal Pages, these young Iranians had been separated from their own moorings. They were encouraged to direct their loyalties and allegiance toward Alexander, and to remember that any prestige or success they achieved would hinge upon the approval and favor of the king and his officer class.

Although it might appear otherwise, Greece was not altogether forgotten by the king. At Susa, in an astonishing move, he ordered the Greek city-states to repatriate all of their exiles.[144] This resulted in a complex process of reabsorption. Among those included were countless numbers of Greek mercenaries, who had recently been disbanded by royal decree in Asia, and many anti-Macedonian exiles who were expelled under the influence of Philip or Alexander in prior years. Once Alexander's father had gained some degree of control over Greece through the Corinthian League, he had forbidden cities to engage in the practice of exiling undesirables. Alexander's measure went one step beyond his father's. It required these cities to take back all but the most objectionable of their own refugees.

At the Olympic Games in the summer of 324, Alexander's envoy, Nicanor of Stagira, who became Aristotle's son-in-law, proclaimed the king's edict of restoration to some 20,000 eager exiles.[145] Their thunderous cheering found no echo, however, among the Greek officials responsible for accommodating them. They had to address vexing questions, such as the restitution of property that by then belonged to others. This startling measure did provide temporary relief for Alexander's problem of vagrant soldiers in Asia, but it also spawned social and political turmoil in Greece, which led to a Greek rebellion shortly after the king's death.[146]

Simon Hornblower comments: "what is interesting is that Alexander thought he could resolve the difficulty at a stroke, indifferent both to opposition (Athens) and to the sheer complexity of the operation . . . . It seems that Alexander now saw himself in a superhuman role, imposing global solutions – like a god: it is Zeus who makes men exiles, 'wandering driven by the gadfly over the earth' (*Iliad* xxiv, 531f.), and who but a god can reverse the process on the necessary scale?"[147]

> You have some local Zeus
> who spawns
> new gods?
> (*Ba*. 467)

## DEIFICATION (324 BC)

Late in 324 a debate was held in Athens over the granting of divine honors to Alexander.[148] This issue seems to have been prompted by the king. A decision to deify Alexander would have meant that the king could be worshiped as a god during his own lifetime, and a spirited argument ensued. Speakers like Demosthenes and Lycurgus protested, in a sarcastic vein, about the king's overbearing pride. Demades, who had once challenged Philip's drunken deportment and thereby earned his respect, pointed out to his fellow citizens that they had better be careful not to lose the soil under their feet while safeguarding the heavens.[149] In the end there seems to have been general agreement that, under the circumstances, it was best to humor Alexander. Even Demosthenes saw an advantage in letting Alexander be the son of Zeus – and Poseidon as well – if that is what he wanted.[150] This attitude apparently also made sense to other Greeks. Damis of Sparta remarked rather dryly, "if he so wishes, he may be called a god" (P.*Mor*.219e).[151]

Alexander had already been acknowledged as the son of Ammon (or Zeus) by the oracle at Siwah. He was serious enough about his divine descent to be noticeably defensive about it. His position (and opposition to doubters) figured significantly in the prosecution of Philotas, and cast its shadow on the circumstances surrounding the impaling of Cleitus. Nevertheless, it was neither necessary nor wise for him to foresake his mortal father in the interest of divine paternity. There was a considerable difference between being the son of a god and a god in one's own right.[152] The difference is spelled out by Arrian in recounting a debate at a symposium over this very question. It is set in the context of the *proskynesis* affair:

> Anaxarchus began the subject, saying that it would be far more just to reckon Alexander a god than Dionysus and Heracles . . . in any case there was no doubt that when Alexander had departed from men they would honour him as a god; how much more just, then, that they should give him his due in life rather than when he was dead . . . . Callisthenes broke in and said: "Anaxarchus, I declare Alexander unworthy of no honour appropriate for a man; but men have used numerous ways of distinguishing all the honours which are appropriate for men and for gods . . . . It is not, therefore, proper to confuse all this, by raising mortals to extravagant proportions by excesses of honour, while bringing the gods, as far as men can, down to a demeaning and unfitting level by honouring them in the same way as men . . . . Even Heracles himself did not receive divine honours from the Greeks in his own lifetime, nor even after his death till the god of Delphi gave his sanction to honouring him as a god."[153]

(4.10.6–11.7)

Aristotle spoke of "godlike men" in his *Politics*.[154] Isocrates had advised Philip that once he had conquered the Persian Empire, the only thing left to do was to become a god.[155] Philip may have hinted at this intention by initiating the construction of the *tholos* (circular building) at Olympia.[156] By placing his own statue in the company of the Twelve Immortals at Aegae, he certainly wished to be seen within the inner circle of the greater gods, despite the charges of *hybris* that such a gesture was bound to provoke. Philip seems to have been equally unconcerned over the wrath of Dionysus, the original thirteenth god.[157] In any event, it was Alexander rather than Philip who lived to see this supreme gesture of singularity carried out. He proved, once again, that he could succeed where his mortal father had failed.

> Dionysus
> whom you outrage
> by your acts
>
> . . .
>
> will call you
> to account
> (*Ba.* 516–17)

Alexander sought deification in Greece and seems to have been granted that distinction there.[158] Exactly what this meant to either the Greeks or Alexander is another question. The surviving comments of the Greeks make it abundantly clear that their willingness to introduce this new cult implied no quixotic belief that the flesh and blood king here on earth was in any way exhibiting some of the more sensational attributes of the gods. Nor, it seems, did Alexander himself have any illusions about this aspect of his divinity. Thus, Alexander corrected Dioxippus when he referred to the blood oozing from one of the king's wounds as ichor, the blood of the gods (*Il.* 5.340).[159] He had also laughed at Anaxarchus who, on one occasion, had asked whether the king could toss thunderbolts.[160] Nonetheless, Alexander posed for Apelles with a thunderbolt in his hand, and was willing to be depicted brandishing the same celestial weapon on the Porus medallions.[161] When Greek envoys approached Alexander in Babylon shortly before his death, they came as if "on a sacred embassy to honor a god" (A.7.23.2).

Alexander sponsored his own divine cult for what seemed to him to be practical reasons, but it is difficult to fathom how this cult might have actually served him. In Greece the idea merely confirmed a common belief in his megalomania, and seemed to fit more comfortably into their catalogue of Hellenic resentments against him. His Iranian subjects never thought of their ruler as a god. In 324, while Alexander was sedulously attempting to consolidate his image as a Great King in the Achaemenid tradition, it would have been folly to prevail upon Asiatics to take his apotheosis seriously. Also, the introduction of a divine cult in Greece had nothing to do with his Macedonians, although they were certainly aware of it and no doubt feared that the cult would eventually be imposed upon them.

> We do not trifle with divinity
> No
> we are the heirs of customs and traditions
> hallowed by age
> and handed down to us
> by our
> fathers
> (*Ba.* 200–2)

For Alexander, however, personal incentives may have outweighed political considerations. Despite the fact that he had created an empire that made his father's domain look modest by comparison, had fought as courageously as Achilles, had succeeded where Heracles had failed, and had outdistanced Dionysus in traversing the world, these superb achievements seem to have left Alexander with little more than temporary elation. His sense of satisfaction was soon replaced by a compulsion to go elsewhere, to accumulate more credits. Plagued by what Wilcken calls "Alexander's restless brain,"[162] the king's only solution to inner turmoil was to return to the battlefield. It is almost as if he imagined that some extraordinary public achievement might become the catalyst through which his private demons would be exorcised.

Apotheosis held a promise of relief. This process would elevate Alexander above secular criticism and reduce the advice of lesser entities to inane banter. No longer would he be accountable for what admirers called eccentricity and detractors melancholia. Alexander could now operate in a divine guise, which generated its own logic and was *ipso facto* unfathomable to mortals. Dissenters would be guilty of profanation rather than treason. To someone who indulged in the fruit of the vine with ever-increasing intensity, these musings might have appeared to be as reasonable as they were attractive.[163]

> do not mistake for wisdom
> the fantasies
> of your sick mind
> (*Ba.* 311–12)

## THE OPIS "MUTINY" (324 BC)

As spring turned into summer, Alexander, now 31, elected to escape from the sweltering heat of Susa and, like his Achaemenid predecessors, seek some relief in the cooler palace complex at Ecbatana. Before turning north, however, the king fulfilled a *pothos* to see the Persian Gulf, which he anticipated would be of commercial significance in the future.[164]

> For when the god
> enters the body of a man
> he fills him
> with
> the breath
> of prophecy
> (*Ba.* 300–1)

The king founded another of his many Alexandrias in this region (for instance modern Charax) and sailed upriver on the Tigris, pausing to undo the ineffective obstructions left by the Persians to discourage naval attacks.

At Opis Alexander called an assembly and declared his intention to send back home some 10,000 veterans no longer fit for active service.[165] The king promised an extravagant bonus that would make these men the envy of all others in Macedonia. Instead of his announcement prompting the delirious cheering he expected, however, it almost fomented a mutiny.[166] With the most difficult campaigning behind them, Alexander's soldiers saw this act as a reflection of royal ingratitude. It was believed to be the prelude to a general replacement of Macedonians by Persians and a permanent transference of their king's capital to Asia. The soldiers, young and old, healthy and infirm, joined in a mean-spirited chorus of protest.

His men shouted that the king should dismiss all of them and suggested sarcastically that if he wished to go on with the fighting, he could do so with the assistance of his "father," Ammon. Alexander, who, Arrian tells us, "had become by this time quicker-tempered" (7.8.3), was upset over the army's attitude toward him and enraged at having his divine paternity subjected to public ridicule. He jumped down from the platform into the crowd and summarily singled out thirteen of the outspoken agitators for execution. This unanticipated response left his men in a state of disorder.[167]

Alexander then leaped back on to the platform and gave a speech that is related by Arrian and may be based on an eyewitness account from either Ptolemy or Aristobulus.[168] The words reported are characteristic of the Alexander we have seen thus far and offer a striking profile of his personality. In another brilliant *coup de théâtre* Alexander began his speech with a tribute to his father Philip. This disarming affirmation of Philip as his mortal father stole the thunder from those who spoke contemptuously of Alexander and Ammon, and soon left others wondering about the legitimacy of their grievances:

First of all, I shall begin my speech with Philip, my father, as is only fair. Philip took you over when you were helpless vagabonds [a summary of what Philip did for them, followed by his declaration that]. . . . These services . . . great as they are when considered by themselves alone, are actually small in comparison with our own. Inheriting from my father only a few gold and silver cups and not so much as sixty Talents . . . . I at once opened up for you [areas]. . . . I added . . . to your empire . . . I captured . . . and gave you [areas]. . . . I have acquired nothing for myself . . . . which of you is conscious that he exerted himself more in my behalf than I in his? Come then, let any of you strip and display his own wounds, and I will display mine in turn . . . there is no part of the body, or none in front, that has been left unwounded . . . I am often struck by stones and clubs for your interest, your glory and your riches . . . . I have made the same marriages as you, and many of your children will be the kin of mine. Furthermore, if you contracted debts, I did not make it my business to discover why, despite the enormous sums you gained by pay and plunder . . . but I discharged them all. Most of you have gold crowns as memorials of your own courage, but also of the honour that I have accorded you . . . . And now it was my intention to send away only men unfit for war, to be the envy of those at home but, as you all desire to go, let all of you begone [and tell those at home] . . . that your king [who] . . . crossed . . . even the river Indus which no one but Dionysus had crossed before . . . and would have crossed the Hyphasis [Beas] as well but for your apprehensions . . . you deserted him and went off, handing him over to the protection of the barbarians he had conquered. This is a report that will perhaps win you a fine reputation with men and will doubtless be holy in the sight of heaven. Begone!

(7.9.2–10.7)

Alexander then jumped down from the platform and stormed into the palace, where he "paid no attention to his bodily needs, and was not seen by any of the Companions, not even on the following day" (A.7.11.1). Leaving the troops who had been mesmerized by his speech, Alexander kept out of sight until it became clear that his Achillean withdrawal had begun to generate widespread concern.

He proceeded to order his Persian troops to form units that would replace their Macedonian counterparts. Persian noblemen were appointed to command these brigades, and certain Asiatic "kinsmen" were declared to be Companions. Persians so designated were eligible to exchange a loving kiss with the king.

This stratagem played on the lurking suspicion among the Macedonians that they would soon be replaced by barbarians. It also raised the perennial question of their own prospects for survival in the heartland of the Persian Empire without the leadership and approval of their king. Not one of the Royal Companions stepped forward to champion their cause as Coenus had done at the Beas. Even if they did succeed in returning to Macedonia on their own, these men might meet with a cool and contemptuous reception in some quarters, and would be without the small fortune their king had promised them. Alexander had abandoned them, just as he felt that he had been abandoned at the Beas.

> He sits apart
> and cares nothing
> nor thinks of
> us
> (*Il.* 15.106–7)

His troops eventually began flocking to the royal pavilion like penitential pilgrims.[169] Many of the men had tears in their eyes and all of them threw their weapons to the ground in capitulation. They were willing to set aside all of their complaints except one: their deprivation of the royal kiss. They insisted that they would not leave until the king had forgiven them, a sign of abject submission that finally resulted in the king's reappearance. Upon seeing their faces and hearing their lamentations, he began to weep himself.[170] Beneath his effusion of tears we can imagine a secret smile of satisfaction.

He forgave them all. When an older officer articulated their concern that Persians were now able to kiss their king while the Macedonian rank and file enjoyed no such honor, Alexander proclaimed that henceforth all Macedonians would be known as his kinsmen. They were offered the privilege of a kiss there and then, and many availed themselves of the opportunity. His men collected their weapons and departed in a euphoric state, reportedly singing a victory song. It was Alexander who should have been chanting a paean. True to form, he once again transformed a potential disaster into a personal and political triumph. Once certain of his troops' subservience, he showed himself to be a gracious master.

The troops still loved their king, but they understood him less, and the growing distance between their ways of thinking and his contributed to their feelings of confusion and hostility. Alexander's attitudes became more unfathomable, and his actions increasingly unpredictable. There were, it seems, a thousand faces to Alexander. He was capable of rewarding and punishing in the same breath and, like his father, remained inscrutable even among those close to him.

Schachermeyr speaks of the "hero, friend, father of the soldiers [and] the threatening, angry, terrorizing, melancholy king."[171] Wilcken says that Alexander could appear "as a man of demonic passion," adding that this was "part of the wonderful combinations of opposites in Alexander's nature, that by the side of this passion he also exhibits a quite surprisingly cool and calm discretion."[172] Mary Renault elucidates the fundamental ambivalence in Alexander: "Intellectually, he was outstandingly flexible and swift in his adjustments. Emotionally it was another matter. His demands on himself were such that though to his life's end he was equal to any physical hardship, pain or danger, under extreme psychological stress he would break rather than bend."[173] As with Dionysus, the polarity of this ambivalent victor was cast in the extreme.

A lavish banquet was held at Opis to commemorate both the reconciliation between the king and his troops, and between Macedonians and Persians.[174] Alexander played host to 9,000 guests at this affair, and his seating arrangement was based on the relative importance of his various subjects.[175] He "seated all the Macedonians round him, and next to them Persians, and then any persons from the other peoples who took precedence for rank or any other high quality, and he himself and those around him drank from the same bowl and poured the same libations, with the Greek soothsayers and Magi initiating the ceremony. Alexander prayed for various blessings and especially that the Macedonians and Persians should enjoy harmony [*homonoia*] as partners in the government"

(A.7.11.8–9). They then all poured a libation at the same time and let out a victory cry in unison.[176]

> Drawing the wine
> from the mixing bowls
> in the cups
> they poured it forth
> and made their prayer
> to the gods
> who live
> everlasting
> (*Il.* 3.295–6)

In addition to back pay and traveling expenses for their journey home, every discharged Macedonian soldier received the colossal bonus of one talent.[177] They would return home as living proof that there were fortunes to be made by serving Alexander in Asia. Back home these men and their families would enjoy the prerogative of sitting in the seats of honor at the front of the theater where they could display their privilege and affluence.

"If they had children by Asian wives, he ordered them to leave them behind with him, and not take home to Macedonia a source of conflict between foreigners and children of foreign wives and the children and mothers they had left behind them; he promised personally to see that they were brought up in the Macedonian way, particularly in military training; when they were grown to manhood, he would take them back himself to Macedonia and hand them over to their fathers" (A.7.12.2). Although he seems to accept this account, even Arrian refers to these promises as "vague and uncertain" (7.12.3), and it is unlikely that the king ever had any such intention. Alexander was, in fact, both relieving his men of the moral responsibility for children they had sired on the expedition, and helping to ensure himself of adequate manpower for the future.[178]

> I
> shall
> never
> come
> home
> (*Il.* 18.330)

The king ordered Craterus, assisted by Polyperchon (a prominent Macedonian officer), to lead the retirees to Macedon.[179] The assignment of Craterus, perhaps Alexander's best general and a favorite among the men, was good for public relations. It served to reassure his battle-scarred veterans that everything he had done was, after all, in their best interests. It may also have been a welcome assignment for Craterus, a traditionalist who, for all his loyalty, expressed no enthusiasm for the king's orientalization.[180] Polyperchon, who went with him, is reported to have once mocked a Persian performing obeisance, an indication that he too was not among the more zealous supporters of the changes in the king and his court.[181]

It might be recalled that Craterus was an implacable enemy of Hephaestion. It was near the time of Craterus' departure that Hephaestion became Chiliarch, the Greek equivalent of a Persian title that implied the greatest of distinctions under the king. Through Craterus' latest appointment Alexander had removed Hephaestion's only real competitor for royal favor. Although Craterus was an outstanding general, his transfer would have no immediate effect on military operations, because he had been seriously ill and unable to participate in any recent campaigns.

Craterus was ordered to replace Antipater and assume that septuagenarian's responsibilities in Macedonia, Thrace, and Greece. This was the most prestigious of independent commands, and may have provided some recompense for Craterus, who would now function worlds away from the corridors of power. Antipater would join Alexander in Babylon, bringing a fresh contingent of Macedonian troops with him. Before Craterus could embark on the last leg of his journey home, however, he was apparently instructed to supervise an extensive shipbuilding project in Cilicia.[182] The delay caused by Craterus' task in Cilicia perhaps afforded Antipater the opportunity to reflect on what new role the king might have in mind for him.

Olympias had been complaining to Alexander for some time about Antipater's regal posture.[183] In 331, while Antipater still seemed indispensable to Alexander, a confrontation between the king's mother and his regent resulted in Olympias' relocation to Epirus.[184] Now, because of the recent difficulties he had experienced in Asia and a basic change in his attitude, Alexander began to pay more serious attention to his mother. Olympias had been reasonably accurate when pointing out potential threats to the king in the past, and her increasingly suspicious son might well have imagined that it was time for his steward to be retired or transferred to a less powerful position.

This change in the king's attitude toward Antipater can be detected as early as 330, when Alexander is reported to have called his regent's victory over the Spartans "a battle of mice." During the same year Alexander's withdrawal of royal protection from the Lyncestian Alexander, Antipater's son-in-law, was a clear indication that things were changing. One anecdote, probably set in the last year of Alexander's life, has an anonymous courtier praising Antipater's frugalities. The king, having become more defensive about his own life-style of late, commented snidely that although Antipater's exterior appeared to be white, he was decidedly purple (i.e., royal) on the inside.[185]

The announcement that Craterus was to replace Antipater as regent was made at Opis in 324. Although Antipater had been successful enough in his responsibilities during the past decade to avoid any recall by the king, he still might have been concerned about this summons to court. Virtually all of the old-guard Macedonians of any standing had somehow managed to disappear on the expedition. More than one officer had been ordered to appear at court for some apparently routine purpose, only to find his head on the block. It is tempting to speculate, but the fact of the matter is that we have no way of determining what Alexander had in mind for Antipater. The only certainty is that Antipater continued to supervise the king's affairs in Europe, and Craterus remained in southern Asia Minor for the remainder of Alexander's lifetime.[186]

Although Antipater never joined Alexander, in early 323 he sent his eldest son Cassander (who had remained in Europe in 334) to the court at Babylon.[187] There this young man joined his two brothers, the youngest of whom was Iolaus, the king's cupbearer. At court Cassander made the near-fatal mistake of laughing out loud at a Persian subject who was performing *proskynesis* before the king. When this occurred Alexander jumped from his throne, seized Cassander by the hair, and bashed his head up against the wall. Even years later Cassander is said to have trembled when exposed to a statue of Alexander at Olympia.[188]

### THE DEATH OF HEPHAESTION (324 BC)

During the autumn of 324 Alexander led his men north over the Zagros Mountains to Ecbatana, where he would remain until the early spring of his last year. While the army marched toward its destination, Atropates, the satrap of Media, presented the king with 100 horsewomen armed with axes and shields, ready for combat. This gift of "Amazons," we are told, was rejected by Alexander because of his fear that his own troops might abuse them.[189]

Ecbatana, the summer retreat of the Achaemenids, provided the opportunity and ambience for leisure, recreation, and drinking bouts.[190] An extravagant festival was held in honor of Dionysus. Its magnitude was enhanced by the importation of 3,000 performers from the Dionysiac guild in Greece.[191] This panoramic tribute to Dionysus may have had its origin in the king's realization that he was playing a dangerous game in courting favorable comparisons between himself and the god.

> Too late
> When there was
> time
> you
> did not
> know me
> (*Ba.* 1345)

Bosworth has recently pointed out that an extract from the *Ephemerides* (or *Royal Diaries*) cited by Aelian, which contains a record of the drinking bouts in which Alexander participated during the Macedonian month of Dius (October/November), should most likely be set during this sojourn to Ecbatana rather than later in Babylon.[192] It reveals an instructive pattern to the king's carousing:

> They say that on the fifth of the month Dius he drank at Eumaeus', then on the sixth he slept from the drinking; and as much of that day as he was fresh, rising up, he did business with the officers about the morrow's journey, saying that it would be early. And on the seventh he was a guest at Perdiccas' and drank again; and on the eighth he slept. On the fifteenth of the same month he also drank, and on the following day he did the things customary after drinking. On the twenty-fourth he dined at Bagoas' [either the eunuch or the son of Pharnuches]; the house of Bagoas was ten stades from the palace; then on the twenty-eighth he was at rest. Accordingly one of two conclusions must be true, either that Alexander hurt himself badly by drinking so many days in the month or that those who wrote these things lie.[193]

> Your health
> Achilleus
> (*Il.* 9.225)

Bosworth comments that "The drinking-sessions recorded in the *Ephemerides* were hardly exaggerated."[194] We can be sure that Alexander's dearest friend, Hephaestion, was one of those who shared in this epic toping.[195]

> You disparage
> the gift
> that is
> his chiefest
> glory
> (*Ba.* 652)

It was in the midst of these elaborate celebrations that the king's *alter ego* killed himself through overindulgence in wine. Diodorus tells us that Hephaestion drank inappropriately,[196] and Green has commented that Hephaestion's "capacity for alcohol seems to have at least equalled Alexander's."[197] The king was aware of his comrade's excessive drinking, and when Hephaestion became ill and contracted a high fever Alexander assigned the Greek physician Glaucias [198] to monitor his condition and behavior in order to prevent further deterioration. Glaucias was specifically instructed to prevent Hephaestion from drinking. Nevertheless, during the morning of the seventh day of Hephaestion's illness, the patient ignored the advice of his doctor (who may have gone to the theater) and washed down his chicken with a half-gallon of chilled wine at breakfast.[199]

this
was
his
own
death
and
evil
destruction
he was
entreating
(*Il.* 16.46–7)

Hephaestion's matutinal bracer proved to be his last drink. His fever soared, and he relapsed and died shortly thereafter. There is little disagreement that the king's second self "drank himself to death."[200] The man who had been seriously wounded at Gaugamela, and who had fought all along with courage and intelligence, presented a singularly unheroic departure. The circumstances foreshadowed the king's own demise within less than a year.

Informed of Hephaestion's sudden relapse, Alexander rushed to his side, but it was too late. The king was devastated by this loss. Arrian says "that for two days after Hephaestion's death Alexander tasted no food[201] and took no care of his body, but lay either moaning or in a sorrowful silence" (7.14.8). Some say he lay weeping on his comrade for a day and a night before being pried away.

There his strength was washed away
and from his hands
he let fall to the ground
the foot of great-hearted Patroklos
to lie there
and himself collapsed
prone
over the dead man
(*Il.* 17.298–300)

The king personally drove his confidant's funeral chariot. He also executed Hephaestion's physician, Glaucias, for either prescribing wrongly or, more likely, for failing to stop Hephaestion from drinking.[202] The local temple of Asclepius, the god of healing, was razed by order of the king.[203] Alexander's grief knew no limits.[204] Its pathological expression was a reflection of the king's own deepening aberrancy, which was now accelerated by his profound personal loss.

Achilleus wept still
as he remembered
his beloved companion

> . . . the actions . . . the hardships . . . the wars of men
> . . . . Remembering all these things
> he let fall
> the swelling tears
> (*Il.* 24.3–9)

Later, when Alexander met with emissaries from Epidaurus (which housed a famous temple dedicated to Asclepius), he gave these men whatever they asked for, in addition to a handsome offering to the god. Justifying his impious action at Ecbatana, the king pointed out to the Epidaurians that Asclepius had not been kind to him "in failing to save . . . the comrade whom I valued as much as my life" (A.7.14.6).[205] Although he was most likely recognized as a god in Hellas by this time, Alexander still felt obliged to explain his uncivilized behavior. Nevertheless, Hephaestion was irretrievably lost, and there was nothing that even Alexander could do to change that.

> Achilleus
> great
> as he was
> could
> do
> nothing
> to
> help
> you
> (*Il.* 16.837)

Funeral games were held on a grand scale. The king cut his hair for Hephaestion as Achilles had done for Patroclus, and is said to have had his horses shorn as well.[206] No musical instrument, including the flute, which was special to Hephaestion (and associated with Dionysus),[207] was heard in camp.

> and
> nightlong
> swift-footed Achilleus
> from a golden mixing-bowl
> with a two-handled goblet in his hand
> drew the wine and poured it on the ground
> and drenched the ground with it
> and called upon the soul
> of
> unhappy
> Patroklos
> (*Il.* 23.218–21)

The sacred fires of the empire were extinguished *in memoriam*,[208] thereby rendering Hephaestion an honor customarily reserved for Persian rulers. His regiment would from then on be called Hephaestion's troop, and these men would carry their dead leader's image into battle as their standard.

At least 10,000 talents were set aside for his funeral pyre. Alexander sought out Deinocrates,[209] who "was famous for his innovations, which combined an exceptional degree of magnificence, audacity and ostentation" to build it (P.72.5). The structure would be some 200 feet high in the form of a ziggurat, and include "eagles with outspread wings looking downward, while about their bases were serpents looking up at the eagles" (D.17.115.3).

Alexander sent a messenger to Siwah to inquire whether or not divine honors could be paid to his loved one. The answer, ironically, came to him shortly before his own death in Babylon. The oracle said that divine honors were inappropriate, but Hephaestion could be honored as a hero.[210] The king then ordered that such a cult be established in perpetuity, and he became the first to offer heroic sacrifices to Hephaestion. It was on this occasion that the king wrote a peculiar letter to Cleomenes, the satrap of Egypt, intimating his awareness that this governor was involved in corrupt practices, but promising to forgive him for past and future misdeeds if he did justice to Hephaestion's heroic shrines.[211]

> You talked madness before
> but this
> is
> raving
> lunacy
> (*Ba.* 359)

Hephaestion endeared himself to few men other than Alexander. Eumenes, the king's secretary, like Craterus, became embroiled in a personal controversy with him.[212] When Hephaestion died, Eumenes was alert enough to become the first of the king's subjects to dedicate himself and his arms to the memory of the deceased. He was attempting to make it clear beyond the shadow of a doubt that whatever their problems had been in the past, he did not rejoice in Hephaestion's death. A great many Companions followed suit and gold and ivory images of the king's favorite were made.

> Now you go down
> to the house of Death
> in the secret places
> of the earth
> and left me
> here

> behind
> in the sorrow
> of
> mourning
> (*Il.* 22.482–3)

Arrian says that Alexander would have preferred to have died before Hephaestion, just as Achilles had wished to die before Patroclus.[213] His friend was the only man, Alexander believed, who loved him for himself. He was also the only person, other than Olympias, who could be trusted without reservation.[214] Hephaestion had zealously endorsed even the most subtle alterations in the king's person and policies. His role in the prosecution of Philotas and his attempt to introduce *proskynesis* speak for his willingness to undertake any task on the king's behalf. In the end this young lion was swept away by the gift of Dionysus, like a hapless victim of the Gedrosian flood. Ironically, the king, as Lane Fox comments, "drank heavily to drown his grief."[215]

> So I
> likewise
> if such
> is the fate
> which has been wrought
> for me
> (*Il.* 18.120)

After a protracted period of mourning Alexander marched out against the Cossaeans, a nomadic tribe in the Zagros mountain region between Ecbatana and Susa. "To lighten his sorrow he set off on a campaign, as if the tracking down and hunting of men might console him, and he subdued the tribe of the Cossaeans, massacring the whole male population from the youths upwards: this was termed a sacrifice to the spirit of Hephaestion" (P.72.4).[216]

> die all an evil death
> till all of you
> pay
> for
> the death
> of
> Patroklos
> (*Il.* 21.133–4)

Thus, Alexander offered human sacrifices to honor the shade of Hephaestion,[217] as Achilles had done for Patroclus. A military explanation could be offered for the campaign against the Cossaeans, but Badian prudently advises that this is one of the cases in which "it would be unsound to postulate a purely 'rational' Alexander and, from this premise, deny the multiple attestation of irrationality, especially at this period of his life."[218]

You are mad
grievously mad
beyond the power
of any
drugs
to cure
(*Ba.* 326–7)

# 5  Death in Babylon

Alexander's return to the West prompted many states to pay diplomatic respects to a man whose emergence out of India made his "invincibility" appear far less fanciful than it had once seemed. Ambassadors from Europe and Africa greeted the king on his way to, and at his court in, Babylon, and offered their congratulations on a successful conclusion to his triumphant eastern expedition. Envoys from the Corinthian League came garlanded as if they were approaching a god, and carried golden crowns, their highest honor, as gifts. Some came from Libya, the southern Italian peninsula, and Rome, while others were reported to have been sent by Celts and Iberians from the western regions of the Mediterranean. Carthaginians, who feared that they might soon be in conflict with Alexander, also came, as did Scythians and Ethiopians.[1]

The number and variety of these deputations were so proliferous that Alexander found it necessary to arrange to receive them on a regularly scheduled basis once he had settled in Babylon. Their rank and order of reception reflected the king's interests and priorities. Religious issues were dealt with first, presentations to the king second, disputes involving neighbors third, intramural problems fourth, and arguments opposing the Exiles' Decree last.[2]

Some westerners were clearly concerned over whether Alexander might look in their direction for his next campaign. Arrian refers to unnamed historians who cite Alexander's plans to circumnavigate Arabia and Africa, and then sail into the Mediterranean at its western outlet in order to conquer Libya and Carthage.[3] He also refers to those who assert Alexander's resolve to sail through the Black Sea and the Sea of Azov to strike at the Scythians, and to other sources which discuss the king's designs on Sicily and Italy.

Plutarch mentions Alexander's intention to sail around Arabia and Africa, and to pass by the Pillars of Heracles after entering the western Mediterranean.[4] Curtius writes of Alexander's determination to complete a conquest of the eastern seaboard as well as of a march against Carthage.[5]

He also claims that an armada of 700 ships was to be built, taken to Babylon, and then launched against Carthage from Syria. In this plan Alexander would proceed to Spain and then sail along the upper lip of the Mediterranean to Epirus, his mother's native land. In all likelihood this destination would also serve as a point of departure. At any rate, it is difficult to disagree with Aristobulus who said quite simply (through Strabo) that Alexander wished to be "lord of all" (S.16.1.11).

Diodorus offers a detailed discussion of Alexander's last plans.[6] His account seems to be drawn from Hieronymus of Cardia, an exceptionally reliable historian.[7] Hieronymus was a protégé of Eumenes, the king's secretary, and is said to have based his version of Alexander's plans on the king's own memoranda (*hypomnemata*). Through Diodorus he tells us that these plans were discovered after the king's death and brought before the army for consideration by Perdiccas. They were voted down because of the cost involved and the difficulty (without Alexander?) in successfully seeing them through.

> Achilleus alone
> knew how
> (*Il*. 16.142)

Although several of the items included on Diodorus' list of plans have inspired skepticism, and even caused some modern historians to dismiss the entire account as fictitious,[8] a number of the items appear credible, as well as consistent, with the king's patterns of behavior. Included in this category are the following: the construction of an armada of 1,000 ships for an assault on Carthage and the other powers in the western Mediterranean (Alexander had borne ill will against Carthage since the siege of Tyre); the building of a road along the coast of Libya to the Pillars of Heracles, with the simultaneous construction of ports and harbors; the foundation of new cities; a reciprocal transplantation of populations between Asia and Europe (as his father had done within his realm); the erection of seven magnificent temples – three in Greece at Delos, Delphi, and Dodona, three in Macedonia at Dium (Zeus), Amphipolis (Artemis), and Cyrnus (Athena) and another for Athena at Troy "that could never be surpassed by any other";[9] the completion of a memorial to Hephaestion; and the building of a pyramid (probably at Aegae) the size of Cheops' in honor of Philip. This final item would silence those who might question Alexander's devotion to his mortal father.[10]

His immediate goal was nothing less than the conquest of the entire Arabian peninsula.[11] It was the linchpin in a grand plan to connect India and Egypt. His pretext, according to Arrian, was that the Arabs were the only people in this part of the world who had neglected to pay homage to him. The truth of the matter, Arrian adds, "is that Alexander was always insatiate in winning possessions" (7.19.6).

Bosworth suggests that by this time Alexander's "concept of his own greatness had become obsessive."[12] A story told by Arrian, drawn from Aristobulus, supports this hypothesis:

> [Alexander] heard that the Arabs honoured only two gods, Uranus and Dionysus,[13] Uranus because he is visible and contains within himself the stars and especially the sun, from which the greatest and most obvious benefit comes to all human affairs, Dionysus in view of his reported expedition to India, and that Alexander therefore thought himself worthy to be regarded as a third god by the Arabs, since his achievements were as magnificent as those of Dionysus.
>
> 7.20.1[14]

Alexander reasoned that if he conquered this region and then permitted the Arabs to be governed according to their own customs – as he had done in India – then they would be willing to worship him out of gratitude for preserving their way of life.

> if in all seriousness
> this is
> your true argument
> then
> it is the very gods
> who
> ruined
> the brain
> within
> you
> (*Il.* 7.359–60)

A huge basin for a new harbor was to be dug at Babylon that would hold 1,000 of the king's vessels. Phoenician ships were to be taken apart, transported to the Euphrates, and reassembled there. Alexander ordered an exploration of the coastline, and it was reported to him that Arabia was expansive, prosperous, and particularly well endowed with exotic spices. He was advised, however, that the coastline was immense, almost, it seemed, as long as that of India. This did not deter him.

> Thence
> to rich Arabia
> (*Ba.* 16)

Reports also told of an abundance of offshore islands with suitable harbors and good prospects for the foundation of cities. One of his ship captains informed him of an island (Failaka) where Artemis was worshiped and goats and deer roamed freely. Hunting was permitted only if the hunter intended to sacrifice his victim to the goddess. Arrian, again relying on Aristobulus, tells us that "Alexander commanded this island to be called Icarus, after the island Icarus in the Aegean Sea, upon which according to the prevalent story Icarus, son of Daedalus, fell when the wax with which his wings had been fastened melted, because he did not follow his father's injunctions and fly low near the ground, but was mad enough to fly high, allowed the sun to melt and loose the wax, and left his name to both the island Icarus and the Icarian sea" (7.20.5). Could Alexander have been thinking of his own fatal ascent?

In the spring of 323, while approaching Babylon, the king was told a disconcerting story that has also been passed on to us by Aristobulus through Arrian.[15] It concerns Apollodorus, one of the Companions who had been left to command the king's troops in Babylon while Alexander marched toward India and who was now with him again at court. He had become concerned over the severe punishments being issued by the king to those accused of maladministration. He wrote to his brother Pythagoras, a diviner, to inquire about his own fate. Pythagoras, who was in Babylon at the time, wrote back to ask who it was that he feared so much that he resorted to divination. Apollodorus replied that it was Alexander and Hephaestion.

The first sacrifice was made concerning Hephaestion. Pythagoras found that the victim's liver had no visible lobe, an ominous portent. The seer reported this in a sealed letter to his brother, who had moved with the court to Ecbatana, and advised that there was nothing to fear from Hephaestion because he would soon be gone. Ironically, this information is said to have arrived in Ecbatana on the day before Hephaestion died.[16]

> the liver
> was torn
> from its place
> and from it
> the black blood
> drenched
> the fold
> of his tunic
> (*Il.* 20.470–1)

Another victim was then sacrificed with Alexander in mind. Once more no lobe was visible. Rather than keep this news to himself, as his brother probably advised, Apollodorus decided that he had better inform Alexander "with the idea of showing loyalty in higher degree to the king by advising him to beware in case any danger came upon him at this time" (7.18.3). Given his concern over the reports of Alexander's irrational behavior, Apollodorus was taking no chances.

Alexander thanked Apollodorus for his report (which was apparently lacking in detail), and when the king entered Babylon, he made a point of asking Pythagoras the specific nature of the sign that had prompted him to write such things to his brother. Pythagoras replied that the victim's liver was found to be without a lobe. Alexander asked him what he thought this signified, and the diviner replied, "Something very serious" (7.18.4).

> why
> do you prophesy
> my death?
> (*Il.* 19.420)

Rather than expressing anger at this grim news, the king paid his respects to Pythagoras for his candor. Alexander was probably thinking of the same phenomenon as reported by Euripides: "No lobe the liver had . . . [which portended] perilous scathe to him that looked."[17] He may also have been considering, in terms of his attack on the Cossaeans, Thetis' warning to Achilles that if he chose to avenge the death of Patroclus, his own end would soon follow.

Before entering Babylon Alexander was intercepted by a delegation of Chaldaeans, an ancestral priesthood.[18] They told him about a troubling oracle that signified that it was most inauspicious for the king to make his entrance at the present time. If he persisted in it, something most unfortunate would happen. Alexander was deeply troubled over what the priests had to say, but suspicious also because the Chaldaeans had been ordered to rebuild the temple of Marduk during Alexander's first visit to Babylon, and may have used those funds for their own purposes. Apparently little progress had been made on the temple, and they were conceivably attempting to prevent any discovery of their embezzlement.[19]

Anaxarchus reminded Alexander that he was above the superstitions of others. Because the king was anxious to enter the city, he followed the advice of his house philosophers. Alexander is said to have quoted a line from a play (now lost) by Euripides to the effect that the best prophets are those who make the best guesses.[20]

If the king insisted on entering, the Chaldaean priests urged that he use the eastern approach. Alexander honored this advice but soon discovered that marshes in this area made such an entrance impossible. When this became clear, Alexander's suspicions about the priests were reinforced. Despite further protestations, he entered the city through the western gate.

Alexander left Babylon soon after this entrance, probably to circumvent the priests' prophecies or to disprove them by entering and leaving the city with impunity. He went to inspect the Babylonian canal system to determine whether or not the process of irrigation could be improved and then returned to the city. At first it seemed as though his visit to Babylon was going favorably, but bad omens continued to multiply.

Arrian says that shortly thereafter he sailed down the Euphrates into the lake and swamp district near the Arabian border, where the ancient Assyro-Babylonian kings were buried.[21] Alexander was serving as steersman, guiding one of the ships between the royal graves, when the breeze caught his wide-brimmed hat and carried it into the water. The royal diadem-ribbon that was wound around his hat detached and stuck to a reed.

Anxious to be of service to the king, a sailor swam to retrieve the ribbon, but thoughtlessly tied it around his own head in order to prevent the material from becoming wet. Because the purple and white ribbon was emblematic of royalty, this event was interpreted as an omen by the seers. Arrian says that most authorities claim that the king rewarded the retriever with a talent and then beheaded him on the advice of those who insisted that it was the traditional punishment for such a breach of propriety. Aristobulus contends that the sailor, a Phoenician, received a talent and was flogged (not executed) for his *lèse-majesté*.[22]

Another portent occurred after Alexander's return to Babylon.[23] While engaged in incorporation of additional Iranians into his army, Alexander became thirsty and left the throne to quench his thirst. Everyone stood up when the king departed, and an obscure man availed himself of the opportunity to pass through the crowd and sit on the throne. Those present watched in disbelief, while the eunuchs attending the throne beat their breasts and faces ritualistically in testimony of the fact that they had witnessed an unspeakable offense. Alexander ordered the man put to the rack to determine whether he was involved in a conspiracy. According to Arrian, the man would say only that the idea had just come to him. Plutarch tells us that this man, named Dionysius, claimed that he was commanded to do so by the god Sarapis (see below).[24] The seers were troubled over the intruder's vague explanation and prevailed upon the king to execute him.

Plutarch says that Alexander's "confidence now deserted him, he began to believe that he had lost the favour of the gods, and he became increasingly suspicious of his friends" (74.1). He continues by saying that the king "had become so much obsessed by his fears of the supernatural and so overwrought and apprehensive in his own mind, that he interpreted every strange or unusual occurrence, no matter how trivial, as a prodigy or a portent, with the result that the palace was filled with soothsayers, sacrificers, purifiers and prognosticators . . . . unreasoning dread filled Alexander's mind with foolish misgivings, once he had become a slave to his fears" (75.1–2). If this is so, Alexander must have been driven to distraction by another report mentioned in Plutarch, of a tame donkey in the king's menagerie, perhaps crazed by disease, which attacked the most formidable of the royal lions and kicked it to death.[25]

> the day
> of your death
> is
> near
> (*Il.* 19.409)

## THE DEATH OF ALEXANDER (323 BC)

Arrian and Plutarch offer similar accounts of Alexander's last days in Babylon, and both cite the *Royal Diaries* as their source of information.[26] According to this document, on May 29[27] the king made his customary offerings and sacrifices as a prelude to his campaign. He then shared the victims and wine with his soldiers. That night Alexander attended an elaborate symposium in honor of Nearchus, who would lead his fleet.

After Alexander had left this affair and was returning to the royal apartments, he was approached by Medius of Larisa,[28] a Companion from Thessaly. Medius invited him to a more intimate and intense drinking bout. Alexander drank heavily at this second gathering. He then returned to his rooms, bathed, and slept until dinner was served on the following day. On the 30th he dined with Medius and drank heavily again but, believing he felt a fever coming on, bathed and slept in the cool bathhouse. By the 31st Alexander had to be transported on a litter to make his sacrifices.

Although the king continued to brief his officers on the upcoming expedition, he ordered his litter carried across the Euphrates to the more pleasant atmosphere of the gardens on the east bank. At first his body responded favorably to the change. He played dice with Medius on the following day and met with his officers a day later. But his fever rose once more, and his condition began to decline once again. It was therefore thought best to carry him back across the river to the palace. By June 7 Alexander was unable to speak. Over the next two days he continued to deteriorate.

> Stab
> through
> the
> throat
> that
> godless
> man
> the
> mocker
>
> (*Ba.* 991–4)

The troops, fearing that the king's death was being concealed by his generals, demanded to see him. They were permitted to parade past him in single file. Although he was still silent, Alexander raised his head and used his eyes to acknowledge the men.[29] Five of his officers and two Greek seers, we are told, slept in the temple of Sarapis on the night of June 9.[30] They asked at the temple if the king should be brought there, but were told that it would be best to leave him where he was. He died as evening approached on June 10, a month or so short of his thirty-third birthday, not in the midst of a violent encounter or displaying his martial virtue, but frail and ingloriously disabled.[31]

> what
> no man
> expected
> (*Ba.* 1391)

The allusion to Sarapis in the *Royal Diaries* is thought by some scholars to be anachronistic.[32] There is no other evidence of the cult's existence during Alexander's lifetime. Nevertheless, according to the *Diaries*, seven men from the king's retinue slept in a temple clearly identified as that of Sarapis in the hope that their vigil would have a salutary effect on the king. Bosworth offers the attractive hypothesis that the reference pertains to a new Egyptian cult associated with healing that combined the worship of Apis, the sacred bull (sacrificed to by Alexander at Memphis in 332), and Osiris, the Egyptian god of the underworld.[33] In his role as pharaoh Alexander was a living Horus who would fuse with Osiris at death. It should be mentioned here that, according to Herodotus, the Egyptians equated Osiris with the Greek god Dionysus.[34]

The authenticity of the *Royal Diaries* has been called into question by some modern authorities and accepted by others. Recently Badian and Bosworth have offered learned arguments to challenge their legitimacy, and Hammond has argued forcefully for their reliability.[35] Some scholars, contending that the document is a forgery, claim that it was written to camouflage the existence of a cabal of leading officers who poisoned Alexander.[36] The most common version of this story (in Plutarch's account) is that Cassander (Antipater's eldest son, who had only joined Alexander in early 323) transported the poison to court, and his brother, Iolaus, the royal cupbearer, mixed it with the king's wine.[37]

Plutarch writes that at the time of the king's death no one suspected such a plot, but when the story circulated five years later, it was readily believed by Alexander's mother, who had the grave of Iolaus dug up and his ashes scattered to the wind.[38] Olympias, of course, detested the house of Antipater and needed no confirmation of a charge that, in fact, she may have devised herself. Nevertheless, it is significant that Alexander, who took an active interest in *materia medica* and was extremely suspicious of others by this time, as far as we know never raised this question himself. Furthermore, if a clique of officers had truly conspired to poison the king, they were clearly tempting fate by placing their trust in an agent or method that left Alexander alive for such a protracted length of time. Past experience had demonstrated that conspirators could easily become undone by their own plots.

Diodorus tells us that Alexander had become so weak by the evening of June 6 that he turned his signet ring over to Perdiccas, the most influential of his marshals, so that he could conduct necessary business.[39]

This was the same man who had helped kill Pausanias thirteen years earlier, had participated in the undoing of Philotas, and had tried to restrain Alexander during the king's conflict with Cleitus. Perdiccas' name also appears on the list of those who hosted drinking parties for the king during his recent stay in Ecbatana, and he was the man chosen to escort the embalmed body of Hephaestion back to Babylon. Nevertheless, when asked to whom he had left his kingdom, Alexander, according to Diodorus, did not designate Perdiccas, but instead whispered, "To the strongest" (17.117.4).[40]

the spirit

within

does not drive me

to

go

on

living

and

be

among

men

(*Il.* 18.90–1)

Some details of Alexander's last days are contained in accounts apart from but consistent with the outlines suggested in the *Diaries*. All versions point to an excessive consumption of alcohol, with Arrian referring to Alexander's "drinking far into the night" (7.24.4). Most writers mention Medius' party, which was apparently a small gathering of twenty men.[41] An unnamed source cited by Arrian refers to Medius as "one of his most trusted Companions at that time" (7.24.4).[42] This Thessalian, who is named as a trierarch of the flotilla that sailed down the Jhelum, but who was not otherwise associated with any military responsibilities, seems to have been a close friend and a favorite drinking partner of the king. Plutarch refers to him as a "leader and skilled master of the choir of flatterers that danced attendance on Alexander, and were banded together against all good men" (*Mor.*65c). Plutarch rejects some of the dramatic details of Medius' party reported elsewhere, but he does include a reference in his rejection to a *skyphos* (the heroic cup linked with Heracles) wielded by Alexander in the company of Medius.[43]

Ephippus tells us that at his last drinking party Alexander called for a 6-quart cup, the cup of Heracles.[44] After drinking from it, and thus offering a sublime example of Kerényi's "intersection of the Dionysian and heroic spheres,"[45] he saluted the health of Proteas, the son of Alexander's childhood nurse Lanice and the nephew of Cleitus. Despite the circumstances of his uncle's death, Proteas remained a favorite of the king and was, as

Bosworth tells us, "a famous drinker who by a curious twist of fate inspired Alexander to perform his last and fatal feat of drunkenness."[46]

Proteas, whose drinking prowess had made him a folk hero among fellow Macedonians, took the huge vessel, recited the king's praises and drank deeply, to everyone's applause. Shortly thereafter, Proteas called for the same cup once more and repeated the toast. The king then insisted on another turn at the heroic cup himself. "Alexander took it and pulled at it bravely, but could not hold out; on the contrary, he sank back on his cushion and let the cup drop from his hands. As a result, he fell ill and died, because, as Ephippus says, Dionysus was angry at him for besieging his native city, Thebes."[47]

> once again
> the god
> humiliated
> him
> (*Ba.* 632)

Diodorus tells us that Alexander was called away from the celebration in honor of Nearchus to a Dionysiac comus in Medius' quarters. "There he drank much unmixed wine in commemoration of the death of Heracles, and finally, filling a huge beaker, downed it at a gulp. Instantly he shrieked aloud as if smitten by a violent blow and was conducted [away] by his Friends [Companions], who led him by the hand back to his apartments" (17.117.1–2). Alexander's chamberlains then put the king to bed and kept him under close observation. The pain increased and physicians were called in. "No one was able to do anything helpful and Alexander continued in great discomfort and acute suffering" (17.117.3).

> he must die
> in his own house
> of
> a
> painful
> sickness
> (*Il.* 13.667)

Court physicians, who were often held responsible for the premature demise of a king, prudently declined to offer any opinion in the case. They were in an unenviable position. Should the king survive and harbor a suspicion that he had been mistreated, there would be a price to pay. Alexander's case bore a striking resemblance to Hephaestion's, and it was unlikely that anyone at court had forgotten the recent example of royal justice when it came to medical malpractice.

Aristobulus, cited in Plutarch, states explicitly that Alexander "was seized with a raging fever, that when he became very thirsty he drank wine which made him delirious, and that he died" (75.6).

I
seem
to see
two suns
blazing
in
the
heavens
(*Ba.* 918)

Alexander's insistence on wine (probably chilled) to slake his parched palate when potable water was available is at first baffling. It was axiomatic in Greek medical practice to prohibit wine whenever a fever developed.[48] During Hephaestion's extended illness Alexander recognized this principle himself and sought unsuccessfully to ensure that it was enforced.

Your
blasphemies
have
made
you
blind
(*Ba.* 502)

Under the circumstances none of the attending physicians felt secure enough to remind Alexander of the inadvisability of his request, or to make any attempt to prevent him from gulping down the wine. If we follow this version, which is clearly designed to convince the reader that the drinking occurred because of the fever and was not its cause, we are presented with a laconic description of acute alcohol withdrawal.[49] All versions of the event are hauntingly reminiscent of the death of the king's *alter ego*.

The god
will
guide us there
with
no effort
on
our
part
(*Ba.* 194)

There is, however, a general agreement that Alexander died of some sort of disease. Schachermeyr suggests leukemia,[50] and Engels a form of malaria,[51] which was contracted by the king when he sailed through the swampy regions of the lower Euphrates. Engels states that the king's condition was aggravated by his overindulgence in wine.[52] Badian says, "Immoderate feasting, to which, particularly in this last period of his life, he was in any case given, either caused the disease or accelerated it; and on 10 June 323 Alexander died, after (we are told) the gods had refused to help him. . . . He certainly died of disease, undiagnosable to us."[53]

a certain Dionysus
whoever
he
may
be
(*Ba.* 220)

# Epilogue

Not long before Alexander burned down the palace at Persepolis, Aristotle was putting the finishing touches to his celebrated theory on the nature of tragedy.[1] The philosopher suggested that the protagonist of such a work should come from a distinguished family, be virtuous (though not entirely so), suffer from a basic error in judgment, undergo a revelatory experience of some sort, and move from happiness to misery.[2] Alexander, who inherited an impressive lineage, began to exhibit some of the latter characteristics seven years before his death. As he lay feverish and dying in Babylon, Alexander could be seen as a "tragic hero" in his own right.

What playwright might be more useful in examining Alexander's credentials as a "tragic hero" than Euripides,[3] whose plays were of particular interest to the king? Furthermore, which tragedy could be more suitable for exploring parallels in Alexander's life than the *Bacchae*, which the king himself quoted with authority? Admittedly, Alexander, who enjoyed being likened to the hero of the *Iliad*, would have winced at being compared to the hapless king of Thebes.[4] Nonetheless, he was just as much a Pentheus as an Achilles.

Like Pentheus, Alexander passionately nurtured his own reputation and defied any real or imagined obstacles in his path. The Macedonian king was rigid in his outlook and immature in his relationships with other people. Alexander's obsession with conspicuous accomplishment and his preoccupation with reassurances of his uniqueness spoke of fundamental insecurities. They were revealed early in his fear of being deprived of sufficient opportunity to demonstrate his exceptional skills, and later by a gnawing anxiety that something might happen that would stain his accomplishments. The great warrior compensated for his feelings of inadequacy through acts of reckless bravado, but his terrifying anger belied the unsullied image he wished to project.

Determined to astound contemporaries and awe future generations with his unique *arete*, Alexander exploited mankind and god with relentless perseverance. In the process, his *hybris* offended a deity capable of revealing and expiating mortal deficiencies with artful brutality. Dionysus chose wine as the vehicle through which he would unveil and magnify the defects of a brilliant man who was spiritually blind.

At first the grand elixir provided Alexander with a welcome retreat from the disturbing aspects of reality, but eventually it became his most critical problem. When Hephaestion, the king's beloved comrade and *alter ego*, drank himself to death during a festival in honor of Dionysus, his end foreshadowed a similar fate for Alexander. Whatever revelations the king culled from the death of his "second self" were soon lost in a morass of bloodshed and drinking.

Dionysus did not stoop to mundane revenge. He prepared Alexander for the sacrifice by permitting him to attain the success he sought. The rub lay in the victor's inability to tolerate prosperity and enjoy his achievements. The feats themselves had begun to take on the tedious quality of routine. This feeling was accompanied by an unsettling awareness that there were those who remained unimpressed with his accomplishments, regardless of their magnitude. In Babylon Alexander "was at an utter loss to know what he should do during the rest of his life" (P.*Mor*.207d). Unable to envisage a palatable alternative, the disconsolate king retreated into plans for a conquest of the Arabian peninsula. Unaware of his own shortcomings, he continued to seek external solutions to internal problems.

In the end, Alexander, like Pentheus, displayed an uncanny resemblance to his divine adversary. Thus, in the poignant finale of a life that blended triumph and tragedy, Alexander unwittingly fulfilled the role he had played with consummate skill for a lifetime – that of his own worst enemy.

An example to all men
(*Ba.* 967)

# Appendix A
## The Royal Tombs

Tomb II at Vergina (see Chapter 1) held 28 silver, clay, and bronze vessels used to hold wine, among them a representative miscellany of ancient Greek drinking cups:[1] a pair distinctly Dionysiac (*cantharoi*); several of the garden variety (*cylixes*); two without handles (*calyxes*) that feature embossed figures inside at the bottom; and a cup customarily associated with Heracles and heroic drinking (*skyphos*). Manolis Andronicos, who discovered the Royal Tombs, speculates that a particularly large vessel found (*phiale*), which is ordinarily associated with libations, might have been wielded by a devout swiller "who got bored emptying the dainty little vessels designed for more restrained and dignified drinking."[2]

In the same tomb there were four jars (*oinochoe*) bearing the Greek word for wine (*oinos*), a bucket (*situla*), two unusually long and narrow jars (*amphorae*) that Andronicos says may have held a rare and delicate vintage,[3] a mixing bowl (*crater*), and a small jug – all of which could be used for wine. A spoon, ladle, and strainer were also in evidence.

The silver *oinochoe* from this group are all embellished with interesting heads of Silenus, a seasoned veteran in the mythological entourage of Dionysus.[4] In classical Greek art, Silenus is usually depicted as a satyr grown old. Satyrs are often portrayed as radiant with wine, while Sileni are likely to be amusingly drunk. The physical effects of his exacting vocation are often evident in the lined face, puffiness, enlarged breasts, and distended stomach of the aged satyr.

A head of Silenus on one of the silver *oinochoe* from Tomb II depicts the hoary attendant of Dionysus with a bloated look, receding hairline, and a hint of bestial attributes.[5] Another Silenus, nestled at the bottom of a *calyx*, exemplifies years of devoted service to his master. He peers up at any drinker who has drained his cup, with one eye half-closed and the glazed look of a piffled Santa Claus.[6]

Dionysus was also found gracing Tomb II in his mortal dimension. An exquisite ivory carving shows a beardless and feminine Dionysus in front of an altar, sitting quite casually on a rock formation draped with a panther's skin.[7] This idealized young Dionysus is situated directly across from a Silenus whose brutish visage belongs in both the animal and human realms. The panther's skin hints at fury dwelling underneath the illusive serenity of Dionysus. Panthers, leopards, lions, and bulls provided epiphanous vehicles for a god capable of obscuring the borders between man and beast.

Pan, the goat-man, god, and companion of Dionysus, was also provided lodging in this tomb. Two youthful Pans are in evidence at the base of a small *amphora,* and an older head of Pan is attached below the handles of a handsome bronze lantern. On the *amphora* the two young Pans, appearing human except for tiny horns protruding from their foreheads, are depicted as joyous and cheerful.[8] On the lantern, however, we see a grim and menacing Pan, capable of inciting *pan*ic or creating *pande*monium. Here the metamorphic Pan is seen in his animal cast.[9]

The other intact tomb at Vergina, referred to by Andronicos as the "Prince's tomb" (Tomb III), contained an impressive miniature ivory relief of Pan. Here Pan appears rather human but goat-footed, playing his pipe and leading a middle-aged bearded man and young woman in some type of ascent.[10] This bearded man, perhaps a humanized Silenus, perhaps an initiate of the Bacchic cult, wields what appears to be the sacred staff of Dionysus (thyrsus), and wears an inebrious smile. Tomb III also produced relief heads of a youthful Pan at the bottom of several *calyxes* and, like Tomb II, the equipment necessary for a symposium.

# Appendix B
## Attributes of wine in Alexander the Great's readings

The following introduction and chart are reprinted virtually as they appeared in O'Brien 1980b: 94–9, 1980c: 3–5. I am grateful to the editors of the *Annals of Scholarship* and the *Drinking and Drug Practices Surveyor* for permission to include this material in the present volume.

We know that Aristotle instructed Alexander in Homer, and the philosopher is probably also responsible for arousing Alexander's interest in Aeschylus, Sophocles, and Euripides. Beyond these works, and a few others (lost or minor), we may be reasonably certain that the king was familiar with the writings of Pindar, Herodotus, and Xenophon. Alexander certainly did not read these authors in order to seek their opinions on wine, drinking, or drunkenness. Nevertheless, having read them, he was exposed to their views on these subjects, and their views convey explicit and implicit messages. These messages are catalogued in the following chart. The categories summarize most of the familiar assumptions about drinking in Hellenic culture. They represent conventional wisdom on the subject. The chart (1) characterizes the messages according to the positive and negative effects attributed to wine and drinking; (2) notes with a ● when one or more categorical reference is present in a particular author's work, and (3) indicates the source of one specific reference for each category. The chart is derived from consideration of 771 citations. Of these, 603 attribute positive effects to wine and drinking; 117 attribute negative effects; the remaining citations are neutral. The sources consist of sixty-one works, including all of the extant plays, poems, dialogues, and histories of the authors cited.

Positive and negative attributes of wine in Alexander the Great's readings
A dot ● indicates that one or more statements of the listed messages are found in the author's writings. Source reference indicates a specific example.

Parenthetical references are to the Loeb Classical editions; line references are to the Greek text.

| POSITIVE | HOMER | AESCHYLUS | PINDAR | HERODOTUS | EURIPIDES | SOPHOCLES | XENOPHON |
|---|---|---|---|---|---|---|---|
| **PHYSICAL** | | | | | | | |
| Revitalizes | *Iliad* ●<br>(6.258–62) | | | | | | |
| Helps generate strength | *Iliad* ●<br>(9.705–6) | | | | | | |
| Warms the body | | ● | | | *Ion* ●<br>(552–3) | | |
| Slakes thirst | ● | | | | ● | *Philoctetes* ●<br>(713–15) | |
| Accompaniment to food | *Odyssey* ●<br>(5.165–6) | ● | | ● | ● | ● | |
| Pleasant aroma | | ● | ● | | *Electra* ●<br>(497–9) | ● | |
| Looks attractive | *Iliad* ●<br>(5.341) | | ● | | ● | ● | |
| Pleasing taste | ● | | | ● | ● | | *Anabasis* ●<br>(6.4.6) |
| Life-giving | | | *Paean* ●<br>(4.25–6) | ● | | | |
| Relaxant | *Iliad* ●<br>(14.5) | | | | | | |

| POSITIVE | HOMER | AESCHYLUS | PINDAR | HERODOTUS | EURIPIDES | SOPHOCLES | XENOPHON |
|---|---|---|---|---|---|---|---|
| Soporific | • | | | • | *Cyclops* • (573–84) | | |
| **PSYCHOLOGICAL** | | | | | | | |
| Engenders love | | | | | *Bacchae* • (773–5) | | |
| Brings joy and cheer | • | • | • | • | *Bacchae* • (773–5) | • | • |
| Provides bravado | *Iliad* • (20.83–5) | | | | | | • |
| Alleviates despair | | | *Paean* • (4.26) | | • | | |
| Heals grief | | • | | | • | | *Symposium* • (2.24–5) |
| Frees truth | | | | | | *Oedipus Rex* • (799–80) | |
| Excites you | | | | • | | | *Hellenica* • (6.4.8) |
| **SOCIAL** | | | | | | | |
| Cultivates fellowship | • | | | • | | | *Anabasis* • (4.5.32) |
| Solidifies friendship (drinks to health) | • | | | • | • | | *Anabasis* • (7.3.27) |
| Marks special occasions | • | | *Olympian* • (7.1–6) | • | • | | • |
| Makes oaths and compacts binding | • | | | *Histories* • (4.70) | | | |

| POSITIVE | HOMER | AESCHYLUS | PINDAR | HERODOTUS | EURIPIDES | SOPHOCLES | XENOPHON |
|---|---|---|---|---|---|---|---|
| Inspires music, singing and dancing | • | • | Nemean (9.48–50) • | • | • | • | • |
| Reward for work | Iliad (18.544–7) • | | | | | | |
| Conducive to merriment | | • | • | • | Alcestis (343) • | | • |
| Serves as gift | • | | • | • | • | | Anabasis (4.8.23) • |
| Hospitality for guests | | | | | | | Cyropaedia (8.3.35) • |
| Weapon against enemy | | | | Histories (3.4) • | • | | |
| Reward for valor | | | | Histories (4.66) • | | | |
| Celebrate victory | Iliad (6.526–30) • | | | | | | |
| Reward for killing enemy | | | | Histories (4.66) • | | | |
| Assists in decision making | | | | Histories (1.133) • | | | |
| RELIGIOUS Libations, offerings to the gods | Odyssey (2.430–3) • | • | • | • | • | • | • |
| Attendant in prayer and sacrifice | • | • | | • | • | | Cyropaedia (7.1.1) • |

| POSITIVE | HOMER | AESCHYLUS | PINDAR | HERODOTUS | EURIPIDES | SOPHOCLES | XENOPHON |
|---|---|---|---|---|---|---|---|
| Celebrate festivals | | | | | | | Cyropaedia (7.5.15) ● |
| Spiritual lubricant | | | | | ● | | Symposium (2.24–5) ● |
| Honoring the dead (sprinkle on grave) | ● | ● | | ● | Heracleidae (1040–1) ● | ● | |
| Communion with god | | | | | Bacchae (284–5) ● | | |
| Necessary in expiatory rites | | Choephori (538–9) ● | | | | | |
| **ECONOMIC**<br>Medium of exchange | Iliad (7.472–5) ● | | ● | ● | ● | | ● |
| Valuable resource | Iliad (17.248–50) ● | | ● | ● | ● | | ● |
| Drinking vessels & jars valuable commodity | ● | ● | ● | ● | ● | | Cyropaedia (8.8.18) ● |
| **NEGATIVE PHYSICAL**<br>Gets you drunk | ● | ● | | ● | Cyclops (427–36) ● | | ● |
| Drains your strength | Iliad (6.264–5) ● | | | | ● | | ● |

| NEGATIVE | HOMER | AESCHYLUS | PINDAR | HERODOTUS | EURIPIDES | SOPHOCLES | XENOPHON |
|---|---|---|---|---|---|---|---|
| **PSYCHOLOGICAL** | | | | | | | |
| Affects your memory | *Iliad* ● (6.264–5) | | | | | | ● |
| Drives you mad | ● | | | *Histories* ● (6.75–84) | ● | | ● |
| Fogs your mind | ● | | | ● | *Cyclops* ● (427–36) | | ● |
| Evokes violence | ● | ● | | | *Cyclops* ● (434) | | ● |
| Leads to lust | | | | | *Phoenissae* ● (21–2) | | |
| Is an enemy | | | | | *Cyclops* ● (678) | | |
| Brings out bestiality | | | | | ● | | *Cyropaedia* ● (5.2.17) |
| **SOCIAL** | | | | | | | |
| Can leave you in ruin | | | | | | | Socrates' ● *Defense* (31) |
| **RELIGIOUS** | | | | | | | |
| Dionysus can make you do things | | | | | *Bacchae* ● (1296) | | |

# Postscript

Although Aristotle's treatise *On Drunkenness* has been lost, his interest in excessive drinking and its consequences is evident from remarks that are scattered throughout his surviving works.[1] Unlike the Athenian physician Mnesitheus, who viewed Dionysus as another practitioner in the art of healing and emphasized the positive attributes of wine,[2] Aristotle was deeply concerned with its harmful effects. The philosopher's discussion of the results of precipitate abstention on the part of heavy drinkers anticipated our modern understanding of acute alcohol withdrawal.[3] This, as we have seen, is the same syndrome unknowingly alluded to by Aristobulus in his description of Alexander's death (see Chapter 5).

What Aristotle may have said to Alexander regarding wine or anything else is sheer conjecture. Aristotle's basic beliefs were known to echo the maxims inscribed in stone at Delphi: "Know thyself" and "Do nothing in excess." It seems unlikely, however, that the philosopher's most illustrious student, who was so passionately devoted to emulating the heroics of mythological figures, ever dwelt on the question of who he really was, and striking a balance between extremes seems to have been antithetical to his nature.

# Key to abbreviations of frequently cited journals

| | |
|---|---|
| AHB | Ancient History Bulletin |
| AJA | American Journal of Archaeology |
| AJAH | American Journal of Ancient History |
| AJP | American Journal of Philology |
| AM | Archaia Makedonia |
| Anc. Soc. | Ancient Society |
| AncW | Ancient World |
| ASNP | Annali della Scuola Normale Superiore di Pisa. Classe di Lettere e Filosofia |
| CJ | Classical Journal |
| CP | Classical Philology |
| CQ | Classical Quarterly |
| CR | Classical Review |
| CW | Classical World |
| G&R | Greece and Rome |
| GRBS | Greek, Roman and Byzantine Studies |
| HSCP | Harvard Studies in Classical Philology |
| HThR | Harvard Theological Review |
| JHS | Journal of Hellenic Studies |
| LCM | Liverpool Classical Monthly |
| PACA | Proceedings of the African Classical Associations |
| PCPS | Proceedings of the Cambridge Philological Society |
| QJSA | Quarterly Journal of Studies on Alcohol |
| REA | Revue des Etudes Anciennes |
| REG | Revue des Etudes Grecques |
| RFIC | Rivista di Filologia e d'Istruzione Classica |
| RhM | Rheinisches Museum für Philologie |
| SymbOsl | Symbolae Osloenses |
| TAPA | Transactions of the American Philological Association |
| ZPE | Zeitschrift für Papyrologie und Epigraphik |

# Notes

## INTRODUCTION TO THE NOTES

Abbreviations for ancient authors and their works in the following pages (with the exception of those referred to in the Preface above) generally conform to the *Oxford Classical Dictionary* (Hammond and Scullard 1978), ix–xxii. *FGrH* refers to a citation from Felix Jacoby's *Die Fragmente der griechischen Historiker* (see Bibliography under "Ancient Sources"). Ephippus *FGrH* 126 F 1 refers to Fragment 1 from Ephippus, who is no. 126 in Jacoby's categorization of ancient authors. Modern authorities are cited according to the Harvard (author/date) system. Thus Bosworth 1988b: 211 indicates p. 211 of the second of Bosworth's 1988 publications listed in the Bibliography. Dates in the notes and the Bibliography indicate the latest edition available to me. Thus Green 1991 refers to a reprint of the 1974 biography of Alexander by Peter Green. The Bibliography has been organized topically in the hope that this arrangement will prove advantageous to my non-professional audience. All the topics are listed before the Bibliography itself. The disadvantage of this approach lies in the occasional necessity to move from one topic to the next in order to locate the exact reference sought.

Some citations refer to the remarks of editors or commentators. Thus Arrowsmith 1968 refers to his translation and edition of the *Bacchae*; Atkinson 1980 to his Commentary on Quintus Curtius Rufus; Bosworth 1980a to his Commentary on Arrian; Brunt 1976 or 1983 to his edition of Arrian; Dodds 1966 to his edition of the *Bacchae*; Goukowsky 1976 to his edition of Diodorus Siculus; Hamilton, J. R. 1969 to his Commentary on Plutarch's *Life of Alexander*; Rolfe 1914 to his edition of Suetonius; Roux 1970 or 1972 to her edition of *Les Bacchantes*; Welles 1983 to his edition of Diodorus Siculus; Hinüber and Wirth 1985a to their edition of Arrian; Yardley and Heckel 1984 to their edition of Quintus Curtius Rufus. The particulars for all of these works are to be found in the Bibliography under "Ancient Sources" or "Other Relevant Ancient Works."

**PROLOGUE**

1 Among the innumerable references to Dionysus in antiquity see Hom. *Il.*
6.119–43, 14.323–5, *Od.* 11.324–5; Hes. *Scut.* 399–400, *Theog.* 940–2, 947–9;
*Hymn. Hom. Bacch.*; Hdt. 2.48–9, 145–6; Soph. *Ant.* 955–63; Eur. *Ba.* passim;
D. 4.2.1–5.4, 25.4; Ov. *Met.* 3.259–315, 3.513–4.41, 4.389–431, 5.329, 7.294–6,
8.176–82, 11.67–145, 13.650–74; Apollod. *Bibl.* 1.3.2, 6.2, 9.12, 9.16, 2.2.2,
4.3–5.3, 3.14.7, *Epit.* 1.9, 3.10; Hyg. *Fab.* and *Poet. Astr.* passim; Paus. passim;
Nonnus, *Dion.* passim; Macrob. *Sat.* 1.18.1–24; for modern accounts see
Guthrie 1956: 145–82; Rose 1959: 149–57; Otto 1965; Boyancé 1966; Gernet
and Boulanger 1970: 97–129; Gernet 1981: 48–70; Farnell 1971: 85–344; Lewis
1971; Kerényi 1976, 1979: 250–74; Vernant 1976, 1980; Jeanmaire 1978;
McGinty 1978a; Detienne 1979, 1986, 1989; Henrichs 1979, 1982, 1984a, 1987;
Kirk 1983: 128–31, 230–2; Burkert 1985: 161–7, 237–42, 290–5; Daraki 1985;
Carpenter 1986; L'association dionysiaque 1986; Vernant 1990: 208–46.

2 They were mistaken. Mycenaean Linear B tablets (Pylos Xa 102, Xb 1419,
*c.* 1200 BC) record a variation of the god's name [Diwonusojo] and seem to
link the god with wine. For the early presence of Dionysus in Greece see
Kerényi 1976: 68–9 and Burkert 1985: 162–3.

3 For the complexities of the relationship between Bacchus and Dionysus see
Cole 1980: 226–34; Burkert 1985: 290–5.

4 A convenient recitation of these epithets is contained in "A Hymn to Dionysus
(containing his Epithets in Alphabetical Order)," Anonymous, *The Greek
Anthology III* 1968: no. 524, 288–91.

5 Hom. (*Il.* 6.132) refers to "mainomenos Dionysos"; Kerényi 1976: 131–4 trans-
lates this as "mad Dionysus" and explains Homer's usage of the adjective in
regard to the maddening effect Dionysus had on his female followers (*maenads*); see Otto 1965: 133–42; also Burkert 1985: 110 "since the god himself
[Dionysus] is the Frenzied One, the madness is at the same time divine experience, fulfilment, and an end in itself; the madness is then admittedly almost
inseparably fused with alcoholic intoxication."

6 A reminder that all translations from the *Bacchae* in the current text are from
Arrowsmith 1968, while line citations refer to Way 1930; other helpful editions
are: Dodds 1966; Kirk 1970; Roux 1970, 1972; for Pentheus and the *Bacchae*
see Grube 1935; Winnington-Ingram 1948; Festugière 1956, 1957; Kamerbeek
1960; Gallini 1963; de Romilly 1963, 1983; Rosenmeyer 1963: 105–52, 1983;
Willink 1966; La Rue 1968; Wohlberg 1968; Burnett 1970; Devereux 1970;
Cantarella 1971, 1974; Arthur 1972; Ferguson 1972; Seidensticker 1972, 1978,
1979; Hamilton 1974, 1978, 1985; Bremer 1976; Castellani 1976; Segal, C.
1977, 1978/9, 1982a/b, 1985, 1986; McGinty 1978b; Thomson 1979; Coche de
la Ferté 1980; Feder 1980: 56–76; Dihle 1981; Durand and Frontisi-Ducroux
1982; Muecke 1982; Diller 1983; Segal, E. 1983b; Carrière 1984; Erbse 1984;
Oranje 1984; Foley 1985: 205–58; Aélion 1986; Caruso 1987; Neuberg 1987;
Stevens 1988; Zeitlin 1990a: passim, 1990b: passim, especially 135–41.

7 See Arist. *Poet.* 1448^b–1456^a; all citations and quotations relating to Aristotle
are from Barnes's 1985 Princeton edition; see also Jones 1962; Belfiore 1985;
Halliwell 1987.

8 Segal, C. 1982a: 248 "the multiplicity of unintegrated character-traits in his
fragmented and conflicted personality."

9 Grube 1935: 40 "a very pure young man . . . . desperately afraid of the power
of emotions let loose"; Roux 1970, 1972: I 22–4, 22 and II 608, "un tout jeune
homme"; Segal, C. 1982a: 76 "[Pentheus'] immaturity," 134: "like Phaethon,
Icarus, Hippolytus – youths who would escape their mortal nature and the
demands of adult sexuality by flight to the sky but end by crashing disastrously

to earth," 171: "a moody and unpredictable adolescent"; Winnington-Ingram 1948: 160, "Pentheus seeks the glorification of his individual person"; Arrowsmith 1968: 148, "Pentheus' lonely arrogance of the 'exceptional' (*perissos*) individual, superior and contemptuous, defying the community's *nomos* in the name of his own self-will"; Foley 1985: 207, "insisting on his differences from others"; Meagher 1990: 11, "an adolescent king."

10 See Segal, C. 1982a: 121, 169, 171, 223, 245, 250, passim.

11 ibid., 251–4.

12 Represented on stage by a bloody mask and perhaps also symbolizing in conjunction with the smiling mask of Dionysus: Foley 1985: 251, "the division between divine and human nature that lies at the heart of the play."

13 See Méautis 1923; Rosenmeyer 1963: 106–10; Segal 1982a: passim; Foley 1980, 1985: 246–54; Vernant and Vidal-Naquet 1986: 38–43, 246–70; Vernant 1990: 215–46.

## 1 THE COMING OF AGE IN MACEDONIA

1 Andronicos 1977, 1978a/b, 1979a/b, 1980a/b, 1981, 1984, 1987; see also the extensive literature by other authors noted in the Bibliography (under "The Royal Tombs at Vergina").

2 Hammond 1970: 65–7, 1972: 156–8, 435, *Hammond* and Griffith 1979: 13, 157.

3 Andronicos 1977: 41, 1978b: 39, 41, 1979a: 48–9, 51, 1980b: 35, 1981: 212–13, pl. 114, 224 has suggested that the "starburst" is a royal emblem; Borza 1981a: 81–2, however, argues (82) that it "perhaps should be taken as national or ethnic sign"; see also Adams, J. P. 1983; Tripodi 1986: 660, "La differenza nel numero dei raggi che esso presenta [in Tomb II], 16 per il re, 12 per la regina, conferma ancora una volta che non si tratta di un emblema in senso araldico e, mentre serve a sottolineare lo scarto di *time* tra i due personaggi, concorre ad indicare, insieme ad altri, significativi, elementi della tomba, l'appartenenza di entrambi al medesimo *status* di regalità."

4 Advocates of Philip II: Andronicos (see the literature cited supra n. 3 and in the Bibliography) 1984: 226–33, 1987: 4; Hammond 1978, 1982, 1989b; Lane Fox 1980: 84; Burstein 1982: 148; Green 1982: 151 (leaning toward Philip II with reservations) and 1989a: 164 (less convinced of the case for Philip II); Prag, Musgrave, and Neave 1984; Prag 1990. Supporters of Philip III or skeptical of the case for Philip II: Lehmann, P. W. 1980, 1981, 1982; Prestianni Giallombardo and Tripodi 1980, 1981; Prestianni Giallombardo 1983, 1986; Borza initially (1981a) acknowledged Philip II as the leading candidate but gradually (1982c, 1985, 1987b, 1990) came to the conclusion that "the process of elimination" (1990: 265) pointed to Philip III. Uncertain: Fredricksmeyer 1981a, 1983; Calder 1981, 1983.

5 Borza 1990: 256–66 emphasizes the insufficient nature of the evidence but offers the hypothesis (266) that "Tomb 1 belongs to Philip II, his queen, Cleopatra, and their infant; Tomb 2 belongs to Philip III Arrhidaeus and his queen, Eurydice, and contains as well some of the royal paraphernalia of Alexander the Great; and Tomb 3 belongs to Alexander IV, the last of the Argeadae"; cf. Hammond 1989b *contra* Borza.

6 Guthrie 1956: 169 (*melanaigis*); Kerényi 1976: 199 (*chthonios*), 163, 319 (*melanaigis*); Miller, S. G. 1982: 162–6 has called attention to the principle of illusion (a Dionysiac motif) in Macedonian funerary façades.

7 Borza 1990: 270.

8 Ephippus *FGrH* 126 F 1; Ath. 3.120d–e; Ephippus probably joined Alexander

in 324 (see Jacoby 1930: 438); Berve 1926: II no. 331 (Ephippus); on the reliability of Ephippus see Badian 1961a: 662–3; cf. Pearson 1960: 61–6.

9  Pl. *Grg.* 471a–c; McKinlay 1949: 291; *Hammond* and Griffith 1979: 135; Borza 1990: 161–2 with n. 3; see Ath. 5.217d.

10  Younger 1966: 109–11; O'Brien 1980b: 90; see McKinlay 1949, 1951 for a full discussion of Greek drinking habits.

11  McKinlay 1949: 290–4, 1951 argues that the Greeks were not as temperate as some would believe; for Macedonian drinking see O'Brien 1980a/b; Borza 1983: 47–50; Austin 1985: 25.

12  P. *Dem.* 16.4.

13  Theopomp. *FGrH* 115 F 236, F 282; Ath. 10.435b–c; for Theopompus see now Shrimpton 1991, esp. 145–82 relating to Philip, 196–274 for a translation of Theopompus' *Testimonia* and fragments; see also Connor 1967; Bruce 1970.

14  Hamilton, J. R. 1982: 30.

15  Theopomp. *FGrH* 115 F 225, F 236; cf. Polyb. 8.9.6–13 and Ath. 6.260d–261a; Walbank 1967: 82.

16  See D.16.86.6–87.2.

17  Duris *FGrH* 76 F 37b (gold cup), F 37a (gold saucer); Ath. 4.155c (cup), cf. 6.231b; Theopomp. *FGrH* 115 F 236; Ath. 10.435b–c (Philip as *philopotes*), Ath. 10.433b: "a *'philopotes'* (drink-lover) is [always] ready for drinking-bouts."

18  Stob. *Flor.* 13.29; Val. Max. 6.2. ext. 1; cf. P.*Mor.* 178f–179a; McKinlay 1949: 291–2.

19  Theopomp. *FGrH* 115 F 81; Ath. 6.259f–260a.

20  Carystius in Ath. 10.435d.

21  Theopomp. *FGrH* 115 F 162; Ath. 6.260b–c; in this and other respects Thessalian society was very much like Macedonian society.

22  Theopomp. *FGrH* 115 F 236; Ath. 10.435b–c.

23  P.5.4.

24  Theopomp. *FGrH* 115 F 27.

25  For Philip's career and contributions see Momigliano 1934; Wüst 1938; Cloché 1955; Kienast 1973; Cawkwell 1978; esp. Hammond and *Griffith* 1979: 203–726; Hatzopoulos and Loukopoulos 1981; Hornblower, S. 1983: 239–60; Bengtson 1985: 11–129; Wirth 1985c; Ellis 1986.

26  P.6.1–8; Anderson, A. R. 1930; Fraser 1953; Hamilton, J. R. 1969: 14–16; for Alexander's early life see Hamilton 1965; on the depiction of childhood in ancient Greek biography see Pelling 1990b.

27  See Green 1991: 517 n. 9.

28  Anderson, A. R. 1930: 3–7.

29  Throughout this text the term "talent" is used to denote "An ancient weight, a money of account" (*OED*). It is difficult to determine, in today's fluctuating monetary climate, just what this would be worth. Prior to 1914, during the period of the gold standard, a British pound sterling was equal to approximately $5.00. Using the figure given by Tarn (1948: I 53 with n. 4), that the 180,000 talents which Alexander gleaned from the Persian treasuries was worth £44,000,000 (or £250 = one talent) at the pre-First World War value, the value in dollars of a single talent would have been $1,250. Obviously, the number of dollars needed at today's inflated rates to buy one talent would be appreciably higher; Rolfe 1914: 551, "The Attic talent, which is most frequently meant, contained 6000 *drachmae*, and was equal to nearly $1200 [1914]"; cf. Bivar 1985: 623–4, 636.

30  A.5.19.4.

31  P.*Mor.* 178f.

32 See Strasburger 1934; Kornemann 1935; Breebaart 1960; Pearson 1960: 112–211; the appendices and notes of Brunt 1976, 1983; Bosworth 1976a/b, 1980a, 1983b, 1988b; Levi 1976: 43–82, 177–330; Stadter 1980; Pédech 1984: 159–413; Hinüber and *Wirth* 1985a: 719–77; Tonnet 1987a/b.

33 Hammond and *Griffith* 1979: 460, 696; see also Errington 1981b, esp. 83 for his summary of Griffith's Philip, including a reference to the competitive "ethos of Olympia."

34 Dem. 2.15.

35 Cf. P.*Mor.* 179d; for an illuminating analysis of Alexander's ambiguous attitude toward Philip see Fredricksmeyer 1990.

36 Bengtson 1985: 189 "für Alexander war sein Vater das große Vorbild, man braucht nur die Rede, die er in Opis gehalten hat, daraufhin zu lesen"; for the dispute over the authenticity of the speech see Chapter 4, n. 168.

37 P.*Mor.* 328e, although Plutarch seems to include more than *poleis*: see Hamilton, J. R. 1982: 160; Bosworth 1988a: 250, "Plutarch interpreted it [Alexander's foundation of cities] as a work of civilisation, tempering barbarism with an influx of higher culture. Contemporaries might have been excused for thinking that the barbarism had come from the west"; Fredricksmeyer 1990: 306–7 (with notes) points out that there were precedents for founding a city in one's own name.

38 Berve 1926: II no. 581 (Olympias); Macurdy 1932a: 22–46; Hamilton, J. R. 1965: 117–18; Schachermeyr 1973: 72–6; see esp. Carney 1987b; Walcot 1987: 21–2.

39 Tarn 1948 II: 326; in a more judicious account of Olympias, Carney 1987b: 41 says: "Disallowing the most blatantly hostile remarks of the sources, it seems fair to say that Olympias was an unusually determined person, vengeful, ruthless, devoted to her son's success and her own, a better dynast than politician. This list of characteristics would suit her son nearly as well as Olympias herself. The mother, however, lacked the son's arena."

40 Hyperides 4.25 as cited in Macurdy 1932: 35.

41 Hyperides 4.26 as cited in Macurdy 1932: 35.

42 A.7.12.6.

43 Macurdy 1932a: 24; Heckel (1981b) cites Plutarch (*Mor.* 401a–b) in support of Polyxena as the original name of Alexander's mother; Polyxena does suit the Molossian practice of naming family members after Achilles' family and the Trojan royal house (she was a daughter of Priam and Hecuba) in order to help legitimize the Hellenic nature of their dynasty; Pomeroy (1984:10) and Wirth (1985c: 29) also endorse Polyxena.

44 For Arybbas see Errington 1975; Heskel 1988.

45 P.2.2; Witt 1977: 67.

46 Guthrie 1956: 43; Burkert 1985: 281–5.

47 P.2.6, 9, 3.2; cf. *Ba.* 697–8; Dodds 1940: 163–4, 1966: xxiii.

48 Although this is speculative. See P.2.9; Duris *FGrH* 76 F 52; Ath. 13.560f, 14.659f; Hammond 1980a: 265, 321 n. 12; Fredricksmeyer 1966: 181; Goukowsky 1981: 9.

49 P.2.1; A.1.11.8; D.17.1.5; J.17.3.1–14.

50 Theopomp. *FGrH* 126 F 355; Hammond 1967: 412–13.

51 P.2.1; A.7.14.4.

52 Baege 1913: 77–106; Vollgraff 1927: 433–48; Fredricksmeyer 1966: 181; Hammond and Griffith 1979: passim; Goukowsky 1981: 8–10; for a sampling of the numismatic evidence in the region see Price 1974: 5–6, 6, "There are frequent references to the worship of Dionysos in these early coins of Macedonia," 14; Kraay 1976: 137, 150, 155.

53 Although men were not "male maenads": see Henrichs 1984b: 70, "Euripides

[in the *Bacchae*] pushed the concept of the maenad to its very limits, yet in doing so he confirmed the exclusive nature of maenadic rites, participation in which was generally confined to female worshipers of Dionysus."

54  Fredricksmeyer 1966: 182 n. 13.

55  *Hammond* and Griffith 1979: 13; Bosworth 1988a: 278.

56  Fredricksmeyer 1966: 181.

57  Dodds 1966: xxii–xxiii; Lefkowitz 1981: 103 seems overly skeptical in asserting that "it is equally possible that the notion of his [Euripides'] exile in Macedonia was created to explain the presence of these unusual [Macedonian] references in the play"; cf. Harder 1985: 125 n. 1.

58  For Dionysiac ritual see Guthrie 1956: 147–52; Boyancé 1966; Farnell 1971: 150–239; Festugière 1972; Henrichs 1978, 1981, 1984b; Jeanmaire 1978: 105–219; Kerényi 1976: 189–272, 1979: 259–63; Burkert 1983: passim, esp. 213–47, 1985: 161–7, 1987: passim; Kraemer 1979; Seidensticker 1979; Seaford 1981; Bremmer 1984; Hoffman, R. J. 1989.

59  Burkert 1987: 21 says that the promise of life after death is evident in the Dionysiac mysteries from the fifth century BC.

60  Detienne 1979: passim; West 1984: 140–75.

61  P.2.7–9.

62  Henrichs 1984b.

63  *Ba.* 314–18.

64  Kerényi 1979: 273 refers to Dionysiac epithets such as Pseudanor, "the one without true virility," Gynnis, "the womanish," Arsenothelys, "the man/womanly."

65  For Philip's marriages see Satyr. in Ath. 13.557b-e; Ellis 1981c; Martin, T. R. 1982: 66–70; Tronson 1984.

66  Although Satyr. in Ath. 13.557c merely says that he begot a child by her; see Tronson 1984: 121–2.

67  Satyr. in Ath. 13.557c; Tronson 1984: 126 points out that Satyrus "is the only ancient source which explicitly links Philip's marriages with his political advancement."

68  Hammond and *Griffith* 1979: 153, 215.

69  Wilcken (1967: 266) and Schachermeyr (1973: 567–8) suspect an epileptoid condition; see also Hamilton, J. R. 1982: 41; Martin, T. R. 1982; Greenwalt 1985b:74–7; Green 1991: 28, 90–1.

70  D.19.11.5.

71  P.3.5 = 6 Hecatombaeon, according to the Attic calendar; see Hamilton, J. R. 1969: 7.

72  Satyr. in Ath. 13.557d; Berve 1926: II no. 433 (Cleopatra); Macurdy 1932a: 26, 31–48; Carney 1988: 394–404.

73  Carney 1987b: 42.

74  Hammond and *Griffith* 1979: 676–7.

75  For Leonidas and young Alexander's other teachers see P.5.7–8, 22.9–10, 24.10–11, *Mor.* 179e–f; Ps-Call. 1.13.4; Jul. Val. 1.7; Berve 1926: II no. 469 (Leonidas) and no. 481 (Lysimachus).

76  Cf. P.*Mor.* 127b, 180b, 1099c.

77  A. 4.10.1–2.

78  A.4.10.1–2; P.2.3–6, 28.1, Ael. *NA* 12.6; Merkelbach 1977: 77–83.

79  P.3.3–4, although Plutarch is somewhat skeptical on the matter; cf. Jul. Val. 1.47; Berve 1926: II 285.

80  *TGF* F 785.

81  For Aristotle before his acceptance of Philip's invitation see Jaeger 1962: 11–117, 120; Chroust 1966, 1967, 1972a, 1973: 1–124.

82  P.7.2–3, *Mor.* 1043d, 1097b, 1126f; J.12.16.8; Diog. Laert. 5.4; Dio Chrys.

*Or.* 2.79, 47.9; Ael. *VH* 12.54; Alexander is credited with the restoration in Val. Max. 5.6 ext. 5, Pliny *HN* 7.109.

83 Diog. Laert. 5.3; Jaeger 1962: 116.
84 Momigliano 1934: 135, 140; Merlan 1954–5: 60–1 with n. 1; Chroust 1973: I 120; Jaeger 1962: 120–1; Green 1991: 54; cf. Hammond and *Griffith* 1979: 517–22; Guthrie 1981: 35–6.
85 Green 1991: 54.
86 Jaeger 1962: 119–20; Chroust 1972a, 1973: I 120; Schachermeyr 1973: 60–1; Guthrie 1981: 35–6; Vatai 1984: 96; Green 1991: 54; cf. Errington 1981b: 78.
87 Jaeger 1962: 117; see Bosworth 1988a: 18 n. 44 for a cautious approach to assumptions about Hermeias' relations with Philip and his death.
88 P.7.3; Hdt. 8.138 in regard to "the Gardens of Midas."
89 F 44R³; see Jaeger 1962: 48; cf. Ath. 2.45c.
90 P.8.1, 41.6–7; D.17.103.6–8; C.9.8.22–7; J.12.10.3; S.15.2.7; Cic. *Div.* 2.135; Eggermont (1975: 107–16) ascribes the dream to Ptolemaic propaganda; cf. Hughes (1984: 185–8), who finds the dream plausible.
91 F 675R³; tr. from Edmunds 1971: 383–4; Wormell 1935: 61–5; Boyancé 1937: 299–310; Bowra 1938; Jaeger 1962: 117–19; Renehan 1982.
92 P.5.8.
93 P.24.10–14.
94 P.8.2, taken figuratively, as it would have been disconcerting to sleep with two dozen scrolls under one's pillow.
95 P.26.1–2; cf. S.13.1.27; Pliny *HN* 7.107–8.
96 P.8.2, *Mor.* 327f; see Edmunds 1971: 372–91.
97 A.7.14.4; Ameling 1988.
98 Griffin 1980b, 1986, 1987; MacCary 1982; for an excellent interpretation of Achilles' character within the context of the *Iliad* see Schein 1984: 89–167; Van Wees 1988.
99 Homer *Od.* 11.488–91, "O shining Odysseus, never try to console me for dying. I would rather follow the plow as thrall to another man, one with no land alloted him and not much to live on, than be a king over all the perished dead"; Schmiel 1987.
100 Shapiro 1983; Verbanck-Piérard 1987.
101 For the origins and early history of the Argead dynasty see Hdt. 5.22, 8.137–9; Thuc. 2.100; Isoc. *Phil.* 32–4, 111–20; D.7.15.1–3, 17.1; P.2.1; J.7.1.7–12, 11.4.5; Vell. Pat. 1.6.5; Hamilton, J. R. 1969: 2; *Hammond* and Griffith 1979: 3–4 lend credence to the Argive connection; Greenwalt 1985a, 1986a, 1987; Borza 1990: 80–4, 112–13, 179 n. 42, 277–8, emphasizes the mythic nature of the claim, convincingly tracing its origins to the policies of Alexander I.
102 Pollitt 1965: 149–50.
103 P.9.1.
104 P.9.1; see Thuc. 2.98.
105 See n. 35 above.
106 C.8.1.24, when this occurred (perhaps at Chaeronea?) is problematic.
107 Polyaenus *Strat.* 4.2.2,7; P.9.2–4, *Cam.* 19.5; D.16.85.2–86.6; J.9.3.9–11; Frontin. *Str.* 2.1.9; Paus. 9.10.1; Dio Chrys. *Or.* 2.2. Diodorus (16.85.5) tells us that Philip led approximately 30,000 infantry and 2,000 cavalry; Hammond 1938; Hammond and *Griffith* 1979: 596–603; Cawkwell 1978: 144–9; Markle 1978; Pritchett 1958, 1985: 49, 77, 144, 151–2, 222–6.
108 Paus. 9.40.10; S.9.2.37; Rahe 1981; cf. Green 1991: 76.
109 D.16.86.4; Tod 1962: no. 176.
110 See Tod 1962: no. 177 (under "Reference Works"); Roebuck 1948; Ryder 1965; Cawkwell 1978: 166–6, Hammond and *Griffith* 1979: 623–46; Perlman 1985, 1986; Ellis 1986: 204–10.

111  See Brunt 1976: lvi–lvii n. 69; Hammond and *Griffith* 1979: 609–10 with n. 1 (610); Green 1991: 79; Fredricksmeyer 1979a for Philip's cult at Athens.
112  J.9.4.5, along with Alcimachus, a veteran diplomat.
113  Dem. 18.67.
114  The most persuasive analysis is found in Badian 1982a; see also Hoffmann 1906; Kalleris 1954: esp. 304–25, 1976; Lauffer 1978: 15–17; *Hammond* and Griffith 1979: 3–4; Greenwalt 1985a, 1986a; Rosen 1987; Scaife 1989; Borza 1990: 90–7, 277; Errington 1990: 3–4 maintains that this prejudice was political in nature.
115  Hegesander in Ath. 1.18a.
116  Arist. *Pol.* 1324[b].
117  Brunt 1976: xxxvi; Badian 1982a; Hamilton 1982: 23; see also Borza 1990: 92 n. 30.
118  For Socrates see Arist. *Rh.* 1398[a]; Plato's *Gorgias* (see n. 9 above) was less than flattering to Archelaus, and seems to illustrate what Borza (1990: 176) calls the Athenians' "genuine underlying disgust at what Archelaus seemed to represent"; see also Badian 1982a: 46 n. 18.
119  As quoted in Borza 1990: 165 with n. 15; see also Badian 1982a: 35, "Ironically, it is based on a line by Euripides," 46 n. 17.
120  Dem. 9.31.
121  Fredricksmeyer 1958: passim, esp. 259–65.
122  A.1.11.7.
123  Arist. *Poet.* 1449[a], 1453[b]; Archilochus in Ath. 14.628a–b, "For I know how to lead off, in the lovely song of lord Dionysus, the dithyramb, when my wits have been stricken with the thunder-bolt of wine."
124  For "The Artists of Dionysus" see Pickard-Cambridge 1988: 279–305, for Philip and Alexander, 279–80; see also Ghiron-Bistagne 1976.
125  P.10.7, 53.2; *Ba.* 266–7; *TGF* F 905; Nicobule *FGrH* 127 F 2; Ath. 12.537d; Instinsky 1961; Brown, T. S. 1967: 361–2, 364–5.
126  A.3.16.7–8, 7.19.2; Paus. 1.8.5 (restored by Antiochus); Val. Max. 2.10. ext. 1 (restored by Seleucus); cf. Gell. *NA* 7.17.2 (books restored by Seleucus); Bosworth 1980a: 317–18.
127  Miller, S. G. 1973; Hammond and *Griffith* 1979: 691–5; Green 1991: 80–2.
128  Paus. 5.20.10.
129  Satyr. in Ath. 13.557d; see also J.9.5.9, 7.2–6; Badian 1963: 244, and see 1982b for problems with Arrian's use of the name Eurydice for Cleopatra; cf. Heckel 1978a *contra* Badian.
130  Satyr. in Ath. 13.557d; Ellis 1986: 214–15 doubts the historicity of the entire story. Levi 1977a: 72–4 emphasizes the difference between what he calls exogamous (e.g. Olympias) and endogamous (e.g. Cleopatra) marriages of Philip.
131  S.7.7.8; *Hammond* and Griffith 1979: 14; Borza 1990: 191–5.
132  P.9.11; cf. J.9.7.5 and Satyr. in Ath. 13.557e.
133  Satyr. in Ath. 13.557d.
134  Borza 1990: 208.
135  P.9.12–14, *Mor.* 70b–c, 179c; J.9.7.5–6.
136  J.9.7.6.
137  Bosworth 1988a: 21–2, places the event before Philip's marriage to Cleopatra; Ellis 1981c: 135–6 and Hatzopoulos 1982a have questioned its historicity, but see the analyses of French and Dixon 1986a/b.
138  P.29.3, *Mor.* 334e; Berve 1926: II no. 371 (Thessalus); Pickard-Cambridge 1988: 279–80 for actors serving in a diplomatic capacity; Badian 1963: 245–6.
139  Hamilton, J. R. 1969: 26.
140  See Badian's remarks on this event (1963: 245).

141 Cf. Heckel 1985a, who believes that these men were appointed by Philip to be Alexander's advisers and were banished for the advice they gave.

142 See Berve 1926: II nos. 143 (Harpalus), 544 (Nearchus), 668 (Ptolemy); Heckel 1985a.

143 See Xen. *Cyr.* 8.4.10–11 as well as Chapter 2 below for Alexander and Xenophon.

144 Berve 1926: II nos. 466 (Leonnatus), 627 (Perdiccas), 181 (Attalus); cf. Heckel 1978b; 1986c.

145 See Berve 1926: II no. 627 and Chapter 5 n. 39 below.

146 See A.1.25.1, 2.14.5; P.10.6–8; D.16.92.1–95.1; J.9.6.1–8, 7.1–14; POxy. 1798 F 1 (an unnamed assassin); Bosworth 1971a; Ellis 1981c; Kraft 1971: 11–42; Hamilton, J. R. 1969: 27–8, 1982: 40–3; Schachermeyr 1973: 100–1; Lane Fox 1974: 17–25; Fears 1975; Lauffer 1978: 37; Hammond 1983a: 87–92; Bengtson 1985: 112–16; Wirth 1985c: 166–7; Will 1987; Fredricksmeyer 1990: 314–15; Vershinin 1990.

147 D.16.91.2; cf. C.7.1.3; J.9.5.8–9.

148 J.9.7.7.

149 On Alexander of Epirus see D.16.72.1; J.8.6.4–8; Dem. 7.32; Paus. 1.11.3; Berve 1926: II no. 38 (Alexander of Epirus); Hammond and *Griffith*: 1979: 505; Werner 1987.

150 Prestianni Giallombardo 1973–4; Bosworth 1980a: 45–6; Hatzopoulos 1982b; cf. Badian 1989: 68 n. 24; Borza 1990: 227, 249 with n. 37.

151 D.16.92.3.

152 J.9.6.3–4.

153 Kraft 1971: 32–8; Fears 1975; Ellis 1986: 223; Borza 1990: 227, for example, subscribes to the theory of a lone assassin; Bosworth 1988a: 25 n. 3, however, points out that personal motives do not exclude accomplices and reminds us that only Diodorus among the Alexander historians infers that Pausanias acted alone.

154 Arist. *Pol.* 1311^b.

155 Lane Fox 1974: 23, "This [account] may be exaggerated, but there is no reason to dismiss all its detail as false or as malicious rumour; its source cannot be checked independently, but Olympias was a woman of wild emotion, who would later show no scruple in murdering family rivals who threatened her"; Lauffer 1978: 37.

156 This passage is omitted in the Penguin translation, and the quotation cited comes from the Loeb text.

157 P.10.7.

158 P.10.6.

159 Satyr. in Ath. 13.557d.

160 J.9.7.12; cf. Paus. 8.7.7.

161 The possibility of Olympias' involvement was acknowledged earlier by Berve 1926: II 284–5 and Kaerst 1927: 318.

162 Badian 1963.

163 ibid., 250.

164 Milns 1969: 31, "There can be little doubt that Alexander became King by becoming a parricide"; Green 1991: 109.

165 Cf. J.11.11.3–7; Green 1991: 88, 102.

166 Polyaenus *Strat.* 8.60; Arrian *FGrH* 156 F 9.22.

167 Bosworth 1971a: 96; Ellis 1973: 352–3; *Hammond* and Griffith 1979: 152–3, 158; Hatzopoulos 1986; Greenwalt 1989; Borza 1990: 244–6 and 298, where he expresses doubts about the ratification of a successor by the Assembly: "I do not find sufficient evidence to indicate that such a procedure existed"; Errington 1990: 220.

168 Based on J.9.7.2, 11.11.5; see Milns 1969: 27; Lane Fox 1974: 503; *Hammond* and Griffith 1979: 153, "polygamy was desirable"; cf. Bosworth 1988a: 6, who says that Philip was "[u]nashamedly polygamous"; Green 1991:88.
169 Satyr. in Ath. 13.557e.
170 J.9.7.12.
171 See also 11.2.3.
172 Paus. 8.7.7.
173 D.17.2.3, "Cleopatra had borne a child to Philip a few days before his death"; J.11.2.3; Paus. 8.7.7; Brunt 1976: lxi; *Hammond* and Griffith 1979: 5, 112; Lane Fox 1974: 18; Green 1991: 95, 103, cf. Tarn 1948: II 260–2; Hammond and *Griffith* 1979: 681 n. 1; Heckel 1979; Unz 1985: 172.
174 Lane Fox 1980: 68; Berve 1926: II no. 411 (Caranus); Unz 1985; cf. Heckel 1979; Bosworth 1988a: 19 n. 46, 27 n. 10.
175 See n. 101 above.
176 D.16.94.4.
177 Welles 1983: 101 n. 2.
178 Badian 1963: 246–8; Milns 1969: 31, 33; Green 1991: 103, 111.
179 Badian 1963: 247; for Philip and deification see Fredricksmeyer 1979a, 1981b, 1982: 94–8; cf. Badian 1981: 67–71.
180 P.10.6.
181 See now the comments of Carney 1987b: 47–8.
182 C.10.5.30.

## 2  A HOMERIC KING

1 A.1.25.1–2; P.10.8; D.17.2.1; C.7.1.6–7; J.11.2.1–2; Bosworth 1971a: 96–7, 1988a: 25, "The sources strongly indicate that they [the Lyncestian brothers] were involved in the actual murder"; Levi 1977a: 82 accepts Lyncestian culpability and that of the Persian king (see A.2.14.5): both accusations reflect the official position adopted by Alexander; see also Ellis 1982.
2 J.11.2.1.
3 A.1.25.1.
4 A.1.25.1–2; C.7.1.6–7; J.11.2.1–2; see Carney 1980: 23–6 for details regarding this Lyncestian's career.
5 See Hammond and *Griffith* 1979: 686–7.
6 Cawkwell 1978: 27–8; Hammond and *Griffith* 1979: 208–9; Ellis 1971; Hornblower, S. 1983: 239, 261–2; Borza 1990: 200–1 with notes; see Hatzo-poulos 1982b for claims to a 360 accession; Justin (7.5.6–10) is the only source that alleges Philip's regency on behalf of Amyntas, son of Perdiccas.
7 Cf. P.11.1.
8 J.12.6.14; A.1.5.4; C.6.9.17, 10.24.
9 J.11.2.3.
10 D.17.5.2; C.7.1.3; J.11.5.1; the chronology of this sequence of events is problematic: see Bosworth 1988a: 25–8.
11 Badian 1960b: 327, 1964: 193–4; C. 7.1.3.
12 Badian 1960b: 327–8, 1964: 193–4; Green 1991: 159–60.
13 P.10.8.
14 Curtius (10.7.1) attests to Arrhidaeus' presence at the court toward the end of Alexander's life, but it should be noted that there is no hard evidence placing Arrhidaeus with Alexander before that; see Greenwalt 1985b, who believes that Arrhidaeus went along on the expedition.
15 D.17.2.2; J.11.1.7–10.
16 According to Plutarch (*Mor.* 331c), this was Alexander's favorite line from Homer.

17 Aeschin. *In. Ctes.* 77–8; P. *Dem.* 22.1–3.
18 Cf. P.*Mor.* 327c.
19 Philostr. *Heroic.* 326; cf. D.17.4.1; J.11.3.1–2; Fredricksmeyer 1958: 2, 142.
20 D.17.4.2–3.
21 D.17.4.4–5; Hammond 1980d.
22 A.1.1.1–2; P.14.1; D.17.4.9; J.11.2.5.
23 A.1.1.3; Lauffer 1978: 41 n. 5.
24 A.7.2.1; P.14.1–5, *Mor.* 331e–332b, 605e, 782a–b; D.17.93.4; Diog. Laert.
   6.32,38; Cic. *Tusc.* 5.92; Dio Chrys. *Or.* 4.1–139; Apul. *Apol.* 22.24; Berve
   1926: II 417 n.3 rejects the story as fiction; Lauffer 1978: 42 with n. 7 finds
   it credible.
25 D.17.93.4; P.14.6–7; cf. D.17.51.3–4; J.12.2.3; Tarn 1948: II 338–46 argues
   for the historicity of the anecdote; Hamilton, J. R. 1969: 34–5, 1982: 46;
   Lauffer 1978: 42–3; Schepens 1989: 15 with n. 1; cf. Parke and Wormell 1956:
   I 240, "The story, as it appears to me, is fictitious"; II 109 (no. 270).
26 The only comprehensive account of Alexander's religious activity is Fredricksmeyer 1958; for the nature of Alexander's religiosity see Edmunds 1971;
   cf. *Il.* 1.218; Xen. *Cyr.* 8.1.23.
27 See Hamilton, J. R. 1969: 39.
28 Kirk 1983: 128.
29 Stewart 1982: 208; Macrob. *Sat.* 1.18.6–8, "no one may suppose Parnassus to
   be sacred to two different gods . . . Apollo and Liber [Dionysus] are one and
   the same god . . . . In the performance of sacred rites a mysterious rule of
   religion ordains that the sun shall be called Apollo when it is in the upper
   hemisphere, that is to say, by day, and be held to be Dionysus, or Liber
   Pater, when it is in the lower hemisphere, that is to say, at night."
30 Northern frontier campaigns and sacrifices at the Danube: A.1.1.4–6.11 (sacrifices: 1.4.5); P.11.5; D.17.8.1; S.7.3.8; Wilcken 1967: 67–70; Lane Fox 1974:
   81–5; Hammond 1980a: 45–8; Hamilton, J. R. 1982: 46–8; Bosworth 1988a:
   28–32; Green 1991: 124–37.
31 Suet. *Aug.* 94.5; see also Macrob. *Sat.* 1.18.11; Lane Fox 1974: 82, 512;
   Fredricksmeyer 1958: 143 n. 14 (a discussion of controversy surrounding this
   sacrifice, which is viewed as unhistorical), 281.
32 Cf. J.9.2.10–13; Darius the Great's fleet had bridged the Danube and his
   troops had defeated the Getae (Hdt. 4.89–93); *Hammond* and Griffith 1979:
   56; Bosworth 1980a: 62; Brown, T. S. 1988; Green 1991: 127–8.
33 A.1.3.5; cf. C.4.7.8 (*ingens cupido*), 8.3, 7.11.4; Hdt. 1.165.
34 Ehrenberg 1938a: 60, 52–61, 1965: 458–65; cf. Méautis 1924a; Kraft 1971:
   81–118; Schachermeyr 1973: 653–7; Wirth 1973: 98; Brunt 1976: 469–70;
   Goukowsky 1978: 173–4; Bosworth 1980a: 62; Hornblower, S. 1983: 263,
   "when all has been said in sober qualification, the strong 'natural curiosity,'
   which the word denotes at its lowest, was surely an important part of Alexander's motivation throughout his short life."
35 A.1.4.6–8.
36 Cf. S.7.3.8; Kornemann 1935: 45–6; Pearson 1960: 184 n. 176; Brunt 1976:
   18 n. 2; Bosworth 1980a: 64–5.
37 Xen. *An.* 1.5.10; cf. A.3.29.4, where the same method is used.
38 See Anderson, J. K. 1970; Stark 1958a: 203–10; Farber 1979; Rubin 1989;
   Tatum 1989: 11–12, 238–9, "With Xenophon an important inspiration, he
   [Alexander] made an empire by imposing a romantic fiction on the world
   about him; in life and even more in death he was the inspiration for romance
   . . . . You might say that Alexander the Great followed the *Cyropaedia* to
   the letter, its final chapter as well as its prologue."
39 Hornblower, S. 1983: 155.

40 Xen. *Cyr.* 1.6.8.
41 Xen. *Cyr.* 1.6.25.
42 See Hornblower (1983: 320 n. 59) concerning the text and translation.
43 Xen. *Cyr.* 1.6.38.
44 Xen. *Cyr.* 2.1.22–4, 8.2.26.
45 Xen. *Cyr.* 5.3.46–50.
46 Xen. *Cyr.* 5.4.17.
47 Xen. *Cyr.* 1.6.24, 8.2.1–2.
48 Xen. *Cyr.* 8.2.10–12.
49 Xen. *Cyr.* 1.6.23.
50 Xen. *Cyr.* 1.6.21.
51 Xen. *Cyr.* 8.1.40.
52 ibid.
53 Xen. *Cyr.* 8.1.41.
54 Demades *Twelve Years* 17; J.11.2.7–9.
55 P.11.6.
56 A.1.7.4–7; D.17.8.2; J.11.2.10; Hammond 1980d.
57 Pind. *Pyth.* 10.1–12 (tr. Bowra 1969); for Alexander and Pindar see Instinsky 1961: 248–50; A.1.9.10; cf. P.11.12.
58 Hamilton, J. R. 1969: 30–1; Lauffer 1978: 49; Grassl 1987; see Rubinsohn's forthcoming article in *AM V*.
59 Hamilton, J. R. 1982: 50.
60 A.1.10.2–6 with n. 3; P.13.1–2, *Dem.* 23.3–6; *Phoc.* 17.2–3; D.17.15.1–5; J.11.4.9–12; Bosworth 1980a: 84–5.
61 Demades *Twelve Years*, 65.
62 A.1.9.1; Bosworth 1980a: 84–5.
63 P.13.3; Ephippus *FGrH* 126 F 3; Ath. 10.434b; Alexander's special treatment of Theban envoys sent to the Great King before the destruction of the city and captured after Issus (A.2.15.2–3; *P.Mor.* 181b) could be taken as an earlier indication of remorse.
64 As quoted in Edson 1970: 38–9 (with slight rearrangement).
65 A.1.11.2; P.14.8–9; this occurred at Leibethra (in the Loeb but not the Penguin edition) on the Macedonian side of Mt Olympus, which Pausanias (9.30.7–11) connects with Orpheus and Dionysus; see Graf 1986: 87–90.
66 Berve 1926: II no. 117 (Aristander); Greenwalt 1982.
67 A.1.11.2; P.14.9.
68 Arist. *Pol.* 1260ᵃ.
69 Arist. *Rh.* 1361ᵃ; Alexander ignored the sage's opinions in this respect as he did Aristotle's instructions to treat barbarians as if they were animals or plants (in *P.Mor.* 329b); in regard to the latter see Schachermeyr 1973: 525 n. 632.
70 Africa 1982a: 411.
71 P.12.1–6, *Mor.* 259d–260d, 1093d; Stadter 1965: 112–14.
72 Saying, according to Plutarch (21.10), that they were "a torment for our eyes," reminiscent of Hdt. 5.18; cf. *P.Mor.* 338d.
73 Tarn 1948: II 319–26; Africa 1982a: 410–14; see Plutarch (*Mor.* 333a), where Alexander severely rebukes one of his governors for offering to send him a beautiful boy, cf. 1099d and P.22.1–2; see Bengtson (1985: 210) on Alexander and pederasty.
74 Hamilton, J. R. 1969: 130; Africa 1982a: 411–12, 420 n. 101.
75 A.1.12.1 (reported without Arrian's endorsement of the story's authenticity).
76 Cf. D.17.37.5–6; C.3.12.15–17.
77 P.39.8, *Mor.* 180d, 332f–333a, 339f–340a; cf. D.17.114.3; Badian 1964: 203, "the only man he fully trusted."
78 See Carney 1983: 272.

79 Theophr. in Ath. 10.435a.
80 ibid.
81 P.*Mor.* 65f, 717f; cf. Xen. *Cyr.* 8.7.21 on sleep.
82 P.21.7–9, *Eum.* 1.3; D.20.20.1–3; C.10.6.11; J.11.10.2–3, 12.15.9; Paus. 9.7.2; Berve 1926: II nos. 206 (Barsine), 353 (Heracles); Brunt 1975; Schachermeyr 1973: 211–12.
83 Alexander probably met Barsine when her father Artabazus was in exile in Macedonia (*c.* 349 BC); see D.16.52.3–4; C.5.9.1; 6.5.2; Berve 1926: II no. 152 (Artabazus); Lane Fox 1974:50.
84 P.21.7–9; J.11.10.2.
85 See P.77.6; C.10.6.9; J.13.2.5; Ps.-Call. 3.33.11; Jul. Val. 3.58; Green 1991: 467, 562 n. 75.
86 Burn 1962a: 65–6.
87 A.1.11.3–5; Olmstead 1948: 496; Instinsky 1949; Rehork 1969: 254–6.
88 A.1.11.3–5; Ptolemy in P.*Mor.* 327d–e; D.17.17.1,3–5; J.11.6.2–7; Callisthenes in Polyb. 12.19.1–2; Ptolemy *FGrH* 138 F 4; Aristobulus *FGrH* 139 F 4; Anaximenes *FGrH* 72 F 29; Front.4.2.4; modern estimates vary; see Tarn 1948: I 10; Brunt 1963:32–6, 42, 46, 1976: lxix–lxxi; Milns 1968: 53; Schachermeyr 1973: 138–9, 139, "Verlässlich waren hiervon nur etwa 30,000, für einen Alexander gerade genug, damit die Welt zu erobern"; Lane Fox 1974: 116; Engels 1978a: 26–9; Lauffer 1978: 51–3; Hamilton, J. R. 1982: 53; Badian 1985: 423; Bengtson 1985: 137–8; Will 1986: 43; Green 1991: 156–9, 530 n.8.
89 For Alexander's appearance and depiction see P.4.1–3; P.*Mor.* 53d, 179d, 331b, 335a–c; Ps.–Call. 1.13.3; Jul. Val. 1.7; Bieber 1964, 1965; von Schwarzenberg 1967, 1976; Kreft 1981; Hartle 1982; Pollitt 1986: 19–46; Fittschen 1988; Kiilerich 1988; Lauter 1988; Smith 1988: 46–8; Stewart 1990: 186–95; Green 1991: 54–5; see Will (1986: 187) for Alexander's behavior patterns seen as compensation for his small physique.
90 Xen. *Cyr.* 8.3.14.
91 See also *Il.* 2.702; J.11.5.10; Instinsky 1949: 29–40, 69–70; Schmitthenner 1968: 34–7; Schachermeyr 1973: 164.
92 A.1.11.7–8, cf. 6.9.3, 10.2; D.17.18.1, 21.2.
93 A.1.11.8.
94 P.15.9, *Mor.* 331d; cf. D.17.17.3; Ael. 9.38; *Il.* 9.185–91.
95 Hdt. 7.43.
96 A.7.9.6; P.15.2; Aristobulus in *Mor.* 327d, 342d says he had 70 talents; C.10.2.24; Tarn 1948: I 14 "he was bankrupt"; Lauffer 1978: 54 (500-talent deficit, but notes 60 talents in Treasury).
97 Perdiccas was one subject clever enough to respond to Alexander's gestures by refusing to share in anything save the king's prospects: see P.15.4–5, cf. *Mor.* 342d–e.
98 Paus. 6.18.2–4.
99 Seltman 1957: 27.
100 For the diverse and contradictory accounts of the battle of the Granicus River see A.1.13.1–16.4; P.16.1–15, *Mor.* 326f; D.17.18.4–21.6; J.11.6.10–14; Fuller 1960: 147–54; Davis 1964; Seibert 1972a: 83–5; Schachermeyr 1973: 170–4; Brunt 1976: 449–53; Foss and Badian 1977; Hammond 1980c; see now Devine 1986b, 1988: 20, "a relatively peripheral battle, involving comparatively small forces and, from the tactical point of view, simple and straightforward," 1989b: 109–11; Bosworth 1988a: 40–4; Green 1991: 172–81, 489–512, although Green (xiv) no longer endorses this view on the battle.
101 Devine 1989b: 109, "Doubtful about the reliability of his Greek allied and mercenary infantry, Alexander had advanced without them"; cf. Fuller 1960: 147.

102  D.17.19.3.
103  A.1.15.8; cf. P.16.9–11; Berve 1926: II no. 427 (Cleitus).
104  A.1.16.6.
105  A.1.16.4; P.16.16; cf. J.11.6.12.
106  The Lacedaemonians (i.e., Spartans) refused to join the Corinthian League and hence did not participate in the expedition.
107  P.16.19; Ath. 14.659f–660a for reference to the sacrificer-cook; Fredricksmeyer 1966 for an excellent discussion of the sources and Alexander's ancestral rites.
108  S.13.4.8.
109  A.1.17.6; cf. Xen. *Cyr.* 1.6.1.
110  A.1.18.2; Badian 1965c: 167.
111  P.3.5–7.
112  S.14.1.23.
113  As translated in Pollitt 1965: 165, 1986: 22–3; cf. Ael. *VH* 2.3; Bieber 1964: 37–8.
114  P.4.3, *Mor.* 335a, 360d; Pliny *HN* 35.92.
115  In the *Aethopis*, a lost epic, see Schein 1984: 25–6.
116  Tod 1962: nos. 184, 185; for Alexander and Priene see Badian 1966: 47–8; Sherwin-White 1985; Marasco 1987.
117  A.1.18.9; commonly held to be an astute policy but viewed by Bosworth 1988a: 47 as "a military blunder."
118  For Ada see A.1.23.7–8; P.*Mor.* 180a; D.16.69.2, 74.2, 17.24.2; S.14.2.17; Berve 1926: II no. 20 (Ada); Hornblower, S. 1982: 45–51.
119  See A.1.23.8; P.22.7; D.17.24.2; Hornblower, S. 1982: 222 (Alexander's adoption), 358–63 (sister-marriage among the Hecatomnid dynasts).
120  D.17.25.6.
121  Cook 1983: 226, "the one incident that with his love–hate relationship with his father Alexander could not bear to be reminded of."
122  A.1.25.6–8.
123  Arrian (1.25.3) says that Alexander the Lyncestian sent a letter to Darius with a certain Amyntas, who deserted to the Great King.
124  Berve 1926: II no. 37 (Alexander the Lyncestian); Carney 1980: 32–3.
125  A.1.26.1–2; P.17.6–8; cf. S.14.3.9; Mederer 1936: 1–8; Pearson 1960: 36–8; Pédech 1984: 52–4.
126  Wilcken 1967: 97; A.2.1.3; D.17.31.3.
127  A.2.3.1.
128  For the Gordian knot see A.2.3.1–8; P.18.1–4; C.3.1.14–18; J.11.7.3–16; Marsyas *FGrH* 136 F 4; Mederer 1936: 9–14; Tarn 1948: II 262–5; Schmidt, L. 1959; Pearson 1960: 38–9, 157; Fredricksmeyer 1961; Hamilton, J. R. 1969: 46–7; Kraft 1971: 84–92; Frei 1972; Seibert 1972a: 92–6; Bosworth 1980a: 184–8, 1988a: 53–4; Roller 1983, 1984; Pédech 1984: 367–8; Will (1986: 62) suggests that Aristobulus' version may be the most authentic.
129  Hdt. 7.73; Fredricksmeyer 1961; Borza 1990: 65.
130  A.2.3.7; P.18.4.
131  A.2.3.7; P.18.3; C.3.1.17–18; J.11.7.15–16.
132  Xen. *An.* 1.2.21.
133  A.2.4.7–11; P.19.1–10; D.17.31.4–6; C.3.5.1–6.17, 3.7.1–2; J.11.8.3–9; S.14.5.12; POxy 1798 F 44; Engels 1978b: 225–6 links this with malaria (*falciparum*) which he contends played an important role in Alexander's demise; see also Atkinson, J. E. 1980: 145–8; Bosworth 1980a: 190–1, 1988a: 55–7; Green 1991: 220, 537 n. 53 suggests bronchial pneumonia.
134  Berve 1926: II no. 788 (Philip the Acarnanian); Sisti 1982.
135  Cited as C.3.6.13 in the Penguin edition.

136 See Carney 1988.
137 A.3.6.7; P.41.8; Badian 1960a, 1961b; Heckel 1977a; Bosworth 1980a: 284–5, 1988a: 57; Carney 1981a; Jaschinski 1981: 10–18; Kingsley 1986; Worthington 1984a.
138 Perhaps an apocryphal story: see A.2.5.2–4; P.*Mor*. 336c, cf. 330f; S.14.5.9; Aristobulus *FGrH* 139 F 9; Ath. 12.530b–c.
139 Arist. *Eth. Eud.* 1216ᵃ; Jaeger 1962: 253–5 on the credibility of the utterance.
140 Kérenyi 1959: 40–4, 85–6.
141 Hyperides 4.19,26.
142 A.2.5.9; Bosworth 1980a: 197–8.
143 D.17.6.1–3.
144 ibid.; A.3.22.2; C.5.10.14; Berve 1926: II no. 244 (Darius III); Schachermeyr 1973: 298–9, 298, "ein Mann [Darius III], der sich nicht nur als Prinz im Kampfe bewährte, sondern auch als Herrscher alles aufs beste bedachte und vorbereitete"; Bosworth 1980a: 202, 1988a: 61–2; Rutz 1984; Cook 1983: 225; see now Seibert (1987), who depicts Darius as a prudent (not cowardly) and practical man who became unsure and irresolute as a result of his tremendous losses.
145 Hamilton, J. R. 1982: 66 "perhaps 75,000 would not be wildly wrong"; Devine (1985a: 29) has Alexander's total force at 35,000–40,000.
146 See Murison 1972; Bosworth 1988a: 59–60 with n. 109.
147 Arrian tells us (2.6.2) of Alexander's alleged forced march from Mallus to Myriandus, a distance of some 75 miles, in two days; this claim is difficult to believe: see Murison 1972: 409; cf. Brunt 1976: 457–64; Atkinson, J. E. 1980: 177; Bosworth (1980a: 199–201, 1988a: 58–9 with n. 106), on the whole, favors Curtius' account, which depicts Alexander establishing himself in a defensive posture and Darius on the offensive; Devine also inclines toward Curtius (1980, 1984, 1985b: 41, "relatively free from contamination by official Macedonian propaganda and, on the whole, tactically coherent and in conformity with inherent military probability"), 1985a: 30 with n. 47 also raises serious questions concerning the likelihood of Alexander marching from Mallus to Myriandus in two days.
148 A.2.7.1.
149 For Issus see A.2.6.1–11.10; P.20.1–10; D.17.33.1–35.1; C.3.8.16–11.27; J.11.9.1–10; Polyb. 12.17.1–22.7; Walbank 1967: 364–76; Wilcken 1967: 99–105; Fuller 1960: 154–62; Hamilton, J. R. 1969: 50–3; Murison 1972; Hammond 1980a: 94–110; Schachermeyr 1973: 208–11; Devine 1980, 1985a, 1985b: 56, "Not only was the battle bloody, but it was also a near defeat for Alexander"; Hellenkemper 1984; Bosworth 1988a: 55–64; Green 1991: 225–35.
150 A.2.7.3–9.
151 Andreae 1977; Rumpf 1962; Schachermeyr 1973: 209 n. 230; Schefold 1979; Pollitt 1986: 3–4, 45–6, 191–2; Smith 1988: 10, 60, 111; Stewart 1990: 84–5, 194–5.
152 P.20.8–9; *Mor*. 341b–c; cf. A.2.12.1; D.17.34.5; C.3.11.10; J.11.9.9.
153 See A.2.12.3–4; cf. P.21.1–11; D.17.36.1–4; C.3.12.4–26; J.11.9.12–16.
154 See Xen. *Cyr*. 5.1.1–18, 6.1.45–52; on Alexander see Bosworth 1980a: 221 on A.3.12.5.
155 D.17.59.6–7 (probably romantic embellishment); cf. C.4.15.10–11.
156 C.10.5.19–25.
157 Badian 1985: 432.
158 A.2.14.3; Griffith 1968; see also Wirth 1971b: 145.
159 D.17.39.1–2; Diodorus' version supported by Griffith 1968; on the embassies (three in all), see Green 1991: 541 n. 56.

160 Green 1991: 244.
161 A.2.15.3.
162 C.4.1.19; D.17.47.1–6.
163 Schefold 1968; Pollitt 1986: 38–45; Smith 1988: 11, 40, 60, 63–4; Stewart 1990: 193–5.
164 A.2.16.7; C.4.2.2–3; Bosworth 1980a: 238.
165 A.2.18.1 (before the siege); P.24.5 (during); C.4.2.17 (during); Bosworth 1980a: 239; Hughes 1984: 170–4 for an informative discussion of this dream.
166 P.24.8–9; Hughes 1984: 175–9 with notes.
167 For the siege of Tyre see A.2.16.1–24.6; P.24.5–25.3; D.17.40.2–46.5; C.4.2.1–4.19; J.11.10.10–14; Polyaenus *Strat.* 4.3.4; Fuller 1960: 206–16; Rutz 1965; Hamilton, J. R. 1969: 62–5; Atkinson, J. E. 1980: 299–319, especially 315–19; Bosworth 1980a: 251–6, 1988a: 65–7; Romane 1987; Stewart 1987.
168 D.17.45.7; cf. C.4.4.1.
169 C.4.4.17.
170 P.24.6–7; D.17.41.7–8; C.4.3.21–2.
171 A.2.25.2; P.29.8; although it should be noted that this is a topos, and its veracity is suspect.
172 For the siege of Gaza see A.2.25.4–27.7; P.25.4–5; D.17.48.7; C.4.5.10, 6.7–30; Atkinson, J. E. 1980: 334–44; Bosworth 1980a: 257–60; Romane 1988.
173 See A.2.26.4; C.4.6.11; Romane 1988: 25–6.
174 Also Hegesias *FGrH* 142 F 5; deemed credible by Radet 1931: 105–6; Burn 1962a: 99; Lane Fox 1974: 193; Schachermeyr 1973: 220 n. 242; Will 1986: 81; Bosworth 1988a: 68; Romane 1988: 25; Green 1991: 267, 541 n. 58; fictitious to Tarn 1948: II 265–70; Pearson 1960: 247–8; Hammond 1983a: 126–8.
175 Hdt. 2.5.
176 Hdt. 2.37.
177 Although only reported to be enthroned as such in the Ps.-Call. 1.34.2; see Tarn 1948: I 41 "crowned as Pharaoh"; Wilcken 1967: 113–14 (probable); Hamilton, J. R. 1982: 74 "enthroned"; Badian 1985: 433 n. 1, "quite likely that he was never crowned"; Bowman 1986: 22, "may also have been a ceremonial coronation at Memphis"; Will 1986: 83, "Zum Pharao gekrönt"; Bosworth 1988a: 71, "most likely that Alexander assumed the kingship as his right and dispensed with native ceremonial"; Green 1991: 269 "instated as Pharaoh."
178 Ps.-Call. 1.30.4.
179 *Od.* 4.354–5; for the foundation of Alexandria see P.26.3–10; A.3.1.5–2.2; D.17.52.1–7; C.4.8.1–6; J.11.11.13; Plutarch and Arrian (following Ptolemy) say that the city was founded before Alexander's visit to Siwah; Diodorus, Curtius, and Justin (in line with Aristobulus) claim after Siwah; see Welles 1962; Borza 1967; Hamilton, J. R. 1969: 66–8; Fraser 1972: II 3–4; Schachermeyr 1973: 239–42; Brunt 1976: 467–8; Bagnall 1979; Atkinson, J. E. 1980: 359–68; Badian 1985: 501 n. 3, "it is most probable that the site was actually marked out before the visit, but that the formal inauguration had to wait until Ammon's approval had been obtained"; Will 1986: 83–4; Bosworth 1988a: 72, 74, 246–7.
180 For Alexander's visit to Siwah and his relationship with Ammon see A.3.3.1–4.5; P.26.11–27.9, *Mor.* 180d; D.17.49.2–51.4; C.4.7.5–30; J.11.11.2–11; S.17.1.43; Ps.-Call. 1.30.2–7; Jul. Val. 1.23; Radet 1926b; Larsen 1932; Mederer 1936: 37–68; Fakhry 1944; Tarn 1948: II 347–50; Tondriau 1949: 42–3; Classen 1959; Pearson 1960: 33–8, 160–2; Woodward 1962; Parke 1967: 194–237, esp. 222–30; Wilcken 1967: 121–9; Hamilton, J. R. 1969: 68–71; Kraft 1971: 43–67, 92–4; Schachermeyr 1973: 242–56; Lane Fox

1974: 200–14; Brunt 1976: 467–80; Bosworth 1977, 1980a: 269–74, 1988a: 71–4; Lauffer 1978: 88–9; Langer 1981; Jähne 1982–5; Will 1986: 84–6; Kienast 1987.

181 Hdt. 3.26.
182 Hdt. 3.34, cf. 3.33; Pl. *Leg.* 695b; Sen. *De ira* 3.14.1–2; Brown, T. S. 1982; see now the interesting analysis of Munson 1989 and the remarks in Griffiths 1989: 70–2.
183 See n.34 above; Kraft 1971: 92–4; Bosworth 1977: 72 n. 117, 1980a: 62, Brunt 1976: 469–70.
184 See Lane Fox 1974: 204.
185 A.3.3.1; Pl. *Leg.* 738c; Welles 1962: 276 n. 18; Parke 1967: 254–5; Classen 1971; Bosworth 1980a: 269–75.
186 A.3.3.1–2; Schachermeyr 1973: 243 n. 269.
187 See the sections on "The Death of Cleitus" and "The Opis 'Mutiny' " in Chapters 3 and 4 below.
188 C.10.5.4; J.12.15.7.
189 Bieber: 1964: 61–2; Pollitt 1986: 26–8; Smith 1988: 40, 44, 60, 111.
190 Wilcken 1967: 127; cf. Levi 1977a: 307; for Alexander's greeting as the god's son see P.27.5, *Mor.* 180d; D.17.51.1; C.4.7.25; J.11.11.7; Pearson 1960: 33–8; Hamilton, J. R. 1969: 71–2; Atkinson, J. E. 1980: 355–7.
191 Burn 1962a: 104.
192 Schachermeyr 1973: 252 n. 285; 672–5.
193 See Fakhry 1944: 39; Parke 1967: 225.
194 P.27.8; cf. J.11.11.2–8; Tarn 1948: II 348 with n. 2 and Hamilton, J. R. 1961b: 13 find it credible enough; but cf. Kaerst 1892: 612.
195 Gitti 1951: 18; Hamilton, J. R. 1969: 5.
196 Parke 1967: 207–8; 255.
197 P.3.4 (but see Hamilton 1969: 7 regarding translation); cf. Gell. 13.4.2–3.
198 Cf. Hamilton, J. R. 1953.
199 At the Danube, Hellespont (twice), Issus (twice), Aornus, Jhelum, Carmania; see Fredricksmeyer 1958: 265–74.
200 A.3.4.5 (Ptolemy), Aristobulus in the same passage and Curtius (4.8.1) indicate that Alexander returned the way he had arrived; the latter version is preferred by many historians, including Borza 1967; Bosworth 1980a: 274 suggests that Arrian may have misunderstood Ptolemy, 1988a: 74; cf. Fraser 1967: 30 n. 27.
201 P.48.4–49.2, *Mor.* 339d–f; Berve 1926: II no. 86 (Antigone).
202 Lane Fox 1974: 222.
203 P.29.1–6; A.3.6.1; C.4.8.16; Pickard-Cambridge 1988: 280.
204 P.29.4.
205 P.29.4–5.
206 P.29.5, *Mor.* 334.d–e; *IG* $2^2$, 2318, 2320; Hamilton, J. R. 1969: 25, 76.
207 A.3.6.2.
208 A.3.7.6; P.31.8; C.4.10.1–7; Pliny *HN* 2.180; Cic. *Div.* 1.121.
209 A.3.7.6.
210 P.31.2–5; cf. Xen. *Cyr.* 2.3.17–20.
211 See the analysis in Devine 1986a: 99, 102–3.
212 P.*Cam.* 19.5; A.3.8.7–15.7; P.32.4–33.11, *Mor.* 180c; D.17.56.4–61.3; C.4.15.1–16.33; J.11.14.1–7; Polyaenus *Strat.* 4.3.6; Griffith 1947; Tarn 1948: II 182–90; Burn 1965: 150–1; Fuller 1960: 163–80; Hamilton, J. R. 1969: 83–90; Schachermeyr 1973: 267–76; Marsden 1964; Devine 1975, 1986a, "It is commonly agreed by military historians that Alexander's victory at Gaugamela was a tactical masterpiece . . . . Alexander's tactics, though on the whole brilliantly original and subtle in conception, were not altogether flawless in

execution. The masterpiece was marred by the victor's heroic pretensions and misconceived order of priorities. Gaugamela, we must remember, was after all the victory of a very great but as yet immature general," 1989a; Welwei 1979; Atkinson, J. E. 1980: 436–55; Bosworth 1980a: 293–313, 1988a: 74–85; Wirth 1980/1; Will 1986: 92–4.

213 A.3.10.2–4.
214 D.17.56.1–4; C.4.13.17–24; J.11.13.1–3.
215 P.32.4.
216 Cf. P.*Mor.* 623e; the possibility of a connection between Alexander's late rising on this occasion and his drinking has been suggested by Will (1986: 93).
217 P.33.1; Brunt 1976: 475; Bosworth 1977: 56–60.
218 P.33.2.
219 A.3.15.1; cf. P.32.5–7, 33.9–11; D.17.60.7; C.4.15.6–8; Polyaenus *Strat.* 4.3.6; Hamilton, J. R. 1969: 89; Atkinson, J. E. 1980: 439–40; Bosworth 1980a: 309–11.
220 Griffith 1947: 87; cf. Devine 1986a: 106, "It is almost certain, despite statements to the contrary in our sources, that this message was never delivered . . . . Alexander was already far advanced in his all-out pursuit of Darius and [the messengers] returned without having accomplished their mission," 1989b: 123, "Alexander's tactical masterpiece was marred by his unrestrained pursuit of Darius, which endangered his left."
221 P.34.1; cf. J.11.14.6.
222 C.5.1.17–18,44; Berve 1926: II no. 484 (Mazaeus).
223 Bosworth 1988a: 235–6.
224 P.34.2.
225 C.5.2.13–15; D.17.66.3–7; cf. P.37.7, 56.1, *Mor.* 329d, *Ages.* 15.3.
226 D.17.66.6–7; see Hammond 1986.
227 D.17.67.1.
228 C.5.1.40–2.
229 P.*Ages.* 15.4; for the battle of Megalopolis see P.*Agis* 3.2; D.17.63.1–4; C.6.1.1–21; J.12.1.6–11; Badian 1967, 1985: 447; *Hammond* and Walbank 1988: 77–8; Noethlichs 1988: 391, "soll . . . gesagt haben."

## 3 THE METAMORPHOSIS

1 Tarn 1948: I 55; cf. Badian 1964.
2 Tarn 1948: II 97.
3 Hamilton, J. R. 1969: lxiii, who also notes that "Alexander is twice described [in Plutarch's *Alexander*] as 'cruel (fearsome) and implacable' (42.4, 57.3)."
4 In the *Moralia* Plutarch addresses charges of "drunkenness and a passion for wine" (337f, cf. 623d–f) made against Alexander, and in his *Life* (23.1) says that Alexander was "less addicted to drink than he was thought to be" (tr. Hamilton, J. R. 1969: 58). Hamilton also notes that Plutarch apparently felt compelled to retract this opinion at *Mor.* 623e on the basis of the evidence in the *Royal Diaries* pointed out to him by his friend Philinus; see Teodorsson 1989: 116–21.
5 Theog. *Eleg.* 499–500, tr. in Rolleston 1927: 105.
6 *The Greek Anthology IV* 1963: 11.232.
7 Philochorus in Ath. 2.37e; Pl. *Symp.* 217e.; Pliny *HN* 14.141 (basis for *in vino veritas*); Eubulus utilizes Dionysus to (in Ath. 2.36b–c) offer a graphic description of escalating revelations: "Three bowls [of wine] only do I mix for the temperate – one to health, which they empty first, the second to love and pleasure, the third to sleep. When this is drunk up wise guests go home.

The fourth bowl is ours no longer, but belongs to violence; the fifth to uproar, the sixth to drunken revel, the seventh to black eyes. The eighth is the policeman's, the ninth belongs to biliousness, and the tenth to madness and hurling the furniture."

8 Ath. 10.427e–f.
9 P.*Mor.* 715d–f.
10 Cf. P.*Mor.* 406b, 437d–e; Teodorsson 1989: 97.
11 Borza 1983: 52 citing Ephippus in Ath. 4.146c.
12 Borza 1983: 47: Borza's article is definitive; see also Tomlinson 1970; for the background and Greek context of the symposium see Dentzer 1982; Garland 1982; Vetta 1983; Lissarrague 1990; Murray 1983, 1984, 1990b; Pellizer 1990; Rösler 1990.
13 (1) 334: Dium (D.17.16.3–4), a nine-day festival sponsored by Alexander (2) 333: Phaselis (P.17.9), Alexander, drunk, crowns a statue (3) 333: Issus (C.3.12.2), Alexander invites close friends to a banquet after the battle (4) 330: Persepolis (P.38.1–8; D.17.72.1–6; C.5.7.2–7), Alexander, drunk, burns down the palace (5) 328: Bazaira near Maracanda (C.8.1.19), Alexander and troops feast after a great hunt (6) 328: Maracanda (A.4.8.1–9.1; P.50.1–51.11; C.8.1.22–52; J.12.6.1–3), Alexander, drunk, kills Cleitus (7) 328/327: Uncertain location (C.8.4.22–30), banquet wherein Alexander meets Roxane (8) 327: Uncertain location (P.54.4–6), symposium wherein Callisthenes refuses to perform *proskynesis* (9) 327: Uncertain location (P.53.3–6), the symposium wherein Callisthenes is politically undone (10) 327: Bactria (A.4.13.5–6; C.8.6.14–27), Alexander drinking heavily while a conspiracy unfolds (11) 327: Nysa (A.5.2.5–7; C.8.10.15–17; J.12.7.7–8), a revel on "Mt Merus" (12) 326/325: "India" (D.17.100.1–2; C.9.7.15–18), conflict between a drunken Macedonian and the boxer Dioxippus at a symposium (13) 326/325: "India" (C.9.7.24–6), Dioxippus accused of stealing a golden cup at a subsequent symposium (14) 325: Carmania (A.6.28.1–3; P.67.1–6; D.17.106.1; C.9.10.24–9), a seven-day drunken revel (15) 324: Persis (P.70.1–2; Ath. 437a–b; Ael. *VH* 2.41), a contest in drinking neat wine after the suicide of Calanus (16) 324: Susa (e.g. P.70.3–6), feasting in celebration of mass marriages (17) 324: Opis (A.7.11.8–9), a general feast in celebration of the reconciliation between the king and his troops (18–21) 324: Ecbatana (Ael. *VH* 3.23), Alexander's heavy drinking at the houses of four friends (22) 324: Ecbatana (A.7.14.1; P.72.1–2; D.17.110.7–8), a Dionysiac festival and the death of Hephaestion (23) 323: Babylon (D.17.116.1; J.12.13.6–7), festivals after Hephaestion's funeral (24) 323: Babylon (A.7.24.4; P.75.3–4), drinking party (25) 323: Babylon (A.7.24.4; P.75.4–5; D.17.117.1–2; J.12.13.7–10, ?14.8–9; ?Ephippus *FGrH* 126 F 3; ?Nicobule *FGrH* 127 F 1), Alexander joins Medius after the above and continues to drink (26) 323: Babylon (A.7.25.1; ?J.12.14.8–9), more drinking with Medius until late into the night. This list is partial and tentative. It contains the locations where verifiable symposia occurred. At least one symposium took place at each of the locations given. This does not mean, of course, that these were necessarily the only symposia held at each respective site – or elsewhere. Our sources generally mention only one symposium per location in order to highlight an unusual event that took place there. Numbers in the present text are higher than those found in O'Brien 1980b: 100. In this case, as in others where there are apparent contradictions between my earlier work and this book, the latter takes precedence; on Alexander's drinking cf. Hammond 1980a: 297–9.
14 Wirth 1973: 132, "Die Quellen sprechen von immer hektischeren Gelagen und einem sich steigernden Alkoholgenuß. Daß solche Exzesse angesichts einer Jahre hindurch physisch überbeanspruchten Konstitution und einer nur

notdürftig ausgeheilten Lungenverletzung in Indien [see Chapter 4 below] eines Tages zum Ruin führen werden, mußte jeder erkennen, der dies miterlebte."

15 Borza 1983: 47; Borza concludes (54–5) by suggesting four uses of the symposium: (1) relief from exacting campaigns, (2) a customary social gathering for Alexander and his comrades, (3) a means of defining the inner court, and (4) a testing ground for one's loyalty to Alexander.

16 O'Brien 1980b: 100–2.

17 See esp. Appendix B below.

18 Ath. 10. 434d; P.*Mor.* 454d–e, 623f–624a; Macurdy 1930.

19 Borza 1983: 50–2.

20 Ephippus *FGrH* 126 F 3; Ath. 10.434a, presuming this to have occurred on that momentous occasion.

21 A.7.29.4; Brunt 1976: 534–5 who says Arrian "was at pains to deny that Al[exander] was given to hard drinking. . . . [f]or an apologist the best course was to say as little as possible."

22 See n. 4. above.

23 Hamilton, J. R. 1982: 30, "Alexander, despite the assertions of his apologists both ancient and modern, drank heavily, particularly towards the end of his life."

24 Pope 1957; Frye 1962: 101, Borza 1972: 242 n. 52, 1990: 167; for the physical remains of the complex at Persepolis see Schmidt, E. F. 1953, 1957, 1970; Wheeler 1968; see Hallock (1985) for contents of the Persepolis Tablets.

25 For the golden vine see Chares *FGrH* 125 F 2; Ath. 12.514e–f; Phylarchus *FGrH* 81 F 41; Ath. 12.539d; Amyntas in Ath. 12.514f; Green 1991: 316.

26 P.37.3–5; D.17.70.1–6; C.5.6.1–8.

27 See Heckel 1980.

28 C.5.5.5–24; D.17.69.2–9; J.11.14.11–12; Heckel 1980; 173, "undoubtedly fictitious."

29 Ransacking: D.17.70.1–6; C.5.6.4–8. 120,000 talents: D.17.71.1; C.5.6.9; cf. P.37.4; D.17.80.3; J.12.1.3; S.15.3.9.

30 Engels 1978a: 79.

31 J. 13.1.9 reports that only 50,000 talents were to be found in the Treasury after Alexander's demise. The king, of course, was a heavy tipper.

32 For the burning of Persepolis see: Cleitarchus *FGrH* 137 F 11; Ath. 13.576d–e; A.3.18.11–12, 6.30.1; P.38.1–8; D.17.72.1–6; C.5.7.3–8,11; S.15.3.6; Ps.-Call. 2.17.11; modern accounts offer a wide spectrum of interpretation: Berve 1926: II no. 359 (Thais); Radet 1931: 188–9 (197 "Ce fut la première épiphanie dionysiaque"); Mederer 1936: 69–83; Olmstead 1948: 521–3 (521, "an act of sheer vandalism"); Tarn 1948: II 47–8 (48, "I need hardly say that there is not a word of truth in the Thais story"); Andreotti 1950: 590 ("deliberato"); Schmidt, E. 1957: 172, 178–9, Pearson 1960: 215, 218–19; Griffith 1964: 37 n. 3; Badian 1967: 186–90, 1985: 446; Wilcken 1967: 144–5; Hamilton, J. R. 1969: 99–101, 1982: 88–9; Wirth 1971b: 149–52; Borza 1972; Schachermeyr 1973: 287–92, 290 n. 335, "Vielleicht war der Akt also nüchtern geplant, dann aber als rauschende Festlichkeit ausgeführt"; Lane Fox 1974: 258–64 (262, "Alexander had done more damage than he intended, and sobriety was followed by repentance"); Brunt 1976: 514–17; Goukowsky's Diodore 1976: 222, "Les deux traditions [premeditated and extemporaneous] n'ont rien de contradictoire, car Thaïs peut avoir offert au roi l'occasion d'accomplir un dessein longuement médité, le délire dionysiaque des participants ajoutant une dimension surnaturelle à ce qui n'eût été qu'un acte de vandalisme"; Levi 1977a: 346–51 (349 "stato deciso"); Balcer 1978; Lauffer 1978: 104–6 with n. 14; Bosworth 1980a: 330–3, 1988a: 91–4 (93 with n. 199, "There is a measure

of agreement that Alexander regretted the action at the time"); Hammond 1980a: 167; Hornblower, S. 1983: 283, 321 n. 61; Bengtson 1985: 163; Will 1986: 98 "Es kann . . . keinerlei Zweifel bestehen, daß diese Tat ganz bewußt geplant und sorgfältig durchgeführt wurde"; Green 1991: 314–21.

33 Bosworth 1988a: 93 suggests that this "exchange between Parmenio and Alexander . . . is probably apocryphal."

34 See Hdt. 8.53.

35 *SIG* I 314; P.38.2; Cleitarchus *FGrH* 137 F 11; Ath. 13.576d–e.

36 A.6.30.1; cf. C.5.7.11; Schmidt, E. 1957: 91–111.

37 Badian 1985: 446.

38 ibid.: 447; Bosworth 1988a: 202–3; *Hammond* and Walbank 1988: 77–8; cf. Borza 1971, 1972: 236, who places Agis' defeat in 331; see Chapter 2, n. 223 above.

39 Badian 1985: 447.

40 Hamilton, J. R. 1982: 89.

41 D.17.74.3–5; cf. A.3.19.5–6; P.42.5; C.6.2.10,17; J.12.1.1.43. See Bosworth 1980a: 336.

42 Bosworth 1980a: 336.

43 A.3.21.10; D.17.73.2; C.5.13.14–17; J.11.15.5.

44 P.43.3–4; C.5.13.24; J.11.15.5.

45 P.43.5, *Mor.* 332f; Hamilton, J. R. 1969: 114, "Plutarch is the only author to mention this incident"; see also A.3.21.10; cf. D.17.73.2; J.11.15.5–15; for a fictionalized encounter between Alexander and Darius see D.17.73.4 and Ps.-Call. 2.20.5–12; see Schachermeyr 1973: 300–3.

46 C.6.6.6.

47 P.43.7; C.6.2.11; cf. D.17.77.4; Berve 1926: II no. 586 (Oxyathres).

48 Cf. P.67.8, *Mor.* 65d; cf. Dicaearchus in Ath. 13.603a–b; Carystius in Ath. 603e; Tarn (1948: II 320–3) dismisses Bagoas the eunuch as fictitious, but Badian (1958b) demonstrates his historicity. Hammond 1983a: 157, 194 n. 24, and Gunderson 1981: 188 still adhere to Tarn's position; Berve 1926: II no. 195 (Bagoas), cf. no. 194 (Bagoas).

49 Ael. *VH* 3.23; I follow Bosworth 1988b: 170–3 in his suggestion that these events probably occurred at Ecbatana in the autumn of 324; cf. O'Brien 1980a: 41.

50 Cf. Xen. *Cyr.* 7.5.60–5.

51 D.17.77.6–7; C.3.3.24, 6.6.8; J.12.3.10.

52 For Alexander's adoption of Persian customs see A.4.7.4, 8.4, 9.9; P.45.1–4, 47.5, *Mor.* 329c–d, 330a–d; D.17.77.4–7; C.6.6.1–12; J.12.3.8–4.1.

53 P.45.2.

54 Ritter 1965: 41–55; see now Fredricksmeyer 1986, "Rather than being a new Oriental monarchy, it was a creation *sui generis*, in which Macedonian and Persian elements were combined, but in which, in the balance, the Macedonian-Greek component prevailed"; *contra* Kingsley 1981, 1984, 1991; Arrian (4.7.4) claims that Alexander also wore the tiara, a conical Persian head-dress worn upright rather than to the side – this emblem of royalty could be exhibited only by the Great King – but most scholars reject Arrian's assertion.

55 P.47.9.

56 *Mor.* 181d; D.17.114.2.

57 A.3.3.1–2; S.17.1.43; P.*Mor.* 332b; Brunt 1976: 464–5.

58 See Chapter 2, n. 89 above.

59 Kerényi 1976: 179–80.

60 See Hdt. 7.61, cf. 6.53–4, 7.150.

61 Lane Fox 1974: 201.

62 See A.3.25.3; C.6.6.13; D.17.74.1–2; see also Fischer 1987.

63  D.17.74.3–4; C.6.2.15–3.18; J.12.3.2–4; cf. P.47.1–4; the entire incident con-
    spicuously ignored by Arrian.
64  C.6.3.1–5; Keegan (1987: 54–9), in a general discussion of Alexander's ora-
    tory, rightly emphasizes the king's calculated theatricality; Bosworth (1988a:
    97), referring to the situation at hand, states that "in practice the issue
    was his [Alexander's] categorical insistence on total unchallenged autocratic
    power. His men were prevailed upon to advance that ambition, fired by
    the king's rhetoric and perhaps more by the hope of donatives present and
    future."
65  Cf. A.5.25.3–26.8, 7.9.1–10.7; P.47.1–4; D.17.74.3–4; J.12.3.2–4; for a bal-
    anced appraisal of Curtius see Yardley and *Heckel* 1984: 1–15.
66  Cf. Xen. *Cyr.* 8.2.7–9, 13–22.
67  P.39.7; accepted by Tarn 1948: II 302 as authentic but rejected by Kaerst
    1892: 616–17 as spurious; see Hamilton 1969: 104.
68  For the Philotas affair see A.3.26.1–27.5; P.48.1–49.15; D.17.79.1–80.4;
    C.6.7.1–7.2.38; J.12.5.1–8; S.15.2.10; Cauer 1894: 8–38; Berve 1926: II no.
    802 (Philotas); Tarn 1948: I 62–5; Badian 1960b, 1961b: 21–3, 1964: 193–7,
    1985: 452–3 (453 n. 1, "the plot against the house of Parmenio"); Wilcken
    1967: 163–6; Hamilton, J. R. 1969: 132–8; Milns 1969: 159–65 (165, "The
    execution of Philotas after a farce of a trial was a judicial murder; the killing
    of Parmenion was a purely political assassination and was carried out in the
    best traditions of an Oriental despot"); Edmunds 1971: 363, 366–8; Schacher-
    meyr 1973: 328–36; Lane Fox 1974: 282–91; Brunt 1976: 517–21; Heckel
    1977b, 1982b, 1983b; Rubinsohn 1977; Lauffer 1978: 119–20 with n. 13;
    Bosworth 1980a: 359–67, 1988a: 101–4 (101–2, "perhaps best to concede that
    he [Philotas] had some sympathy with the conspirators without being actively
    involved in the plot"); Carney 1980; Hammond 1980a: 180–5; Hornblower,
    S. 1983: 284–5 (284, "The real issue was the relationship between the more
    intransigent Macedonian nobility . . . and the new Alexander"); Will 1986:
    118–23; Green 1991: 339–49.
69  C.6.7.33–4.
70  C.6.8.16.
71  Arrian (3.26.2) interpreted this as proof of Philotas' involvement in the plot.
72  C.6.11.12.
73  P.49.12.
74  A.3.25.4; C.6.6.18–19, 9.27; Berve 1926: II no. 554 (Nicanor).
75  For the murder of Parmenio see A.3.26.3–4; P.49.13; D.17.80.1, 3;
    C.7.2.11–34; J.12.5.3; S.15.2.10.
76  A.3.26.3; C.7.2.11–29; cf. D.17.80.3; Berve 1926: II no. 648 (Polydamas).
77  C.7.2.32; even the apologetic Tarn 1948: I 64 refers to Parmenio's death as
    "plain murder."
78  P.49.1.
79  Badian 1960b, esp. 326.
80  Rubinsohn 1977; Heckel 1977b, 1978b, 1982b, 1983b, 1986b, esp. 302, 1986c.
81  P.48.3–4; Schachermeyr 1973: 329; see also Hamilton, J. R. 1969: 134–5.
82  P.48.3.
83  And with Philip, who is said to have referred to Parmenio as his only real
    general (P.*Mor.* 177c).
84  A.1.13.3–7, 18.6–9, 2.25.2–3, 3.10.1–2; P.16.3; the ultimate source for these
    disagreements is generally thought to be Callisthenes, who may have retro-
    actively impugned Parmenio in order to make the general's liquidation appear
    more justified; Bearzot 1987.
85  C.7.1.36–40.
86  C.7.1.10–40.

87 Cf. Xen. *Cyr.* 8.2.4.
88 A.3.27.5; cf. C.6.11.35–8; to Bosworth (1988a: 101) Demetrius was the "central figure" in the conspiracy.
89 Strasburger 1934; Kornemann 1935; Pearson 1960: 188–211; Brunt 1976: xxx–xxxi; Bosworth 1980a: 22–7; Pédech 1984: 215–329.
90 D.17.80.2; C.7.1.5–9; Berve 1926: II no. 37 (Alexander the Lyncestian); Badian 1960b: 335–6 (336, "this cold-blooded execution of a harmless man"); Carney 1980; Heckel 1983b.
91 Bosworth 1988a: 103.
92 D.17.80.4; C.7.2.35–8; J.12.5.4–8; Polyaenus *Strat.* 4.3.19; Badian 1960b: 335; Bosworth 1980a: 363, 1988a: 104.
93 Steph. Byz. s.v. *Phrada*; P.*Mor.* 328f; S.11.8.9.
94 A.5.3.2, *Ind.* 5.11; D.17.83.1; C.7.3.22; S.11.5.5.
95 Cf. P.43.6.
96 P.*Mor.* 557b; C.7.5.28–35; D.17. Summary 20; S.11.11.4.
97 S.11.11.4, cf. 14.1.5.
98 Hdt. 6.19; see Brown, T. S. 1978 for Herodotus' account of a consultation of the oracle within "the larger context of Lydian history."
99 Parke 1985b: 65, 67–8; cf. Tarn 1948: II 272–5.
100 Parke 1985b: 68.
101 A.4.3.1–4; cf. C.7.6.19–23.
102 A.4.4.1.
103 C.7.7.8–22; cf. A.4.4.3.
104 C.7.7.23–9.
105 A.4.4.6–8; C.7.9.9–16; Fuller 1960: 236–41.
106 A.4.4.8–9; P.45.5–6; cf. C.7.9.11–14, referring only to the lingering effect of a previously acquired neck-wound.
107 C.7.9.15; Pliny *HN* 6.49.
108 A.4.5.3–6.2; C.7.7.31–9.
109 C.7.7.39.
110 C.7.11.1–29; *Metz Epitome* 18; A.4.18.4–19.5.
111 P.50.1–52.7, *Mor.* 71c; A.4.8.1–9.8; Diodorus summary 27; C.8.1.19–2.13; J.12.6.1–17; Sen. *Ep.* 83.19; *De ira* 3.17.1; Cauer 1892: 38–58; Kornemann 1935: 248–51; Aymard 1949; Brown, T. S. 1949b: 236–9; Pearson 1960: 60, 169–70; Instinsky 1961: 250–3; Hamilton, J. R. 1969: 139–45; Milns 1969: 189–94; Schachermeyr 1973: 362–70; Lane Fox 1974: 309–14; Bosworth 1977: 62–4, 1988a: 114–16; Lauffer 1978: 130–1 (131, "Der Mord an Kleitos bedeutete für Alexander wohl die schwerste persönliche Krise seines Lebens"); Hammond 1980a: 194–5; Carney 1981c; Badian 1982a: 41; Will 1986: 129–32; Green 1991: 361–6; the chronology is problematic: see Tarn 1948: I 73 with n. 1 and Lauffer 1978: 132 with n. 27, who place the episode at Maracanda in the summer of 328; Berve 1926: II 207 (winter).
112 P.50.3.
113 A.4.8.1–2, 9.5; see Piganiol 1940 on Alexander's celebration of Dionysiac festivals and the absence of the god's name when one might expect to see it in the sources; Fredricksmeyer 1958: 274–83 for details of Alexander and Dionysus.
114 Curtius (8.5.8), in his discussion of the the *proskynesis* episode, has flatterers "publicly declaring that Hercules, Father Liber [Dionysus] and Castor and Pollux would make way before the new divinity [Alexander]!"
115 P.50.8.
116 Schachermeyr 1973: 366; Bosworth 1988a: 111.
117 A.4.9.3–4; C.8.1.21; J.12.6.10; cf. Jul. Val. 1.7 (called Alacrinis); Ael. *VH* 12.26; Ath. 4.129a; Berve 1926: II no. 462 (Lanice).

118 C.8.1.20,39.

119 C.8.1.19, 2.14; cf. A.4.17.3.

120 P.51.8.

121 A.4.9.4; C.8.2.11; J.12.6.15; Plutarch (52.1) says that night and the following day.

122 P.52.2.

123 P.52.4.

124 Cf. *Mor.* 781b and Hdt. 3.31, "they [Persian royal judges] had also found a law whereby the King of Persia might do whatsoever he wished."

125 See the speech preceding his suicide in Soph. *Aj.* 815–65.

126 A.4.9.5; Curtius 8.2.6, "He [Alexander] wondered whether it was divine anger that had driven him to this heinous crime, and it occurred to him that he had failed to offer the annual sacrifice to Father Liber [Dionysus] at the appointed time. So it was that the god's anger had displayed itself against him – for the crime was committed amid drinking and feasting." The "sin against Dionysus" is referred to in Diodorus' summary of Book 17.

127 C.8.2.12.

128 Arist. *Rh.* 1379$^a$–1379$^b$.

129 C.8.4.30.

130 A.4.16.2–3; cf. C.8.1.1.

131 A.4.17.7; cf. C.8.3.1–15.

132 A.4.19.5–6, 20.4; P.47.7–8, *Mor.* 332e, 338d; D.18.3.3, Summary of Book 17; C.8.4.21–30; J.12.15.9, 13.2.5,9; S.11.11.4; *Metz Epitome* 28–31; Berve 1926: II 688 (Roxane); Renard and Servais 1955; Hamilton, J. R. 1969: 129–30; Bosworth 1988a: 117.

133 P.47.7, *Mor.* 332e, 338d.

134 C.8.4.27; Renard and Servais 1955.

135 The *Metz Epitome* (70) refers to another son who died at the Jhelum (Hydaspes) in the autumn of 326.

136 O'Brien 1980b: 100–1; Borza 1983: 55.

137 For background and general issues related to *proskynesis* see Hdt. 1.134, 7.136; Isoc. *Paneg.* 151; Xen. *An.* 3.2.13; Cauer 1894: 62–6; Richards 1934; Méautis 1942b; Balsdon 1950: 375; Bickerman 1963b: 244–55; Hamilton 1969: 150; Seibert 1972a: 192–204; Schachermeyr 1973: 371–5; Lane Fox 1974: 320–1; Brunt 1976: 538–41 calls attention to the fact that the nature of *proskynesis* varied according to the rank of the person performing it and doubts if prostration played a role at Alexander's banquet; Badian 1981: 48 with n. 30, 52; Bosworth 1988a: 284, "It [*proskynesis*] might involve a slight stooping forward and the simultaneous blowing of a kiss, as is depicted on the Persepolis Treasury relief, or it could be a complete prostration before the monarch."

138 For Alexander and *proskynesis* see A.4.10.5–12.5; P.54.3–55.1; C.8.5.5–24; J.12.7.1–3; Brown, T. S. 1949b: 240–6; Balsdon 1950: 371–82; Radet 1931: 256–70; Wilcken 1967: 168–70; Hamilton, J. R. 1969: 150–3, 1982: 105–6, Schachermeyr 1973: 375–85; Lane Fox 1974: 320–5; Lauffer 1978: 136 with n. 34; Badian 1981: 48–54; Will 1986: 136–8; Bosworth 1988a: 117–18, 284–7; Green 1991: 372–6; Arrian (4.12.6) disapproved of Alexander's *hybris* during this episode; see Schachermeyr 1973: 463, 558 (587, "In seinen späteren Jahren jedoch beobachten wir auch an Alexander die Gefahr der eigenen Hybris").

139 Green 1991: 376.

140 P.55.1.

141 Cf. A.4.12.3–5.

142 See Pearson 1960: 22–49; Pédech 1984: 15–69; Levi 1977b: 19–28.

143 A.4.12.6–7, 14.1.

144 P.54.2; cf. Diog. Laert. 5.5, who says that Aristotle advised Callisthenes not to take so many liberties in speaking before the king. Aristotle is said to have quoted Homer: "Then I must lose you soon, my child, by what you are saying" (*Il.* 18.95). Plutarch (54.1), citing Hermippus, says that Callisthenes quoted a Homeric phrase on several occasions that could have nettled the king: "Patroklos also is dead, who was better by far than you are" (*Il.* 21.107).

145 P.53.1, *Mor.* 1043d; Brown, T. S. 1949b: 233 n. 42.

146 P.53.2; A.4.10.1, 12.6–7.

147 P.*Mor.* 329b.

148 A.4.28.4, 30.4, 5.2.1, 26.5, 6.3.4, 14.2, 7.10.6, 20.1; S.3.5.5.

149 P.53.3.

150 Alexander may have left out *sophos* because he felt it did not apply to Callisthenes: see Hamilton, J. R. 1969: 148.

151 For the conspiracy see A.4.12.7–14.3; P.55.3–9; C.8.6.2–8.20; Berve 1926: II no. 305 (Hermolaus); Cauer 1894: 66–79; Hamilton, J. R. 1969: 153–7; Milns 1969: 197–9; Schachermeyr 1973: 386–90; Lane Fox 1974: 325–8; Lauffer 1978: 137–8 with n. 35; Carney (1981b) offers the most persuasive account of the episode and raises questions (227) about the use of the term "pages"; Will 1986: 138–9; Bosworth 1988a: 117–19; see Hammond (1990) for a thorough discussion of "the School of Pages"; I have also benefited from an unpublished paper on the subject by Thomas J. Byrne.

152 Hammond 1990: 268, "It was only in 331 BC that 50 Pages came to join him near Susa. As they were to serve as bodyguards, these Pages were beginning the last year of their course. Their juniors continued to attend the School in Macedonia. Thereafter until Alexander's death each graduating year of Pages must have joined him."

153 Cf. A.4.10.3–4 and P.55.4 for the view that the youths may have thought of themselves as tyrannicides.

154 A.4.13.5–6; C.8.6.16–17.

155 C.8.6.19. cf. Xen. *Cyr.* 8.2.3.

156 Cf. C.8.7.1–15.

157 C.8.8.20; Plutarch (55.7) cites a letter (rejected by Kaerst 1892: 608 and accepted by Hamilton, J. R. 1961: 16) saying that the "youths were stoned to death by the Macedonians," a view supported by Arrian (4.14.3).

158 For discussion, see Brown, T. S. 1949b: 247–8; Hamilton, J. R. 1961b: 16; Prandi 1985: 29–33; Golan 1988.

159 A.4.14.3; Curtius (8.8.21) says that Callisthenes died under torture; Justin (15.3.3–6) and Diogenes Laertius (5.5) claim that he was kept in an iron cage; cf. Diodorus' summary of Book 17; also see Rubinsohn's forthcoming article on Callisthenes in *AM* 5.

160 P.55.9.

161 P.57.1; cf. A.4.22.3; Polyaenus *Strat.* 4.3.10; C.6.6.14–17.

162 C.8.5.4; cf. A.*Ind.* 19.5; P.66.5; again, wide divergence among modern historians: see Tarn 1948: I 84, II 168–9; Fuller 1960: 124; Hamilton, J. R. 1969: 184; Schachermeyr 1973: 404; Brunt 1976: 530–1; Lauffer 1978: 139; Hammond 1980a: 203; Bosworth 1988a: 272; Green 1991: 381.

163 Brunt 1976: 530.

164 For example, Hdt. 3.94, 98–106, 4.40,44; Scylax *FGrH* 709 F 1–7; Arist. *Mete.* 350ᵃ, *Pol.* 1332ᵇ; Ctesias *FGrH* 688 F 45–52; A.*Ind.* 7.4–9.10; D.2.38.1–42.4, 3.63.3–5; C.8.9.1–37; S.11.5.5; Tarn 1948: I 85–7; Cary 1949: 194–205; Radet 1931: 277–8; Dihle 1964; Narain 1965; Woodcock 1966: 17–21; Wilcken 1967: 174–5; Schwarz 1972; Seibert 1972a: 147–65; Schachermeyr 1973: 413–17; Hammond 1980a: 202–3; Brunt 1983: 443–74; see now Karttunen 1989: 65–229.

165 J.12.7.4; Radet 1950: 299; Hamilton, J. R. 1969: 171; Badian 1985: 465–6; Schachermeyr 1973: 402; Brunt 1983: 465.
166 See citations in Brunt 1983: 435–42; cf. C.8.10.1; Hartman 1965; Schachermeyr 1973: 110–13; Bosworth 1988a: 119; Karttunen 1989: 210–19.
167 D.2.38.5.
168 Badian 1985: 461–3 with n. 1 on 462–3.
169 A.4.22.6; P.59.1–5, *Mor.* 181c; C.8.10.1–2; Berve 1926: II no. 739 (Taxiles); Yardley and *Heckel* 1984: 316, 322.
170 A.4.26.1–27.4; P.59.6–7; D.17.84.1–6; cf. C.8.10.22–36; Polyaenus *Strat.* 4.3.20; *Metz Epitome* 39–45; Narain 1965: 157; for an alternative chronology relating to this sequence of events see Bosworth 1988a: 121–2, 1990; cf. Narain 1965: 157; Badian 1987a.
171 A.4.27.3.
172 P.59.6–7; D.17.84.2.
173 Tarn 1948: I 89.
174 On Nysa see A.5.1.1–3.4; P.58.6–9; Diodorus' Summary of Book 17; C.8.10.7–18; J.12.7.6–8; S.15.1.7–8; the credibility of the Nysa episode has been treated with undue skepticism by Goukowsky (1981: 24–33); cf. the more convincing position of Bosworth 1988a: 121 with n. 300; see also Mederer 1936: 97–9; Radet 1931: 285–7; Woodcock 1966: 21–25; McCrindle 1969: 338–40; Kraft 1971: 97–8; Schachermeyr 1973: 410–13; Brunt 1983: 438; Dihle 1987: 48 n. 7; Karttunen 1989: 56 n. 404, 59.
175 A.5.2.3.
176 See Prologue, n. 4 above.
177 A.5.2.1.
178 See now Karttunen 1989: passim.
179 Bosworth 1988a: 119.
180 For Aornus see A.4.28.1–30.4; D.17.85.1–86.1; C.8.11.2–25; J.12.7.12–13; S.15.1.8; *Metz Epitome* 46–7; Radet 1931: 287–9; Fuller 1960: 248–54; McCrindle 1969: 335–8; Kraft 1971: 94–7; Bosworth 1988a: 123, 1990.
181 Stein 1929: 120–54; on Heracles' failure to take the rock see A.4.28.1–4; P.*Mor.* 181d; D.17.85.2; C.8.11.2.
182 A.4.30.4; C.8.11.24.
183 A.4.30.5–8; D.17.86.2–3.

## 4 THE AMBIVALENT VICTOR

1 See Chapter 3, nn. 164–6 above; A.5.4.1–6.8; D.17.86.3; Seibert 1985: 143–70 for the geography of the Indian expedition; Hammond 1980a: 202, "For Alexander, 'India' lay east of the Indus and projected eastwards into the Ocean, as Aristotle had taught him."
2 A.5.3.5–6; C.8.12.11; For Taxila see Marshall 1951: I 11–19.
3 An abbreviated version of this conversation (which may be fictitious) can be found in P.*Mor.* 181c.
4 C.8.12.17–18.
5 For the Gymnosophists see A.7.1.5–6, 2.2–4; P.64.1–65.8; S.15.1.63–6,68; Pfister 1941; Brown, T. S. 1949a: 38–51; Pearson 1960: 96–100; Hansen 1965; Wilcken 1967: 180–1; Hamilton, J. R. 1969: 178–81; Kraft 1971: 99; Schachermeyr 1973: 420–1; Lane Fox 1974: 348–50; Brunt 1983: 491–3; Pédech 1984: 104–14.
6 Berve 1926: II no. 583 (Onesicritus); Brown, T. S. 1949a; Pearson 1960: 83–111; Pédech 1984: 71–157.
7 S.15.1.64.
8 Once again the numbers in the sources are diverse and contradictory: see

A.5.15.4; P.62.1; D.17.87.1–2; C.8.13.6 (85 elephants); I follow Devine 1987, 1989b: 124–7 in regard to these numbers.

9 For the battle of the Hydaspes (Jhelum) River see A.5.8.4–18.7; P.60.1–15; D.17.87.1–89.3; C.8.13.3–14.44; J.12.8.1–4; Polyaenus *Strat.* 4.3.9,22; Front. *Str.* 1.4.9–9a; Breloer 1933; Radet 1935; Hamilton 1956, 1969: 163–9; Fuller 1960: 180–99; Burn 1965: 148, 150–1, 153–4; Goukowsky 1972; Brunt 1983: 457–9, 485–7; Devine 1987, 1989b: 124–7; Hammond 1980a: 204–12; Bosworth 1988a: 125–30; Ferrill 1988a: 211–15, 1988b; Kulak 1988a/b.

10 C.8.13.20–1.

11 P.60.14, *Mor.* 181e, 332e, 458b; cf. C.8.14.41–5.

12 Arist. *Eth. Nic.* 1159ᵃ.

13 A.6.2.1; cf. D.17.89.6; C.8.14.45; J.12.8.7; S.15.1.33; Pliny *HN* 6.59; *Metz Epitome* 61.

14 See A.5.14.4, 19.4–6; cf. D.17.95.5; C.8.14.34; S.15.1.29; Gell. *NA* 5.2.4–5; however, cf. Plutarch (61.1–2), who also records the story (based on Onesicritus) that Bucephalas died of exhaustion and old age, supported by A.5.19.4; see Anderson, A. R. 1930.

15 A.5.19.4; C.9.3.23; P.61.2; J.12.8.5.

16 P.61.3.

17 Philostr. *VA* 2.24, cf. 2.20; Ael. *NA* 7.37; Tarn 1938: 164; Oikonomides 1985: 71.

18 A.5.19.4.

19 Schachermeyr 1973: 443–51; Burstein 1976.

20 See Engels 1980.

21 Green 1991: 404–6.

22 A.5.23.1.

23 A.5.24.5.

24 Schachermeyr 1973: 184, "Bedingungslose Übergabe verlangte Alexander von allen . . . . Denn im Grund seines Herzens liebte der König alle Menschen, sofern sie ihm nur gehorchten."

25 C.9.1.27–34; D.17.91.4–92.3; S.15.1.31; Ael. *NA* 8.1; Hdt. 1.192; Berve 1926: II no. 734 (Sophithes).

26 Oikonomides 1985: 71.

27 D.17.94.2–3; S.15.1.17.

28 On the problem of snakes see A.*Ind.* 15.10–11; D.17.90.1–7; C.9.1.12; S.15.1.28, 2.7; Ael. *NA* 12.32, 15.21, 16.39, 17.2.

29 On the "mutiny" at the Beas River see A.5.24.8–29.2; P.62.1–8; D.17.93.1–95.2; C.9.2.1–3.19; J.12.8.10–17; S.3.5.5, 15.1.27,32; Philostr. *VA* 2.43; Pliny *HN* 6.62; Radet 1931: 299–307; Schachermeyr 1966, 1973: 434–42; Hamilton, J. R. 1969: 170–5; Kraft 1971: 103–6; Lauffer 1978: 151–3; Hammond 1980a: 213–15; Holt 1982; Brunt 1983: 531–3; Will 1986: 151–2; Bosworth 1988a: 132–4; Green 1991: 406–11.

30 D.17.94.1–4.

31 D.17.94.4.

32 Cf. C.9.2.12–13.5; see Kornemann 1935: 78–81; Tarn 1948: II 287–90; Schachermeyr 1973: 436 with n. 530; Brunt 1983: 528–34 for a general discussion of Arrian's speeches and letters, 531, "It is quite possible that A. [Arrian] had authority for supposing that on each occasion Al. [Alexander] spoke in the sense he conveys"; cf. Bosworth 1988b: 123–34; see also C.9.2.12–13.5.

33 A.5.28.1.

34 A.5.28.3; P.62.5–6; C.9.3.18–19.

35 A.5.28.4; S.15.1.27.

36 Hammond 1980a: 214.

37 S.3.5.5.

38 D.17.95.1–2; C.9.3.19; P.62.6–8; J.12.8.16–17.
39 Bosworth 1988a: 133, "Alexander had bowed to their pressure and he never forgot it."
40 P.13.4.
41 A.6.2.1; cf. C.9.3.20; Will 1986: 152–3.
42 A.6.2.3, *Ind.* 18.9–10; cf. P.66.3; S.15.2.4–5, 1.28.
43 A.*Ind.* 18.3–10; for the role of the trierarchs see Berve 1926: I 165–6 with notes; Wilcken 1967: 188.
44 A.6.3.1–2, *Ind.* 18.11.
45 A.6.2.2–3.5, *Ind.* 19.7; cf. D.17.95.5–96.1; C.9.3.21–4; S.15.1.17; *Metz Epitome* 70.
46 According to Arrian (*Ind.* 19.5).
47 P.*Mor.* 337a.
48 Arist. *Eth. Nic.* 1166ᵃ.
49 A.6.4.4–5.4; D.17.97.1–3; C.9.4.1, 8–14.
50 D.17.97.1–3; C.9.4.9–14 says that Alexander was ready to leap into the sea; this testimony and the swimming pool excavated at Pella (Hammond 1990: 289 n. 79), cast serious doubt on Plutarch's assertion that Alexander could not swim (58.6).
51 Badian 1985: 469–70.
52 A.6.7.5–6.
53 A.6.9.1–11.8; P.63.2–14, *Mor.* 327b, 341c, 343d–345b; D.17.98.3–99.5; C.9.4.26–6.1; J.12.9.5–10.1; S.15.1.33.
54 A.6.11.1.
55 ibid. (erroneously called Critodemus), *Ind.* 18.7; C.9.5.22–7.
56 A.6.12.1–13.3; P.63.11; C.9.5.19, 29–6.1.
57 See Arist. *Eth. Nic.* 1115ᵃ-1117ᵇ.
58 Arist. *Eth. Nic.* 1115ᵇ.
59 Arist. *Eth. Nic.* 1168ᵇ.
60 Arist. *Eth. Nic.* 1166ᵃ.
61 Arist. *Eth. Nic.* 1166ᵇ.
62 See Brunt 1983: 139 n. 1.
63 D.17.103.7–8; C.9.8.22–7; J.12.10.3; S.15.2.7.
64 Snyder 1966: 164; cf. Xen. *Cyr.* 8.2.24–6.
65 P.*Mor.* 521b; Pliny *HN* 35.139; Dioxippus was an Olympian victor: see Berve 1926: II no. 284 (Dioxippus).
66 Cf. D.17.100.1–101.6.
67 Tarn 1948: I 103.
68 A.6.18.4–19.2; for Alexander's journey on the Indus to Ocean see also A.6.19.3–20.5, *Ind.* 20.10; C.9.8.28–9.27; D.17.104.1; P.66.1–2; Brunt 1983: 155–61 (notes).
69 A.6.19.3–4; P.66.1; D.17.104.1; Hamilton, J. R. 1969: 182.
70 For Alexander's sacrifices (those mandated by Ammon were made on both islands) see A.6.19.4–5; *Ind.* 20.10; P.66.2; D.17.104.1; C.9.9.27; Hamilton, J. R. 1969: 182.
71 P.65.6–8.
72 A.6.17.3; J.12.10.1 (says Polyperchon); S.15.2.11.
73 For the Gedrosian disaster see A.6.21.3–26.5; P.66.4–7; D.17.104.3–106.1; C.9.10.4–18; J.12.10.7; S.15.1.5, 2.3–7; Pliny *HN* 12.34; Stein 1943; Strasburger 1952; Wilcken 1967: 199–200; Hamilton, J. R. 1969: 181–4; Kraft 1971: 106–18; Schachermeyr 1973: 464–71; Engels 1978a: 110–18, 135–43; Brunt 1983: 474–83; Badian 1985: 471–3; Bosworth 1988a: 139–46; Will 1986: 157–9; Green 1991: 433–7.
74 See Hamilton, J. R. 1972.

75  Cf. P.42.7–10; C.7.5.10–12; Front. *Str.* 1.7.7; Polyaenus *Strat.* 4.3.25; the incident is located in various places: see Hamilton, J. R. 1969: 113.
76  A.6.24.1; P.66.7; S.15.2.7.
77  Estimates of how many people were brought into and out of the desert range widely: see Tarn 1948: I 107; Strasburger 1952: 487; Kraft 1971: 116–17; Engels 1978a: 111, 114; Brunt 1983: 481–3; Badian 1985: 471; Will 1986: 157; Bosworth 1988a: 145; Green 1991: 435.
78  Put into proper perspective by Schepens 1985; Bengtson 1986: 178, "Man kann das Unternehmen nicht anders als den Ausdruck eines gesteigerten Selbstbewußtseins Alexanders bezeichnen, der hier in seiner Hybris den Tod vieler seiner Gefährten verschuldet hat."
79  Badian 1985: 472–3.
80  Hamilton, J. R. 1969: 183.
81  See now Högemann 1985.
82  See Pearson 1960: 112–49; Badian 1975; Brunt 1983: 518–25; Pédech 1984: 159–214; Sofman and Tsibukidis 1987; Meister 1989: 66–7; Wirth 1988.
83  A.*Ind.* 30.1–7; cf. D.17.106.6–7; C.10.1.11–12.
84  A.7.5.5, *Ind.* 23.5.
85  A.7.4.1; P.68.7; Tarn 1948: II 299 rejects Plutarch's version.
86  Hamilton, J. R. 1982: 128.
87  For Harpalus' second flight see Berve 1926: II no. 143 (Harpalus); Badian 1961b; Schachermeyr 1973: 476; Jaschinski 1981: 23–44; Ashton 1983; Will 1983: 110–27, esp. 113–19; Worthington 1984a/b; 1986a/b/c; Bosworth 1988a: 149–50, 215–20.
88  P.35.15, *Mor.* 648c; Theophr. *Hist. Pl.* 4.4.1.
89  See Bosworth 1988a: 149–50.
90  Python in Ath. 13.586d, 595e–596b; Snell 1964: 99–138; Goukowsky 1981: 72–7; Jaschinski 1981: 94; Bosworth 1988a: 149–50 containing the most persuasive discussion; for genre and play see Sutton 1980.
91  Badian 1961b: 16–19, 1985: 476, 480.
92  A.7.4.3.
93  C.9.10.21,29.
94  A.6.27.3–5; C.10.1.1–8; J.12.10.8; Berve 1926: II nos. 354 (Heracon), 422 (Cleander), 712 (Sitalces).
95  See also C.10.1.1–8.
96  C.10.1.8.
97  Badian 1985: 477.
98  Bosworth 1988a: 149.
99  Curtius (9.7.1–11) tells us of 3,000 mercenaries who abandoned their posts and returned to Europe while Alexander was in "India"; cf. D.17.99.5–6.
100  D.17.106.2–3, cf. 111.1, 18.9.1–2.
101  Badian 1961b: 26–8; Jaschinski 1981: 45–61; Bosworth 1988a: 148–9.
102  A.6.28.1–3; P.67.1–6; D.17.106.1; C.9.10.24–9; Radet 1931: 337–41; Mederer 1936: 99–101; Wilcken 1967: 201, "legend"; Goukowsky 1981: 47–64 (64, "si la Bacchanale de Carmanie a bien été, comme nous le croyons, un *kômos épinikios*, ils n'ont fait que développer un aspect triomphal qui existait dès l'origine, à ceci près qu'Alexandre voulait remercier Dionysos et non pas imiter les fastes et la divine ivresse de son triomphe"); Bosworth 1988a: 147, "Some of the story, the imitation of Dionysus, may be a late accretion, but the majority of the details, independently described by Plutarch and Curtius, look authentic."
103  A.6.28.1.
104  Badian 1985: 479; Will 1986: 145, "Feierlichkeiten, vor allem Orgien und Trinkgelage, konnten nun unter dem Namen des Dionysos zu quasi religiös-

kultischen Handlungen erhöht werden, das Zechgelage wurde Staats– und Gottesdienst. Mehrtägige Festlichkeiten mit entsprechendem Alkoholkonsum häuften sich nun bezeichnenderweise in Indien und wurden gleichsam Bestandteil von Alexanders 'Programm.' "

105 A.6.28.4.

106 A.6.28.5–6, *Ind*. 33.2–36.9; P.68.1; D.17.106.4–5; C.10.1.10; Pearson 1960: 134–5 draws attention to Nearchus's use of Homer as a model; see Badian 1975: 147–8, 160–6 for a discussion of the chronology of Nearchus' arrival in Carmania and related issues; cf. Bosworth 1987.

107 A.*Ind*. 35.3.

108 A.*Ind*. 36.3.

109 Cf. Dicaearchus in Ath. 13.603a–b.

110 Green 1991: 443.

111 Refuted by Nock 1985 (the reprint of a 1928 article), who claimed that Alexander was likened to Dionysus posthumously; cf. Kern 1938: 47; Piganiol 1940; Servais 1959; Seibert 1972: 204–6; Schachermeyr 1973: 409–13; Jeanmaire 1978: 351–72; Goukowsky 1981: 79–83; Brunt 1983: 435–42 (439, "there is no evidence that he [Alexander] ever claimed to be a re-incarnation of Dionysus"); see now Will 1986: 141–7.

112 A.6.30.1–2.

113 A.6.28.3.

114 P.69.1–2; *Mor*. 246a–b; J.1.6.13–16; Polyaenus *Strat*. 7.45.2; cf. Xen. *Cyr*. 8.5.21.

115 See Phylarchus *FGrH* 81 F 41; Ath. 12.539d–f.

116 To continue Ephippus *FGrH* 126 F 5 as translated in Ath. 537e–538a: "Alexander sprinkled the very floor with valuable perfumes and scented wine. In his honour myrrh and other kinds of incense went up in smoke; a religious stillness and silence born of fear held fast all who were in his presence. For he was hot-tempered and murderous, reputed, in fact, to be melancholy-mad." Ephippus' testimony is rejected by Pearson 1960: 65; cf. Berve 1926: I 15–17; Neuffer 1929: 51–3; Badian 1961a: 663, "As far as our slender evidence goes, the account is confirmed; why, therefore, should we believe that Ephippus, writing shortly after the King's death about matters known to tens of thousands, made himself a laughing-stock by silly invention?," 1985: 488 n. 2; Bosworth 1980b: 8.

117 Who was special to Alexander because of her alleged involvement in his birth, but also to Dionysus, with whom there was a divine rivalry of sorts, see Jeanmaire 1978: 210–14 (214, "une sorte de rivalté"); Detienne 1989: 69 n. 22, "Artemis and Dionysos exerted a mutual influence on each other."

118 Kern 1938: 47, "Alexandros und Dionysos wurden unzertrennlich."

119 A.6.29.4–30.2; P.69.3–5; C.10.1.30–5; S.15.3.7; cf. Ps.-Call. 2.18.1; see Bosworth 1988b: 46–55 for a comparison of accounts (particularly Arrian and Strabo).

120 C.10.1.25–38; Badian 1958b: 147–50; cf. Tarn 1948: II 321.

121 P.69.3; Berve 1926: II no. 679; Hamilton, J. R. 1969: 192.

122 P.*Dem*. 25.1–7; 10.2.1–3; D.17.108.4–8, 18.19.2; S. 17.3.21; Paus. 1.37.5, 2.33.3–5; Ath. 8.341e–f, 13.586b–d, 594d–596b; Hyperides *In Dem*. 10–12; see above, n. 87; Bosworth (1988a: 215–20) for the effects of Harpalus' flight in Athens.

123 A.7.3.1–6; P.69.6–70.1; D.17.107.1–6; S.15.1.68; Ael. *VH* 5.6.

124 Cf. A.7.3.1–6; Cic. *Div*. 1.47; Val. Max. 1.8 ext. 10.

125 Athen. 10.437a–b; P.70.1–2; Ael. *VH* 2.41; Will 1986: 145, "Des Königs Helden fielen in Erfüllung ihrer staatsbürgerlichen Pflichten nun nicht mehr nur auf den Schlachtfeldern."

126 Bosworth 1988a: 155.

127 A.*Ind*. 42.5–10; Pliny *HN* 6.100.

128 On the Susa marriages see Chares *FGrH* 125 F 4; Ath. 12.538b–539a; Phylarchus *FGrH* 81 F 41; Ath. 12.539b–540a (Phylarchus and Agatharchides); A.7.4.4–8, 6.2; P.70.3, *Mor*. 329e–f, 338d; D.17.107.6; C.10.3.11–12; J.12.10.9–10; Ael. *VH* 8.7; Radet 1931: 342–50; Tarn 1948: I 110–11, II 333 n. 1; Badian 1964: 201, 1985: 480; Wilcken 1967: 207–9; Hamilton 1969: 194–5; Milns 1969: 239–40; Schachermeyr 1973: 483–7; Lane Fox 1974: 417–19; Lauffer 1978: 169–70 with n. 12; Hammond 1980a: 261; Will 1986: 166; Bosworth 1980b: 11–12, 1988a: 156–7.

129 A.7.4.5.

130 Referred to by Diodorus (17.16.4) in relation to Alexander's celebration at Dium.

131 Chares *FGrH* 125 F 4; Ath. 12.538c–f, quoted from the latter.

132 Tarn 1948: I 111, for a full discussion of this vision in relation to the feast at Opis, see Tarn 1933.

133 That is, the notion of the brotherhood of man: see Badian 1958a; Todd 1964; Thomas, C. G. 1968.

134 Frye 1962: 132; Schachermeyr 1973: 479–87; Hamilton, J. R. 1982: 133; cf. Bosworth 1988a: 156–7.

135 Hamilton, J. R. 1987.

136 Bosworth 1980b: 20, "There is little that can be said to approximate to careful premeditated policy; rather Alexander seems to have reacted promptly to the various challenges confronting him during his reign. The result is piecemeal and certainly less romantic than a visionary policy of fusion and conciliation but it is far truer to the evidence as it stands"; 1988a: 156–7; cf. Hornblower, S. 1982: 105, 220, 1983: 281–4, 320 n. 56.

137 Hamilton J. R. 1969: 195, "if this [the marriage to Parysatis] is true, Alexander will have intended to link himself with *both* [*sic*] the royal houses of Persia."

138 Badian (1964: 201) in regard to the children of Macedonian veterans left with him at Opis: "His purpose, ultimately, was the creation of a royal army of mixed blood and no fixed domicile – children of the camp, who knew no loyalty but to him"; see also Bosworth 1988a: 273.

139 A.7.4.8.

140 A.7.5.1–3; P.70.3–6, *Mor*. 339b–c; D.17.109.2; C.10.2.9–11; cf. J.12.11.1–3.

141 See the accounts above in n. 140.

142 A.7.6.1; P.47.6, 71.1; D.17.108.1–3; C.8.5.1.

143 And to provide a counterpart to his Macedonians: see Bosworth 1980b: 17–18; the impact of Alexander's manpower drain on Macedonia is outlined in Bosworth 1986a; cf. Hammond 1989c.

144 For the Exiles' Decree see D.17.109.1, 18.8.2–7; C.10.2.4–7; J.13.5.2–5; Hyperides 1.18; Dinarchus 1.81–2; Tod 1962: nos. 201–2; Heisserer 1980: 188–93, 205–29; Bagnall and Derow 1981: 5–8; Tarn 1948: I 111–112 (112, "a wise and statesman-like measure"); Sealey 1960; Badian 1961b: 25–31; Wilcken 1967: 214–17; Bosworth 1988a: 215–28 (220, "inflicting grave disruption upon thousands of communities"); Green 1991: 450–1.

145 D.18.8.3–5; see also Diog. Laert. 5.12; Steph. Byz. s.v. *Mieza*; Berve 1926: II no. 557 (Nicanor).

146 Hamilton, J. R. 1982: 137 "Alexander explicitly disclaimed responsibility for the banishment of the exiles and claimed credit for their restoration." Restored exiles qualified as yet another group owing everything to Alexander.

147 Hornblower, S. 1983: 290, for an interesting and percipient interpretation; cf. Hamilton 1982: 136–8.

148 On deification see P.*Mor*. 187e, 219e, 804b, 842d; Hyperides 5.31–2, 6.21;

Dinarchus 1.94; Timaeus in Polyb. 12.12b 3; Ael. *VH* 2.19, 5.12; Ath. 6.58; Diog. Laert. 6.63; Val. Max. 7.2 ext 13; Berve 1926: I 97; Kaerst 1927: 482–5; Sanctis 1940; Tarn 1948: II 370–4; Balsdon 1950: 383–8; Taeger 1951, 1957: passim; Hamilton, J. R. 1953, 1969: 73–4; 1982: 138–41; Bickerman 1963a; Wilcken 1967: 210–14; Habicht 1970: 17–25, 28–36, 243–6, 251–2; Edmunds 1971; Schachermeyr 1973: 525–31; Rosen 1978; Fredricksmeyer 1979a/b; Badian 1981: 54–66; Brunt 1983: 495–7; Walbank 1987: 366–8; Bosworth 1988a: 219, 288–90; Green 1991: 451–3.

149 Aelian *VH* 5.12.
150 Hyperides *In Demo.* 31; Atkinson, K. M. T. 1973.
151 Ael. *VH* 2.19; Ath. 6.251b.
152 Badian 1981: 31.
153 Cf. C.8.5.8–12.
154 Arist. *Pol.* 1253ᵃ, 1284ᵃ⁻ᵇ, 1288ᵃ, 1332ᵇ, also *Eth. Nic.* 1145ᵃ.
155 Isoc. *Ep.* 3.5, *Phil.* 113–14; Perlman 1957, 1973, 1976, 1983.
156 Miller, S. G. 1973; Fredricksmeyer 1979a: 52–6; Badian 1981: 71; Green 1991: 80–2.
157 See Chapter 1 above; three late sources attest to Demades' proposal to recognize Alexander as a thirteenth god: Ael. *VH* 5.12; Val. Max. 7.2. ext. 13; Ath. 6.251b.
158 Damis in P.*Mor.* 219e; Ael. *VH* 2.19; see above, n. 148.
159 P.28.3, *Mor.* 180e, 341b; Aristobulus *FGrH* 139 F 47; Ath. 6.251a; C.8.10.29; Sen. *Ep.* 59.12; Tarn 1948: II 358–9 n. 5.
160 P.28.4.
161 Seltman 1955: 213–27; Kaiser 1962; Bellinger 1979: 27; Oikonomides 1981; Dürr 1974; Goukowsky 1978: 61–5; Price, M. J. 1982b.
162 Wilcken 1967: 223; cf. Dem. 1.14.
163 Hamilton, J. R. 1953: 156–7; Badian 1964: 202; Green 1991: 453, "He became a god when he ceased wholly to trust his powers as a man, taking the divine shield of invincibility to combat his inner fear of failure, the divine gift of eternal youth as a talisman against the spectres of old age, sickness, death: the perils of the flesh that reminded him of his own mortality. Alcoholism bred paranoia: his dreams became grandiose lunacies. He was formidable still; but he had come very near the end of the road."
164 A.7.1.1, *Ind.* 20.1–2 with n. 1.
165 A.7.8.1; P.71.2; C.10.2.12–4.2; J.12.11.4.
166 On the so-called "mutiny" at Opis see A.7.8.1–12.3; P.71.1–9; D.17.108.3, 109.1; C.10.2.8–4.3; J.12.11.5–12.7; Wilcken 1967: 218–22; Milns 1969: 246–7 (247, "a masterpiece of psychological manipulation"); Schachermeyr 1973: 492–7; Lane Fox 1974: 424–9; Lauffer 1978: 173–6; Hammond 1980b: 469–71; Hornblower, S. 1983: 291–2; Will 1986: 167–8; Bosworth 1988a: 159–61; Green 1991: 453–7.
167 A.7.8.3; D.17.109.2; C.10.2.30, 4.2–3; J.12.11.8.
168 A.7.9.1–10.7; C.10.2.15–29; for the various judgments on the validity of these speeches (particularly Arrian's) see Kornemann 1935: 158–66, who argues that the speech is based on Ptolemy; Tarn 1948 II: 290–6 (295, "came through Ptolemy and is genuine"); Wüst 1953–4a/b stresses its rhetorical nature; Griffith 1965:137 acknowledges problems but contends that it is "founded on fact"; Stadter 1980, "highly rhetorical"; Hamilton 1982: 26, "The speech is Arrian's own composition, but the substance may go back, if not to Alexander, at least to Ptolemy. Rhetorical it undoubtedly is, but a solid basis of fact underlies it"; Brunt 1983: 532–3 "lack of authenticity is much more evident in the speech at Opis, though not all the objections of F. R. Wüst . . . are well-founded"; Montgomery 1985 supports Wüst; Bosworth 1988b: 113,

"Neither in its shape nor in its detailed content can it bear any relation to what was actually said by Alexander"; however, Bosworth 112 does presume that "Arrian had a vestigial report of the Opis speech which began with a brief review of Philip's successes and contrasted them with Alexander's even greater triumphs."

169 A.7.11.4; P.71.5–7; D.17.109.3; J.12.12.5–6.
170 A.7.11.5; P.71.8.
171 Schachermeyr 1973: 232, "Auf der einen Seite der strahlende Held, bestrickend als Freund seiner Vertrauten, als Anführer der Truppe, als Soldatenvater; auf der anderen Seite der dräuende, zürnende, schreckenverbreitende, düstere König."
172 Wilcken 1967: 54; cf. Yavetz (1983: 161–5) on Julius Caesar.
173 Renault 1976: 59–60.
174 For the banquet at Opis see A.7.11.8–9; cf. Ps.-Call. 3.28.9; Tarn 1933; Badian 1958a.
175 A.7.11.8.
176 A.7.11.9.
177 A.7.12.1–3; P.71.8; J.12.12.7,10.
178 Cf. P.71.9; D.17.110.3; J.12.4.5–10; Badian 1964: 201.
179 A.7.12.3–4; J.12.12.8–9.
180 P.47.9; *Eum.* 6.2.
181 C.8.5.2–6.1; Berve 1926: II no. 654 (Polyperchon).
182 Deduced from 18.4.1–2, cf. A.7.12.3–4; Schachermeyr 1973: 516–19, 553; Heckel 1985a; Bosworth 1988a: 161 with n. 424, 1988b: 207–11, esp. 208 with n. 90.
183 A.7.12.5–7; P.*Mor.*180d; D.17.118.1; J.12.14.3.
184 D.18.49.4; Paus.1.11.3; Livy 8.24.17.
185 P.*Mor.*180e; Griffith 1965b.
186 Suidas s.v. *Antipatros* (2703), however, speaks of Antipater's unsympathetic response to Alexander's divine pretensions and "blasphemy."
187 P.74.2–4, *Mor.* 180f; cf. A.4.12.2; D.17.118.2, see also 19.49.1–51.6; C.8.5.22–4, 10.10.19; Berve 1926: II no. 414 (Cassander).
188 P.74.6.
189 A.7.13.2–6; Bosworth 1988a: 163, "The march itself had been a relaxed affair with repeated carousing en route."
190 A.7.14.1; P.72.1; D.17.110.7.
191 Ephippus *FGrH* 126 F 5; Ath. 12.538a–b.
192 Bosworth 1988b: 170–3.
193 Ael. *VH* 3.23, translated in Robinson 1953: 31.
194 Bosworth 1988b: 174.
195 For the death of Hephaestion see A.7.14.1–15.1; P.72.2–5; D.17.110.8; J.12.12.11–12; Hamilton, J. R. 1969: 199–202; Schachermeyr 1973: 511–15; Lane Fox 1974: 433–8; Bosworth 1988a: 163–5; Green 1991: 464–7.
196 D.17.110.8: "ἐν οἷς [πότους] Ἡφαιστίων ἀκαίροις μέθαις χρησάμενος = in which [drinking parties] Hephaestion drank inappropriately," left untranslated in the Loeb edition: see therein 445 n. 1.
197 Green 1991: 464; Bengtson 1985: 183, "Hephaistion war an seinem frühen Ende nicht schuldlos. Wie so viele andere Makedonen kannte er weder Maß noch Ziel beim Trinken, auch Alexander stand ihm hier nicht viel nach."
198 Berve 1926: II no. 228 (Glaucias).
199 P.72.2.
200 Badian 1964: 203.
201 Cf. Arrian's account of Alexander after the death of Cleitus (A.4.9.4, "refused

firmly all food or drink for three days"); no reference to food or drink at the Beas (A.5.28.3) or Opis (A.7.11.1).

202 Arrian (7.14.4) mentions this report without endorsing its credibility.

203 Arrian reports this at 7.14.5 but doubts its authenticity; Epictetus 2.22.17; Brunt 1983: 251 n. 3.

204 A.7.14.2–9; P.72.3; *Il*. 19.319–20, "But now you lie here torn before me, and my heart goes starved for food and drink, though they are here beside me, by reason of longing [*pothos*] for you."

205 Cf. *Il*. 18.81–2.

206 A.7.14.4; P.72.3; see Hdt. 9.24 and Ael. *VH* 7.8.

207 P.72.3; Kerényi 1976: 66–7, 271.

208 D.17.114.4.

209 P.*Mor*. 335c–e, where Plutarch also (mistakenly) says it was Stasicrates instead of Deinocrates: see Berve 1926: II no. 249 (Deinocrates); A.7.14.8 (10,000); D.17.115.5 (12,000); J.12.12.12 (12,000); Hamilton, J. R. 1969: 201–2; Schachermeyr 1973: 514–15.

210 A.7.14.6–7, 23.6; P.72.3, 75.3; D.17.115.6 (a god); J.12.12.12 (a god); Hyperides *Epitaph*. 21; Lucian *Calumn*. 17–18; Treves 1939; Bickerman 1963a; Habicht 1970: 28–36.

211 A.7.23.6–8; Hamilton, J. R. 1953: 157; Vogt 1971; Seibert 1972b; Schachermeyr 1973: 476–7; Bosworth 1988a: 234–5.

212 A.7.13.1, 14.9; P.*Eum*. 2.1–5.

213 A.7.16.8.

214 Badian 1964: 203.

215 Lane Fox 1974: 447, who also insists that Alexander "was not an alcoholic."

216 Regarding Alexander's victory and the foundation of cities for the settlement of survivors see A.7.15.1–3, *Ind*. 40.6–8; cf. D.17.111.4–6; S.11.13.6.

217 P.72.4; Hamilton, J. R. 1969: 201.

218 Badian 1985: 486.


## 5 DEATH IN BABYLON

1 A.7.15.4–6, 19.1–2, 23.2; D.17.113.1–4; J.12.13.1–2; Pliny *HN* 3.57; Tarn 1948: II 21–6, 374–8; Hampl 1953; Andreotti 1957: 133–66; Sordi 1965, 1985; Schachermeyr 1970: 218–23; Brunt 1983: 495–9; Pacella 1984; Bosworth 1988a: 165–7, 1988b: 83–93; Green 1991: 469–70.

2 D.17.113.3–4.

3 A. 7.1.2–3, cf. 4.7.5.

4 P.68.1.

5 C.10.1.17–19.

6 D.18.4.2–6; Andreotti 1953: 133–66; Hampl 1953; Schachermeyr 1954, 1970: 187–94, 1973: 547–56; Wilcken 1967: 224–6; Badian 1968, 1985: 490–1; Hamilton, J. R. 1969: 187–9; Hammond 1980a: 300–4; Brunt 1983: 500–4; Bosworth 1988a: 164–5, 1988b: 185–211.

7 Following Schachermeyr (1954) and Wilcken (1967: 226), among others, in accepting Hieronymus of Cardia as the source and the plans as basically authentic; cf. Hornblower, J. 1981: 94–6 and Hornblower, S. 1983: 290–1.

8 Tarn 1948: II 378–98; Pearson 1960: 261–2.

9 D.18.4.5.

10 Cf. Hamilton, J. R. 1969: 188.

11 A.7.19.6–20.2; S.16.1.11; Högemann 1985: 120–43; Bosworth 1988a: 168–70, 1988b: 56–60.

12 Bosworth 1988b: 211.

13 Cf. S.16.11; Brunt 1983: 270 n. 1 says Strabo "substitutes Zeus for Uranus"; Herodotus (3.8) has Dionysus and Aphrodite.

14 Cf. P.*Mor.* 326b.

15 A.7.18.1–5; cf. P.73.3–5; Mederer 1936: 124–6.

16 A.7.18.2–3.

17 Eur. *El.* 827–9; see Hamilton, J. R. 1969: 203.

18 A.7.16.5–6; cf. P.73.1; D.17.112.2–6; J.12.13.3–6; S.16.1.6; Mederer 1936: 120–4; Smelik 1978–9; van der Spek 1985.

19 A.7.17.1–4, cf. 3.16.4; S.16.1.5; Schachermeyr 1973: 282, 508–9.

20 A.7.16.6.

21 A.7.22.1–5; D.17.116.5–6; S.16.1.11; Mederer 1936: 126–30.

22 A.7.22.3–5.

23 A.7.24.1–3; cf. P.73.7–74.1; D.17.116.2–4; see also Berosus in Ath. 14.639c; Mederer 1936: 130–3; Derchain and Hubaux 1950; Lane Fox 1974: 459–60.

24 P.73.8; Berve 1926: II no. 278 (Dionysios); Hamilton, J. R. 1969: 204.

25 P.73.6.

26 Cf. the accounts of Alexander's death from the *Royal Diaries* in Arrian (7.25.1–26.3) and Plutarch (76.1–77.1); for full versions from the basic accounts see A.7.24.4–28.1; P.75.4–77.5; D.17.117.1–118.1; C.10.5.1–6; J.12.13.3–16.1; see also Ephippus *FGrH* 126 F 3; Ath. 10.434a–b; Nicobule *FGrH* 127 F 1, F2; Ath. 10.434c, 12.537d; *Metz Epitome* 97–113; Ps.-Call. 3.31–5; Mederer 1936: 133–60; Pearson 1954–5; Hamilton, J. R. 1969: 208–15; Milns 1969: 255–8; Bosworth 1971b, 1988a: 171–3, 1988b: 157–84; Schachermeyr 1970: 65–71, 1973: 556–63; Brunt 1976: xxiv–xxvi, 1983: notes on pp. 288–96; Renault 1976: 257–66; Merkelbach 1977: 75–7; Engels 1978b; Lauffer 1978: 186–8; Hammond 1980a: 295–9, 1983a: 4–11, 1988b, 1989d; Strasburger 1982b: 1101; Heckel 1988; Badian 1985: 489–90, 1987b; Will 1986: 175–80.

27 For chronology see Samuel, A. E. 1965: 8; Hamilton, J. R. 1969: 208–10; Bosworth 1988b: 164–7.

28 A.7.24.4; D.17.117.1; J.12.13.6–10; Berve 1926: II no. 521 (Medius).

29 A.7.26.1; P.76.8; C.10.5.1–3; Val. Max. 5.1 ext. 1; cf. Ps.-Call. 3.32.12–15; *Metz Epitome* 105–6.

30 A.7.26.2–3; P.76.9.

31 P.75.5, 76.9; A.7.28.1; Dio Chrys. *Or.* 64.21, "after escaping from the Theban hoplites, the Thessalian cavalry, the Aetolian javelin-throwers, the Thracians with their daggers, the martial Persians, the tribe of irresistible Medes, from lofty mountains, impassable rivers, unscalable cliffs, from Darius, Porus, and many other tribes and kings I might name, yet in Babylon, remote from battle and from wounds, our warrior died!"; Samuel, A. E. 1965: 8; Lewis, D. M. 1969: 272; Seibert 1972a: 173–5; Bosworth 1980b: 45–6; cf. Hamilton, J. R. 1969: 7, 28.

32 Pearson 1954–5: 438–9 with n. 40; Fraser, P. M. 1967, 1972: I 246–50; Brunt 1983: 292–3 with n. 2; cf. Welles 1962; Bosworth 1988b: 167–70.

33 Bosworth 1988b: 168–70.

34 Hdt. 2.42.

35 Badian 1987b; Bosworth 1988b: 183–4; Hammond 1980a: 295–9, 1983a: 4–11, 1988b, 1989d.

36 Bosworth (1971b) has developed the most elaborate justification for this thesis.

37 Assertions of poisoning are based on A.7.27.1–2; P.77.1–5, *Mor.* 849f; D.17.118.1–2; C.10.10.14–18; J.12.13.10–14.9; Paus. 8.17.6; Jul. Val. 3.56; Ps.-Call. 3.31.2–32.3; *Metz Epitome* 87–100 passim; Pliny *HN* 30.149; Dio Chrys. *Or.* 64.19; Vitr. *De Arch.* 8.3.16; see Berve 1926: II no. 386 (Iolaus); Mederer 1936: 140–55; Milns 1969: 257 (strychnine); Hamilton 1969: 213–15; Bosworth 1971b; Engels 1978b: 224–5; Levi 1977a: 406 ("probabilmente arsenico");

Green 1991: 476–77 (477, "If the king was not poisoned, the chances are that he succumbed either to raging pleurisy, or else, more probably, to malaria . . . . In either case, advanced alcoholism, combined with the terrible wound he sustained in India, had finally lowered even his iron resistance to a point where he could no longer hope to survive").

38  P.77.2; cf. C.10.10.14.

39  D.17.117.3, 18.2.4; C.10.5.4; J.12.15.12–13; *Metz Epitome* 112; Mederer 1936: 157–9; Schachermeyr 1973: 564 n. 679; Badian 1987b; Hammond 1989d.

40  Or "the most capable" (Τῷ κρατίστῳ), Alexander thus absolving himself of the responsibility that came with designating a successor; see also D.18.1.4–5; A.7.26.3; P.*Mor.* 181f; C.10.5.2, 5–6; J.12.15.5–8; Xen. *Cyr.* 8.7.8; Mederer 1936: 155–7; Badian 1987b; Hammond 1989d.

41  The names of the alleged participants in Medius' party are listed in Ps.-Call. 3.31.8–10 and *Metz Epitome* 97–8; see now Samuel 1986: 435–7.

42  Cf. P.23.7.

43  P.75.5; Ephippus *FGrH* 126 F 3; Ath. 10.434a–b, see also 11.469d; Hamilton, J. R. 1969: 209.

44  Ephippus *FGrH* 126 F 3; Ath. 10.434a, cf. 11.469d; Macrob. *Sat.* 5.21.16-19; Suidas s.v. *skyphos*; Sen. *Ep.* 83.23.

45  Kerényi 1976: 329.

46  Bosworth 1988a: 115–16; Ephippus *FGrH* 126 F 3; Ath. 10.434a–b; Berve 1926: II no. 665 (Proteas).

47  Ephippus *FGrH* 126 F 3; Ath. 10.434b; Nicobule *FGrH* 125 F 2; Ath. 12.537d as translated in Robinson 1953: 89, "and at his very last banquet, Alexander, remembering an episode in the *Andromeda* of Euripides, recited it in a declamatory manner, and then drank a cup of unmixed wine with great eagerness, and compelled all the rest to do so too"; A.7.27.2; P.75.5; Paus. 8.7.8, "some god . . . extinguished so relentlessly the life of Alexander"; Dio Chrys. *Or.* 64.20 "he [Alexander] abused Dionysus, though indulging so lavishly in that god's gifts"; *Metz Epitome* 99; J.12.13.7–10, "Taking up a cup, he suddenly uttered a groan while he was drinking, as if he had been stabbed with a dagger, and being carried half dead from the table, he was excruciated with such torture that he called for a sword to put an end to it, and felt pain at the touch of his attendants as if he were all over wounds"; Bosworth 1971b: 114–15; Will 1986: 178.

48  McKinlay 1950: 233, "Athenaeus refers to a wine of the Thebaid in Egypt that may be safely given in fevers [Athen. 33f: "it may be given even to fever patients without injury"] although, in general, wine was forbidden in such cases except to the aged"; cf. Pliny *HN* 23.48-9.

49  See O'Brien 1980b: 103 n. 1.

50  In addition to malaria and perhaps pneumonia: see Schachermeyr 1970: 65–9 and 1973: 563 with n. 678.

51  Engels 1978b.

52  Engels 1978b: 225, "*falciparum* malaria . . . . The king's weakened physical condition – his many wounds and heavy drinking – may have helped induce a pernicious manifestation of the disease which led to his death"; Will 1986: 178, "Eine bestimmte Krankheit, sei es nun Leberzirrhose oder Malaria, läßt sich aus den Berichten zwar nicht diagnostizieren, doch sind die mittelbaren Ursachen des Todes offensichtlich: totale physische Zerrüttung aufgrund von Marschstrapazen, Verletzungen, Krankheiten und vor allem natürlich eines permanenten übermäßigen Alkoholgenusses. Es verwundert letzlich nur, daß Alexander das für einen Militär durchaus stolze Alter von rund 33 Jahren erreichte."

53  Badian 1985: 489.

**EPILOGUE**

1 Arist. *Poet.* passim; see Jones 1962; Belfiore 1985; Halliwell 1987; Rist 1989: 286 places the (Revised) *Poetics* in Aristotle's last Athenian period *c.* 333.
2 See Prologue, n. 7 above.
3 Described by Aristotle (*Poet.* 1453ᵃ) as "the most tragic certainly of the dramatists."
4 Winnington-Ingram (1948: 160–1) argued that Pentheus himself is not much of a "tragic hero," and he may very well be right. Oddly enough Alexander supplies the elements Winnington-Ingram saw lacking in Pentheus. Alexander has "stature," occupies stage-center at the first opportunity, and establishes himself as "the dominant figure" in his own tragic saga.

**APPENDIX A**

1 See Andronicos 1984: 146–60.
2 Andronicos 1984: 149.
3 ibid.
4 Andronicos 1984: 156–57.
5 ibid., pls 115–16 (pp. 152–3).
6 Andronicos 1984: 157, pls 112–14 (pp. 150–1).
7 Andronicos 1984: 136, pl 90 (p. 133).
8 Andronicos 1984: 153.
9 Andronicos 1984: 165, pls 130–1.
10 Andronicos 1984: 208, pl 169.

**POSTSCRIPT**

1 For references to this treatise see Arist. *Frag.* F103R³, F104R³, F106R³, F107R³, F108R³, F110R³, F111R³; Ath. 2.44d, 11.496f, 14.641d. Various comments attributed to Aristotle on drinking and drunkenness may be found in: Arist. [*Pr.*] 871ᵃ–876ᵃ, 949ᵃ, 953ᵃ–954ᵃ, *Eth. Nic.* 1113ᵇ, 1114ᵃ, 1117ᵃ, 1151ᵃ, 1152ᵃ, 1154ᵇ, *Eth. Eud.* 1231ᵃ, 1235ᵇ, *Pol.* 1274ᵇ, *Frag.* F109R³, Ath. 2.40d, 15.674b–c.
2 Ath. 2.36a–b; McKinlay 1950.
3 Arist. [*Pr.*] 949a; cf. *Frag.* F588R³.

# Topics in the bibliography

General                                    279
Reference works                            279
Ancient sources                            280
    Diodorus Siculus                       280
    Quintus Curtius Rufus                  280
    Plutarch                               280
    Arrian                                 280
    Justin                                 281
Related texts                              281
Other relevant ancient works              281
Modern general treatments                  284
Recent collections                         285
Historiography                             285
Dionysus                                   289
Macedonian background                      296
The Royal Tombs at Vergina                 297
Young Alexander                            299
Aristotle                                  303
Religion                                   304
Military                                   307
Political                                  310
The metamorphosis                          314
India                                      317
Deification                                317
Alexander's death                          318
Miscellaneous                              320

# Bibliography

## GENERAL

Badian, E. (1971) "Alexander the Great, 1948–67," *CW* 65: 37–56, 77–83.
Seibert, J. (1972a) *Alexander der Grosse*. Darmstadt.
Tarn, W. W. (1927) *Cambridge Ancient History VI*. Cambridge. 590–603.
Walser, G. (1956) "Zur neueren Forschung über Alexander den Grossen," *Schweizer Beiträge zur allgemeinen Geschichte*. 14: 156–89.
Consult bibliographical references in the general works and commentaries of Atkinson, Badian, Bengtson, Bosworth, Brunt, Goukowsky, Green, Hamilton, Hammond, Hornblower, Lane Fox, Lauffer, Schachermeyr, Will, and Wirth along with entries in *L'Année Philologique*.

## REFERENCE WORKS

Ackermann, H. C., Augé, C., Gisler, J.-R., Jaeger, B., and Müller, P. eds (1981–90) *Lexicon Iconographicum Mythologicae Classicae I–V* (all double volumes). Zurich.
Bagnall, R. S. and Derow, P. eds (1981) *Greek Historical Documents: The Hellenistic Period*. Chico.
Bernhardy, G. ed. (1986) *Suidas. Suidae Lexicon I–V*. Osnabrück. Greek with Latin notes.
Berve, H. (1926) *Das Alexanderreich auf prosopographischer Grundlage I–II*. Munich.
Bickerman, E. J. (1968) *Chronology of the Ancient World*. Ithaca.
Buchwald, W., Holweg, A. and Prinz, O. eds (1982) *Tusculum-Lexikon griechischer und lateinischer Autoren des Altertums und des Mittelalters*. Zurich.
Cary, M. (1949) *The Geographic Background of Greek and Roman History*. Oxford.
Dittenberger, W. ed. (1915–24) *Sylloge Inscriptionum Graecarum I–IV*. Leipzig.
Hammond, N. G. L. and Scullard, H. H. eds (1978) *The Oxford Classical Dictionary*. Oxford.
Heisserer, A. J. (1980) *Alexander the Great and the Greeks. The Epigraphic Evidence*. Norman, Oklahoma.
Nauck, A. and Snell, B. (1964) *Tragicorvm Graecorvm Fragmenta. Svpplementvm*. Hildesheim. Greek with Latin notes.
Olshausen, E. (1991) *Einführung in die historische Geographie der Alten Welt*. Darmstadt.
Pauly, A. F. von, Wissowa, G., and Kroll, W. eds (1894–1972) *Real-Encyclopädie der klassischen Altertumswissenschaft*. Stuttgart.
Pédech, P. (1976) *La géographie des grecs*. Paris.

*Reallexikon für Antike und Christentum* (1950–64). Stuttgart.

Roscher, W. H. ed. (1965) *Ausführliches Lexikon der griechischen und römischen Mythologie*. Hildesheim.

Seibert, J. (1985) *Die Eroberung des Perserreiches durch Alexander den Grossen auf kartographischer Grundlage*. Wiesbaden.

Thomson, J. O. (1948) *History of Ancient Geography*. Cambridge.

Tod, M. N. (1962) *A Selection of Greek Historical Inscriptions II*. Oxford.

Wellington, J. S. (1983) *Dictionary of Bibliographic Abbreviations Found in the Scholarship of Classical Studies and Related Disciplines*. Westport, Connecticut and London.

## ANCIENT SOURCES

No contemporary account of Alexander's career has survived intact. Extant fragments from his own era have been printed and commented upon in F. Jacoby (1926,1929,1930), *Die Fragmente der griechischen Historiker IIA, IIB and IID*. Berlin. The fragments were translated into English by C. A. Robinson Jr (1953), *The History of Alexander the Great I*. Providence, RI. They are discussed in L. Pearson (1960), *The Lost Histories of Alexander the Great*. New York. Five connected accounts have survived from the first century BC through the third century AD. They are listed in chronological order.

### Diodorus Siculus (second half of the first century BC)

Welles, C. B. ed. (1983) *Diodorus of Sicily VIII. Books XVI.66–95 and XVII*. London and Cambridge, Mass. Loeb. Greek and English. With notes.

Goukowsky, P. ed. (1976) *Diodore de Sicile XVII*. Paris. Budé. Greek and French. With notes.

### Quintus Curtius Rufus (first century AD)

Rolfe, J. C. tr. and ed. (1971, 1976) *Quintus Curtius. History of Alexander I–II*. London and Cambridge, Mass. Loeb. Latin and English. With notes.

Bardon, H. tr. and ed. (1961, 1965) *Quinte-Curce: Histoires I–II*. Paris. Budé. Latin and French. With notes.

Yardley, J. tr. and Heckel, W. ed. (1984) *Quintus Curtius Rufus. The History of Alexander*. Harmondsworth. English. With notes.

Atkinson, J. E. (1980) *A Commentary on Q. Curtius Rufus' Historiae Alexandri Magni Books 3 & 4*. Amsterdam.

### Plutarch (second half of the first and early second century AD)

Perrin, B. tr. and ed. (1971) *Plutarch's Lives VII (Alexander)*. London and Cambridge, Mass. Loeb. Greek and English. With notes.

Flacelière, R. and Chambry, E. trs and eds (1975) *Plutarque. Vies IX (Alexandre)*. Paris. Budé. Greek and French. With notes.

Scott-Kilvert, I. tr. and ed. with an introduction by Griffith, G. T. (1983) *The Age of Alexander*. Harmondsworth. English. With notes.

Hamilton, J. R. (1969) *Plutarch*, Alexander: *A Commentary*. Oxford.

### Arrian (first half of the second century AD)

Brunt, P. A. tr. and ed. (1976, 1983) *History of Alexander and Indica I–II*. London and Cambridge, Mass. Loeb. Greek and English. With notes.

Sélincourt, A. de tr. with introduction and notes by Hamilton, J. R. (1971) *Arrian: The Campaigns of Alexander*. Harmondsworth. Penguin. English. With notes.
Savinel, P. tr. with an afterword by Vidal-Naquet, P. (1984) *Histoire d'Alexandre . . . et L'Inde*. Paris. French. With notes.
Hinüber, O. von and Wirth, G. trs and eds (1985a) *Der Alexanderzug* (Wirth). *Indische Geschichte* (Hinüber). Munich. Greek and German. With notes.
Goralski, W. J. tr. and ed. (1989) "Arrian's *Events After Alexander*. Summary of Photius and Selected Fragments," *AncW* 19: 81–108.
Bosworth, A. B. (1980a) *A Historical Commentary on Arrian's History of Alexander I. Books I–III*. Oxford.


**Justin (a third-century AD epitome of Pompeius Trogus' *Philippic Histories* from the Augustan era)**

Seel, O. ed. (1972) *M. Iuniani Iustini. Epitoma Historiarum Philippicarum Pompei Trogi*. Stuttgart. Teubner. Latin. With notes.
Watson, J. S. tr. and ed. (1875) *Justin, Cornelius Nepos and Eutropius*. London. Bohn. English. With notes.


**RELATED TEXTS**

Jones, H. L. tr. and ed. (1923–83) *The Geography of Strabo I–VIII*. London and Cambridge, Mass. Loeb. Greek and English. Especially VII. With notes.
Kroll, W. tr. and ed. (1926) *Historia Alexandri Magni (Pseudo-Callisthenes)*. Berlin. Latin. With notes.
Pfister, F. tr. and ed. (1978) *Der Alexanderroman mit einer Auswahl aus den verwandten Texten*. Meisenheim. Latin and German. With notes.
Stoneman, R. tr. and ed. (1991) *The Greek Alexander Romance*. Harmondsworth. Penguin. English. With notes.
Thomas, P. H. ed. (1960) *Epitoma Rerum Gestarum Alexandri Magni et Liber de Morte Eius*. Leipzig. Teubner edition of the *Metz Epitome*. Latin. With notes.
Wolohojian, A. M. tr. and ed. (1969) *The Romance of Alexander the Great by Pseudo-Callisthenes*. New York. *The Alexander Romance* in an English translation of the Armenian version. English. With notes.


**OTHER RELEVANT ANCIENT WORKS**

**(arranged alphabetically according to ancient authors)**

Aelian. (1958–9) *On the Characteristics of Animals I–III*. tr. and ed. A. F. Scholfield. London and Cambridge, Mass. Loeb. Greek and English.
(1974) *Claudii Aeliani. Varia Historia*. ed. M. R. Dilts. Leipzig. Teubner. Greek.
(1989) "Aelian's *Manual of Hellenistic Military Tactics*. A New Translation from the Greek with an Introduction," *AncW* 19: 31–64.
Aeschines. (1968) *The Speeches of Aeschines*. tr. and ed. C. D. Adams. London and Cambridge, Mass. Loeb. Greek and English.
Apollodorus. (1921) *Apollodorus. The Library*. tr. and ed. J. G. Frazer. London and New York. Loeb. Greek and English.
Apuleius. (1909) *The Apologia and Florida of Apuleius of Madaura*. tr. and ed. H. E. Butler. Oxford. English.
(1914) *Apvlei Apologia*. eds H. E. Butler and A. S. Owen. Oxford. Latin.
Aristotle. See the twenty-three volumes in the Loeb Classical Library for the Greek texts with English translations.
(1985) *The Complete Works I–II*. ed. J. Barnes. Princeton. English.

Athenaeus. (1928–63) *The Deipnosophists I–VII*. tr. and ed. C. B. Gulick. London and Cambridge, Mass. Loeb. Greek and English.

Cicero. (1960) *Cicero. Tusculan Disputations*. tr. and ed. J. E. King. London and New York. 1960. Loeb. Latin and English.

(1979) *Cicero XX (De Divinatione)*. tr.and ed. W. A. Falconer. London and Cambridge, Mass. Loeb. Latin and English.

Demosthenes. (1962–84) *Demosthenes. Speeches I–VII*. trs and eds J. H. Vince, C. A. Vince, A. T. Murray, N. W. De Witt, N. J. De Witt. London and Cambridge, Mass. Loeb. Greek and English.

Dinarchus. (1954) *Minor Attic Orators II*. tr. and ed. J. O. Burtt. London and Cambridge, Mass. Loeb. Greek and English.

Dio Chrysostom. (1951–61) *Discourses I–V*. trs and eds J. W. Cohoon and H.L. Crosby. London and Cambridge, Mass. Loeb. Greek and English.

Diodorus Siculus. (1933–61) *Diodorus of Sicily I–VI & VIII–XII*. trs and eds R. M. Geer, C. H. Oldfather, and F. R. Walton. London, New York and Cambridge, Mass. Loeb. Greek and English. See above for VII, the key volume.

Epictetus. (1926) *The Discourses as Reported by Arrian, the Manual, and Fragments I*. tr. and ed. W. A. Oldfather. London and Cambridge, Mass. Loeb. Greek and English.

Euripides. (1919) *Euripides II (Electra)* tr. and ed. A. S. Way. London and New York. Loeb. Greek and English.

(1930) *Euripides III (Bacchanals)*. tr. and ed. A. S. Way. London and Cambridge, Mass. Loeb. Greek and English.

(1966) Euripides *Bacchae*. ed. E. R. Dodds. Oxford. Greek with introduction and commentary.

(1968) *Euripides V (The Bacchae)* tr. and ed. W. Arrowsmith. Chicago and London. English. 141–228.

(1970) *The Bacchae by Euripides: A Translation with Commentary*. tr. and ed. G. S. Kirk. Englewood Cliffs.

(1970, 1972) *Euripide. Les Bacchantes I–II*. ed. J. Roux. Paris. Greek and French with introduction and commentary.

Frontinus. (1969) *The Stratagems and The Aqueducts of Rome*. trs C. E. Bennett and C. Herschel, ed. M. B. McElwain. London and Cambridge, Mass. Loeb. Latin and English.

Gellius. (1927–8) *The Attic Nights of Aulus Gellius I–III*. tr. and ed. J. C. Rolfe. London and New York. Loeb. Latin and English.

*The Greek Anthology III–IV*. (1963, 1968) tr. and ed. W. R. Paton. London and Cambridge, Mass. Loeb. Greek and English.

Herodotus. (1928–81) *Herodotus I–IV*. tr. and ed. A. D. Godley. London and Cambridge, Mass. Loeb. Greek and English.

Hesiod. (1977) *Hesiod. The Homeric Hymns and Homerica*. tr. and ed. H. G. Evelyn-White. London and Cambridge, Mass. Loeb. Greek and English.

Homer. (1961) *Homer. The Iliad*. tr. and ed. R. Lattimore. Chicago and London. English.

(1966) *Homer. The Odyssey I–II*. tr. and ed. A. T. Murray. London and Cambridge, Mass. Loeb. Greek and English.

(1967) *Homer. The Odyssey*. tr. and ed. R. Lattimore. New York. English.

(1978, 1985) *Homer. The Iliad I–II*. tr. and ed. A. T. Murray. London and Cambridge, Mass. Loeb. Greek and English.

Hyginus. (1934) *Hygini. Fabvlae*. ed. H. J. Rose. Leiden. Latin.

(1960) *The Myths of Hyginus*. tr. and ed. M. Grant. Lawrence. English.

(1983) *Hygin. L'Astronomie*. tr. and ed. A. Le Bœuffle. Paris. Budé. Latin and French.

Hyperides. (1954) *Minor Attic Orators II*. tr. and ed. J. O. Burtt. London and Cambridge, Mass. Loeb. Greek and English.

Isocrates. (1966, 1968) *Isocrates I, III*. tr. and ed. L. van Hook. London and Cambridge, Mass. Loeb. Greek and English.

Julius Valerius. (1888) *Iuli Valeri. Alexandri Polemi Res Gestae Alexandri Macedonis*. ed. B. Keubler. Leipzig. Teubner. Latin.

Livy. (1926, 1968) *Livy IV, XIII*. trs B. O. Foster and A. C. Schlesinger. London, New York, and Cambridge, Mass. Loeb. Latin and English.

Lucian. (1921) *Lucian I*. tr. and ed. A. M. Harmon. London and New York. Loeb. Greek and English.

Macrobius. (1963) *Macrobivs*. ed. J. Willis. Leipzig. Teubner. Latin.

(1969) *Macrobius. The Saturnalia*. tr. and ed. P. V. Davies. New York and London.

Nonnus. (1940) *Nonnos. Dionysiaca*. tr. W. H. D. Rouse, eds H. J. Rose and L. R. Lind. London and Cambridge, Mass. Loeb. Greek and English.

Orosius. (1990) *Orose. Histoires (Contre les Païens)*. tr. and ed. M-P Arnaud-Lindet. Paris. Budé. Latin and French.

Ovid. (1916) *Ovid. Metamorphoses I–II*. tr. and ed. F. J. Miller. London and New York. Loeb. Latin and English.

Pausanias. (1971–9) *Pausanias. Description of Greece I–V*. trs and eds W. H. S. Jones, H. A. Ormerod, and R. E. Wycherley. London and Cambridge, Mass. Loeb. Greek and English.

Philostratus. (1969) *Philostratus. The Life of Apollonius of Tyana I*. tr. and ed. F. C. Conybeare. London and Cambridge, Mass. Loeb. Greek and English.

(1977) *Flavii Philostrati. Heroicvs*. ed. L. de Lannoy. Leipzig. Teubner. Greek with Latin notes.

Pindar. (1946) *The Odes of Pindar*. tr. and ed. J. Sandys. London and Cambridge, Mass. Loeb. Greek and English

(1969) *Pindar. The Odes*. tr. C. M. Bowra. Harmondsworth. Penguin. English.

Plato. (1926) *Plato. Laws IX (first of two volumes)*. tr. and ed. R. G. Bury. London and New York. Loeb. Greek and English.

(1959) *Plato. Gorgias. A Revised Text with Introduction and Commentary*. ed. E. R. Dodds. Oxford.

(1967) *Plato V (Symposium, Gorgias)*. tr. and ed. W. R. M. Lamb. London and Cambridge, Mass. Loeb. Greek and English.

Pliny the Elder. (1938–66) *Pliny. Natural History I–X*. trs and eds H. Rackham, W. H. S. Jones, and D. E. Eichholz. London and Cambridge, Mass. Loeb. Latin and English.

Plutarch. (1914–20) *Plutarch's Lives II (Camillus), V (Agesilaus), VIII (Eumenes), IX (Pyrrhus)*. tr. and ed. B. Perrin. London and New York. Loeb. Greek and English.

(1928–86) *Plutarch. Moralia I–XV*. trs and eds F. C. Babbitt, W. C. Helmbold, P. H. De Lacy, B. Einarson, P. A. Clement, H. B. Hoffleit, E. L. Minar, F. H. Sandbach, H. N. Fowler, L. Pearson, and H. Cherniss. London and Cambridge, Mass. Loeb. Greek and English.

(1988, 1990) *Plutarque. Œuvres morales V 1ᵉ et 2ᵉ parties*. trs and eds F. Frazier and C. Froidefond. Paris. Budé. Greek and French.

Polyaenus. (1970) *Polyaenus. Strategemata*. eds. E. Woelfflin and J. Melber. Leipzig. Greek.

(1974) *Polyaenus. Stratagems of War*. tr. and ed. R. Shepherd. Chicago. English.

Polybius. (1922–60) *Polybius. The Histories I–VI*. tr. and ed. W. R. Paton. London, New York, and Cambridge, Mass. Loeb. Greek and English.

Seneca. (1928) *Seneca. Moral Essays I*. tr. and ed. J. W. Basore. London and New York. Loeb. Latin and English.

(1967, 1970) *Seneca. Ad Lucilium. Epistulae Morales I–II*. tr. and ed. R. M. Gummere. London and New York. Loeb. Latin and English.

Sophocles (1968, 1961) *Sophocles I (Antigone) II (Ajax)*. tr. and ed. F. Storr. London and Cambridge, Mass. Loeb. Greek and English.

Stephanus Byzantius. (1849) *Stephani Byzantii*. ed. A. Meinekii. Greek with Latin notes.

Stobaeus. (1893) *Ioannis Stobaei. Florilegium I–III*. ed. O. Holze. Leipzig. Greek.

Suetonius. (1970) *Suetonius I*. tr. and ed. J. C. Rolfe. London and Cambridge, Mass. Loeb. Latin and English.

Tacitus. (1969–70) *Tacitus III–V (Annals)*. tr. and ed. J. Jackson. London and Cambridge, Mass. Loeb. Latin and English.

Theognis. (1962) *Théognis. Poèmes élégiaques*. Paris. Budé. Greek and French.

Theophrastus. (1916) *Theophrastus. Enquiry Into Plants I*. tr. and ed. A. Hort. London and New York. Loeb. Greek and English.

(1961) *Theophrastus. The Characters*. tr. and ed. J. M. Edmonds. London and Cambridge, Mass. Loeb. Greek and English.

Thucydides. (1928) *Thucydides I*. tr. and ed. C. F. Smith. London and New York. Loeb. Greek and English.

Valerius Maximus. (1966) *Valerii Maximi*. ed. C. Kempf. Stuttgart. Teubner. Latin.

Velleius Paterculus. (1967) *Velleius Paterculus. Compendium of Roman History*. tr. and ed. F. W. Shipley. London and Cambridge, Mass. Loeb. Latin and English.

Vitruvius. (1934) *Vitruvius. On Architecture II*. tr. and ed. F. Granger. London and New York. Loeb. Latin and English.

Xenophon. (1961) *Xenophon. Anabasis Bks. I–VII (in two volumes)*. tr. and ed. C. L. Brownson. London and Cambridge, Mass. Loeb. Greek and English.

(1983, 1979) *Cyropaedia I–II*. tr. and ed. W. Miller. London and Cambridge, Mass. Loeb. Greek and English.

## MODERN GENERAL TREATMENTS

Badian, E. (1985) "Alexander in Iran," *Cambridge History of Iran II*. ed. I. Gershevitch. Cambridge. 420–501, 897–903.

Beloch, K. J. (1927) *Griechische Geschichte I–IV*. Berlin and Leipzig.

Bengtson, H. (1985) *Philipp und Alexander der Grosse. Die Begründer der hellenistischen Welt*. Munich.

Bosworth, A. B. (1988a) *Conquest and Empire: The Reign of Alexander the Great*. Cambridge.

Briant, P. (1974) *Alexandre le Grand*. Paris.

Burn, A. R. (1962a) *Alexander the Great and the Hellenistic World*. New York.

Citati, P. and Sisti, F. (1985) *Alessandro Magno*. Milan.

Cloché, P. (1953) *Alexandre le Grand et les essais de fusion entre l'Occident gréco-macédonien et l'Orient*. Neuchâtel.

Droysen, J. G. (1833) *Geschichte Alexanders des Grossen*. Hamburg.

Green, P. (1991) *Alexander of Macedon. 356–323 BC. A Historical Biography*. Berkeley and Oxford.

Hamilton, J. R. (1982) *Alexander the Great*. Pittsburgh.

Hammond, N. G. L. (1980a) *Alexander the Great. King, Commander and Statesman*. Park Ridge, NJ.

Hammond, N. G. L. and Walbank, F. W. (1988) *A History of Macedonia 336–167 BC III*. Oxford.

Hampl, F. (1958) *Alexander der Grosse*. Göttingen.

Hornblower, S. (1983) *The Greek World 479–323 BC*. London. 239–93, 312–22.

Jouguet, P. (1978) *Alexander the Great and the Hellenistic World*. Chicago.
Kaerst, J. (1927) *Geschichte des Hellenismus I*. Leipzig. 286–513.
Lane Fox, R. (1974) *Alexander the Great*. New York.
(1980) *The Search for Alexander*. Boston and Toronto.
Lauffer, S. (1978) *Alexander der Grosse*. Munich.
Levi, M. A. (1977a) *Alessandro Magno*. Milan.
Milns, R. D. (1969) *Alexander the Great*. New York.
Radet, G. (1931) *Alexandre le Grand*. Paris.
Renault, M. (1976) *The Nature of Alexander*. New York.
Robinson, C. A. (1947) *Alexander the Great*. New York.
Schachermeyr, F. (1973) *Alexander der Grosse: Das Problem seiner Persönlichkeit und seines Wirkens*. Vienna.
Snyder, J. W. (1966) *Alexander the Great*. New York.
Tarn, W. W. (1948) *Alexander the Great I–II*. Cambridge.
Weedman, G. E. A. (1976) "Alexander the Great. The Misunderstanding of a King". Diss. Bloomington, Ind.
Welles, C. B. (1970) *Alexander and the Hellenistic World*. Toronto. 5–48.
Wilcken, U. (1967) *Alexander the Great*. tr. G. C. Richards, notes and introduction E. N. Borza. New York.
Will, W. (1986) *Alexander der Grosse. Geschichte Makedoniens II*. Stuttgart.
Wirth, G. (1973) *Alexander der Grosse*. Hamburg.

## RECENT COLLECTIONS

Adams, W. L. and Borza, E. N. eds (1982) *Philip II, Alexander the Great and the Macedonian Heritage*. Washington.
*The Ancient World*. Six special Alexander issues. 1981 (IV:3–4); 1982 (V:1–2); 1985 (XII:1–2); 1986 (XIII:3–4); 1987 (XVI:3–4); 1988 (XVIII:1–2); 1989 (XIX:1–2).
*Archaia Makedonia 1–4* (1970, 1977, 1983, 1986). Thessaloniki.
Badian, E. ed. (1976a) *Alexandre le Grand. Image et réalité. Entretiens Hardt XXII*. Geneva.
Barr-Sharrar, B. and Borza, E. N. eds (1982) *Macedonia and Greece in Late Classical and Early Hellenistic Times*. Washington.
Borza, E. N. ed. (1974) *The Impact of Alexander the Great*. Hinsdale.
Dell, H. D. ed. (1981) *Ancient Macedonian Studies in Honor of Charles F. Edson*. Thessaloniki.
Ehrenberg, V. (1965) *Polis und Imperium*. eds K. J. Stroheker and A. J. Graham. Zurich and Stuttgart. 399–501.
*G&R 12, no. 2* (1965). Alexander issue.
Green, P. (1989a) *Classical Bearings*. New York.
Griffith, G. T. ed. (1966) *Alexander the Great: The Main Problems*. Cambridge.
*Megas Alexandros*. (1980) Thessaloniki.
Ozols, J. and Thewalt, V. (1984) *Aus dem Osten des Alexanderreiches*. Cologne.
Sordi, M. ed. (1984) *Alessandro Magno tra storia e mito*. Milan.
Strasburger, H. (1982a, 1990) *Studien zur Alten Geschichte II–III*. eds W. Schmitthenner and R. Zoepffel. Hildesheim and New York.
Will, W. and Heinrichs, J. (1987, 1988) *Zu Alexander d. Gr. I–II*. Amsterdam.
Wirth, G. (1985b) *Studien zur Alexandergeschichte*. Darmstadt.

## HISTORIOGRAPHY

Alfieri, T. T. (1988) "Problemi di fonti nei libri XVI e XVII di Diodoro," *Acme* 41: 21–9.

Ameling, W. L. (1984) "L. Flavius Arrianus Neos Xenophon," *Epigraphica Anatolia* 4: 119–22.

Andreotti, R. (1950) "Il problema di Alessandro Magno nella storiografia dell' ultimo decennio," *Historia* 1: 583–600.

Atkinson, J. E. (1963) "Primary Sources and the Alexanderreich," *Acta Classica* 6: 125–37.

Badian, E. (1958a) "Alexander the Great and the Unity of Mankind," *Historia* 7: 425–44.

(1961a) Review of L. Pearson's *The Lost Histories of Alexander the Great*, *Gnomon* 33: 660–7.

(1965a) "The Date of Clitarchus," *PACA* 8: 5–11.

(1976b) "Some Recent Interpretations of Alexander," *Alexandre le Grand. Image et réalité. Entretiens Hardt XXII*. ed. E. Badian. Geneva. 279–311.

(1989) "History from 'square Brackets,' " *ZPE* 79: 59–70.

Bailey, D. R. S. (1981) "Curtiana," *CQ* 1: 175–80.

Barigazzi, A. (1984) "Plutarco e il corso futuro della storia," *Prometheus* 10: 264–86.

Barrow, R. H. (1968) *Plutarch and His Times*. London.

Barzano, A. (1985) *Curzio Rufo e la sua epoca*. Milan.

Berg, B. (1973) "An Early Source of the Alexander Romance," *GRBS* 14: 381–7.

Bigwood, J. M. (1989) "Ctesias' *Indica* and Photius," *Phoenix* 43: 302–16.

Boncquet, J. (1982–3) "Polybius on the Critical Evaluation of Historians," *Anc. Soc.* 13–14: 277–91.

Borza, E. N. (1968) "Cleitarchus and Diodorus' Account of Alexander," *PACA* 11: 25–45.

Bosworth, A. B. (1972) "Arrian's Literary Development," *CQ* 22: 163–85.

(1976a) "Arrian and the Alexander Vulgate," *Alexandre le Grand. Image et réalité. Entretiens Hardt XXII*. ed. E. Badian. Geneva. 1–46.

(1976b) "Errors in Arrian," *CQ* 26: 117–39.

(1983a) "History and Rhetoric in Curtius Rufus," *CP* 78: 150–61.

(1983b) "Arrian and the Caspian Gates: A Study in Methodology," *CQ* 33: 265–76.

(1988b) *From Arrian to Alexander. Studies in Historical Methodology*. Oxford.

(1990) "Plutarch, Callisthenes and the Peace of Callias," *JHS* 110: 1–13.

Breebaart, A. B. (1960) *Enige historiografische Aspecten van Arrianus' Anabasis Alexandri*. Leiden.

Brown, T. S. (1949a) *Onesicritus. A Study in Hellenistic Historiography*. Berkeley.

(1950) "Clitarchus," *AJP* 71: 134–55.

Bruce, I. A. F. (1970) "Theopompus and Classical Greek Historiography," *History and Theory* 9: 86–109.

Brunt, P. A. (1974) "Notes on Aristobulus of Cassandria," *CQ* 24: 65–9.

Clarysse, W. and Schepens, G. (1985) "A Ptolemaic Fragment of an Alexander History," *Chronique d'Egypte* 60: 30–47.

Connor, W. R. (1967) "History Without Heroes: Theopompus' Treatment of Philip of Macedon," *GRBS* 8: 133–54.

Curiazi, D. (1983) "Hist. Fragm. Novum," *Museum Criticum* 18: 209–13.

Demandt, A. (1972) "Politische Aspekte im Alexanderbild der Neuzeit," *Archiv für Kulturgeschichte* 54: 325–63.

(1984) *Ungeschehene Geschichte*. Göttingen.

Egge, R. (1978) *Untersuchungen zur Primärtradition bei Q. Curtius Rufus*. Freiburg.

Errington, R. M. (1969) "Bias in Ptolemy's History of Alexander," *CQ* 19: 233–42.

Fears, J. R. (1974) "The Stoic View of the Career and Character of Alexander the Great," *Philologus* 118: 113–30.

Fisch, M. H. (1937) "Alexander and the Stoics," *AJP* 58: 59–82, 129–44.

Frazier, F. (1987) "A propos de la composition des couples dans les 'Vies parallèles' de Plutarque," *Revue de Philologie de Littérature et d'Histoire Anciennes* 61: 65–75.

Gawlowska, W. (1984) "Alexandre le Grand – créateur de sa propre légende (à la lumière des sources greco-latines)," *Concilium Eirene* 16: 65–9.

Geiger, J. (1981) "Plutarch's Parallel Lives: The Choice of Heroes," *Hermes* 109: 85–104.

Goodyear, F. R. D. (1982) "On the Character and Text of Justin's Compilation of Trogus," *PACA* 16: 1–24.

Goukowsky, P. (1969) " 'Clitarque Seul?' Remarques sur les sources du livre xvii de Diodore de Sicile," *REA* 71: 320–6.

Gray, V. J. (1990) "The Moral Interpretation of the 'Second Preface' to Arrian's *Anabasis*," *JHS* 110: 180–6.

Griffith, G. T. (1968) "The Letter of Darius at Arrian 2.14," *PCPS* 14: 33–48.

Habicht, C. (1985) *Pausanias' Guide to Ancient Greece*. Berkeley.

Hamilton, J. R. (1955) "Three Passages in Arrian," *CQ* 5: 217–21.

(1961a) "Cleitarchus and Aristobulus," *Historia* 10: 448–59.

(1961b) "The Letters in Plutarch's *Alexander*," *PACA* 4: 9–20.

(1969) *Plutarch, Alexander: A Commentary*. Oxford.

(1977) "Cleitarchus and Diodorus 17," *Greece and the Ancient Mediterranean in History and Prehistory*. ed. K. H. Kinzl. Berlin. 126–46.

Hammond, N. G. L. (1980b) "Some Passages in Arrian Concerning Alexander," *CQ* 30: 455–76.

(1983a) *Three Historians of Alexander the Great. The So-called Vulgate Authors, Diodorus, Justin and Curtius*. Cambridge.

Hampl, F. (1954) "Alexander der Grosse und die Beurteilung geschichtlicher Persönlichkeiten in der modernen Historiographie," *Nouvelle Clio* 6: 91–136.

Harrison, G. W. M. (1987) "Rhetoric, Writing and Plutarch," *Anc. Soc.* 18: 271–9.

Hatzopoulos, M. B. (1981) "A Century and a Lustrum of Macedonian Studies," *AncW* 4: 91–108.

Heckel, W. (1988) *The Last Days and Testament of Alexander the Great: A Prosopographic Study*. Stuttgart.

(1991) "Q. Curtius Rufus and the Date of Cleander's Mission to the Peloponnese," *Hermes* 119: 124–5.

Hornblower, J. (1981) *Hieronymus of Cardia*. Oxford.

Hunt, J. M. (1985) "More Emendations in the Epitoma Metensis," *CP* 80: 335–7.

Iliescu, V. (1987) "Histrianorum rex? Zu Just. 9,2,2," *Zu Alexander d. Gr.I.* eds W. Will and J. Heinrichs. Amsterdam. 193–218.

Kaerst, J. (1892) "Der Briefwechsel Alexanders des Grossen," *Philologus* 51: 602–22.

Kornemann, E. (1935) *Die Alexandergeschichte des Königs Ptolemaios I. von Aegypten. Versuch einer Rekonstruktion*. Leipzig.

Kraus Reggiani, C. (1982) "I frammenti di Aristobulo, esegeta biblico," *Bollettino dei Classici, Accademia dei Lincei* 3: 87–134.

Levi, M. A. (1977b) *Introduzione ad Alessandro Magno*. Milan.

Lund, A. A. (1987) "Neues zu Curtius 3,5,1; 3,10,5; 4,10,3," *Gymnasium* 94: 438–41.

Lytton, R. H. (1973) "Justin's Account of Alexander the Great: A Historical Commentary." Dissertation. Pennsylvania State University.

McQueen, E. I. (1967) "Quintus Curtius Rufus," *Latin Biography*. ed. T. A. Dorey. London.

Marincola, J. M. (1989) "Some Suggestions on the Proem and " 'Second Preface' of Arrian's *Anabasis*," *JHS* 109: 186–9.

Martin, T. R. (1983) "Quintus Curtius' Presentation of Philip Arrhidaeus and Josephus' Accounts of the Accession of Claudius," *AJAH* 8: 161–90.

Mederer, E. (1936) *Die Alexanderlegenden bei den ältesten Alexanderhistorikern.* Stuttgart.

Meister, K. (1989) "Das Bild Alexanders des Grossen in der Historiographie seiner Zeit," *Festschrift Robert Werner.* eds Werner Dahlheim, Wolfgang Schuller, and Jürgen von Ungern-Sternberg. Konstanz. 63–79.

Mensching, E. (1963) "Peripatetiker über Alexander," *Historia* 12: 274–82.

Merkelbach, R. (1977) *Die Quellen des griechischen Alexanderromans.* Munich.

Merlan, P. (1950) "Alexander the Great or Antiphon the Sophist?," *CP* 45: 161–6.

Milns, R. D. (1983) "A Note on Arrian's Anabasis," *CP* 78: 47–50.

Moles, J. L. (1985) "The Interpretation of the " 'Second Preface' in Arrian's *Anabasis*," *JHS* 105: 162–8.

Mossman, J. M. (1988) "Tragedy and Epic in Plutarch's *Alexander*," *JHS* 108: 83–93.

Oost, S. I. (1981) "The Alexander Historians and 'Asia,' " *Ancient Macedonian Studies in Honor of Charles F. Edson.* ed. H. J. Dell. Thessaloniki. 265–82.

Pacella, D. (1982) "Alessandro e gli ebrei nella testimonianza dello Ps. Callistene," *ASNP* 12: 1255–69.

Palmer, D. W. (1981) "The End of Alexander in PS.-Callisthenes," *Prudentia* 13: 75–9.

Pearson, L. (1954–5) "The Diary and Letters of Alexander the Great," *Historia* 4: 429–55.

(1960) *The Lost Histories of Alexander the Great.* New York.

Pédech, P. (1974) "Strabon Historien d'Alexandre," *Grazer Bëitrage II.* Amsterdam. 129–45.

(1984) *Historiens, compagnons d'Alexandre.* Paris.

Pelling, C. B. R. (1980) "Plutarch's Adaption of his Source-Material," *JHS* 100: 127–40.

(1988) "Aspects of Plutarch's Characterization," *Illinois Classical Studies* 13: 257–74.

(1990a) *Characterization and Individuality in Greek Literature.* Oxford.

(1990b) "Childhood and Personality in Greek Biography," *Characterization and Individuality in Greek Literature.* ed. C. Pelling. Oxford. 213–44.

Robinson, C. A. Jr (1953) *The History of Alexander the Great I.* Providence, RI.

Roisman, J. (1983–4) "Why Arrian Wrote the Anabasis," *Rivista Storica dell'Antichità* 13–14: 253–63.

(1984) "Ptolemy and his rivals in his History of Alexander the Great," *CQ* 34: 373–85.

Rubincam, C. (1987) "The Organization and Composition of Diodoros' Bibliotheke," *Classical Views = Echos du Monde Classique* 6: 313–28.

Rubinsohn, W. Z. (1986) "Some Remarks on Soviet Historiography of Ancient Macedonia and Alexander the Great," *AM* 4: 525–40.

(1988) "Hellenism in Recent Soviet Perspective," *East European History.* ed. S. J. Kirschbaum. Columbus. 41–66.

Runia, D. T. (1989) "Polis and Megalopolis: Philo and the Founding of Alexandria," *Mnemosyne* 42: 398–412.

Russell, D. A. (1972) *Plutarch.* London.

Sacks, K. S. (1990) *Diodorus Siculus and the First Century.* Princeton.

Shrimpton, G. S. (1991) *Theopompus the Historian.* Montreal.

Sordi, M. (1987) "Diodoro e il 'dopo Alessandro,' " *Aevum* 61: 29–36.

Stadter, P. A. (1965) *Plutarch's Historical Works.* Cambridge, Mass.

(1967) "Flavius Arrianus: The New Xenophon," *GRBS* 8: 155–61.

(1980) *Arrian of Nicomedia*. Chapel Hill, NC.

(1981) "Arrian's Extended Preface," *Illinois Classical Studies* 6: 157–71.

(1988) "The Proems of Plutarch's *Lives*," *Illinois Classical Studies* 13: 275–95.

Strasburger, H. (1934) *Ptolemaios und Alexander*. Leipzig.

Sumner, G. V. (1961) "Curtius Rufus and the *Historiae Alexandri*," *Journal of the Australasian Universities Language and Literature Association* 15: 30–9.

Swain, S. (1989) "Plutarch: Chance, Providence, and History," *AJP* 110: 272–302.

Syme, R. (1982) "The Career of Arrian," *HSCP* 86: 181–211.

Tarn, W. W. (1933) "Alexander the Great and the Unity of Mankind," *PCPS* 19: 123–66.

Teodorsson, S.-T. (1989, 1990) *A Commentary on Plutarch's Table Talks I–II. Books I–III, IV–VI*. Göteborg.

Thérasse, J. (1968) "Le moralisme de Justin (Trogue Pompée) contre Alexandre le Grand; son influence sur l'œuvre de Quinte-Curce," *AC* 37: 551–88.

(1973) "Le jugement de Quinte-Curce sur Alexandre: une appréciation morale indépendante," *Etudes Classiques* 41: 23–42.

Thomas, C. G. (1968) "Alexander the Great and the Unity of Mankind," *CJ* 63: 258–60.

Todd, R. A. (1964) "W. W. Tarn and the Alexander Ideal," *The Historian* 27: 48–55.

Tonnet, H. (1987a) *Recherches sur Arrien*. Amsterdam.

(1987b) "La 'Vulgate' dans Arrien," *Zu Alexander d. Gr. I*. eds W. Will and J. Heinrichs. Amsterdam. 635–56.

Verdin, H., Schepens, G., and Keyser, E. de eds (1990) *Purposes of History. Studies in Greek Historiography from the 4th to the 2nd Centuries BC*. Leuven.

Walbank, F. W. (1957, 1967) *A Historical Commentary on Polybius I–II*. Oxford.

Wardman, A. E. (1955) "Plutarch and Alexander," *CQ* 5: 96–107.

Watt, W. S. (1983) "Curtiana," *PCPS* 29: 77–86.

Welles, C. B. (1963) "The Reliability of Ptolemy as an Historian," *Miscellanea di studi alessandri in memoria di A. Rostagni*. Turin. 101–16.

Wirth, G. (1964) "Anmerkungen zur Arrianbiographie," *Historia* 13: 209–45.

Wüst, F. R. (1953–4a) "Die Rede Alexanders des Grossen in Opis, Arrian VII 9–10," *Historia* 2: 177–88.

Zambrini, A. (1987) "A proposito degli *Indika* di Arriano," *ASNP* 17: 139–54.

## DIONYSUS

Aélion, R. (1986) *Quelques grands mythes héroïques dans l'oeuvre d'Euripide*. Paris.

Arnott, G. (1973) "Euripides and the Unexpected," *G&R* 20: 49–64.

Arnott, P. D. (1989) *Public and Performance in the Greek Theater*. London and New York.

Arthur, M. (1972) "The Choral Odes of the *Bacchae* of Euripides," *Yale Classical Studies* 22: 145–79.

*L'association dionysiaque dans les sociétés anciennes. Actes de la table ronde organisée par l'Ecole française de Rome*. Paris and Rome. 1986.

Baltazar, E. (1982) "The Divine Darkness," *The Journal of Religion and Psychical Research* 5: 94–102.

Barr-Sharrar, B. (1979) "Towards an Interpretation of the Frieze on the Derveni Krater," *Bronzes hellénistiques et romains: Tradition et renouveau*. Lausanne. 55–9.

Baslez, M.-F. (1984) *L'étranger dans la Grèce antique*. Paris.

Bérard, C. ed. (1987) *Images et sociétés en Grèce ancienne*. Lausanne.

Boyancé, P. (1965–6) "Dionysos et Sémélé," *Rendiconti della Pontificia Accademia Romana di Archeologia* 38: 79–104.

(1966) "Dionysiaca," *REA* 68: 33–60.

Bremer, J. M. (1976) "De interpretatie van Euripides' Bacchen," *Lampas* 9: 2–7.

Bremmer, J. N. (1984) "Greek Maenadism Reconsidered," *ZPE* 55: 267–86.

ed. (1986a) *Interpretations of Greek Mythology*. Totowa.

Brion, C. (1987) "Porteurs de thyrse ou bacchants," *Images et sociétiés en Grèce ancienne*. ed. C. Bérard. 145–53.

Brown, C. (1982) "Dionysus and the Women of Elis: *PMG* 871," *GRBS* 23: 305–14.

Burian, P. ed. (1985) *Directions in Euripidean Criticism*. Durham, NC.

Burkert, W. (1977) *Orphism and the Bacchic Mysteries. New Evidence and Old Problems of Interpretation*. Berkeley.

(1979) *Structure and History in Greek Mythology and Ritual*. Berkeley.

(1983) *Homo Necans. The Anthropology of Ancient Greek Sacrificial Ritual and Myth*. tr. P. Bing. Berkeley.

(1985) *Greek Religion*. tr. J. Raffan. Cambridge, Mass.

(1987) *Ancient Mystery Cults*. Cambridge, Mass. and London.

Burnett, A. P. (1970) "Pentheus and Dionysus: Host and Guest," *CP* 65: 15–29.

Cantarella, R. (1971) "Il Dioniso delle *Baccanti* e la teoria aristotelica sulle origini del dramma," *Studi in onore di Vittorio De Falco*. Naples. 123–32.

(1974) "Dioniso, fra *Baccanti* e *Rane*," *Serta Turyniana*. eds J. L. Heller and J. K. Newman. Urbana, Ill. 291–310.

Carpenter, T. H. (1986) *Dionysian Imagery in Archaic Greek Art*. Oxford.

Carrière, J. (1984) "Quelques mots encore sur les Bacchantes d'Euripide," *Delebecque Mélanges* 1: 89–99.

Caruso, C. (1987) "Travestissements dionysiaques," *Images et sociétés en Grèce ancienne*. ed. P. Bérard. Lausanne. 103–10.

Casadio, G. (1989) "Dionysos entre historie et sociologie," *Dialogues d'histoire ancienne* 15: 285–308.

Castellani, V. (1976) "That Troubled House of Pentheus in Euripides' *Bacchae*," *TAPA* 106: 61–83.

Coche de la Ferté, E. (1980) "Penthée et Dionysos: Nouvel essai d'interprétation des 'Bacchantes' d'Euripide," *Recherches sur les religions de l'antiquité classique*. ed. R. Bloch. Geneva and Paris. 105–257.

Cole, S. G. (1980) "New Evidence for the Mysteries of Dionysos," *GRBS* 21: 223–38.

(1984) *Theoi Megaloi: The Cult of the Great Gods at Samothrace*. Leiden.

Conacher, D. J. (1967) *Euripidean Drama: Myth, Theme and Structure*. Toronto.

Dale, A. M. (1969) "Seen and Unseen on the Greek Stage," *Collected Papers*. Cambridge. 119–29.

Daraki, M. (1980) "Aspects du sacrifice dionysiaque," *Revue de l'Histoire des Religions* 197: 131–57.

(1982) "Oinops Pontos: la mer dionysiaque," *Revue de l'Histoire des Religions* 199: 3–22.

(1985) *Dionysos*. Paris.

Detienne, M. (1979) *Dionysos Slain*. trs M. Muellner and L. Muellner. Baltimore and London.

(1986) "Dionysos en ses parousies: un dieu épidemique," *L'Association dionysiaque dans les sociétés anciennes. Actes de la table ronde organisée par l'Ecole française de Rome*. Paris and Rome.

(1989) *Dionysos at Large*. tr. A. Goldhammer. Cambridge, Mass. and London.

Deutsch, H. (1969) *A Psychoanalytic Study of the Myth of Dionysus and Apollo*. New York.

Devereux, G. (1970) "The Psychotherapy Scene in Euripides' *Bacchae*," *JHS* 90: 35–48.

Dihle, A. (1981) *Der Prolog der "Bacchen" und die antike Überlieferungsphase des Euripides-Textes*. Heidelberg.

(1987) "Dionysos in Indien," *India and the Ancient World. History, Trade and Culture Before AD 650*. ed. G. Pollet. Leuven. 47–57.

Diller, H. (1983) "Euripides' Final Phase: The Bacchae," *Oxford Readings in Greek Tragedy*. ed. E. Segal. Oxford. 357–69.

Dodds, E. R. (1940) "Maenadism in the Bacchae," *HThR* 33: 155–76.

(1963) *The Greeks and the Irrational*. Berkeley.

Dover, K. J. (1974) *Greek Popular Morality in the Times of Plato and Aristotle*. Berkeley.

Durand, J.-L. and Frontisi-Ducroux, F. (1982) "Idoles, figures, images: autour de Dionysos," *Revue Archéologique* 1: 81–108.

Easterling, P. E. and Knox, B. M. W. (1985) *The Cambridge History of Classical Literature I*. Cambridge.

Ehrenberg, V. (1938a) "Pothos," *Alexander and the Greeks*. Oxford.

Eisner, R. (1987) *The Road to Daulis: Psychoanalysis, Psychology, and Classical Mythology*. Syracuse. 107–38.

Elderkin, G. W. (1924) *Kantharos. Studies in Dionysiac and Kindred Cult*. Princeton.

Erbse, H. (1984) *Studien zum Prolog der euripideischen Tragödie*. Berlin and New York.

Farnell, L. R. (1971) *The Cults of the Greek States V*. Chicago.

de Fátima Sousa e Silva, M. (1985–86) "Elementos visuais e pictóricos na tragédia de Euripides," *Humanitas* 37–8: 9–86.

Feder, L. (1980) *Madness in Literature*. Princeton.

Ferguson, J. (1972) *A Companion to Greek Tragedy*. Austin.

Festugière, A. J. (1956) "La signification religieuse de la Parodos des Bacchantes," *Eranos* 54: 72–86.

(1957) "Euripide dans les 'Bacchantes,' " *Eranos* 55: 127–44.

(1972) "Les mystères de Dionysos," *Etudes de religion grecque et hellénistique*. Paris. 13–63.

Fol, A. B. and Mazarov, J. (1977) *Thrace and the Thracians*. New York. 32–59.

Foley, H. P. (1980) "The Masque of Dionysus," *TAPA* 110: 107–33.

(1985) *Ritual Irony. Poetry and Sacrifice in Euripides*. Ithaca and London.

Fontenrose, J. (1959) *Python. A Study of the Delphic Myth and its Origins*. Berkeley.

(1981) *The Delphic Oracle*. Berkeley.

Forbes Irving, P. M. C. (1990) *Metamorphosis in Greek Myths*. Oxford.

Gallini, C. (1963) "Il travestismo rituale di Penteo," *Studi e Materiali di Storia delle Religioni* 34: 211–28.

Gernet, L. (1953) "Dionysos et la religion dionysiaque. Eléments hérités et traits originaux," *REG* 66: 377–95.

(1981) *The Anthropology of Ancient Greece*. trs J. Hamilton and B. Nagy. Baltimore and London.

Gernet, L. and Boulanger, A. (1970) *Le génie grec dans la religion*. Paris.

Ghiron-Bistagne, P. (1976) *Recherches sur les acteurs dans la Grèce antique*. Paris.

Gill, C. (1990) "The Character-Personality Distinction," *Characterization and Individuality in Greek Literature*. ed. C. B. R. Pelling. Oxford. 1–31.

Gimbutas, M. (1990) *The Goddesses and Gods of Old Europe: Myths and Cult Images*. Berkeley.

Girard, R. (1977) *Violence and the Sacred*. tr. P. Gregory. Baltimore and London.

Goldhill, S. (1986) *Reading Greek Tragedy*. Cambridge.

(1990a) "The Greater Dionysia and Civic Ideology," *Nothing to Do with Dionysos? Athenian Drama in its Social Context.* eds J. J. Winkler and F. I. Zeitlin. Princeton. 97–129.

(1990b) "Character and Action, Representation and Reading. Greek Tragedy and its Critics," *Characterization and Individuality in Greek Literature.* ed. C. B. R. Pelling. Oxford. 100–27.

Goukowsky, P. (1978, 1981) *Essai sur les origines du mythe d'Alexandre (336–270 av. J.-C.) I–II.* Nancy.

Graf, F. (1985) *Griechische Mythologie.* Munich and Zurich.

(1986) "Orpheus: A Poet Among Men," *Interpretations of Greek Mythology.* ed. J. N. Bremmer. Totowa. 80–106.

Grube, G. M. A. (1935) "Dionysus in the *Bacchae*," *TAPA* 66: 37–54.

Guépin, J.-P. (1968) *The Tragic Paradox. Myth and Ritual in Greek Tragedy.* Amsterdam.

Guthrie, W. K. C. (1956) *The Greeks and their Gods.* Boston.

Halliwell, S. (1990) "Traditional Greek Conceptions of Character," *Characterization and Individuality in Greek Literature.* ed. C. B. R. Pelling. Oxford. 32–59.

Hamilton, R. (1974) "*Bacchae* 47–52: Dionysus' Plan," *TAPA* 104: 139–49.

(1978) "Prologue Prophecy and Plot in Four Plays of Euripides," *AJP* 99: 277–302.

(1985) "Euripidean Priests," *HSCP* 89: 53–73.

Harder, A. (1985) *Euripides' Kresphontes and Archelaos.* Leiden.

Harrison, J. E. (1922) *Prolegomena to the Study of Greek Religion.* Cambridge.

Hartle, R. W. (1986) "An Interpretation of the Derveni Krater: Symmetry and Meaning," *AM* 4: 257–78.

Henrichs, A. (1969) "Die Maenaden von Milet," *ZPE* 4: 223–41.

(1978) "Greek Maenadism from Olympias to Messalina," *HSCP* 82: 121–60.

(1979) "Greek and Roman Glimpses of Dionysos," *Dionysos and his Circle: Ancient Through Modern.* ed. C. Houser. Cambridge, Mass. 1–11.

(1981) "Human Sacrifice in Greek Religion: Three Case Studies," *Entretiens Hardt XXVII*: 195–242.

(1982) "Changing Dionysiac Identities," *Jewish and Christian Self-Definition III.* eds Ben F. Meyer and E. P. Sanders. Philadelphia. 137–60.

(1984a) "Loss of Self, Suffering, Violence: The Modern View of Dionysus from Nietzsche to Girard," *HSCP* 88: 205–40.

(1984b) "Male Intruders Among the Maenads: the So-called Male Celebrant," *Classical Studies in Memory of Karl K. Hulley.* Chico. 69–91.

(1987) *Die Götter Griechenlands. Ihr Bild im Wandel der Religionswissenschaft.* Bamberg.

Hillman, J. (1972) *The Myth of Analysis.* Evanston, Ill.

Hoffman, R. J. (1989) "Ritual License and the Cult of Dionysus," *Athenaeum* 67: 91–115.

Hubert, H. and Mauss, M. (1964) *Sacrifice: Its Nature and Function.* tr. W. D. Halls. Chicago.

Hughes, J. D. (1984) "The Dreams of Alexander the Great," *The Journal of Psychohistory* 12: 168–92.

Jeanmaire, H. (1978) *Dionysos. Histoire du culte de Bacchus.* Paris.

Kamerbeek, J. C. (1960) "Mythe et réalité dans l'oeuvre d'Euripide," *Entretiens Hardt XIII.* ed. O. Reverdin. Geneva. 1–25.

Kerényi, C. (1976) *Dionysos. Archetypal Image of Indestructible Life.* tr. R. Manheim. Princeton.

(1979) *The Gods of the Greeks.* tr. N. Cameron. Guildford.

Keuls, E. C. (1984) "Male–Female Interaction in Fifth-Century Dionysiac Ritual as Shown in Attic Vase Painting," *ZPE* 55: 287–97.

Kirk, G. S. (1983) *The Nature of Greek Myths.* Harmondsworth.

Kitto, H. D. F. (1954) *Greek Tragedy*. New York.

Knox, B. M. W. (1986) *Word and Action. Essays on the Ancient Theater*. Baltimore and London.

Kraemer, R. S. (1979) "Ecstasy and Possession: The Attraction of Women to the Cult of Dionysus," *HThR* 72: 55–80.

La Rue, J. (1968) "Prurience Uncovered: The Psychology of Euripides' Pentheus," *CJ* 63: 209–14.

Lefkowitz, M. R. (1981) *The Lives of the Greek Poets*. Baltimore.

Leineiks, V. (1984) "Euripides, *Bakchai* 877–81 = 897–901," *JHS* 104: 178–9.

Lesky, A. (1972) *Die tragische Dichtung der Hellenen*. Göttingen.

Lewis, I. M. (1971) *Ecstatic Religion*. Baltimore.

Lissarrague, F. (1987) "Dionysos s'en va-t-en guerre," *Images et sociétés ancienne*. ed. P. Bérard. Lausanne. 111–20.

McGinty, P. (1978a) *Interpretation and Dionysos. Method in the Study of a God*. The Hague.

(1978b) "Dionysos's Revenge and the Validation of the Hellenic World-View," *HThR* 71: 77–94.

MacNally, S. (1984) "The Maenad in Early Greek Art," *Women in the Ancient World*. eds J. Peradotto and J. P. Sullivan. Albany, 107–41.

Martin, L. M. (1987) *Hellenistic Religions. An Introduction*. Oxford.

Massenzio, M. (1969) "Cultura e crisi permanente: La 'xenia' dionisiaca," *Studi e Materiali di Storia delle Religioni* 40: 27–113.

Meagher, R. E. (1989) *Mortal Vision: The Wisdom of Euripides*. New York.

(1990) "Revel and Revelation in the *Bakkhai*: Reflections on the Poetics of Euripides," *Willamette Journal* 5: 1–20.

Méautis, G. (1923) "Recherches sur l'expression des masques dans quelques tragédies d'Euripide," *REG* 36: 172–82.

(1942a) "Recherches sur l'époque d'Alexandre: Le *pothos* d'Alexandre le Grand," *REA* 44: 300–4.

Meillier, C. (1983) "Une étude sur la poésie dionysiaque," *REG* 96: 282–5.

Merkelbach, R. (1988) *Die Hirten des Dionysos*. Stuttgart.

Muecke, F. (1982) " 'I Know You – By Your Rags': Costume and Disguise in Fifth-century Drama," *Antichthon* 16: 17–34.

Neuberg, M. (1987) "Whose Laughter Does Pentheus Fear? (Eur. Ba. 842)," *CQ* 37: 227–30.

Nietzsche, F. (1956) *The Birth of Tragedy and the Genealogy of Morals*. tr. F. Golffing. Garden City.

Nilsson, M. P. (1957) *The Dionysiac Mysteries of the Hellenistic and Roman Age*. Lund.

(1961) *Geschichte der griechischen Religion I–II*. Munich.

Norwood, G. (1954) *Essays in Euripidean Drama*. Berkeley.

O'Connor-Visser, E. A. M. E. (1987) *Aspects of Human Sacrifice in the Tragedies of Euripides*. Amsterdam.

O'Flaherty, W. D. (1980) "Dionysus and Siva: Parallel Patterns in Two Pairs of Myths," *History of Religions* 20: 81–111.

Olson, S. D. (1989) "Traditional Forms and Euripidean Adaptation: The Hero Pattern in *Bacchae*," *CW* 83: 25–8.

Oranje, H. (1984) *Euripides' Bacchae. The Play and its Audience*. Leiden.

Otto, W. F. (1965) *Dionysus. Myth and Cult*. tr. R. B. Palmer. Bloomington and London.

Parke, H. W. and Wormell, D. E. W. (1956) *The Delphic Oracle*. Oxford.

Peradotto, J. and Sullivan, J. P. eds (1984) *Women in the Ancient World*. Albany.

Philippart, H. (1930) "Iconographie des 'Bacchantes' d'Euripide," *Revue Belge de Philologie et d'Histoire* 9: 5–72.

Pickard-Cambridge, A. W. (1962) *Dithyramb. Tragedy and Comedy*. Oxford.
(1988) *The Dramatic Festivals of Athens*. eds J. Gould and D. M. Lewis. Oxford.
Privitera, G. A. (1970) *Dioniso in Omero*. Rome.
Puig, M.-C. V. (1987) "Sur l'identité de la figure féminine assise sur un taureau dans la céramique attique à figures noires," *Images et sociétés en Grèce ancienne*. ed. C. Bérard. Lausanne. 131–43.
Quandt, W. (1913) *De Baccho ab Alexandri Aetate in Asia Minore Culto*. Halle.
Rizzo, I. G. (1981) "Euripide, *Baccanti* 406," *Siculorum Gymnasium* 34: 1–24.
Rohde, E. (1966) *Psyche*. tr. W. B. Hillis. New York.
Rohdich, H. (1968) *Die Euripideische Tragödie: Untersuchungen zu ihrer Tragik*. Heidelberg.
Romilly, J. de. (1963) "Le thème du bonheur dans les *Bacchantes*," *REG* 76: 361–80.
(1983) "Fear and Suffering in Aeschylus and Euripides," *Oxford Readings in Greek Tragedy*. ed. E. Segal. Oxford. 390–5.
(1985) *A Short History of Greek Literature*. tr. L. Doherty. Chicago and London.
Rose, H. J. (1956) "Divine Disguisings," *HThR* 49: 63–72.
(1959) *A Handbook of Greek Mythology*. New York.
Rosenmeyer, T. G. (1963) *The Masks of Tragedy*. Austin.
(1983) "Tragedy and Religion: The *Bacchae*," *Oxford Readings in Greek Tragedy*. ed. E. Segal. Oxford. 370–89.
Roth, P. (1984) "Teiresias as *Mantis* and Intellectual in Euripides' *Bacchae*," *TAPA* 114: 59–69.
Roux, G. (1966) "Testimonia Delphica II: Note sur l'Hymne homérique à Apollon, vers 298," *REG* 79: 1–5.
(1976) *Delphes. Son oracle et ses dieux*. Paris.
Sansone, D. (1978) "The *Bacchae* as Satyr-Play?," *Illinois Classical Studies* 3: 40–6.
Schmoll, E. A. (1987) "The Wig of Pentheus: Euripides, Bacchae 831," *LCM* 12: 70–2.
Seaford, R. (1981) "Dionysiac Drama and the Dionysiac Mysteries," *CQ* 31: 252–75.
(1987) "Pentheus' Vision: *Bacchae* 918–22," *CQ* 37: 76–8.
Segal, C. (1961) "The Character and Cults of Dionysus and the Unity of the *Frogs*," *HSCP* 65: 207–42.
(1977) "Euripides' *Bacchae*: Conflict and Mediation," *Ramus* 6: 103–20.
(1978/9) "Pentheus and Hippolytus on the Couch and on the Grid: Psychoanalytic and Structuralist Readings of Greek Tragedy," *CW* 72: 129–48.
(1982a) *Dionysiac Poetics and Euripides' Bacchae*. Princeton.
(1982b) "Etymologies and Double Meanings in Euripides' *Bacchae*," *Glotta* 60: 81–93.
(1985) "The *Bacchae* as Metatragedy," *Directions in Euripidean Criticism*. ed. P. Burian. Durham, NC. 156–73, 221–5.
(1986) *Interpreting Greek Tragedy: Myth, Poetry, Text*. Ithaca.
Segal, E. ed. (1983a) *Oxford Readings in Greek Tragedy*. Oxford.
Segal, E. (1983b) "Euripides: Poet of Paradox," *Oxford Readings in Greek Tragedy*. ed. E. Segal. Oxford.
Seidensticker, B. (1972) "Pentheus," *Poetica* 5: 35–63.
(1978) "Comic Elements in Euripides' *Bacchae*," *AJP* 99: 303–20.
(1979) "Sacrificial Ritual in the *Bacchae*," *Arktouros. Hellenic Studies Presented to B. M. W. Knox*. eds G. W. Bowersock, W. Burkert, and M. C. J. Putnam. Berlin and New York. 18: 181–90.
Simon, B. (1978) *Mind and Madness in Ancient Greece*. Ithaca and London.
Simon, E. (1980) *Die Götter der Griechen*. Munich. 269–94.

(1983) *Festivals of Attica. An Archaeological Commentary*. Madison.
Slater, P. E. (1968) *The Glory of Hera. Greek Mythology and the Greek Family*. Boston.
Stevens, E. (1988) "Whose Laughter Does Pentheus Fear?," *CQ* 38: 246–7.
Stewart, A. (1982) "Dionysos at Delphi: The Pediments of the Sixth Temple of Apollo and Religious Reform in the Age of Alexander," *Macedonia and Greece in Late Classical and Early Hellenistic Times*. eds B. Barr-Sharrar and E. N. Borza. Washington. 205–27.
Taplin, O. P. (1979) *Greek Tragedy in Action*. Berkeley.
(1986) "Fifth-century Tragedy and Comedy: A Synkrisis," *JHS* 106: 163–74.
Thomson, G. (1979) "The Problem of the *Bacchae*," *Epistemonike Epeteris tes Philosophikes Scholes tou Aristoteleiou Panepistemiou*. Thessaloniki. 424–46.
Vellacott, P. (1975) *Ironic Drama: A Study of Euripides' Method and Meaning*. Cambridge.
Vernant, J.-P. (1976) *Religion grecque, religions antiques*. Paris.
(1980) *Myth and Society in Ancient Greece*. tr. J. Lloyd. Sussex, NJ.
(1985) "Le Dionysos masqué des *Bacchantes* d'Euripide," *L'Homme* 93: 39–58.
(1990) *Figures, idoles, masques*. Paris. 41–50, 208–46.
Vernant, J.-P. and Vidal-Naquet, P. (1981) *Tragedy and Myth in Ancient Greece I*. tr. J. Lloyd. Sussex, NJ.
(1986) *Mythe et tragédie en Grèce ancienne II*. Paris.
Vernel, H. S. (1990) *Ter unus. Isis, Dionysos, Hermes. Three Studies in Henotheism*. Leiden.
Vickers, B. (1973) *Towards Greek Tragedy. Drama, Myth, Society*. London.
Vidal-Naquet, P. (1986) "The Black Hunter Revisited," *PCPS* 32: 126–44.
Vollgraff, W. (1927) "Le péan delphique à Dionysos," *Bulletin de Correspondance Hellénique* 51: 423–68.
Wace, A. J. B. (1909–10) "North Greek Festivals and the Worship of Dionysos," *Annual. British School at Athens* 16: 232–53.
Wasson, R., Gordon, A., and Carl, A. (1978) *The Road of Eleusis: Unveiling the Secret of the Mysteries*. New York.
Webster, T. B. L. (1965) "The Poet and the Mask," *Classical Drama and its Influence*. New York.
(1967) *The Tragedies of Euripides*. London.
West, M. L. (1984) *The Orphic Poems*. Oxford.
Willink, C. W. (1966) "Some Problems of Text and Interpretation in the *Bacchae*," *CR* 16: 27–50, 220–42.
Winkler, J. J. and Zeitlin, F. I. eds (1990) *Nothing to do with Dionysos? Athenian Drama in its Social Context*. Princeton.
Winnington-Ingram, R. P. (1948) *Euripides and Dionysus. An Interpretation of the Bacchae*. Cambridge.
Wohlberg, J. (1968) "The Palace-Hero Equation in Euripides," *Acta Antiqua Academiae Scientiarum Hungaricae* 16: 149–55.
Zeitlin, F. I. (1982) "Cultic Models of the Female: Rites of Dionysus and Demeter," *Arethusa* 15: 129–57.
(1990a) "Playing the Other: Theater, Theatricality, and the Feminine in Greek Drama," *Nothing to Do with Dionysos? Athenian Drama in its Social Context*. eds J. J. Winkler and F. I. Zeitlin. Princeton. 64–96.
(1990b) "Thebes: Theater of Self and Society in Athenian Drama," *Nothing to Do with Dionysos? Athenian Drama in its Social Context*. eds J. J. Winkler and F. I. Zeitlin. Princeton. 130–67.
Zimmerman, B. (1991) *Greek Tragedy. An Introduction*. tr. T. Marier. Baltimore and London. 123–8.

## MACEDONIAN BACKGROUND

Adams, W. L. (1986) "Macedonian Kingship and the Right of Petition," *AM* 4: 43–52.

Anson, E. M. (1984) "The Meaning of the Term Macedones," *AncW* 10: 67–8.

(1985a) "Macedonia's Alleged Constitutionalism," *CJ* 80: 303–16.

Aymard, A. (1950) "Sur l'assemblée macédonienne," *REA* 52: 115–37.

Badian, E. (1982a) "Greeks and Macedonians," *Macedonia and Greece in Late Classical and Early Hellenistic Times*. eds B. Barr-Sharrar and E. N. Borza. Washington. 33–51.

Bellen, H. (1974) "Der Rachegedanke in der griechisch–persischen Auseinandersetzung," *Chiron* 4: 184–205.

Blanchaud, M.-H. (1986) "Les cultes orientaux en Macédoine grecque dans l'antiquité," *AM* 4: 83–6.

Borza, E. N. (1982a) "The History and Archaeology of Macedonia: Retrospect and Prospect," *Macedonia and Greece in Late Classical and Early Hellenistic Times*. eds B. Barr-Sharrar and E. N. Borza. Washington. 17–30.

(1982b) "Athenians, Macedonians, and the Origins of the Macedonian Royal House," *Studies in Attic Epigraphy History and Topography*. Princeton. 7–13.

(1987a) "Timber and Politics in the Ancient World: Macedon and the Greeks," *Proceedings of the American Philosophical Society* 131: 32–52.

(1989) "Some Toponym Problems in Eastern Macedonia," *AHB* 3: 60–9.

(1990) *In the Shadow of Olympus. The Emergence of Macedon*. Princeton.

Carlier, P. (1984) *La royauté en Grèce avant Alexandre*. Strasburg.

Carney, E. D. (1983) "Regicide in Macedonia," *Parola del Passato* 38: 260–72.

Cloché, P. (1960) *Histoire de la Macédoine jusqu'à l'avènement d'Alexandre le Grand (336 avant J.-C)*. Paris.

Dascalakis, A. (1965) *The Hellenism of the Ancient Macedonians*. Thessaloniki.

Edson, C. F. (1970) "Early Macedonia," *AM* 1: 17–44.

(1981) "Early Macedonia," *Philip of Macedon*. eds M. B. Hatzopoulos and L. D. Loukopoulos. London. 10–35.

Errington, R. M. (1981a) "Alexander the Philhellene and Persia," *Ancient Macedonian Studies in Honor of Charles F. Edson*. ed. H. J. Dell. Thessaloniki. 139–43.

(1983) "The Historiographical Origins of Macedonian 'Staatsrecht,' " *AM* 3: 89–101.

(1990) *A History of Macedonia*. tr. C. Errington. Berkeley and Oxford.

Granier, F. (1931) *Die makedonische Heeresversammlung*. Munich.

Greenwalt, W. S. (1985) "The Introduction of Caranus into the Argead King List," *GRBS* 26: 43–9.

(1986a) "Herodotus and the Foundation of Argead Macedonia," *AncW* 13: 117–22.

(1987) "Argaeus in the Macedonian Religious Tradition," *AHB* 1: 51–3.

(1988a) "Amyntas III and the Political Stability of Argead Macedonia," *AncW* 18: 35–44.

Griffith, G. T. (1965a) "The Macedonian Background," *G&R* 12: 125–39.

Gude, M. (1933) *A History of Olynthus*. Baltimore.

Hammond, N. G. L. (1970) "The Archaeological Background to the Macedonian Kingdom," *AM* 1:53–67.

(1972) *A History of Macedonia I*. Oxford.

(1989a) *The Macedonian State: The Origins, Institutions and History*. Oxford.

Hammond, N. G. L. and Griffith, G. T. (1979) *A History of Macedonia II*. Oxford.

Hatzopoulos, M. B. (1986) "Succession and Regency in Classical Macedonia," *AM* 4: 279–92.
Hoddinott, R. F. (1981) *The Thracians*. Over Wallop, UK.
Hoffmann, O. (1906) *Die Makedonen. Ihre Sprache und ihr Volkstum*. Göttingen.
Isaac, B. (1986) *The Greek Settlements in Thrace until the Macedonian Conquest*. Leiden.
Islami, S. (1985) *et al. Les Illyriens*. Tirane.
Kalléris, J. N. (1954, 1976) *Les anciens Macédoniens I–II*. Athens.
Masson, O. (1984) "Quelques noms de femmes en Macédoine," *ZPE* 55: 133–6.
Rizakis, A. and Touratsoglou, J. eds (1985) *Epigraphes Ano Makedonias I*. Athens.
Scaife, R. (1989) "Alexander I in the Histories of Herodotos," *Hermes* 117: 129–37.
Tataki, A. B. (1988) *Ancient Beroea. Prosopography and Society*. Athens.
*Treasures of Ancient Macedonia: Archaeological Museum of Thessaloniki*. (1977). Athens.


**THE ROYAL TOMBS AT VERGINA**

Adams, J. P. (1983) "The *Larnakes* from Tomb II at Vergina," *Archaeological News* 12: 1–7.
Adams, W. L. (1980) "The Royal Macedonian Tomb at Vergina: An Historical Interpretation," *AncW* 3: 67–72.
Andronicos, M. (1977) "Vergina: The Royal Graves in the Great Tumulus," *Archaiologika Analekta ex Athēnon* 10: 1–72.
(1978a) "Regal Treasures from a Macedonian Tomb," *National Geographic* 154: 54–77.
(1978b) "The Royal Tomb of Philip II," *Archaeology* 31: 33–41.
(1979a) "The Tombs at the Great Tumulus of Vergina," *Greece and Italy in the Classical World. Acta of the XI International Congress of Classical Archaeology*. London. 39–56.
(1979b) "The Finds from the Royal Tombs at Vergina," *PCPS* 65: 355–67.
(1980a) "The Royal Tomb at Vergina and the Problem of the Dead," *Archaiologika Analekta ex Athēnon* 13: 168–78.
(1980b) "The Royal Tombs at Vergina," *The Search for Alexander*. Boston. 26–38.
(1981) "The Royal Tombs at Aigai (Vergina)," *Philip of Macedon*. eds M. B. Hatzopoulos and L. D. Loukopoulos. London. 188–231.
(1984) *Vergina. The Royal Tombs and the Ancient City*. Athens.
(1987) "Some Reflections on the Macedonian Tombs," *Annual. British School at Athens* 82: 1–16.
Andronovski, H. (1978) "Rich Archeological Discoveries in Vergina," *Macedonian Review* 8: 109–12.
Borza, E. N. (1981a) "The Macedonian Royal Tombs at Vergina: Some Cautionary Notes," *Archaeological News* 10: 73–87.
(1982c) "Those Vergina Tombs Again," *Archaeological News* 11: 8–10.
(1985) "A Macedonian Skull," *Newsletter of the Association of Ancient Historians* 36: 3–4.
(1987b) "The Royal Macedonian Tombs and the Paraphernalia of Alexander the Great," *Phoenix* 41: 105–21.
Burstein, S. M. (1982) "The Tomb of Philip II and the Succession of Alexander the Great," *Classical Views = Echos du Monde Classique* 26: 141–63.
Cadelo, E. (1987) "The New Vergina," *Athena Magazine* 19: 272.
Calder III, W. M. (1981) "Diadem and Barrel-Vault: A Note," *AJA* 85: 334–5.
(1983) " 'Golden Diadems' Again," *AJA* 87: 102–3.

Daux, G. (1977) "Aigeia: sites des tombes royales de la Macédoine antique," *Comptes rendus de l'Academie des inscriptions et belles lettres*. 620–30.

Fredricksmeyer, E. A. (1981a) "Again the So-Called Tomb of Philip II," *AJA* 85: 330–4.

(1983) "Once More the Diadem and Barrel-Vault at Vergina," *AJA* 87: 99–102.

Green, P. (1982) "The Royal Tombs of Vergina: A Historical Analysis," *Philip II, Alexander the Great and the Macedonian Heritage*. eds W. L. Adams and E. N. Borza. Washington. 129–51.

(1989b) "The Macedonian Connection," *Classical Bearings*. 151–64.

Hammond, N. G. L. (1978) " 'Philip's Tomb' in Historical Context," *GRBS* 19: 331–50.

(1982) "The Evidence for the Identity of the Royal Tombs at Vergina," *Philip II, Alexander the Great and the Macedonian Heritage*. eds W. L. Adams and E. N. Borza. Washington. 111–27.

(1989b) "Arms and the King: The Insignia of Alexander the Great," *Phoenix* 43: 217–24.

Lehmann, P. W. (1980) "The So-Called Tomb of Philip II: A Different Interpretation," *AJA* 84: 527–31.

(1981) "Once Again the Royal Tomb at Vergina," *Archaiologika Analekta ex Athēnon* 14: 134–44.

(1982) "The So-called Tomb of Philip II. An Addendum," *AJA* 86: 437–42.

Markle, M. M. (1980) "Weapons from the Cemetery at Vergina and Alexander's Army," *Megas Alexandros*. Thessaloniki. 243–67.

Miller, S. G. (1982) "Macedonian Tombs: Their Architecture and Architectural Decoration," *Macedonia and Greece in Late Classical and Early Hellenistic Times*. eds B. Barr-Sharrar and E. N. Borza. Washington.

Neverov, O. Ya. (1990) "The Finds in the Large Tumulus in Vergina and the Problems of the Toreutics of the Early Hellenistic Period," *Vestnik Drevnei Istorii* 192: 161–6. [Russian with English summary].

Oikonomides, Al. N. (1988a) "Coins, Archaeological Finds and the 'Macedonian Shield,' " *Classical Bulletin* 64: 77–84.

(1989) "The Portrait of King Philip II of Macedonia," *AncW* 20: 5–16.

Prag, A. J. N. W. (1990) "Reconstructing King Philip II: The 'Nice' Version," *AJA* 94: 237–47.

Prag, A. J. N. W., Musgrave, J. H. and Neave, R. A. H. (1984) "The Skull from Tomb II at Vergina: King Philip II of Macedon," *JHS* 104: 60–78.

Prestianni Giallombardo, A. M. (1983) "Riflessioni storiografiche sul Grande Tumulo e le tombe reali di Vergina," *Acta of the XII International Congress of Classical Archaeology*. Athens.

(1986) "Il diadema di Vergina e l'iconografia di Filippo II," *AM* 4: 497–509.

Prestianni Giallombardo, A. M. and Tripodi, B. (1980) "Le tombe regali di Vergina: quale Filippo?," *ASNP* 10: 889–1001.

(1981) "La tomba e il tesoro di Filippo II di Macedonia: una nuova proposta d'attribuzione," *Magna Graecia* 16: 14–17.

Rotroff, S. I. (1984) "Spool Saltcellars in the Athenian Agora," *Hesperia* 53: 343–54.

Tomlinson, R. A. (1987) "The Architectural Context of the Macedonian Vaulted Tombs," *Annual. British School at Athens* 82: 305–12.

Tripodi, B. (1986) "L'emblema' della casa reale macedone," *AM* 4: 653–60.

Xirotiris, N. I. and Langenscheidt, F. (1981) "The Cremations from the Royal Macedonian Tombs of Vergina," *Archaiologike Ephemeris* 142–60, pls.52–5.

## YOUNG ALEXANDER

Africa, T. W. (1982a) "Homosexuals in Greek History," *The Journal of Psychohistory* 9: 401–20.

Agostinetti, A. S. (1988) "Presenze femminili nei libri XVIII–XX della Biblioteca Storica di Diodoro Siculo," *Acme* 41: 31–9.

Anderson, A. R. (1930) "Bucephalas and his Legend," *AJP* 51: 1–21.

Badian, E. (1963) "The Death of Philip II," *Phoenix* 17: 244–50.

—— (1982b) " 'Eurydice,' " *Philip II, Alexander the Great and the Macedonian Heritage*. eds W. L. Adams and E. N. Borza. Washington. 99–110.

Bliquez, L. J. (1981) "Philip II and Abdera," *Eranos* 79: 65–79.

Borza, E. N. (1978) "Philip II and the Greeks," *CP* 73: 236–43.

Bosworth, A. B. (1971a) "Philip II and Upper Macedonia," *CQ* 21: 93–105.

Bowersock, G. W. (1988) "Erodoto, Alessandro e Roma," *Rivista Storica Italiana* 100: 724–38.

Bremmer, J. N. (1989) "Greek Pederasty and Modern Homosexuality," *From Sappho to De Sade*. ed. J. N. Bremmer. London and New York. 1–14.

Brown, T. S. (1967) "Alexander's Book Order (Plut. *Alex.* 8)," *Historia* 16: 359–68.

—— (1977) "Alexander and Greek Athletics, in Fact and Fiction," *Greece and the Eastern Mediterranean in Ancient History and Prehistory*. ed. K. K. Kinzl. 76–88.

Brunt, P. A. (1975) "Alexander, Barsine and Heracles," *RFIC* 103: 22–34.

Carney, E. D. (1987a) "The Career of Adea-Eurydike," *Historia* 36: 496–501.

—— (1987b) "Olympias," *Anc. Soc.* 18: 35–62.

—— (1988) "The Sisters of Alexander the Great: Royal Relicts," *Historia* 37: 385–404.

Carson, A. (1986) *Eros, the Bittersweet: An Essay*. Princeton.

Cawkwell, G. L. (1978) *Philip of Macedon*. London.

—— (1981) "Philip and Athens," *Philip of Macedon*. eds M. B. Hatzopoulos and L. D. Loukopoulos. London. 100–10.

Cloché, P. (1955) *Un fondateur d'empire. Philippe II, roi de Macédoine*. Saint-Etienne.

Dascalakis, A. (1965) "La jeunesse d'Alexandre et l'enseignement d'Aristote," *Studii Clasice* 7: 168–80.

—— (1966) *Alexander the Great and Hellenism*. Thessaloniki.

De Bruyn, O. (1989) "L'aréopage et la Macédoine à l'époque de Démosthène," *Etudes classiques* 57: 3–12.

Develin, R. D. (1981) "The Murder of Philip II," *Antichthon* 15: 86–99.

Dover, K. J. (1979) *Greek Homosexuality*. Cambridge, Mass.

—— (1984) "Classical Greek Attitudes to Sexual Behaviour," *Women in the Ancient World*. eds J. Peradotto and J. P. Sullivan. Albany. 143–57.

Ellis, J. R. (1969) "Population-transplants by Philip II," *Makedonika* 9: 9–17.

—— (1971) "Amyntas Perdikka, Philip II and Alexander the Great," *JHS* 91: 15–24.

—— (1973) "The Step-brothers of Philip II," *Historia* 22: 350–4.

—— (1977) "The Dynamics of Fourth-Century Macedonian Imperialism," *AM* 2: 103–14.

—— (1981a) "Macedonia under Philip," *Philip of Macedon*. eds M. B. Hatzopoulos and L. D. Loukopoulos. London. 146–65.

—— (1981b) "The Unification of Macedonia," *Philip of Macedon*. eds M. B. Hatzopoulos and L. D. Loukopoulos. London. 35–47.

—— (1981c) "The Assassination of Philip II," *Ancient Macedonian Studies in Honor of Charles F. Edson*. ed. H. J. Dell. Thessaloniki. 99–137.

—— (1982) "The First Months of Alexander's Reign," *Macedonia and Greece in Late Classical and Early Hellenistic Times*. eds B. Barr-Sharrar and E. N. Borza. Washington. 69–73.

(1986) *Philip II and Macedonian Imperialism.* Princeton.

Errington, R. M. (1974) "Macedonian 'Royal Style' and its Historical Significance," *JHS* 94: 20–37.

(1975) "Arybbas the Molossian," *GRBS* 16: 41–50.

(1978) "The Nature of the Macedonian State under the Monarchy," *Chiron* 8: 77–133.

(1981b) "Review-Discussion: Four Interpretations of Philip II," *AJAH* 6: 69–88.

Farber, J. J. (1979) "The *Cyropaedia* and Hellenistic Kingship," *AJP* 100: 497–514.

Fears, J. R. (1975) "Pausanias, the Assassin of Philip II," *Athenaeum* 53: 111–35.

Flacelière, R. (1962) "Homosexuality," *Love in Ancient Greece.* tr. J. Cleugh. New York. 62–100.

Fraser, A. D. (1953) "The 'Breaking' of Bucephalus," *CW* 47: 22–3.

Fredricksmeyer, E. A. (1979a) "Divine Honors for Philip II," *TAPA* 109: 39–61.

(1981b) "On the Background of the Ruler Cult," *Ancient Macedonian Studies in Honor of Charles F. Edson.* ed. H. J. Dell. Thessaloniki. 145–56.

(1982) "On the Final Aims of Philip II," *Philip II, Alexander the Great and the Macedonian Heritage.* eds W. L. Adams and E. N. Borza. Washington. 85–98.

(1990) "Alexander and Philip: Emulation and Resentment," *Classical Views = Echos du Monde Classique* 85: 300–15.

French, V. and Dixon, P. (1986a) "The Pixodaros Affair: Another View. Appendix: The Reliability of Plutarch," *AncW* 13: 73–86.

(1986b) "The Source Traditions for the Pixodaros Affair," *AncW* 14: 25–40.

Gonzalez-Reigosa, F. and Velez-Diaz, A. (1983) "Psychohistorians Discuss Psychohistory," *The Journal of Psychohistory* 10: 511–20.

Grassl, H. (1987) "Alexander der Grosse und die Zerstörung Thebens," *Zu Alexander d. Gr.* eds W. Will and J. Heinrichs. Amsterdam. 271–8.

Greenwalt, W. S. (1984) "The Search for Arrhidaeus," *AncW* 10: 69–77.

(1986b) "Macedonia's Kings and the Political Usefulness of the Medical Arts," *AM* 4: 213–22.

(1988b) "The Marriageability Age at the Argead Court: 360–317 BC," *CW* 82: 93–7.

(1989) "Polygamy and Succession in Argead Macedonia," *Arethusa* 22: 19–43.

Grzybek, E. (1986) "Zu Philipp II. und Alexander dem Grossen," *AM* 4: 223–9.

Hamilton, C. D. (1982) "Problems of Alliance and Hegemony in Fourth Century Greece Reconsidered," *Classical Views = Echos du Monde Classique* 1: 297–318.

Hamilton, J. R. (1965) "Alexander's Early Life," *G&R* 12: 117–24.

Hammond, N. G. L. (1967) *Epirus.* Oxford.

(1981) "The End of Philip," *Philip of Macedon.* eds M. B. Hatzopoulos and L. D. Loukopoulos. London. 166–75.

(1988a) "The King and the Land in the Macedonian Kingdom," *CQ* 38: 382–91.

(1990a) "Royal Pages, Personal Pages, and Boys Trained in the Macedonian Manner during the Period of the Temenid Monarchy," *Historia* 39: 261–90.

Hampl, F. (1934) *Der König der Makedonen.* Leipzig.

Hatzopoulos, M. B. (1982a) "A Reconsideration of the Pixodarus Affair," *Macedonia and Greece in Late Classical and Early Hellenistic Times.* eds B. Barr-Sharrar and E. N. Borza. Washington. 59–66.

(1982b) "The Oleveni Inscription and the Dates of Philip II's Reign," *Philip II, Alexander the Great and the Macedonian Heritage.* eds W. L. Adams and E. N. Borza. Washington. 21–42.

Hatzopoulos, M. B, and Loukopoulos, L. D. eds. (1981) *Philip of Macedon.* London.

Hauben, H. (1975) "Philippe II. Fondateur de la marine macédonienne," *Anc. Soc.* 6: 51–9.

Heckel, W. (1978a) "Kleopatra or Eurydike?," *Phoenix* 32: 155–8.

(1979) "Philip II, Kleopatra and Karanos," *RFIC* 107: 385–93.

(1981a) "Philip and Olympias (337/6 BC)," *Classical Contributions*. Locust Valley. 51–7.

(1981b) "Polyxena, the Mother of Alexander the Great," *Chiron* 11: 79–86.

(1983a) "Adea-Eurydike," *Glotta* 61: 40–2.

(1983–4) "Kynnane the Illyrian," *Rivista Storica dell'Antichità* 13–14: 193–200.

(1985a) "The 'Boyhood Friends' of Alexander the Great," *Emérita* 53: 285–9.

Heskel, J. (1988) "The Political Background of the Arybbas Decree," *GRBS* 29: 185–96.

Kelly, D. H. (1980) "Philip II of Macedon and the Boeotian Alliance," *Antichthon* 14: 64–83.

Kienast, D. (1973) *Philipp II. von Makedonien und das Reich der Achaimeniden*. Munich.

Klees, H. (1987) "Die Expansion Makedoniens unter Philip II. und der Friede des Philokrates," *Zu Alexander d. Gr. I.* eds W. Will and J. Heinrichs. Amsterdam. 131–91.

Lehmann, K. (1983) *Samothrace*. Locust Valley.

Lévêque, P. (1981) "Philip's Personality," *Philip of Macedon*. tr. W. Phelps, eds M. B. Hatzopoulos and L. D. Loukopoulos. London. 176–87.

McKinlay, A. P. (1939) "The 'Indulgent' Dionysius," *TAPA* 70: 51–61.

Macurdy, G. H. (1927) "Queen Eurydice and the Evidence for Woman Power in Early Macedonia," *AJP* 48: 201–14.

(1932a) *Hellenistic Queens*. Baltimore and London.

Markle, M. M. (1974) "The Strategy of Philip in 346," *CQ* 24: 253–68.

(1976) "Support of Athenian Intellectuals for Philip: A Study of Isocrates' *Philippus* and Speusippus' *Letter to Philip*," *JHS* 96: 80–99.

(1981) "Demosthenes, *Second Philippic*: A Valid Policy for the Athenians against Philip," *Antichthon* 15: 62–85.

Martin, T. R. (1981) "Diodorus on Philip II and Thessaly in the 350's BC," *CP* 76: 188–201.

(1982) "A Phantom Fragment of Theopompus and Philip II's First Campaign in Thessaly," *HSCP* 86: 55–78.

Miller, S. G. (1973) "The Philippeion and Hellenistic Macedonian Architecture," *Mitteilungen des Deutschen Archäologischen Instituts. Athenische Abteilung* 88: 189–218.

Momigliano, A. D. (1934) *Filippo il Macedone*. Florence.

Montgomery, H. (1985) "The Economic Revolution of Philip II – Myth or Reality?" *SymbOsl* 60: 37–47.

Moscati Castelnuovo, L. (1986) "Eleno e la tradizione troiana in Epiro," *RFIC* 114: 411–24.

Oikonomides, Al. N. (1982) "The Epigram on the Tomb of Olympias at Pydna," *AncW* 5: 9–16.

Ostwald, M. (1969) *Nomos and the Beginnings of the Athenian Democracy*. Oxford.

Parsons, P. J. (1979) "The Burial of Philip II?," *AJAH* 4: 97–101.

Perlman, S. (1957) "Isocrates' *'Philippus'* – a Reinterpretation," *Historia* 6: 306–17.

ed. (1973) *Philip and Athens*. Cambridge.

(1976) "Panhellenism, the Polis and Imperialism," *Historia* 25: 1–30.

(1983) "Isocrates, *'Patris'* and Philip II," *AM* 3: 211–27.

(1985) "Greek Diplomatic Tradition and the Corinthian League of Philip of Macedon," *Historia* 34: 153–74.

(1986) "Fourth Century Treaties and the League of Corinth of Philip of Macedon," *AM* 4: 437–42.

Petsas, P. (1958) "New Discoveries at Pella, Birthplace and Capital of Alexander," *Archaeology* 11: 246–54.

Peyrefitte, R. (1977) *La jeunesse d'Alexandre*. Paris.

Pomeroy, S. B. (1984) *Women in Hellenistic Egypt. From Alexander to Cleopatra*. New York.

Prestianni Giallombardo, A. M. (1973–4) "Aspetti giuridici e problemi cronologici della reggenza di Filippo II di Macedonia," *Helikon* 13–14: 191–209.

(1980) "Eurydike-Kleopatra. Nota ad Arr. Anab. 3,6,5," *ASNP* 10: 295–306.

Price, S. R. F. (1984) *Rituals and Power*. Cambridge.

Roux, G. (1981) "Samothrace, le sanctuaire des Grands Dieux et ses mystères," *Bulletin de l'Association Guillaume Budé*. 2–23.

Rosen, K. (1987) "Alexander I., Herodot und die makedonische Basileia," *Zu Alexander d. Gr. I*. eds W. Will and J. Heinrichs. Amsterdam. 25–51.

Rubin, L. G. (1989) "Love and Politics in Xenophon's *Cyropaedia*," *Interpretation* 16: 391–413.

Ryder, T. T. B. (1965) *Koine Eirene*. Oxford.

Roebuck, C. (1948) "The Settlements of Philip II with the Greek States in 338 BC," *CP* 43: 73–92.

Sadourny, J. (1979) "A la recherche d'" une politique en les rapports d'Eschine et de Philippe de Macédoine de la prise d'Olynthe à Chèronée," *REA* 81: 19–36.

Samuel, A. E. (1988) "Philip and Alexander as Kings: Macedonian Monarchy and Merovingian Parallels," *American Historical Review* 93: 1270–86.

Schmitt, H. H. ed. (1969) *Die Staatsverträge des Altertums III*. Munich.

Seiler, F. (1986) *Die griechische Tholos*. Mainz.

Strauss, B. S. (1984) "Philipp II of Macedon, Athens, and Silver Mining," *Hermes* 112: 418–27.

Tatum, J. (1989) *Xenophon's Imperial Fiction. On the Education of Cyrus*. Princeton.

Thomas, C. G. (1983) "Philip II, Alexander III, and Hellenistic Kingship," *LCM* 8: 86–7.

Tritsch, W. (1936) *Olympias, die Mutter Alexanders des Grossen. Das Schicksal eines Weltreiches*. Frankfurt.

Tronson, A. (1984) "Satyrus the Peripatetic and the Marriages of Philip II," *JHS* 104: 116–26.

Unz, R. K. (1985) "Alexander's Brothers?," *JHS* 105: 171–4.

Velkov, V. (1987) "Alexander der Grosse und Thrakien," *Zu Alexander d. Gr I*. eds W. Will and J. Heinrichs. Amsterdam. 257–69.

Vershinin, L. R. (1990) "The Circumstances of the Conspiracy against Philip II of Macedonia," *Vestnik Drevnei Istorii* 20: 139–53 [Russian with English summary].

Walcot, P. (1987) "Plato's Mother and Other Terrible Women," *G&R* 34: 12–31.

Welwei, K.-W. (1987) "Zum Problem der frühmakedonischen Heeresversammlung," *Zu Alexander d. Gr. I*. eds W. Will and J. Heinrichs. Amsterdam. 1–24.

Will, W. (1987) "Ein sogenannter Vatermörder. Nochmals zur Ermordung Philipps," *Zu Alexander d. Gr. I*. eds W. Will and J. Heinrichs. Amsterdam. 219–32.

Wirth, G. (1985c) *Philipp II. Geschichte Makedoniens I*. Stuttgart.

Witt, R. E. (1977) "The Kabeiroi in Ancient Macedonia," *AM* 2: 67–80.

Wüst, F. R. (1938) *Philipp II. von Makedonien und Griechenland (346–338)*. Munich.

**ARISTOTLE**

Ackrill, J. L. (1981) *Aristotle the Philosopher*. Oxford.

Barnes, J. (1982) *Aristotle*. Oxford and New York.

Barnes, J., Schofield, M., and Sorabji, R. eds (1977) *Articles on Aristotle II*. London.

Belfiore, E. (1985) "Pleasure, Tragedy and Aristotelian Psychology," *CQ* 35: 349–61.

Bosworth, A. B. (1970) "Aristotle and Callisthenes," *Historia* 19: 407–13.

Bowra, C. M. (1938) "Aristotle's Hymn to Virtue," *CQ* 32: 182–9.

Boyancé, P. (1937) *Le culte des Muses chez les philosophes grecs*. Paris.

Charles, D. (1984) *Aristotle's Philosophy of Action*. Ithaca.

Chroust, A.-H. (1966) "Aristotle and Callisthenes of Olynthus," *Classical Folia* 20: 32–41.

—— (1967) "Aristotle Leaves the Academy," *G&R* 14: 39–43.

—— (1972a) "Aristotle's Sojourn in Assos," *Historia* 21: 170–6.

—— (1972b) "Aristotle and the Foreign Policy of Macedonia," *Review of Politics* 34: 367–94.

—— (1973) *Aristotle. New Light on his Life and on Some of his Lost Works I–III*. Notre Dame and London.

Dahl, N. O. (1984) *Practical Reason, Aristotle, and Weakness of the Will*. Minneapolis.

Engberg-Pederson, T. (1983) *Aristotle's Theory of Moral Insight*. Oxford.

Fortenbaugh, W. W. (1975) *Aristotle on Emotion*. London.

Gauthier, R. A. and Jolif, J. Y. (1970) *Aristote: L'Ethique à Nicomaque I–IV*. Paris and Louvain.

Guthrie, W. K. C. (1981) *A History of Greek Philosophy VI. Aristotle. An Encounter*. London, New York and Melbourne.

Halliwell, S. (1987) *The Poetics of Aristotle. Translation and Commentary*. London.

Hardie, W. F. R. (1980) *Aristotle's Ethical Theory*. Oxford.

Jaeger, W. (1962) *Aristotle*. tr. R. Robinson. Oxford.

Jones, J. (1962) *On Aristotle and Greek Tragedy*. London.

Jordan, J. N. (1987) *Western Philosophy. From Antiquity to the Middle Ages*. New York. 128–71.

Jürgen, W. von. (1985) *Werk und Wirkung. Aristoteles und seine Schule I*. Berlin and New York.

Kelsen, H. (1937/8) "The Philosophy of Aristotle and the Hellenic-Macedonian Policy," *International Journal of Ethics* 48: 1–64.

Kenny, A. J. P. (1978) *The Aristotelian Ethics*. Oxford.

—— (1979) *Aristotle's Theory of the Will*. London.

Kraut, R. (1989) *Aristotle on the Human Good*. Princeton.

Merlan, P. (1954–5) "Isocrates, Aristotle, and Alexander the Great," *Historia* 3: 60–81.

Mulgan, R. G. (1974) "Aristotle and Absolute Rule," *Antichthon* 8: 21–8.

Plezia, M. (1968) "Aristoteles gegenüber der Monarchie Alexanders d. Gr.," *Studien zur Geschichte und Philosophie des Altertums*. ed. J. Harmatta. Amsterdam. 84–9.

Prandi, L. (1984) "La lettera di Aristotele ad Alessandro: il problema di Callistene," *RISA* 1: 31–45.

Raz, J., ed. (1978) *Practical Reasoning*. Oxford.

Renehan, R. (1982) "Aristotle as Lyric Poet: The Hermias Poem," *GRBS* 23: 251–74.

Richter, M. (1990) "Aristotle and the Classical Greek Concept of Despotism," *History of European Ideas* 12: 175–87.

Rist, J. M. (1989) *The Mind of Aristotle: A Study in Philosophical Growth.* Toronto, Buffalo, and London.

Romm, J. S. (1989) "Aristotle's Elephant and the Myth of Alexander's Scientific Patronage," *AJP* 110: 566–75.

Rorty, A. O. ed. (1980) *Essays on Aristotle's Ethics.* Berkeley.

Schütrumpf, E. (1991) *Aristoteles. Politik II–III.* Berlin.

Sordi, M. (1984) "La Lettera di Aristotele ad Alessandro e i rapporti tra greci e barbari," *Aevum* 58: 3–12.

Stern, S. M. (1968) *Aristotle on the World-State.* London.

Vatai, F. L. (1984) *Intellectuals in Politics in the Greek World.* London, Sydney, and Dover, N.H.

Wormell, D. E. W. (1935) "The Literary Tradition concerning Hermias of Atarneus," *Yale Classical Studies* 5: 57–92.

## RELIGION

Ameling, W. L. (1988) "Alexander und Achilleus. Eine Bestandsaufnahme," *Zu Alexander d. Gr II.* eds W. Will and J. Heinrichs. Amsterdam. 657–92.

Arafat, K. W. (1990) *Classical Zeus. A Study in Art and Literature.* Oxford.

Baege, W. (1913) *De Macedonum Sacris.* Halle.

Bérard, C. et al. (1984) *La cité des images. Religion et société en Grèce antique.* Lausanne and Paris.

Bernard, P. (1980) "Heracles, les Grottes de Karafto et le sanctuaire de Mont Sambulos en Iran," *Studia Iranica* 9: 301–24.

Beye, C. R. (1968) *The Iliad, the Odyssey and the Epic Tradition.* London.

(1987) *Ancient Greek Literature and Society.* Ithaca and London.

Bonnet, C. (1988) *Melgart. Cultes et mythes de L'Héraclès tyrien en Méditerrannée.* Leuven.

Borza, E. N. (1967) "Alexander and the Return from Siwah," *Historia* 16: 369.

Bosworth, A. B. (1977) "Alexander and Ammon," *Greece and the Ancient Mediterranean in History and Prehistory.* ed. K. Kinzl. Berlin and New York. 51–75.

Bowra, C. M. (1969) *The Greek Experience.* New York.

Bremmer, J. N. (1986b) "Greek Mythology: A Select Bibliography (1965–1986)," *Interpretations of Greek Mythology.* ed. J. N. Bremmer. Totowa, NJ. 278–83.

Brenk, F. E. (1986) "Dear Child: The Speech of Phoinix and the Tragedy of Achilleus in the Ninth Book of the *Iliad*," *Eranos* 84: 77–86.

Brommer, F. (1986) *Heracles. The Twelve Labors of the Hero in Ancient Art and Literature.* New Rochelle, NY.

Brundage, B. C. (1958) "Herakles the Levantine: A Comprehensive View," *Journal of Near Eastern Studies* 17: 225–36.

Classen, D. J. (1959) "The Libyan God Ammon in Greece before 331 BC," *Historia* 8: 349–55.

Clay, J. S. (1989) *The Politics of Olympus. Form and Meaning in the Major Homeric Hymns.* Princeton.

Dow, S. (1985) "The Cult of the Hero Doctor," *Bulletin. American Society of Papyrologists* 22: 33–47.

Dull, S. (1970) "De Macedonum Sacris. Gedanken zu einer Neubearbeitung der Götterkulte in Makedonien," *AM* 1: 316–23.

Easterling, P. E. and Muir, J. V. eds (1985) *Greek Religion and Society.* Cambridge.

Edson, C. F. (1971) "Macedonian Cults," *Oxford Classical Dictionary.* Oxford. 634.

Edmunds, L. (1979) "Alexander and the Calendar (Plut. *Alex.* 16.2)," *Historia* 28: 112–17.

ed. (1990) *Approaches to Greek Myth*. Baltimore and London.

Edwards, M. W. (1987) *Homer. Poet of the Iliad*. Baltimore and London.

Fakhry, A. (1944) *Siwa Oasis. Its History and Antiquities*. Cairo.

Ferguson, J. (1989) *Among the Gods. An Archaeological Exploration of Ancient Greek Religion*. London and New York.

Festugière, A. J. (1954) *Personal Religion among the Greeks*. Berkeley.

Fontenrose, J. (1978) *The Delphic Oracle: Its Responses and Operations*. Berkeley.

Fraser, P. M. (1967) "Current Problems concerning the Early History of the Cult of Sarapis," *Opuscula Atheniensia* 7: 23–45.

(1972) *Ptolemaic Alexandria I–III*. Oxford.

Fredricksmeyer, E. A. (1958) "The Religion of Alexander the Great". Dissertation. Wisconsin.

(1961) "Alexander, Midas and the Oracle at Gordium," *CP* 56: 160–8.

(1966) "The Ancestral Rites of Alexander the Great," *CP* 61: 179–82.

Frei, P. (1972) "Der Wagen von Gordion," *Museum Helveticum* 29: 110–23.

Gitti, A. (1951) *Quando nacque in Alessandro Magno l'idea della filiazione divina*. Bari.

Greenwalt, W. S. (1982) "A Macedonian Mantis," *AncW* 5: 17–25.

Griffin, J. (1980a) *Homer*. Oxford.

(1980b) *Homer on Life and Death*. Oxford.

(1986) "Heroic and Unheroic Ideas in Homer," *Chios* 1: 3–13.

(1987) "Homer and Excess," *Homer: Beyond Oral Poetry. Recent Trends in Homeric Interpretation*. eds J. M. Bremer, I. J. F. de Jong and J. Kalff. Amsterdam.

Grottanelli, C. and Parise, N. F. eds (1988) *Sacrificio e società nel mondo antico*. Bari.

Hooker, J. T. (1988) "The Cults of Achilles," *RhM* 131: 1–7.

Instinsky, H. U. (1949) *Alexander der Grosse am Hellespont*. Godesberg.

(1961) "Alexander, Pindar, Euripides," *Historia* 10: 248–55.

Jähne, A. (1982–5) "Alexander und Amon," *An. U. Sci. Budapestinensis Rolando Eötvös* 9–10: 49–55.

Kerényi, C. (1959) *Asklepios. Archetypal Image of the Physician's Existence*. tr. R. Manheim. New York.

Kern, O. (1938) "Der Glaube Alexanders des Grossen," *Die Religion der Griechen III*. Berlin. 38–57.

Kienast, D. (1987) "Alexander, Zeus und Ammon," *Zu Alexander d. Gr. I*. eds W. Will and J. Heinrichs. 309–33.

King, K. C. (1987) *Achilles. Paradigms of the War Hero from Homer to the Middle Ages*. Berkeley. 1–49.

Kirk, G. S. (1962) *The Songs of Homer*. Cambridge.

Knapp, R. C. (1986) "La via Heraclea en el occidente: mito, arqueologia, propaganda, historia," *Emérita* 54: 103–22.

Knox, B. M. W. (1983) *The Heroic Temper. Studies in Sophoclean Tragedy*. Berkeley.

Langer, P. (1981) "Alexander the Great at Siwah," *AncW* 4: 109–27.

Larsen, J. A. O. (1932) "Alexander at the Oracle of Ammon," *CP* 27: 70–5.

Lefkowitz, M. R. (1986) *Women in Greek Myth*. Baltimore.

Lloyd-Jones, H. (1971) *The Justice of Zeus*. Berkeley.

MacCary, W. T. (1982) *Childlike Achilles. Ontogeny and Phylogeny in the Iliad*. New York.

Mastrocinque, A. (1987) "Alessandro a Menfi," *Zu Alexander d. Gr. I*. eds W. Will and J. Heinrichs. 289–307.

Mazon, P. (1948) *Introduction a l'Iliade*. Paris.
Nagy, G. (1979) *The Best of the Achaeans: Concepts of the Hero in Archaic Greek Poetry*. Baltimore and London.
(1990) *Greek Mythology and Poetics*. Ithaca and London.
Nock, A. D. (1933) *Conversion. The Old and the New in Religion from Alexander the Great to Augustine of Hippo*. Oxford.
(1944) "The Cult of Heroes," *HThR* 37: 141–74.
Palagia, O. (1986) "Imitation of Heracles in Ruler Portraiture. A Survey from Alexander to Maximinus Daza," *Boreas* 9: 137–51.
Parke, H. W. (1967) *The Oracles of Zeus. Dodona. Olympia. Ammon*. Oxford.
(1985a) *Oracles of Apollo in Asia Minor*. London.
(1986) "The Temple of Apollo at Didyma: The Building and its Function," *JHS* 106: 121–31.
Parker, R. (1983) *Miasma. Pollution and Purification in Early Greek Religion*. Oxford.
(1985) "Greek States and Greek Oracles," *History of Political Thought* 6: 298–326.
Picard, C. and G.-C. (1964) "Hercule et Melqart," *Hommages à J. Bayet*. eds M. Renard and R. Schilling. Brussels. 569–78.
Pritchett, W. K. (1979) *The Greek State at War III: Religion*. Berkeley.
Radet, G. (1926a) "Tyr, Delphes et l'Apollon de Gèla," *REA* 28: 113–20.
(1926b) "Le pèlerinage au sanctuaire d'Ammon," *REA* 28: 213–40.
Redfield, J. M. (1975) *Nature and Culture in the Iliad*. Chicago.
Rehork, J. (1969) "Homer, Herodot und Alexander," *Beiträge zur Alten Geschichte und deren Nachleben I* eds R. Stiehl and H. E. Stier. Berlin. 251–60.
Roller, L. E. (1983) "The Legend of Midas," *Classical Antiquity* 2: 299–313.
(1984) "Midas and the Gordian Knot," *Classical Antiquity* 3: 256–71.
Schadewaldt, W. (1966) *Iliasstudien*. Darmstadt.
Schein, S. L. (1984) *The Mortal Hero: An Introduction to Homer's Iliad*. Berkeley.
Schmiel, R. (1987) "Achilles in Hades," *CP* 82: 35–7.
Shapiro, H. A. (1983) "Hêrôs Theos: the Death and Apotheosis of Herakles," *CW* 77: 7–18.
Silk, M. S. (1987) *Homer, The Iliad*. Cambridge.
Sissa, G. and Detienne, M. (1989) *La vie quotidienne des dieux grecs*. Paris.
Verbanck-Piérard, A. (1987) "Images et croyances en Grèce ancienne: représentations de l'apothéose Héraklès au VIᵉ siècle," *Images et sociétés en Grèce ancienne*. ed. C. Bérard. Lausanne. 187–99.
(1989) "Le double culte d'Héraklès: légende ou réalité?," *Entre hommes et dieux*. ed. A.-F. Laurens. Paris.
Vernant, J.-P. (1987a) "Formes de croyance et de rationalité en Grèce ancienne," *Arch. Sci. Sociales Relig.* 32: 115–23.
(1987b) "Entre la honte et la gloire," *Métis* 2: 269–98.
Veyne, P. (1983) *Did the Greeks Believe in their Myths?* tr. P. Nissing. Chicago and London.
Wees, H. van (1988) "Kings in Combat: Battles and Heroes in the *Iliad*," *CQ* 38: 1–24.
Welles, C. B. (1962) "The Discovery of Sarapis and the Foundation of Alexandria," *Historia* 11: 271–98.
Woodward, A. M. (1962) "Athens and the Oracle of Ammon," *Annual. British School at Athens* 57: 5–13.

# MILITARY

Adcock, Sir F. E. (1957) *The Greek and Macedonian Art of War*. Berkeley.

Anderson, J. K. (1970) *Military Theory and Practice in the Age of Xenophon*. Berkeley.

Anson, E. M. (1981) "Alexander's Hypaspists and the Argyraspids," *Historia* 30: 117–20.

(1985b) "The Hypaspists: Macedonia's Professional Citzen-Soldiers," *Historia* 34: 246–8.

(1989) "The Persian Fleet in 334," *CP* 84: 44–9.

(1991) "The Evolution of the Macedonian Army Assembly (330–315 BC)," *Historia* 40: 230–47.

Atkinson, J. E. (1987) "The Infantry Commissions Awarded by Alexander at the End of 331 BC," *Zu Alexander d. Gr. I.* eds W. Will and J. Heinrichs. Amsterdam. 413–35.

Badian, E. (1965b) "Orientals in Alexander's Army," *JHS* 85: 160–1.

Borza, E. N. (1977) "Alexander's Communications," *AM* 2: 295–303.

Bosworth, A. B. (1975) "The Mission of Amphoterus and the Outbreak of Agis' War," *Phoenix* 29: 27–43.

(1986a) "Macedonian Manpower under Alexander the Great," *AM* 4: 115–22.

Breloer, B. (1933) *Alexanders Kampf gegen Poros*. Stuttgart.

Brunt, P. A. (1962) "Persian Accounts of Alexander's Campaigns," *CQ* 12: 141–55.

(1963) "Alexander's Macedonian Cavalry," *JHS* 83: 27–46.

Burn, A. R. (1952) "Notes on Alexander's Campaigns, 332–330," *JHS* 72: 81–91.

(1965) "The Generalship of Alexander," *G&R* 12: 140–54.

Davis, E. W. (1964) "The Persian Battle Plan at the Granicus," *The James Sprunt Studies in History and Political Science* 46: 34–44.

Devine, A. M. (1975) "Grand Tactics at Gaugamela," *Phoenix* 29: 374–85.

(1980) "The Location of the Battle of Issus," *LCM* 5: 3–10.

(1984) "The Location of Castabalum and Alexander's Route from Mallus to Myriandrus," *Acta Classica* 27: 127–9.

(1985a) "The Strategies of Alexander the Great and Darius III in the Issus Campaign (333 BC)," *AncW* 12: 25–38.

(1985b) "Grand Tactics at the Battle of Issus," *AncW* 12: 39–59.

(1986a) "The Battle of Gaugamela: A Tactical and Source-Critical Study," *AncW* 13: 87–115.

(1986b) "Demythologizing the Battle of the Granicus," *Phoenix* 40: 265–78.

(1987) "The Battle of Hydaspes: A Tactical and Source-Critical Study," *AncW* 16: 91–113.

(1988) "A Pawn-Sacrifice at the Battle of the Granicus: The Origins of a Favorite Stratagem of Alexander the Great," *AncW* 18: 3–20.

(1989a) "The Macedonian Army at Gaugamela: Its Strength and the Length of its Battle-Line," *AncW* 19: 77–80.

(1989b) "Alexander the Great," *Warfare in the Ancient World*. ed. J. Hackett. New York, Oxford, and Sidney. 104–29.

Dupuy, J. N. (1969) *The Military Life of Alexander the Great of Macedonia*. New York.

Eggermont, P. H. L. (1970) "Alexander's Campaign in Gandhāra and Ptolemy's List of Indo-Scythian Towns," *Orientalia Lovaniensia Periodica* 1: 63–123.

(1975) *Alexander's Campaigns in Sind and Baluchistan and the Siege of the Brahmin Town of Harmatelia*. Leuven.

Engels, D. W. (1978a) *Alexander the Great and the Logistics of the Macedonian Army*. Berkeley.

(1980) "Alexander's Intelligence System," *CQ* 30: 327–40.
Erskine, A. (1989) "The [pezétairoi] of Philip II and Alexander III," *Historia* 38: 385–94.
Faure, P. (1982) *La vie quotidienne des armées d'Alexandre*. Paris.
Ferrill, A. (1988a) *The Origins of War from the Stone Age to Alexander the Great*. New York. 175–217, 230–2.
(1988b) "Alexander in India. The Battle at the Edge of the Earth," *Quarterly Journal of Military History* 1: 76–85.
Fisher, T. (1990) "A proposito di Curzio Rufo 4,3,25," *Rivista di Filologia e d'Istruzione Classica* 118: 56.
Foss, C. and Badian, E. (1977) "The Battle of the Granicus: a New Look," *AM* 2: 271–93, 495–502.
Fuller, J. F. C. (1960) *The Generalship of Alexander the Great*. Rahway.
Goukowsky, P. (1972) "Le roi Poros et son éléphant," *Bulletin de Correspondance Hellenique* 96: 473–502.
(1987) "Makedonika," *REG* 100: 240–55.
Griffith, G. T. (1935) *The Mercenaries of the Hellenistic World*. Cambridge.
(1947) "Alexander's Generalship at Gaugamela," *JHS* 67: 77–89.
(1956) "*Makedonika*. Notes on the Macedonians of Philip and Alexander," *PCPS* 4: 3–10.
(1963) "A Note on the Hipparchies of Alexander," *JHS* 83: 68–74.
(1981a) "Philip As a General and the Macedonian Army," *Philip of Macedon*. eds M. B. Hatzopoulos and L. Loukopoulos. London. 58–77.
(1981b) "Peltast, and the Origins of the Macedonian Phalanx," *Ancient Macedonian Studies in Honor of Charles F. Edson*. ed. H. J. Dell. Thessaloniki. 161–7.
Grupp, G. (1984) "Herrscherethos und Kriegführung bei Achämeniden und Makedonen," *Aus dem Osten des Alexanderreiches*. eds J. Ozols and V. Thewalt. Cologne. 32–42.
Hamilton, J. R. (1956) "The Cavalry Battle at the Hydaspes," *JHS* 76: 26–31.
(1972) "Alexander among the Oreitae," *Historia* 21: 603–8.
Hammond, N. G. L. (1938) "The Two Battles of Chaeronea (338 BC and 86 BC)," *Klio* 13: 186–218.
(1974) "Alexander's Campaign in Illyria," *JHS* 94: 67–87.
(1977) "The Campaign of Alexander against Cleitus and Glaucias," *AM* 2: 503–9.
(1980c) "The Battle of the Granicus River," *JHS* 100: 73–88.
(1980d) "The March of Alexander the Great on Thebes in 335 BC," *Megas Alexandros*. Thessaloniki. 171–81.
(1980e) "Training in the Use of a Sarissa and its Effect in Battle, 359–333 BC," *Antichthon* 14: 53–63.
(1983b) "The Text and the Meaning of Arrian vii 6.2–5," *JHS* 103: 139–44.
(1989c) "Casualties and Reinforcements of Citizen Soldiers in Greece and Macedonia," *JHS* 109: 56–68.
Hauben, H. (1972) "The Command Structure in Alexander's Mediterranean Fleets," *Anc. Soc.* 3: 56–65.
(1976) "The Expansion of Macedonian Sea-Power under Alexander the Great," *Anc. Soc.* 7: 79–185.
(1987) "Onesicritus and the Hellenistic 'Archikybernesis,' " *Zu Alexander d. Gr. I*. eds W. Will and J. Heinrichs. Amsterdam. 569–93.
Heckel, W. (1980) "Alexander at the Persian Gates," *Athenaeum* 58: 168–74.
Hellenkemper, H. (1984) "Das wiedergefundene Issos," *Aus dem Osten des Alexanderreiches*. eds J. Ozols and V. Thewalt. Cologne. 43–50.
Katzenstein, H. J. (1973) *The History of Tyre*. Jerusalem.
Kebric, R. B. (1988) "Old Age, the Ancient Military, and Alexander's Army: Positive Examples for a Graying America," *The Gerontologist* 28: 298–300.

Keegan, J. (1987) *The Mask of Command*. New York.

Khlopin, I. N. (1980/1) "Die Chronologie und Dynamik des Feldzuges Alexanders des Grossen nach Mittelasien," *Anc. Soc.* 11–12: 151–72.

Kulak, M. (1988a) "De Proelio ab Alexandro Magno cum Poro Indorum Rege ad Hydaspem Commiso," *Meander* 43: 229–41 [Polish with Latin summary].

(1988b) "De Alexandri Magni flumine Hydaspe ad Oceanum itinere annis CCCXXVI/CCCXXV facto," *Meander* 43: 331–8 [Polish with Latin summary].

Lock, R. A. (1972) "The Date of Agis III's War in Greece," *Antichthon* 6; 10–27.

(1977a) "The Macedonian Army Assembly in the Time of Alexander the Great," *CP* 72: 91–107.

(1977b) "The Origins of the Argyraspids," *Historia* 26: 373–8.

McCoy, W. J. (1989) "Memnon of Rhodes at the Granicus," *AJP* 110: 413–33.

McCrindle, J. W. (1969) *The Invasion of India by Alexander the Great*. New York and London.

Manti, P. A. (1983) "The Cavalry Sarissa," *AncW* 8: 73–80.

Markle, M. M. (1977) "The Macedonian Sarissa, Spear and Related Armor," *AJA* 81: 323–9.

(1978) "Use of the Sarissa by Philip and Alexander of Macedon," *AJA* 82: 483–97.

(1982) "Macedonian Arms and Tactics under Alexander the Great," *Macedonia and Greece in Late Classical and Early Hellenistic Times*. eds B. Barr-Sharrar and E. N. Borza. Washington. 87–111.

Marsden, E. W. (1964) *The Campaign of Gaugamela*. Liverpool.

(1971) *Greek and Roman Artillery II*. Oxford.

(1977) "Macedonian Military Machinery and its Designers under Philip and Alexander," *AM* 2: 211–23.

Milns, R. D. (1966a) "Alexander's Pursuit of Darius through Iran," *Historia* 15: 256.

(1966b) "Alexander's Seventh Phalanx Battalion," *GRBS* 7: 159–66.

(1971) "The Hypaspists of Alexander III: Some Problems," *Historia* 20: 186–95.

(1976) "The Army of Alexander the Great," *Alexandre le Grand. Image et réalité. Entretiens Hardt XXII*. ed. E. Badian. Geneva. 87–136.

(1982) "A Note on Diodorus and Macedonian Military Terminology in Book XVII," *Historia* 31: 123–6.

(1987) "Army Pay and the Military Budget of Alexander the Great," *Zu Alexander d. Gr. I*. eds W. Will and J. Heinrichs. Amsterdam. 233–56.

Morrison, J. S. (1987) "Athenian Sea-Power in 323/2 BC: Dream and Reality," *JHS* 107: 88–97.

Murison, C. L. (1972) "Darius III and the Battle of Issus," *Historia* 21: 399–423.

Neumann, C. (1971) "A Note on Alexander's March-Rates," *Historia* 20: 196–8.

Parke, H. W. (1933) *Greek Mercenary Soldiers*. Oxford.

Pritchett, W. K. (1958) "Observations on Chaironeia," *AJA* 62: 307–11.

(1971, 1974, 1979, 1985) *The Greek State at War I–IV*. Berkeley.

Radet, G. (1932) "La dernière campagne d'Alexandre contre Darius," *Mélanges Gustave Glotz II*. Paris. 765–78.

(1935) "Alexandre et Porus. Le passage de l'Hydaspe," *REA* 37: 349–57.

Rahe, P. A. (1981) "The Annihilation of the Sacred Band at Chaeronea," *AJA* 85: 84–7.

Roberts, J. T. (1982) "Chares, Lysicles and the Battle of Chaeronea," *Klio* 64: 367–71.

Romane, P. (1987) "Alexander's Siege of Tyre," *AncW* 16: 79–90.

(1988) "Alexander's Siege of Gaza," *AncW* 18: 21–30.

Rutz, W. (1965) "Zur Erzählungskunst des Q. Curtius Rufus: Die Belagerung von Tyrus," *Hermes* 93: 370–82.

Ruzicka, S. (1983) "Curtius 4.1.34–37 and the 'Magnitudo Belli,' " *CJ* 79: 30–4.

(1988) "War in the Aegean, 333–331 BC: A Reconsideration," *Phoenix* 42: 131–51.

Stark, F. (1958a) *Alexander's Path*. London.

(1958b) "Alexander's March from Miletus to Phrygia," *JHS* 78: 102–20.

Stein, A. (1929) *On Alexander's Track to the Indus*. London.

(1943) "On Alexander's Route into Gedrosia. An Archaeological Tour in Las Bela," *Geographical Journal* 102: 193–227.

Stewart, A. (1987) "Diodorus, Curtius, and Arrian on Alexander's Mole at Tyre," *Berytus* 35: 97–9.

Strasburger, H. (1952) "Alexanders Zug durch die Gedrosische Wüste," *Hermes* 80: 456–93.

Vidal-Naquet, P. (1984) "Alessandro e i cacciatori neri," *Studi Storici per l'Antichità Classica* 25: 25–33.

Welwei, K-W. (1979) "Der Kampf um das makedonische Lager bei Gaugamela," *RhM* 122: 222–8.

Wirth, G. (1971a) "Nearchos, der Flottenchef," *Acta Conventus XI "Eirene"*. 615–39.

(1977) "Erwägungen zur Chronologie des Jahres 333 v. Chr.," *Helikon* 17: 23–55.

(1980/1) "Zwei Lager bei Gaugamela," *Quaderni Catanesi di Studi Classici e Medievali*, 2: 51–100, 3: 5–61.

(1984) "Zu einer schweigenden Mehrheit. Alexander und die griechischen Söldner," *Aus dem Osten des Alexanderreiches*. eds J. Ozols and V. Thewalt. Cologne. 9–31.

## POLITICAL

Andreotti, R. (1956) "Per una critica dell'ideologia di Alessandro Magno," *Historia* 5: 257–302.

(1957) "Die Weltmonarchie Alexanders des Grossen in Überlieferung und geschichtlicher Wirklichkeit," *Saeculum* 8: 120–66.

Anson, E. M. (1988) "Antigonus, the Satrap of Phrygia," *Historia* 37: 471–7.

Ashton, N. G. (1983) "The Lamian War – A False Start?," *Antichthon* 17: 47–61.

Atkinson, J. E. (1981) "Macedon and Athenian Politics in the Period 338 to 323 BC," *Acta Classica* 24: 37–48.

Badian, E. (1960a) "The First Flight of Harpalus," *Historia* 9: 245–6.

(1961b) "Harpalus," *JHS* 81: 16–43.

(1965c) "The Administration of the Empire," *G&R* 12: 166–82.

(1966) "Alexander the Great and the Greeks of Asia," *Ancient Society and Institutions*. Oxford. 37–69.

(1967) "Agis III," *Hermes* 95: 170–92.

(1987a) "Alexander at Peucelaotis," *CQ* 37: 117–28.

Bagnall, R. S. (1979) "The Date of the Foundation of Alexandria," *AJAH* 4: 46–9.

Baldry, H. C. (1965) *The Unity of Mankind in Greek Thought*. Cambridge.

Baumann, R. A. (1990) *Political Trials in Ancient Greece*. London. 128–50.

Bengtson, H. et. al. (1969) *The Greeks and the Persians from the Sixth to the Fourth Centuries*. London.

Bernard, P. (1982a) "Alexandre et Ai-Khanoum," *Journal des Savants* 125–38.

(1982b) "Diodore XVII, 83, I: Alexandrie du Cause ou Alexandrie de l'Oxus?," *Journal des Savants* 217–42.

Bernhardt, R. (1988) "Zu den Verhandlungen zwischen Dareios und Alexander nach der Schlacht bei Issos," *Chiron* 18: 181–98.

Bickerman, E. J. (1934) "Alexandre le Grand et les villes d'Asie," *REG* 47: 346–74.

(1940) "La lettre d'Alexandre le Grand aux bannis grecs," *REA* 42: 25–35.

Borza, E. N. (1971) "The End of Agis' Revolt," *CP* 66: 230–5.

Bosworth, A. B. (1974) "The Government of Syria under Alexander the Great," *CQ* 24: 46–64.

(1980b) "Alexander and the Iranians," *JHS* 100: 1–21.

(1981) "A Missing Year in the History of Alexander the Great," *JHS* 101: 17–39.

(1986b) "Alexander the Great and the Decline of Macedon," *JHS* 106: 1–12.

(1987) "Nearchus in Susiana," *Zu Alexander d. Gr.I.* eds W. Will and J. Heinrichs. Amsterdam. 541–67.

Bowman, A. K. (1986) *Egypt after the Pharaohs. 332 BC–AD 642 from Alexander to the Arab Conquest.* London.

Briant, P. (1980) "Conquête territoriale et stratégie idéologique: Alexandre le grand et l'idéologie monarchique achéménide," *Prace Historyczne* 63: 37–83.

(1982a) *Etat et pasteurs au Moyen-Orient ancien.* Cambridge and Paris.

(1982b) *Rois, tributs et paysans.* Paris.

Brunt, P. A. (1965) "The Aims of Alexander," *G&R* 12: 2005–15.

Buchner, E. (1954) "Zwei Gutachten über die Behandlung der Barbaren durch Alexander den Grossen," *Hermes* 82: 378–84.

Burn, A. R. (1962b) *Persia and the Greeks.* London.

(1985) "Persia and the Greeks," *The Cambridge History of Iran II.* ed. I. Gershevitch. Cambridge. 292–391.

Burstein, S. M. (1976) "Alexander, Callisthenes and the Sources of the Nile," *GRBS* 17: 135–46.

Cargill, J. (1981) *The Second Athenian League.* Berkeley.

Carney, E. D. (1981a) "The First Flight of Harpalus Again," *CJ* 77: 9–11.

Cawkwell, G. L. (1969) "The Crowning of Demosthenes," *CQ* 19: 163–80.

Cook, J. M. (1983) *The Persian Empire.* London.

(1985) "The Rise of the Achaemenids and Establishment of their Empire," *The Cambridge History of Iran II.* ed. I. Gershevitch. Cambridge. 200–91.

De Callataÿ, F. (1989) "Les trésors achéménides et les monnayages d'Alexandre: espèces immobilisées et espèces circulantes?," *REA* 91: 259–76.

Ehrenberg, V. (1938b) *Alexander and the Greeks.* Oxford.

Fischer, K. (1967) "Zur Lage von Kandahar an Landverbindungen zwischen Iran und Indien," *Bonner Jarhbücher* 167: 129–232.

(1987) "Bessos im Gelände zwischen Areia und Baktria. Landschaft und Siedlung an Wegestrecken der Zeit Alexanders III. von Makedonien," *Zu Alexander d. Gr. I.* eds W. Will and J. Heinrichs. Amsterdam. 457–66.

Fortina, M. (1965) *Cassandro, re di Macedonia.* Turin.

Frye, R. N. (1962) *The Heritage of Persia.* London.

Graf, D. F. (1984) "Medism: The Origin and Significance of the Term," *JHS* 104: 15–30.

Griffith, G. T. (1964) "Alexander the Great and an Experiment in Government," *PCPS* 10: 23–39.

(1965b) "Alexander and Antipater in 323 BC," *PACA* 8: 12–17.

Gunderson, L. L. (1981) "Alexander and the Attic Orators," *Ancient Macedonian Studies in Honor of Charles F. Edson.* ed. H. J. Dell. Thessaloniki. 183–91.

Hallock, R. T. (1985) "The Evidence of the Persepolis Tablets," *The Cambridge History of Iran II.* ed. I. Gershevitch. Cambridge. 588–609.

Hamilton, J. R. (1987) "Alexander's Iranian Policy," *Zu Alexander d. Gr. I.* eds W. Will and J. Heinrichs. Amsterdam. 467–86.

Hammond, N. G. L. (1985) "Some Macedonian Offices c. 336–309 BC," *JHS* 105: 156–60.

Harris, N. (1986) *Alexander the Great and the Greeks.* Watts.

Heckel, W. (1977a) "The Flight of Harpalus and Tauriskos," *CP* 72: 133–5.

(1981c) "Two Doctors from Kos?," *Mnemosyne* 34: 396–8.

(1986a) "Chorienes and Sisimithres," *Athenaeum* 74: 223–6.

(1987a) "Fifty-Two Anonymae in the History of Alexander," *Historia* 36: 114–19.

(1987b) "*Anonymi* in the History of Alexander the Great," *Antiquité Classique* 56: 130–47.

Heinrichs, J. (1987) " 'Asiens König.' Die Inschriften des Kyrosgrabs und das achämenidische Reichsverständnis," *Zu Alexander d. Gr. I.* eds W. Will and J. Heinrichs. Amsterdam. 487–540.

Herzfeld, E. (1968) *The Persian Empire*. Wiesbaden.

Heuss, A. (1954) "Alexander der Grosse und die politische Ideologie des Altertums," *Antike und Abendland* 4: 65–104.

Higgins, W. E. (1980) "Aspects of Alexander's Imperial Administration: Some Modern Methods and Views Reviewed," *Athenaeum* 58: 129–52.

Holt, F. L. (1982) "The Hyphasis 'Mutiny': A Source Study," *AncW* 5: 33–59.

(1984) "Discovering the Lost History of Ancient Afghanistan," *AncW* 9: 3–11.

(1986a) "Alexander's Settlements in Central Asia," *AM* 4: 315–23.

(1988) *Alexander the Great and Bactria. The Formation of a Greek Frontier in Central Asia*. Leiden and New York.

Holzberger, N. (1988) "Hellenistisches und Römisches in der Philippos-Episode bei Curtius Rufus (III 5,1–6,20)," *Klassische Sprachen und Literaturen* 22: 86–104.

Hornblower, S. (1982) *Mausolus*. Oxford.

Jaschinski, S. (1981) *Alexander und Griechenland unter dem Eindruck der Flucht des Harpalos*. Bonn.

Jones, T. B. (1935) "Alexander and the Winter of 330–329 BC," *CW* 28: 124–5.

Kingsley, B. M. (1986) "Harpalos in the Megarid (333–331 BC) and the Grain Shipments from Cyrene," *ZPE* 66: 165–77.

Kuhrt, A. (1990) "Alexander and Babylon," *Achaemenid History V*. eds H. Sancisi-Weerdenburg, A. Kuhrt, and J. W. Drijvers. Leiden. 121–30.

McQueen, E. I. (1978) "Some Notes on the Anti-Macedonian Movement in the Peloponnese in 331 BC," *Historia* 27: 40–64.

Mallowan, M. (1985) "Cyrus the Great (558–529 BC)," *The Cambridge History of Iran II*. ed. I. Gershevitch. Cambridge. 392–419.

Marasco, G. (1985) "La 'Profezia dinastica' e la resistenza babilonese alla conquista di Alessandro," *ASNP* 15: 529–37.

(1987) "Alessandro Magno e Priene," *Sileno* 13: 59–77.

Mendels, D. (1984) "Aetolia 331–301: Frustration, Political Power and Survival," *Historia* 33: 129–80.

Meyer, E. (1924) *Alexander der Grosse und die absolute Monarchie*. Halle.

Miltner, F. (1952) "Der Okeanos in der persischen Weltreichidee," *Saeculum* 3: 522–55.

Missitzis, L. (1985) "A Royal Decree of Alexander the Great on the Lands of Philippi," *AncW* 12: 3–14.

Mitchel, F. W. (1965) "Athens in the Age of Alexander," *G&R* 12: 189–204.

Noethlichs, K. L. (1987) "Sparta und Alexander: Überlegungen zum 'Mäusekrieg' und zum 'Sparta-Mythos,' " *Zu Alexander d. Gr. I.* eds W. Will and J. Heinrichs. Amsterdam. 391–412.

Olmstead, A. T. (1948) *History of the Persian Empire*. Chicago.

Piejko, F. (1985) "The 'Second Letter' of Alexander the Great to Chios," *Phoenix* 39: 238–49.

Prandi, L. (1983) "Alessandro Magno e Chio: considerazioni su *Syll.*³ 283 E *SEG* XXII, 506," *Aevum* 57: 24–32.

Rebuffat, F. (1983) "Alexandre le Grand et les problèmes financiers au début de son règne (été 336 – printemps 334)," *Revue Numismatique* 25: 43–52.

Renard, M. and Servais, J. (1955) "A propos du mariage d'Alexandre et de Roxane," *Acta Classica* 24: 29–50.

Rutz, W. (1984) "Das Bild des Dareios bei Curtius Rufus," *Würzburger Jahrbücher für die Altertumswissenschaft* 10: 147–59.

Sancisi-Weerdenburg, H., Kuhrt, A. and Drijvers, J. W. eds (1987–1990) *Achaemenid History I–V*. Leiden.

Schmidt, L. (1959) "Der gordische Knoten und seine Lösung," *Antaios* 1: 305–18.

Schmitthenner, W. (1968) "Über eine Formveränderung der Monarchie seit Alexander d. Gr.," *Saeculum* 19: 31–46.

Schwartz, M. (1985) "The Religion of Achaemenian Iran," *The Cambridge History of Iran II*. ed. I. Gershevitch. Cambridge. 664–97.

Seager, R. (1981) "The Freedom of the Greeks of Asia: From Alexander to Antiochus," *CQ* 31: 106–12.

Sealey, R. (1960) "The Olympic Festival of 324 BC," *CR* 10: 185–6.

Seibert, J. (1972b) "Nochmals zu Kleomenes von Naukratis," *Chiron* 2: 99–102.

(1987) "Dareios III," *Zu Alexander d. Gr. I*. eds W. Will and J. Heinrichs. Amsterdam. 437–56.

Sherwin-White, S. M. (1985) "Ancient Archives: The Edict of Alexander to Priene, A Reappraisal," *JHS* 105: 69–89.

Sisti, F. (1982) "Alessandro e il medico Filippo: analisi e fortuna di un aneddoto," *Bollettino dei Classici* 3: 139–51.

Snell, B. (1964) *Scenes from Greek Drama*. Berkeley.

Sofman, A. S. and Tsibukidis, D. I. (1987) "Nearchus and Alexander," *AncW* 16: 71–7.

Sordi, M. (1965) "Alessandro e i Romani," *Rendiconti dell'Istituto Lombardo di Scienze e Lettere* 99: 445–52.

(1983) "Alessandro Magno e l'eredità di Siracusa," *Aevum* 57: 14–23.

(1985) "Alessandro Magno, i Galli e Roma," *Scritti in onore di Piero Treves. A Cura di Fulviomario Briolo*. ed. X. Teves. Rome.

Stronach, D. (1978) *Pasargadae*. Oxford.

Stroud, R. S. (1984) "An Argive Decree from Nemea concerning Aspendos," *Hesperia* 53: 193–216.

Tarn, W. W. (1938) *The Greeks in Bactria and India*. Cambridge.

Thomas, C. G. (1974) "Alexander's Garrisons: A Clue to his Administrative Plans?," *Antichthon* 8: 11–20.

Tripodi, B. (1979) "La *immunitas cunctarum rerum* concessa da Alessandro Magno ai macedoni (Iust., 11,1,10)," *ASNP* 9: 513–25.

Tronson, A. (1985) "The Relevance of IG II (2) 329 to the Hellenic League of Alexander the Great," *AncW* 12: 15–19.

Vogt, J. (1971) "Kleomenes von Naukratis – Herr von Ägypten," *Chiron* 1: 153–7.

Walser, G. (1966) *Die Völkerschaften auf den Reliefs von Persepolis*. Berlin.

ed. (1972) *Beiträge zur Achämenidengeschichte*. Wiesbaden.

Werner, R. (1987) "Alexander der Molosser in Italien," *Zu Alexander d. Gr. I*. eds W. Will and J. Heinrichs. Amsterdam. 335–90.

Will, W. (1983) *Athen und Alexander. Untersuchungen zur Geschichte der Stadt von 338 bis 322 v. Chr.* Munich.

Wirth, G. (1971b) "Dareios und Alexander," *Chiron* 1: 133–52.

(1971c) "Alexander zwischen Gaugamela und Persepolis," *Historia* 20: 617–32.

(1972) "Die *SYNTAXEIS* von Kleinasien 334 v. Chr.," *Chiron* 2: 91–8.

Wolski, J. (1985–8) "Alexandre le Grand et l'Iran. Contribution à l'histoire de l'époque séleucide et arsacide," *Acta Antiqua et Archaeologica* 31: 3–11.

Worthington, I. (1984a) "The First Flight of Harpalus Reconsidered," *G&R* 31: 161–9.

(1984b) "Harpalus and the Macedonian Envoys," *LCM* 9: 47–8.

(1985a) "Plutarch *Demosthenes* 25 and Demosthenes' Cup," *CP* 80: 229–33.
(1985b) "Pausanias II 33,4–5 and Demosthenes," *Hermes* 113: 123–5.
(1986a) "I. G. II² 1631, 1632 and Harpalus' Ships," *ZPE* 65: 222–4.
(1986b) "The Chronology of the Harpalus Affair," *SymbOsl* 61: 63–76.
(1986c) "Hyper. 5 *Dem.* 18 and Alexander's Second Directive to the Greeks," *Classica et Mediaevalia* 37: 115–21.
(1990) "Alexander the Great and the Date of the Mytilene Decree," *ZPE* 83: 194–214.
Wüst, F. R. (1953–4b) "Die Meuterei von Opis," *Historia* 2: 418–31.
Young, R. S. (1963) "Gordion of the Royal Road," *Proceedings of the American Philosophical Society* 107: 348–64.

## THE METAMORPHOSIS

Africa, T. W. (1982b) "Worms and the Death of Kings: A Cautionary Note on Disease and History," *Classical Antiquity* 1: 1–17.
Austin, G. A. (1985) *Alcohol in Western Society from Antiquity to 1800*. Santa Barbara, Denver, and Oxford.
Aymard, A. (1949) "Sur quelques vers d'Euripide qui poussèrent Alexandre au meurtre," *Annuaire de l'Institut de Philologie et d'Histoire Orientales* 9: 43–74.
Badian, E. (1958b) "The Eunuch Bagoas. A Study in Method," *CQ* 8: 144–57.
(1960b) "The Death of Parmenio," *TAPA* 91: 324–38.
(1964) "Alexander the Great and the Loneliness of Power," *Studies in Greek and Roman History*. ed. E. Badian. Oxford. 192–205.
Balcer, J. M. (1978) "Alexander's Burning of Persepolis," *Iranica Antiqua* 13: 119–33.
Bearzot, C. (1987) "La tradizione su Parmenione negli storici di Alessandro," *Aevum* 61: 89–104.
Belfiore, E. (1986) "Wine and *Catharsis* of the Emotions in Plato's *Laws*," *CQ* 36: 421–37.
Bernard, P. (1984) "Le philosophe Anaxarque et le roi Nicocréon de Salamine," *Journal des Savants* 3–49.
Borza, E. N. (1972) "Fire from Heaven: Alexander at Persepolis," *CP* 67: 233–45.
(1981b) "Anaxarchus and Callisthenes: Academic Intrigue at Alexander's Court," *Ancient Macedonian Studies in Honor of Charles F. Edson*. ed. H. J. Dell. Thessaloniki. 73–86.
(1983) "The Symposium at Alexander's Court," *AM* 3: 45–55.
Brown, T. S. (1949b) "Callisthenes and Alexander," *AJP* 70: 225–48.
(1978) "Aristodicus of Cyme and the Branchidae," *AJP* 99: 64–78.
(1982) "Herodotus' Portrait of Cambyses," *Historia* 31: 387–403.
Buijs, J. A. J. M. (1983) "Abermals Persepolis," *Gymnasium* 90: 513–29.
Cahill, N. (1985) "The Treasury at Persepolis: Gift-Giving at the City of the Persians," *AJA* 89: 373–89.
Carney, E. D. (1980) "Alexander the Lyncestian: the Disloyal Opposition," *GRBS* 21: 23–33.
(1981b) "The Conspiracy of Hermolaus," *CJ* 76: 223–31.
(1981c) "The Death of Clitus," *GRBS* 22: 149–60.
Cauer, F. (1894) "Philotas, Kleitos, Kallisthenes," *Jahrbücher für classische Philologie* Suppl. 20: 8–38.
Clark, L. P. (1923) "The Narcissism of Alexander the Great," *Psychoanalytic Review* 9: 56–9.
Dentzer, J. M. (1982) *Le motif du banquet couché dans le Proche-Orient et le monde grec du VIIe au IVe siècles av. J.-C.* Rome.
Edmunds, L. (1971) "The Religiosity of Alexander," *GRBS* 12: 363–91.

Emboden, W. (1977) "Dionysus as a Shaman and Wine as a Magical Drug," *Journal of Psychedelic Drugs* 9: 187–92.

Forbes, R. J. (1955) *Studies in Ancient Technology III*. Leiden.

Fredricksmeyer, E. A. (1986) "Alexander the Great and the Macedonian Kausia," *TAPA* 116: 215–27.

Garland, R. (1982) "Greek Drinking Parties," *History Today* 32: 18–21.

Golan, D. (1988) "The Fate of a Court Historian, Callisthenes," *Athenaeum* 66: 99–120.

Graf, F. (1980) "Milch, Honig und Wein," *Perennitas*. Rome. 209–21.

Griffiths, A. (1989) "Was Kleomenes Mad?," *Classical Sparta. Techniques behind her Success*. ed. A. Powell. 51–78.

Hagenow, G. (1982) *Aus dem Weingarten der Antike*. Mainz.

Hallock, R. T. (1985) "The Evidence of the Persepolis Tablets," *The Cambridge History of Iran II*. ed. I. Gershevitch. Cambridge. 588–609.

Hammond, N. G. L. (1990) "Royal Pages, Personal Pages, and Boys Trained in the Macedonian manner During the Period of the Temenid Monarchy," *Historia* 39: 261–90.

Harris, R. I. (1968) "The Dilemma of Alexander the Great," *PACA* 11: 46–54.

Heckel, W. (1977b) "The Conspiracy *against* Philotas," *Phoenix* 31: 9–21.

(1978b) "The Somatophylakes of Alexander the Great: Some Thoughts," *Historia* 27: 224–8.

(1982a) "The Early Career of Lysimachos," *Klio* 64: 373–81.

(1982b) "Who was Hegelochos?," *RhM* 125: 78–87.

(1983b) "Alexandros Lynkestes and Orontas," *Eranos* 81: 139–42.

(1986b) "Factions and Macedonian Politics in the Reign of Alexander the Great," *AM* 4: 293–305.

(1986c) "*Somatophylakia*: A Macedonian *Cursus Honorum*," *Phoenix* 40: 279–94.

Kraft, K. (1971) *Der "rationale" Alexander*. Kallmünz.

Leibowitz, J. O. (1967) "Studies in the History of Alcoholism – II. Acute Alcoholism in Ancient Greek and Roman Medicine," *British Journal of Addiction* 62: 83–6.

Lissarrague, F. (1990) *The Aesthetics of the Greek Banquet. Images of Wine and Ritual*. tr. A. Szegedy-Maszak. Princeton.

Lissarrague, F. and Schmitt-Pantel, P. (1988) "Spartizione e communità nei banchetti greci," *Sacrificio e società nel mondo antico*. eds Cristiano Grottaneli and Nicola F. Parise. Bari. 211–29.

Lukinovich, A. (1990) "The Play of Reflections between Literary Form and the Sympotic Theme in the *Deipnosophistae* of Athenaeus," *Sympotica*. tr. M. Shipway. ed. O. Murray. Oxford. 263–71.

McKinlay, A. P. (1948) "Ancient Experience with Intoxicating Drinks: Non-Classical Peoples," *QJSA* 9: 388–414.

(1949) "Ancient Experience with Intoxicating Drinks: Non-Attic Greek States," *QJSA* 10: 289–315.

(1950) "Bacchus as Health-Giver," *QJSA* 11: 230–46.

(1951) "Attic Temperance," *QJSA* 12: 61–102.

(1953) "New Light on the Question of Homeric Temperance," *QJSA* 14: 78–93.

Macurdy, G. H. (1930) "The Refusal of Callisthenes to Drink the Health of Alexander," *JHS* 50: 294–7.

(1932b) "The Grammar of Drinking Healths," *AJP* 53: 168–71.

Meyer, H. (1986) "Der Berg Athos als Alexander. Zu den realen Grundlagen der Vision der Deinokrates," *Revue Archéologique* 10: 22–30.

Miller, S[teph.] G. (1979) "Drinking Uncut-Wine . . . to Death: Unpublished Greek Epigram for a Youth from Ephesus," *AncW* 2: 29–30.

Munson, R. V. (1991) "The Madness of Cambyses (Herodotus 3.16–68)," *Arethusa* 24: 43–65.

Murray, O. (1983) "The Greek Symposion in History," *Tria Corda*. ed. E. Gabba. Como. 257–72.

(1984) "Symposion and Männerbund," *Concilium Eirene XVI/I*. eds P. Oliva and A. Frolíková. Prague. 47–52.

ed. (1990a) *Sympotica*. Oxford.

(1990b) "Sympotic History," *Sympotica*. ed. O. Murray. Oxford. 3–13.

Neuffer, E. (1929) *Das Kostüm Alexanders d. Gr*. Giessen.

O'Brien, J. M. (1980a) "The Enigma of Alexander: The Alcohol Factor," *Annals of Scholarship* 1: 31–46.

(1980b) "Alexander and Dionysus: The Invisible Enemy," *Annals of Scholarship* 1: 83–105.

(1980c) "The Grand Elixir 2,300 Years Removed: Attributes of Wine in Alexander the Great's (d.323 BC) Reading," *Drinking and Drug Practices Surveyor* 16: 3–5.

(1981) "Alexander the Great," *British Journal on Alcohol and Alcoholism* 16: 39–40.

Parke, H. W. (1985b) "The Massacre of the Branchidae," *JHS* 105: 59–68.

Pellizer, E. (1990) "Outlines of a Morphology of Sympotic Entertainment," *Sympotica*. tr. C. McLaughlin. ed. O. Murray. Oxford. 177–84.

Piganiol, A. (1940) "Les Dionysies d'Alexandre," *REA* 42: 285–92.

Pigeaud, J. (1981) *La maladie de l'âme*. Paris. 477–503.

Pope, A. V. (1957) "Persepolis as a Ritual City," *Archaeology* 10: 123–30.

Prandi, L. (1985) *Callistene: uno storico tra Aristotele e i re macedoni*. Milan.

Prieur, J. (1987) *Alexandre le grand et les mystères de l'Orient*. Paris.

Ritter, H. W. (1965) *Diadem und Königsherrschaft*. Munich.

(1987) "Die Bedeutung des Diadems," *Historia* 36: 290–301.

Rolleston, J. D. (1927) "Alcoholism in Classical Antiquity," *The British Journal of Inebriety* 24: 101–20.

Rösler, W. (1990) "*Mnemosyne* in the *Symposion*," *Sympotica*. ed. O. Murray. Oxford. 230–7.

Rubinsohn, W. Z. (1977) "The 'Philotas Affair' – A Reconsideration," *AM* 2: 409–20.

Schepens, G. (1985) "Alexander de Grote, onoverwinnelijk? Een historisch-methodologische kanttekening bij het moderne onderzoek," *Tijdschrift voor Geschiedenis* 98: 493–512.

(1989) "Zum Problem der 'Unbesiegbarkeit' Alexanders des Grossen," *Anc. Soc.* 20: 15–53.

Schmidt, E. F. (1953, 1957, 1970) *Persepolis I–III*. Chicago.

Scholl, R. (1987) "Alexander der Grosse und die Sklaverei am Hofe," *Klio* 69: 108–21.

Seltman, C. (1957) *Wine in the Ancient World*. London.

Servais, J. (1959) "Alexandre-Dionysos et Diogène-Sarapis," *Antiquité Classique* 28: 98–106.

Slater, W. J. (1976) "Symposium at Sea," *HSCP* 80: 161–70.

ed. (1991) *Dining in a Classical Context*. Ann Arbor.

Stagakis, G. S. (1970) "Observations on the *Hetairoi* of Alexander the Great," *AM* 1: 86–102.

Strasburger, H. (1982b) "Psychoanalyse und Alte Geschichte," *Studien zur Alten Geschichte II*. eds W. Schmitthenner and R. Zoepffel. Hildesheim and New York. 1098–1110.

Taylor, M. W. (1981) *The Tyrant Slayers*. New York.

Tecuşan, M. (1990) "*Logos Sympotikos*: Patterns of the Irrational in Philosophical

Drinking: Plato Outside the *Symposium*," *Sympotica*. ed. O. Murray. Oxford. 238–60.

Toohey, P. (1990) "Some Ancient Histories of Literary Melancholia," *Illinois Classical Studies* 15: 143–61.

Tomlinson, R. A. (1970) "Ancient Macedonian Symposia," *AM* 1: 308–15.

Vetta, M. ed. (1983) *Poesia e simposia nella Grecia antica. Guida storica e critica*. Rome.

Vickers, M. (n.d.) *Greek Symposia*. London.

Villard, P. (1984) "Pathologie et thérapeutique de l'ivresse dans l'Antiquité classique," *Cahiers de nutrition et de diététique* 19: 225–7.

(1988) "Ivresses dans l'Antiquité classique," *Histoire, économie et société* 7: 443–59.

Vivante, P. (1982) "The Syntax of Homer's Epithets of Wine," *Glotta* 60: 13–23.

Wheeler, M. (1968) *Flames over Persepolis*. New York.

Younger, W. (1966) *Gods, Men, and Wine*. Cleveland.

## INDIA

Badian, E. (1975) "Nearchus the Cretan," *Yale Classical Studies* 24: 147–70.

Bosworth, A. B. (1983c) "The Indian Satrapies under Alexander the Great," *Antichthon* 17: 37–46.

Dihle, A. (1964) "The Conception of India in Hellenistic and Roman Literature," *PCPS* 10: 15–23.

Ghosh, P. K. (1988) "The Gangaridai of the Classical Writers," *Quarterly Review of Historical Studies* 27: 44–52.

Hansen, G. C. (1965) "Alexander und die Brahmanen," *Klio* 43/45: 351–80.

Hartman, S. S. (1965) "Dionysus and Heracles in India according to Megasthenes: A Counter-argument," *Temenos* 1: 55–64.

Karttunen, K. (1989) *India in Early Greek Literature*. Helsinki.

Kienast, D. (1965) "Alexander und der Ganges," *Historia* 124: 180–8.

Marshall, J. H. (1951) *Taxila I–III*. Cambridge.

Narain, A. K. (1965) "Alexander and India," *G&R* 12: 155–65.

Oikonomides, Al. N. (1988b) "The Real End of Alexander's Conquest of India," *AncW* 18: 31–4.

Pfister, F. (1941) "Das Nachleben der Überlieferung von Alexander und den Brahmanen," *Hermes* 76: 143–69.

Radet, G. (1938) "Explorations Indo-Iraniennes," *REA* 40: 421–32.

Schachermeyr, F. (1966) "Alexander und die Ganges-Länder," *Alexander the Great: The Main Problems*. ed. G. T. Griffith. Cambridge. 137–50.

Schwarz, V.-F. F. (1972) "Neue Perspektiven in den griechisch-indischen Beziehungen," *Orientalistische Literaturzeitung* 17: 5–26.

Woodcock, G. (1966) *The Greeks in India*. London.

## DEIFICATION

Atkinson, K. M. T. (1973) "Demosthenes, Alexander and Asebeia," *Athenaeum* 51: 310–35.

Badian, E. (1981) "The Deification of Alexander the Great," *Ancient Macedonian Studies in Honor of Charles F. Edson*. ed. H. J. Dell. Thessaloniki. 27–71.

Balsdon, J. P. V. D. (1950) "The 'Divinity' of Alexander," *Historia* 1: 363–88.

Bickerman, E. J. (1963a) "Sur un passage d'Hypéride," *Athenaeum* 41: 70–83.

(1963b) "A propos d'un passage de Chares de Mytilène," *Parola del Passato* 18: 241–55.

Dascalakis, A. (1967) "La déification d'Alexandre le Grand en Egypte et la réaction en Grèce," *Studii Classici Bucharest IX*. 93–105.

Flower, M. A. (1988) "Agesilaus of Sparta and the Origins of the Ruler Cult," *CQ* 38: 123–34.

Fredricksmeyer, E. A. (1979b) "Three Notes on Alexander's Deification," *AJAH* 4: 1–9.

Frye, R. N. (1972) "Gestures of Deference to Royalty in Ancient Iran," *Iranica Antiqua* 9: 102–7.

Habicht, C. (1970) *Gottmenschentum und griechische Städte*. Munich.

Hamilton, J. R. (1953) "Alexander and his 'So-called' Father," *CQ* 3: 151–7.

Heckel, W. (1978c) "Leonnatos, Polyperchon and the Introduction of *Proskynesis*," *AJP* 99: 459–61.

Marasco, G. (1983) "Alessandro, i diadochi e il culto dell'eroe eponimo," *Prometheus* 9: 57–63.

Méautis, G. (1942b) "Recherches sur l'époque d'Alexandre II: A propos de la proskynèse," *REA* 44: 305–8.

Nock, A. D. (1986) "Notes on Ruler-Cult I–IV," *Essays on Religion and the Ancient World*. ed. Z. Stewart. Oxford. 134–52.

Oikonomides, Al. N. (1985) "The Deification of Alexander in Bactria and India," *AncW* 12: 69–71.

Richards, G. C. (1934) "Proskynesis," *CR* 48: 168–70.

Rosen, K. (1978) "Der 'göttliche' Alexander, Athen und Samos," *Historia* 27: 20–39.

Sanctis, G. De (1940) "Gli ultimi di Alessandro ai Greci," *RFIC* 68: 1–21.

Schnabel, P. (1926) "Zur Frage der Selbstvergötterung Alexanders," *Klio* 20: 398–414.

Scott, K. (1929) "Plutarch and the Ruler Cult," *TAPA* 60: 117–35.

Straten, F. T. van. (1974) "Did the Greeks Kneel before their Gods?," *Bulletin Antieke Beschaving* 49: 159–89.

Taeger, F. (1937) "Isokrates und die Anfänge des hellenistischen Herrscherkults," *Hermes* 72: 355–60.

(1951) "Alexander der Grosse und die Anfänge des hellenistischen Herrenkultes," *Historische Zeitschrift* 172: 225–44.

(1957, 1960) *Charisma: Studien zur Geschichte des Antiken Herrscherkultes I–II*. Stuttgart.

Taylor, L. R. (1927) "The 'Proskynesis' and the Hellenistic Ruler Cult," *JHS* 47: 53–62.

Tondriau, J. (1949) "Alexandre le Grand assimilé à différentes divinités," *Revue de Philologie de Littérature et d'Histoire Anciennes* 23: 41–52.

(1952) "Dionysos, dieu royal: du Bacchus tauromorphe primitif aux souverains hellénistiques Neoi Dionysoi," *Annuaire de l'Institut de Philologie et d'Histoire Orientales et Slaves* 12: 441–66.

Treves, P. (1939) "Hyperides and the Cult of Hephaestion," *CR* 53: 56–7.

Walbank, F. W. (1987) "Könige als Götter. Überlegungen zum Herrscherkult von Alexander bis Augustus," *Chiron* 17: 365–82.

Weinstock, S. (1957) "Victor and Invictus," *HThR* 50: 211–47.

## ALEXANDER'S DEATH

Alonso-Núñez, J. M. (1987) "Alexander der Grosse und die Iberische Halbinsel (Zu Arrian, Anabasis II 16, 4–6 und VII 15, 4)," *Zu Alexander d. Gr. I*. eds W. Will and J. Heinrichs. Amsterdam. 605–25.

Badian, E. (1968) "A King's Notebooks," *HSCP* 72: 183–204.

(1987b) "The Ring and the Book," *Zu Alexander d. Gr. I.* eds W. Will and J. Heinrichs. Amsterdam. 605–25.

Bendinelli, G. (1965) "Cassandro di Macedonia nella Vita Plutarchea di Alessandro Magno," *RFIC* 93: 150–64.

Borza, E. N. (1987c) "Malaria in Alexander's Army," *AHB* 1: 36–8.

Bosworth, A. B. (1971b) "The Death of Alexander the Great: Rumour and Propaganda," *CQ* 21: 112–36.

Brandes, M. A. (1979) "Alexander der Grosse in Babylon," *Antike Kunst* 22: 87–98.

Coulomb, J. (1984) "La mort d'Alexandre le Grand," *Histoire des Sciences Médicales* 18: 137–45.

Derchain, Ph.-J. and Hubaux, J. (1950) "Le fantôme de Babylone," *Antiquité Classique* 19: 367–82.

Engels, D. W. (1978b) "A Note on Alexander's Death," *CP* 73: 224–8.

Greenwalt, W. S. (1988c) "Argaeus, Ptolemy II and Alexander's Corpse," *AHB* 2: 39–41.

Habicht, C. (1988) "Argeus, Ptolemy II and Alexander's Corpse," *AHB* 2: 88–9.

Hackl, U. (1988) "Alexander der Grosse und der Beginn des Hellenistischen Zeitalters," *Zu Alexander d. Gr. II.* eds W. Will and J. Heinrichs. Amsterdam. 693–716.

Hammond, N. G. L. (1984) "Alexander's Veterans after his Death," *GRBS* 25: 51–61.

(1987) "An Unfulfilled Promise by Alexander the Great," *Zu Alexander d. Gr. I.* eds W. Will and J. Heinrichs. Amsterdam. 627–34.

(1988b) "The Royal Journal of Alexander," *Historia* 37: 129–50.

(1989d) "Aspects of Alexander's Journal and Ring in his Last Days," *AJP* 110: 155–60.

Hampl, F. (1953) "Alexanders des Grossen *Hypomnemata* und letzte Pläne," *Studies Presented to D. M. Robinson II.* St Louis. 816–29.

Heckel, W. (1985b) "The Macedonian Veterans in Kilikia," *LCM* 10: 109–10.

Högemann, P. (1985) *Alexander der Grosse und Arabien.* Munich.

Holt, F. L. (1986b) "The Missing Mummy of Alexander the Great," *Archaeology* 39: 80.

Landucci Gattinoni, F. (1984) "La morte di Alessandro e la tradizione su Antipatro," *Alessandro Magno tra storia e mito.* ed. M. Sordi. 91–111.

Lewis, D. M. (1969) "Two Days: (1) Epicurus' Birthday (2) Alexander's Death-day," *CR* 19: 271–2.

Samuel, A. E. (1965) "Alexander's 'Royal Journals,' " *Historia* 14: 1–12.

(1986) "The Earliest Elements in the Alexander Romance," *Historia* 35: 427–37.

Schachermeyr, F. (1954) "Die letzten Pläne Alexanders des Grossen," *Jahreshefte des Österreichischen Archäologischen Instituts in Wien* 41: 118–40.

(1970) *Alexander in Babylon und die Reichsordnung nach seinem Tode.* Vienna.

Skoda, F. (1988) *Médecine ancienne et métaphore. Le vocabulaire de l'anatomie et de la pathologie en grec ancien.* Paris.

Smelik, K. A. D. (1978–9) "The 'Omina Mortis' in the Histories of Alexander the Great: Alexander's Attitude Towards the Babylonian Priesthood," *Talanta* 10–11: 92–111.

Spek, R. J. van der (1985) "The Babylonian Temple during the Macedonian and Parthian Domination," *Bibliotheca Orientalis* 42: 541–62.

Welles, C. B. (1965) "Alexander's Historical Achievement," *G&R* 12: 216–28.

Wirth, G. (1988) "Nearch, Alexander und die Diadochen. Spekulationen über einen Zusammenhang," *Tyche* 3: 241–59.

(1989) "Alexander, Kassander und andere Zeitgenossen. Erwägungen zum Problem ihrer Selbstdarstellung," *Tyche* 4: 193–220.

Wüst, F. R. (1959) "Zu den Hypomnemata Alexanders des Grossen: Das Grabmal des Hephaistion," *Jahreshefte des Österreichischen Archäologischen Instituts in Wien* 44: 147–57.


## MISCELLANEOUS

Andreae, B. (1977) *Das Alexandermosaik aus Pompeji*. Recklinghausen.

Baldus, H. R. (1987) "Die Siegel Alexanders des Grossen. Versuch einer Rekonstruktion auf literarischer und numismatischer Grundlage," *Chiron* 17: 395–449.

Barr-Sharrar, B. (1982) "Macedonian Metal Vases in Perspective: Some Observations on Context and Tradition," *Macedonia and Greece in Late Classical and Early Hellenistic Times*. eds B. Barr-Sharrar and E. N. Borza. Washington. 123–39.

Bauslaugh, R. A. (1984) "The Numismatic Legacy of Alexander the Great," *Archaeology* 37: 34–41.

Bellinger, A. R. (1979) *Essays on the Coinage of Alexander the Great*. New York.

Bieber, M. (1964) *Alexander the Great in Greek and Roman Art*. Chicago.

(1965) "The Portraits of Alexander," *G&R* 12: 183–8.

Biers, W. R. (1980) *The Archaeology of Greece*. Ithaca and London.

Bivar, A. D. H. (1985) "Achaemenid Coins, Weights and Measures," *The Cambridge History of Iran II*. ed. I. Gershevitch. Cambridge. 610–39.

Blanckenhagen, P. H. von. (1982) "Painting in the Time of Alexander and Later," *Macedonia and Greece in Late Classical and Early Hellenistic Times*. eds B. Barr-Sharrar and E. N. Borza. Washington. 251–60.

Boardman, J. (1981) *Greek Art*. London.

Bouzek, J. and Ondrejova, I. (1987) "Some Notes on the Relations of the Thracian, Macedonian, Iranian and Scythian Arts in the Fourth Century BC," *Eirene* 24: 67–93.

Bright, D. F. and Bowen, B. C. (1983) "Emblems, Elephants, and Alexander," *Il. Stud. Philol.* 80: 14–24.

Brown, T. S. (1988) "Herodotus and Justin 9.2," *AHB* 2: 1–3.

Calder III, W. M. (1982) "Alexander's House (Pausanias 8.32.1)," *GRBS* 23: 281–7.

Cresci, G. M. (1983–4) "Alessandro in età neroniana: victor o praedo?," *Atti dell'Istituto Veneto di Scienze. Lettere e Arti* 142: 75–93.

Develin, R. D. (1985) "Anaximenes (*FGrHist* 72) F 4," *Historia* 34: 493–6.

Draganov, D. (1984) "Hat Alexander der Grosse Silbermünzen in Kabyle prägen lassen?," *Klio* 66: 74–84.

Dull, S. (1986) "Makedonische Funde im Istanbuler Museum," *AM* 4: 183–206.

Dürr, N. C. (1974) "Neues aus Babylonien," *Schweizer Münzblätter* 24: 33–6.

Fittschen, K. ed. (1988) *Griechische Porträts*. Darmstadt.

Fraser, P. M. (1979–80) "The Son of Aristonax at Kandahar," *Afghan Studies* 2: 9–21.

Green, P. (1989c) "Caesar and Alexander: aemulatio, imitatio, comparatio," *Classical Bearings: Interpreting Ancient History and Culture*. New York. 193–209.

Hadley, R. A. (1974) "Seleucus, Dionysus, or Alexander?," *Numismatic Chronicle and Journal of the Royal Numismatic Society* 7: 9–13.

Hammond, N. G. L. (1986) "The Kingdom of Asia and the Persian Throne," *Antichthon* 20: 73–85.

(1990b) "Inscriptions concerning Philippi and Calindoea in the Reign of Alexander the Great," *ZPE* 82: 167–75.

Hartle, R. W. (1982) "The Search for Alexander's Portrait," *Philip II, Alexander the Great and the Macedonian Heritage*. eds W. L. Adams and E. N. Borza. Washington. 153–76.

(1983) "The Bust of Alexander in Thiene, Florence, and Versailles: Ancient and Modern Baroque," *AM* 3: 107–16.

Hoistadt, R. (1948) *Cynic Hero and Cynic King*. Uppsala. 204–20.

Houser, C. (1982) "Alexander's Influence on Greek Sculpture as Seen in a Portrait in Athens," *Macedonia and Greece in Late Classical and Early Hellenistic Times*. eds B. Barr-Sharrar and E. N. Borza. Washington. 228–38.

Huxley, G. (1985) "Sogdian Tanais in Aristobulus," *Bulletin of the American Society of Papyrologists* 22: 117–21.

Janson, H. W. ed. (1965) *The Art of Greece 1400–31 BC Sources and Documents*. Englewood Cliffs.

Kaiser, W. B. (1962) "Ein Meister der Glyptik aus dem Umkreis Alexanders des Grossen," *Jahrbuch des Deutschen Archäologischen Instituts* 77: 227–39.

Kiilerich, B. (1988) "Physiognomics and the Iconography of Alexander," *SymbOsl* 63: 51–66.

Kingsley, B. M. (1981) "The Cap that Survived Alexander," *AJA* 85: 39–46.

(1984) "The Kausia Diadematophoros," *AJA* 88: 66–8.

(1991) "Alexander's *Kausia* and Macedonian Tradition," *Classical Antiquity* 10: 59–76.

Kraay, C. M. (1976) *Archaic and Classical Greek Coins*. London.

Lauter, H. (1988) "Alexanders wahres Gesicht," *Zu Alexander d. Gr. II*. eds W. Will and J. Heinrichs. Amsterdam. 717–43.

Lehmann, P. W. (1980) "A New Portrait of Alexander the Great," *Megas Alexandros*. Thessaloniki. 183–87.

Le Rider, G. (1977) *Le monnayage d'argent et d'or de Philippe II*. Paris.

Litvinskii, B. and Pitchikjan, I. (1981) "The Temple of the Oxus," *Journal of the Hong Kong Branch [of the] Royal Asiatic Society* 20: 133–67.

Martin, T. R. (1985) *Sovereignty and Coinage in Classical Greece*. Princeton.

Michel, D. (1968) *Alexander als Vorbild für Pompeius, Caesar und Marcus Aurelius*. Brussels.

Miller, S. G. (1986) "Alexander's Funeral Cart," *AM* 4: 401–12.

Moon, W., ed. (1983) *Ancient Greek Art and Iconography*. Madison and London.

Oikonomides, Al. N. (1981) "Decadrachm Aids in Identification of Alexander," *Coin World International* 11/25: 31–2.

Pacella, D. (1984) "Sui rapporti di Alessandro con Roma e Cartagine nella leggenda," *Studi classici e Orientali* 34: 103–25.

Pédech, P. (1980) "L'expédition d'Alexandre et la science grecque," *Megas Alexandros*. Thessaloniki. 135–56.

Perlman, S. (1965) "The Coins of Philip II and Alexander the Great and their Pan-Hellenic Propaganda," *Numismatic Chronicle and Journal of the Royal Numismatic Society* 5: 57–67.

Pfister, F. (1964) "Alexander der Grosse. Die Geschichte seines Ruhms im Lichte seiner Beinamen," *Historia* 13: 37–79.

Pieper, J. (1984) "Der Berg Athos in Riesengestalt," *Aus dem Osten des Alexanderreiches*. eds J. Ozols and V. Thewalt. Cologne. 57–65.

Pollitt, J. J. (1965) *The Art of Greece 1400–31 BC Sources and Documents*. Englewood Cliffs.

(1986) *Art in the Hellenistic Age*. Cambridge.

Price, M. J. (1974) *Coins of the Macedonians*. London.

(1982a) "Alexander's Reform of the Macedonian Regal Coinage," *Numismatic Chronicle and Journal of the Royal Numismatic Society* 142: 180–90.

(1982b) "The 'Porus' Coinage of Alexander the Great. A Symbol of Concord and Community," *Studia Paulo Naster Oblata I*. ed. S. Scheers. 75–85.

Robertson, M. (1982) "Early Greek Mosaic," *Macedonia and Greece in Late Classical and Early Hellenistic Times*. eds B. Barr-Sharrar and E. N. Borza. Washington. 241–9.

Ross Holloway, R. (1980–1) "Alexander the Great's Choice of Coin Types," *A. 1st. Ital. Numismatica* 27–8: 57–60.

Rouveret, A. (1989) *Histoire et imaginaire de la peinture ancienne*. Paris and Rome.

Rumpf, A. (1962) "Zum Alexander Mosaik," *Mitteilungen des Deutschen Archäologischen Instituts. Athenische Abteilung* 77: 229–41.

Ruschenbusch, E. (1979) "Die soziale Herkunft der Epheben um 330," *ZPE* 35: 173–6.

Schefold, K. (1968) *Der Alexander-Sarkophag*. Berlin.

—— (1979) *Die Antwort der griechischen Kunst auf die Siege Alexanders des Grossen*. Munich.

Schwarzenberg, E. von. (1967) "Der lysippische Alexander," *Bonner Jarhbücher* 167: 58–118.

—— (1976) "The Portraiture of Alexander," *Alexandre le Grand. Image et réalité. Entretiens Hardt XXII*. ed. E. Badian. Geneva. 223–78.

Seltman, C. (1955) *Greek Coins*. London.

Slowikowski, S. S. (1989) "Alexander the Great and Sport History. A Commentary on Scholarship," *Journal of Sport History* 16: 70–8.

Smith, R. R. R. (1988) *Hellenistic Royal Portraits*. Oxford.

Stewart, A. (1990) *Greek Sculpture*. New Haven.

Sutton, D. F. (1980) *The Greek Satyr Play*. Meisenheim am Glan.

Thompson, M. (1982) "The Coinage of Philip II and Alexander III," *Macedonia and Greece in Late Classical and Early Hellenistic Times*. eds B. Barr-Sharrar and E. N. Borza. Washington. 112–21.

Vickers, M. (1986) "Persepolis, Athènes, et Sybaris: questions de monnayage et de chronologie," *REG* 99: 239–70.

Volk, J. G. (1984) "A Lysippan Zeus," *Classical Antiquity* 3: 272–83.

Yavetz, Z. (1983) *Julius Caesar and his Public Image*. Ithaca.

Zervos, O. H. (1982) "The Earliest Coins of Alexander the Great," *Numismatic Chronicle and Journal of the Royal Numismatic Society* 22: 166–79.

# Index

The reader is also referred to "Frequently cited sources in the text."

Abdalonymus 82
Abisares 154, 155, 157, 161
Abreas 174
Abulites 184–5
Abydos 60
Academy (Plato's) 19, 26
Acesines, River (Chenab) 155, 162, 171, 173, 175
Achaeans (Achaians) 61, 169
Achaemenian(s), Achaemenid(s) 65, 75, 79, 86, 105, 111–12, 113, 150, 197, 198, 203, 204, 210; see also Persian(s), Persian Empire
Achilles (Achilleus), son of Peleus, Achillean ix, 9, 10, 12, 13, 14, 20–3, 42, 46, 57, 61, 64, 66, 77, 86, 90, 112, 114, 120, 125, 131, 132, 134, 143, 157, 168, 173, 183, 187, 197, 204, 206, 211, 212, 213, 215, 218, 221, 229
Achilles of Athens 92
Acrisius 114
Acropolis (Athens) 26, 27, 64, 97, 107
acting, actors 27, 31–2, 36, 75, 92, 104, 119, 198
Acuphis 151–2
Ada 57, 68
Adriatic 50
Aegae (Vergina) 5–6, 14, 35, 40, 43, 45, 55, 202, 218, 231–2
Aegean Sea 13, 70, 79, 219
Aelian 210–11
Aeropus 43, 44, 69; see also Alexander the Lyncestian; Lyncestis
Aeschylus 27, 177, 233–8
Afghanistan 117
Africa 217

Africa, T.W. 57
Agamemnon 7, 22, 60
Agathon 187
Agave 4
*Agen* (Python's) 185
*agones* 75
agora (Athens) 26
Ajax 20–1, 137
Ajax, Porus' elephant 161
*Alcestis* (Euripides') 236
alcohol: see wine
alcoholism: see Alexander III, drinking
Alexander I of Macedon 54, 55–6
Alexander III of Macedon (the Great):
  accession 42, 43–6; Achilles, relationship with: see Achilles; administration 45–6, 65, 66–7, 73, 97–8, 181 *passim*; alcoholism: see drinking; ambassador to Athens 26–8; ambitions 8, 9, 10–11, 12, 60, 71, 156–7, 165–7, 179, 181, 191, 217–20 *passim*; anger 66, 72, 85, 101–2, 130–1, 136–40, 143, 146, 167–8, 170, 177, 184–5, 186, 205–6, 207, 229; *aniketos* (invincible) 47, 73, 176, 185, 217; anxiety: see insecurities; apotheosis: see deification; *arete* (excellence) 45–6, 229 *passim*; appearance 26, 60, 63, 94, 96, 98, 113, 151, 159, 193; autocratic 127, 138; birth 17, 18, 143; boyhood 8–23, 66; bravery 63–4, 74, 77, 84, 85, 139, 173–7, 229 *passim*; "Brotherhood of Man" 197–201, 206–8; Chaeronea, battle of: see Chaeronea; charisma 32, 77, 115–17, 148, 181, 183 *passim*;

children of 58–9, 141, 205; cities, foundation of 11, 24, 87, 130, 161–2, 181, 204, 218, 219; clemency 44, 54, 59, 67, 69, 84, 126, 186; compassion 44–5, 81, 105–6, 111, 126; conspiracies against 33, 44, 69, 74, 117–28, 145–8, 222, 224; courage: *see* bravery; curiosity 20, 50, 123, 127, 147, 150; Cyrus the Great, relationship with: *see* Cyrus the Great; death 33, 58, 157, 202, 203, 212, 214, 215, 223–8, 229–30, 239; deification 11, 18, 66, 86, 88, 137, 142–3, 144, 152, 183, 194–5, 201–4, 210, 217; Dionysus, relationship with: *see* Dionysus; diplomacy 26–8, 46, 52–4, 64, 68, 70, 73, 75, 78, 79–82, 84, 92–3, 97–9, 127, 142–3, 162–3, 178, 197–201, 205–8 *passim*; divine sonship 18, 72–3, 87–91, 92, 96, 135, 139, 143, 156, 177, 201–2, 205; divinity: *see* deification; dreams 82–3, 87, 133–4, 137; drinking 8, 14, 33, 50, 55, 58, 69–70, 93, 94–5, 102–4, 106–10, 112, 130, 133–9, 146–7, 188–9, 190, 191, 194, 196, 197–8, 204, 207–8, 210–16, 223–8, 230, 239, 259; education 17–18, 19–23; fear: *see* insecurities; finances 45, 54, 61–2, 67, 81, 92, 106, 110–11, 199–200, 205, 214; flattery 21, 95, 225; fusion, policy of 98, 114, 197–201, 206–8; genealogy 13–14, 22–3, 48, 61, 75, 87–91, 114, 137, 149; genius ix, x, 46, 49–50, 52, 56, 71–2, 94, 120–8, 133, 150, 204–8, 218, 230; geographical knowledge 149, 155; as Great King 97, 98, 113, 142–3, 150, 193, 203; Greeks, relations with: *see* Greeks; Heracles, relationship with: *see* Heracles; heroic models 21–3; hostages, use of 92, 124, 141, 151, 177, 200; humor 62, 84; *hybris* 48, 73, 229; illnesses 73–5, 131, 223–8, 229–30; image 10, 21, 42, 54, 81, 83, 85, 87, 88, 94, 101, 113, 127, 128, 136–7, 139, 143–4, 149, 156, 179, 180, 184, 185, 187, 190, 193, 198, 208, 229–30; inner circle of friends 32–3, 69, 74, 78, 91, 113–14, 118–20, 123, 125, 126, 131, 137, 167, 189–90, 197–8, 223, 225–6; insecurities 8, 9, 10, 11, 19, 23, 33, 39–41, 46, 101–2, 117, 127, 128, 132, 136, 138, 139, 157, 179, 180, 184, 188, 190, 191, 204, 222, 229; intrepid 87–91, 106, 173–4, 179–84, 185 *passim*; largesse 59, 66, 92, 97, 104, 106, 110, 112, 117, 156, 192, 197–201, 205–6, 208, 213; Last Plans (*hypomnemata*) 217–20; Macedonians, relations with 73, 98, 101, 102, 109, 113, 115, 127–8, 136, 145–8, 204–10; marriages 140–1, 144, 197–8, 205; massacres 84–5, 129–30, 151, 154, 163, 173, 174, 178, 215; medical involvements 20, 59, 64, 79, 164, 177–8, 211–12, 224; megalomania ix, 139, 191, 193, 203, 204, 218–19; metamorphosis ix, 101–54, 191, 194, 195, 205, 209, 214; military prowess 20, 24, 25, 46, 49–51, 52–4, 56, 62–3, 67–8, 76–8, 82–5, 93–7, 117, 131, 132–3, 150, 153, 155, 157–63, 173–6, 180–4, 193, 217–19, 229; Olympias, relations with: *see* Olympias; orientalization 102, 113, 115, 122, 125, 127, 138, 139, 142–3, 147, 192–3, 197–8, 199–201, 208–9; *oxyteros* 186; paranoia ix, 224; Perseus, relationship with: *see* Perseus; pharaoh 86, 89, 91, 224; Philip II, relations with: *see* Philip II; poisoning of (alleged) 224; *pothos* 50, 56, 71, 87–8, 151, 153, 156, 180–1, 184, 204; pragmatism 20, 65, 198, 199, 208; purges 43–6, 117–28, 184–8, 192; rapidity 46, 52, 73, 106, 140; regent 24; religiosity 14, 22, 27, 42, 47–8, 49, 50, 54, 60–1, 62, 64, 65, 67, 71, 72, 76, 83, 84, 85, 86, 87–91, 92, 93, 97, 101, 107, 115, 129–30, 131, 133–9, 142–3, 146–7, 152, 154, 155, 162, 168–9, 171, 172, 179, 180, 183, 189, 190, 191, 207–8, 212–13, 215, 217, 219, 220–1, 221–3; remorse 107–8, 137, 139, 196; sacking of cities 52–5, 84, 85, 105–6, 130, 163; suicide 137–8; sexuality 56–9, 112–13; violence (personal) ix, 85–6, 136–7, 184–5, 187, 191, 195, 196, 210, 212; women, attitude toward and treatment of 56–9, 61, 68, 78–9, 81, 99, 135, 146–7, 165, 192, 210; wounds 77–8, 85, 130, 150, 174–7, 183, 205; youth: *see* boyhood

Alexander IV of Macedon (son of Alexander the Great) 59, 141
Alexander of Epirus (the Molossian) 35–6, 40
Alexander the Lyncestian 41, 44, 69, 74, 127, 209
*Alexander Mosaic* 77, 114
*Alexander Sarcophagus* 82
Alexandria (Charax) 204
Alexandria (Egypt) 5, 87, 162
Alexandria Eschate 130
Alexandropolis 24
Alkmene 149
Amazons 210
Ammon 86–91, 135, 171, 172, 179, 190, 193, 202, 205; *see also* Zeus
Amphilochus 75
Amphipolis 49, 59, 218
Amphitrite 171
*amphora(e)* 231–2
Amu Darya, River: *see* Oxus
Amyntas (son of Andromenes) 126
Amyntas (son of Perdiccas III, cousin of Alexander the Great) 40, 44, 121
Amyntas III of Macedon (father of Philip II) 19, 28
Amyntas, Macedonian exile 76
*Anabasis* (Arrian's): *see* Arrian
*Anabasis* (Xenophon's) 51, 234–6
Anatolia(n) 19, 68, 76, 91
Anaxarchus 137, 202, 203, 221
Anaximenes 62
Anchiale 74
Ancyra 73
Andromache 13, 136
*Andromache* (Euripides') 136–7
Andromeda 114
*Andromeda* (Euripides') 276, n.47
Andromenes 126
Andronicos, M. 5, 231–2
Antigone 91
Antipater 7, 12, 24, 26, 39, 41, 44, 52–3, 59, 69, 99, 109–10, 114, 127, 209–10, 224
Aornus (Aornos), "rock" of (Pir-Sar) 148, 153–4, 166
Apelles 66, 134, 203
Apis 86, 224
Aphrodite 56, 185
Apollo(nian) 13, 22, 35, 38, 47–8, 66, 75, 84, 129, 190 (Averter of Evil), 193, 202
Apollodorus 220–1
Apollophanes 181, 184, 186

apotheosis: *see* Alexander III, deification
Arabia(n), Arab(s) 85, 124, 184, 217–21, 230
Arabian Sea 178
Arbela 93, 97
Archelaus of Macedon 6, 26, 55
Areia 117
*arete* 2, 20–1, 22; *see also* Alexander III, *arete*
Argead 14, 40–1, 43–4, 90–1
Argos, Argive(s) 22, 75, 102, 114
Ariadne 114
Ariamazes 133
Aristander 56, 62, 69, 83, 85, 93, 94, 96, 131, 137
Aristobulus 71–2, 91, 104, 146–8, 192, 195, 205, 218, 219–20, 222, 226, 239
Aristogeiton 27, 146
Aristotle x, 19–23, 26–7, 37, 50, 57, 58, 69–70, 71, 74, 88, 134, 139, 143–4, 148, 149, 161, 172–3, 176–7, 201, 202, 229, 233, 239
Armenians 105
Arrhidaeus: *see* Philip III of Macedon
Arrian: *Anabasis* 108, cited 10–11, 18–19, 21, 23, 28, 43, 50, 53, 54, 57–8, 63, 64, 67–9, 70, 72, 74, 76–7, 79–81, 82, 84–5, 87–8, 90, 94–5, 102, 107–8, 116, 122, 126, 129, 138–9, 146–7, 149, 150, 151–2, 153, 155, 156–7, 159–61, 162–3, 164, 165–7, 169, 171, 173, 176–7, 180, 182–3, 185, 186, 189–90, 192, 196, 199–200, 202, 203, 205–8, 212–13, 215, 217, 218–22, 223, 225; *Indica* 180, cited 112, 153, 164, 180–1, 183, 189–90
Arsames 73
Arses: *see* Artaxerxes IV
Artabazus 58, 66, 112, 197
Artacoana 117
Artaxerxes III (Ochus) of Persia 19, 80, 197; as Great King, 24
Artaxerxes IV (Arses) of Persia 80
Artaxerxes V of Persia: *see* Bessus
Artemis 66, 193, 218, 219
Artemisios 48
Arybbas 13
ascetics: *see* Gymnosophists
Asclepius 75, 212–13
Ashurbanipal: *see* Sardanapalus
*askesis* 51
Asia(n)(s) (Orient), Asiatic ix, 3, 6, 11, 12, 15, 18, 19, 21, 23, 25–6, 28,

30, 31, 32, 34, 35, 39, 44, 45, 54, 56, 57, 59, 60, 61, 64, 68, 71, 73, 77, 80–1, 90, 97, 107, 112, 113, 114, 116, 140, 141, 149, 164, 166, 167, 190, 193, 198, 199, 200, 201, 203, 205, 208, 209
Asia Minor 18, 19, 31, 32, 35, 44, 51, 57, 65–70, 79, 91, 171, 210
Assyrian(s) 74, 105
Assyro-Babylonian, royal graves 221
Astaspes 186
Atarneus 19, 21
Atarrhias 119
Athamas 15
Athena 27, 61, 62, 64, 67 (Polias), 74, 75, 79, 97, 114, 154 (Nike), 161–2, 218
Athenian Assembly 52
Athenodorus 92
Athens, Athenian(s) 7, 8, 11, 12, 19, 23–4, 25–8, 31, 36, 41, 45, 46, 51, 52, 53, 54, 64, 67, 70, 75, 81, 82, 92, 97, 103, 107, 108, 146, 171, 178, 185, 195, 201, 239
Atropates 210
Attalus (son of Andromenes) 33, 41, 126
Attalus (uncle of Cleopatra, Philip II's last wife) 28–9, 34–5, 37, 38, 39, 41, 44
Attic, Attica 25, 26, 27, 48, 107
Attock 155
Audata (wife of Philip II) 17
Axius, River 93
Azov, Sea of 217

Babylon(ians) 93, 97–8, 101, 105, 170, 180, 183, 185, 196, 203, 209, 210, 211, 214, 217–30 *passim*; Hanging Gardens 185
*Bacchae* (Euripides') x, 1–4, 6, 14, 15–16, 18, 23, 35, 36, 47, 49, 50, 55, 56, 61, 64–5, 70, 71, 72, 73, 83, 84, 87, 89, 91, 92, 99–100, 104, 106–7, 108, 109, 110, 112, 113, 118, 120, 124, 132, 133, 134, 137, 138, 139, 141, 144, 145, 148, 149, 152, 153, 154, 164, 172, 174, 175, 178, 179, 182, 186, 188–9, 190, 191, 193, 194, 195, 196, 201, 203, 204, 210, 211, 214, 216, 219, 223, 224, 226, 227, 228, 229, 230, 235, 237, 238
Bacchanalian: *see* Dionysus
Bacchantes: *see* Dionysus, cult

Bacchic: *see* Dionysus
Bacchic cult: *see* Dionysus, cult
Bacchus: *see* Dionysus
Bacchylides 55–6
Bactra 132
Bactria, Bactria(n)(s) 111, 115, 116, 117, 128, 129, 132, 135, 140, 145, 148, 153, 156, 167
Badian, E. 39, 44, 79, 109, 125, 183–4, 186, 187, 189, 198, 215–16, 224, 228
Bagoas (the eunuch) 112, 190, 192, 195, 211
Bagoas (son of Pharnuches) 171, 211
Bagoas the Vizier 75, 80
Bahmanabad 178
Bajaur 150
Balkan (mountains) 49
Baluchistan: *see* Gedrosia
banquet: *see* symposium
barbarian(s), barbaric, barbarity, barbarization 6, 11, 25, 26, 31, 34, 45, 52, 57, 64, 70, 73, 77, 94, 102, 115, 121, 129, 135, 136, 144, 165, 175, 199, 200, 206
Barsine (mistress of Alexander the Great) 58–9, 66, 81, 112, 197
Batis 84–6
Beas, River: *see* Ganges; Hyphasis
Beqaa Valley 93
Bermium (mountains) 20, 71
Berve, H. 125
Bessus (Artaxerxes V) 111–12, 115–16, 117, 128–9
Black Sea 217
Bodrum: *see* Halicarnassus
bodyguards: *see* Royal Bodyguards
Boeotian 55, 177
Bolan pass 180
Bolon 123
Borza, E. N. 6, 103,
Bosworth, A. B. x, 127, 153, 196, 198–9, 200, 210–11, 218–19, 224, 226
Brahmans 173–4
Branchidae 129–30
Brigians 71; *see also* Phrygia
Briseis 22
Britannic Islands 18
British Museum 67
Bromius: *see* Dionysus
"Brotherhood of Man": *see* Alexander III, "Brotherhood of Man"
Bucephala 9, 161, 170
Bucephalas 8–9, 30, 161
Burn, A. R. 59, 89

Byzantium 23–4, 83

Cadmus 40, 54, 84
Cadousian 75
Calanus 157, 179–80, 195–6
Callias 102
Calliope 60
Callisthenes 18, 65, 80–1, 88, 89, 96, 104, 129, 137, 142–8, 202
Callixeina 58
*calyxes* 231–2
Cambyses 51, 88
*candys* 113
*cantharus, cantharoi* 1, 14, 231
Cappadocia, Cappadocian(s) 73, 105
Caranus (founder of Argead dynasty) 41
Caranus (possible son of Philip II and Cleopatra) 40–1, 44
Cardia 171, 218
Caria, Carian(s) 31–3, 57, 68, 92
Carmania 180, 184–92, 196
Carthage, Carthaginian(s) 217–18
Cassander 210, 224
Castor, Polydeuces and: *see* Dioscuri
Cathaean(s) 162–3
Caucasus 128–9
Cebalinus 117–18, 122
Celts 50, 217
Chaeronea, battle of 7, 24–6, 28, 41, 150
Chaldaeans 221
Charax: *see* Alexandria
Chares 77, 133, 148, 196, 197–8
Chenab, River: *see* Acesines
Cheops 218
Chiliarch (Grand Vizier) 112, 209
Chios 7, 70
*Choephori* (Aeschylus') 237
chorus, Greek x; *see also* tragedy
*chthonios*: *see* Dionysus
Cilicia 69, 73, 74, 76, 116, 209
Cilician Gates 73
Cilluta 179
Citium 96
Cleander 111, 124–5, 186–8
Cleitus (Clitus) 55, 63, 90, 127, 128, 133–40, 144, 146, 147, 156, 171, 185, 202, 225
Cleomenes 214
Cleopatra (daughter of Philip II and Olympias) 17, 35, 39
Cleopatra (Philip II's last wife) 28–41, 44

Clio 60
Codomannus: *see* Darius III
Coenus 119, 121, 123, 124, 140, 160, 166, 167, 171, 186, 187–8, 206
Common Peace 53
Companion Cavalry 25, 63, 64, 77, 96, 120, 127, 133, 135, 151, 183; *see also* Royal Companions
Companions: *see* Royal Companions
comus 25, 107, 226
Conga line: *see* comus
Cophen, River (Kabul) 150
Corinth, Corinthian(s) 9, 30, 32, 46, 47, 63, 102
Corinthian League 26, 45, 46, 53, 54, 64, 67, 91, 110, 148, 201, 217
Corragus 178
Cos 66, 174
Cossaeans 215, 221
*crater* 48, 231
Craterus 91, 113, 114, 118–19, 123, 158, 160, 162, 170, 171, 172, 180, 185, 197, 209–10
Creon, King 38, 54
Crete 195
Critobulus 174
Croesus 65
Ctesias 149
Curtius 12, 42, 74, 76, 78, 83, 84, 85–6, 91, 93, 94, 98–9, 102, 106, 107, 112, 115–16, 118–25, 140, 147, 163, 178, 187, 189, 192, 195, 217–18
Cyclopean 169
*Cyclops* (Euripides') 235, 237–8
Cydnus, River 73
*cylixes* 231
Cynane 17, 40
Cynic 156; *see also* Diogenes
Cypris: *see* Aphrodite
Cypriot 92
*Cyropaedia* (Xenophon's) 51–2, 78, 236–8
Cyropolis (Ura-Tyube) 130
Cyrnus 218
Cyrus the Great of Persia 51–2, 60, 65, 77, 78, 88, 97, 142, 150, 181, 183, 192, 193; tomb of 192, 194–5

Daedalus 220
Daisios (May) 47–8
Damascus 81
Damghan: *see* Hecatompylus
Damis 202
Dandamis 156

Danube, River (Ister) 11, 24, 49–50, 129; Spirit of 50
Danubian 17
Dardanelles: *see* Hellespont
Darius I (the Great) of Persia 105, 149, 150; as Great King 67
Darius III (Codomannus) of Persia 21, 33, 36, 75–9, 80, 81, 82, 84, 85, 93–7, 98, 99, 106, 109, 110, 111, 112, 113, 115, 129, 160, 190, 197; as Great King 53, 69, 76, 77, 78, 79, 80, 81, 96, 111, 113; wife of 78
Deinocrates 214
Delos 218
Delphi, Delphic Oracle 28, 35, 47, 48, 49, 88, 202, 218, 239
Delta: *see* Nile, River
Demades 7, 25, 54, 201
Demaratus 9, 30, 63
Demeter: *see* Earth
Demetrius (the Besieger) 79
Demetrius (the Bodyguard) 126
Demetrius (the Companion) 142
democracies, democratic 65
Demosthenes 7, 10, 25, 26, 44, 45, 52, 54, 201
Didyma 129
Dimnus 117, 118, 120, 121
Diodorus 7, 25, 34, 35, 36, 37, 40, 41, 44, 52, 53, 56, 61, 63, 64, 70, 80, 83–4, 97, 107, 151, 163, 173, 211, 214, 218, 224–5, 226
Diogenes 46–7, 156
Dionysius 222
Dionysodorus 81
Dionysus (Dionysos), Dionysia(c)(n), (Bacchus, Bacchic) ix–x, 1–6, 13, 14–16, 20, 23, 25, 27, 31, 40, 48, 49, 54, 55, 56, 59, 62, 64, 72–3, 75, 81, 84, 88, 90, 92, 99–100, 102–3, 104, 107, 108, 110, 114, 131, 132, 133, 134, 138–9, 144, 149–50, 151–3, 164, 166, 169, 170, 172, 175, 177, 182, 183, 186, 188–9, 190, 191, 193, 194, 198, 202, 203, 204, 206, 207, 210, 213, 215, 219, 224, 225, 226, 228, 229–30, 231–2, 239; Bromius 55, 61; *chthonios* 6; cult 3, 4, 13, 14–16, 23, 54, 64, 114; Dionysia 27, 64, 92; "disease" 3; gift of: *see* wine; guild 27, 92, 210; *melanaigis* 6; *orgia*, orgiastic 15–16; Triumph 23; *see also* Aegae; drinking; ivy; maenads; wine

Dioscuri (Castor and Polydeuces) 20–1, 90, 134, 138
Dioxippus 178, 203
dithyramb; 27 *see also* Dionysus
Dium 55–6, 64, 218
Dius 211
Dodona 12–13, 88, 90, 218
drama, Greek: *see* tragedy
Drangiana 117, 185
drinking, drinkers and drunkenness 1–2, 6–8, 14, 23, 25, 26, 28, 29, 33, 34, 36, 50, 56, 57, 58, 68, 69–70, 74, 81, 90, 91, 93, 95, 102–4, 106–8, 112, 130, 133, 134, 135, 136, 138, 139, 144, 146, 147, 156, 171, 178, 188–9, 190, 196, 201, 207, 210, 211, 212, 215, 223, 225, 226–7, 230, 231–9; *see also* Alexander III; Dionysus; symposium; wine
Dropides 63
Drypetis 197

Earth (Demeter) 49, 93
East 169; *see also* India
Ecbatana 33, 97, 105, 106, 110, 112, 124, 125, 129, 130, 204, 210, 211, 213, 215, 220, 225
Egypt, Egyptian(s) 56, 82, 83, 84, 86–91, 97, 108, 117, 118, 162, 171, 214, 218, 224
Elaeus 60
*Electra* (Euripides') 234
Electra Gate 53
elephants 93, 150, 154, 155, 157–61, 164, 172
Elimiotis 17, 188
*entheos* 1
Engels, D.W. 106, 227–8
Epaminondas 54
*Ephemerides*: see *Royal Diaries*
Ephesus, Ephesian(s) 65–7
Ephippus 6, 193, 225, 226
Epidaurus, Epidaurians 213
*Epigoni* 141, 200
Epirus, Epirote 12, 13, 17, 30, 31, 35, 40, 209, 218
Erigyius 119, 131
Eros 30
E-Sagila 97
Ethiopia, Ethiopia(n)(s) 114, 150, 217
Eumaeus 211
Eumenes 171, 197, 214, 218
Euphrates, River 51, 84, 93, 180, 196, 219, 221, 223, 227

Euripides x, 2, 14, 15, 16, 27, 38, 136, 144, 153, 221, 229, 233–8
Europa (possible daughter of Cleopatra and Philip II) 40
Europe, European(s) 8, 11, 12, 18, 25, 28, 37, 41, 58, 60, 61, 66, 76, 79, 91, 99, 106, 112, 127, 143, 149, 195, 198, 199, 200, 210, 217, 218
Eurydice (mother of Philip II) 28, 29
Eurydice: *see* Cleopatra, Philip II's last wife
Exiles' Decree 200–1

Failaka, island: *see* Icarus
Farah: *see* Phrada
Fear: *see* Phobos
feast(ing): *see* symposium
Furies 128
fusion, policy of: *see* Alexander III, fusion

Gallipoli peninsula: *see* Thracian Chersonese
Gandhara 150
Ganges, River 55, 164, 165; plain 149, 156; *see also* Hyphasis
Gardens of Midas: *see* Midas, Gardens of; Mieza
Gaugamela (Tell Gomel), battle of 79, 91–7, 98, 109, 111, 150, 158, 159, 212
Gaza 84–5, 105
Gedrosia (Gadrosia), Gedrosian Desert (Makran) 179–84, 189, 191, 215
Getae 50
Ghazni 128
Gibraltar 23
Glaucias 211–12
Glycera ("Sugar") 185, 195
Gordian knot ix, 70–3, 141
Gordium ix, 69, 70–3
*Gorgias* (Plato's) 6
Gorgon 114
Grand Vizier: *see* Chiliarch
Granicus, River (Koçabas), battle of 47, 62–4, 66, 67, 70, 73, 92, 135
Great King 97, 105, 142; *see also* Alexander III; Artaxerxes III; Darius I; Darius III; Xerxes
Greece, Greek(s), Hellas, Hellene(s), Hellenic x, 1, 2, 3, 6, 11, 14, 17, 20, 24, 25, 26, 28, 30, 35, 36, 45, 46–9, 51, 52, 53, 54, 55, 57, 59, 60, 62, 63, 64, 65, 67, 70, 74, 75, 77, 80, 81, 82, 84, 85, 86, 88, 89, 90, 91, 92, 93, 94, 96, 98, 99, 105, 107, 108, 109, 110, 114, 115, 121, 123, 130, 133, 136, 141, 142, 143, 144, 145, 146, 149, 151, 153, 165, 166, 167, 171, 185, 190, 193, 195, 197, 200, 201, 202, 203, 207, 209, 210, 211, 213, 218, 223, 224, 227, 231, 233; Hellenization 65; Panhellenic 26, 130
Green, P. 162, 191, 211
Gymnosophists (ascetics, naked philosophers) 150, 156–7

Hades 21, 143
Haemus, Mount 49
Hagnon 117
Halicarnassus (Bodrum) 68, 69, 82
Halys, River 80
Hamadan: *see* Ecbatana
Hamilton, J. R. 7, 54, 101–2, 185, 198
Hammond, N. G. L. 5, 169, 224
Haranpur 157
Harmodius 27, 146
Harpalus (Imperial Treasurer) 27, 32, 74, 110, 185–6, 187–8, 195
Hecataeus 44
Hecatompylus (Damghan) 115
Heckel, W. 125
Hector (Hektor) 13, 43, 86
Hector (son of Parmenio) 91
*hegemon* of the Corinthian League 46, 54, 64, 91
*hegemon* of the Hellenes 46, 80
*Helen* (Euripides') 27
Helenus 13
Helicon 96
Heliopolis 86
Helios (Sun) 93, 161, 163
Hellas: *see* Greece
Hellene(s): *see* Greece
*Hellenica* (Xenophon's) 235
Hellenization: *see* Greece
Hellespont 11, 12, 21, 23, 30, 34, 55, 59–61, 63, 116, 149, 164, 168, 171
Hellespontine Phrygia 62, 65, 66
Hephaestion 6, 57–8, 81–2, 113–14, 119, 123, 127, 140, 142, 146, 150, 154, 155, 162, 171, 172, 173, 189, 197, 209, 210–16, 218, 220, 225, 226, 227, 230
Hera 14–15, 90, 152
Heracles (Herakles, Hercules), Herculean 14, 20–3, 46, 48, 50, 51,

53, 54, 61, 65, 66, 75, 79, 82, 83, 84, 87–8, 90, 91, 92, 93, 128, 129, 134, 138, 144, 149, 153, 154, 166, 169, 181, 183, 190, 193, 202, 204, 225, 226, 231; Krishna 153; Pillars of 23, 217, 218; Propator 171; *see also* Melcarth

Heracles (illegitimate son of Alexander the Great) 58, 59, 66, 112

Heracon 187

Herat 117

Hermias 19–21, 50

Hermes 15, 193; Psychopompus 194

Hermocrates 37

Hermolaus 145–6, 147

Herodotus, Herodotean 86, 114, 129–30, 149, 180, 184, 224, 233–8

*heros theos* 22

Hestia 1

Hieronymus 218

Himalayas 157

Hindu: *see* Sind

Hindu Kush (mountains) 116, 128, 129, 149, 150, 185

Hipparchus 146

*Histories* (Herodotus') 86, 235, 236, 238

*History of Sicily* (Philistus') 27

*HN* (Pliny the Elder's *Naturalis Historia*) 60, 66

Homer ix, 21, 27, 87, 233–8; Homeric 7, 21, 43, 52, 57, 61, 63, 137, 161, 173, 189; Homeric King 43–100; *see also Iliad*; *Odyssey*

*homonoia* 207

Hormuz, Strait of 189

Hornblower, S. 51, 201

Horus 86, 224

hostages 26; *see also* Alexander III, hostages

*hybris* 202; *see also* Alexander III, *hybris*

Hydaspes, River (Jhelum) 9, 155, 170, 171, 172, 173, 174, 178, 225; battle of 157–62, 163

Hydraotes, River (Ravi) 155, 162, 173, 175

Hygeia 75

*Hymn to Virtue* (Aristotle's) 20–1, 22, 50

Hyperboreans 48, 114

Hyperides 12

Hyphasis, River (Beas) 155, 161, 162,

163, 164–70, 171, 184, 186, 187, 206; *see also* Ganges

*hypomnemata*: *see* Alexander III, Last Plans

Iberians 217

Icarian sea 220

Icarus, island 219–20

ichor 203

Ida, Mount 62

*Iliad* (Homer's) ix, 21–3, 43, 57, 61, 81, 114, 229; cited 9, 10, 11, 12, 22, 23, 24, 25, 28–9, 31–2, 38, 42, 43, 45, 47, 53, 58, 59, 63, 64, 71, 75, 77, 79, 82, 85, 86, 88, 89, 94, 95–6, 111, 112, 114, 116, 119, 120, 122–3, 124, 125, 126, 128, 129, 130, 131, 132, 135, 136, 139–40, 141, 143, 145, 149–50, 156, 157, 158–9, 161, 164–5, 166, 168, 169, 170, 171, 172, 173, 174–5, 176, 177, 179, 180, 187, 192, 197, 201, 203, 206, 208, 211, 212–13, 214–15, 218, 219, 220, 221, 222, 225, 226, 234–7

Ilium 62; *see also* Troy

Illyria, Illyrian(s) 10, 17, 29, 30, 34, 40, 52

Immortals: *see* Olympian gods

Imperial Treasurer: *see* Harpalus

"India," Indian(s) 55, 98, 105, 133, 148–81 *passim*, 183, 185, 187, 188, 189, 192, 193, 195, 197, 198, 217, 218, 219, 220

Indian Ocean 105

*Indica* (Arrian's): *see* Arrian

Indus, River 105, 149, 150, 153, 154, 155, 162, 170, 171, 178, 180, 206

Ino 15

Iolaus 53

Iolaus (son of Antipater) 210, 224

*Ion* (Euripides') 234

Ionia 65, 66, 165

Iphicrates 81

Iran, Iranian(s) 77, 98, 141, 149, 181, 187, 193, 194, 197, 198, 199, 200, 203, 222

Isocrates 80, 202

Issus, battle of 57, 75–9, 80, 81, 93, 96

Ister, River: *see* Danube

Italy, Italian 217

ivy 1, 151, 152, 185; *see also* Dionysus

Jalalabad 171

Jalalpur 158

Jaxartes, River 105, 130, 131
Jhau 181
Jhelum, River: *see* Hydaspes
Justin 13, 37–9, 40, 42, 43, 44, 53, 102

Kabul Valley 128, 148; *see also*
　Cophen, River
Karachi 181
Karnak 86
Kashmir 154, 155, 156, 157, 161
*kausia* 113
Kerényi, C. 225
Khawak pass 128
Kirk, G. S. 48
Koçabas, River: *see* Granicus
Krishna: *see* Heracles

Lacedaemonians: *see* Sparta
Lagus 126
Lampsacus 62
Lane Fox, R. 41, 92, 215
Lanice 135, 225
Larisa 17, 171
Last Plans: *see* Alexander III, Last
　Plans
Leda 21
Leochares 28
Leonidas (Alexander's tutor) 17–18, 68
Leonidas (Spartan king) 17–18
Leonnatus 33, 41, 78, 117, 119, 171,
　174, 181, 184, 189, 197
Lerna 114
Lesbos 70
leukemia 227
Levant 91
libation(s) 2, 60, 133, 142, 171, 179,
　196, 207, 208, 213, 231
Libya, Libyan(s) 87–91, 181, 190, 217,
　218; Desert 88, 89, 91, 181
Little Star: *see* Roxane
Luxor 86
Lycian 132
Lycurgus 201
Lydia, Lydian(s) 65, 105, 149
Lyncestis, Lyncestian(s) 41, 43, 44, 69,
　74, 127, 209
Lysimachus of Acarnania 21
Lysimachus (Royal Bodyguard) 171,
　189
Lysippus, Lysippean 60, 64, 66

Macedon, Macedonia,
　Macedonia(n)(s): *see* Alexander III
Macedonian army 8, 10–11, 14, 20,

24–5, 26, 34, 41, 44, 46, 49–50, 52–4,
　55, 57, 58, 59–61, 62–4, 65–70, 74,
　75–9, 80–6, 90, 92, 93–8, 99, 103,
　105–11, 112, 113, 115–39, 140, 141,
　144, 146, 148–9, 150–4, 156, 157–60,
　162–70, 171–2, 173–6, 177–8, 179,
　180, 181–4, 185, 186–7, 188–90, 193,
　196–7, 198–200, 205–10, 211, 214,
　215, 218, 220, 222, 223–4
Macedonian drinking 6–8; *see also*
　Alexander III, drinking; drinking
Macurdy, G. 13
Maedi 24
maenads 15, 56; *see also* Dionysus, cult
Magarsus 75
Magi 185, 195, 207
Makran: *see* Gedrosia
malaria 227
Malavas: *see* Malli
Malli (Malavas), Mallian(s) 170, 173,
　177, 179, 189
Mallus 75
Maracanda (Samarkand) 130, 132,
　133, 152, 156, 168
Marathus 79
Marduk, temple 97, 221
Mareotis, Lake 87
Margites 52
Massaga 150, 151, 154
Massagetae 140
Mazaeus 93, 97–8
Meda (wife of Philip II) 17
Medea 38
Media, Median(s) (Medes) 51, 105,
　106, 113, 119, 129, 136, 147, 186,
　187, 197, 199, 210
Mediterranean 62, 67, 79, 87, 92, 179,
　217
Medius 104, 171, 223, 225, 226
Medusa 114
Megalopolis, battle of 99
Megara 74
*melanaigis*: *see* Dionysus
Melcarth 82, 84; *see also* Heracles
Meleager 156
Memnon 62, 66, 68, 70, 73, 81
Memphis 86, 91, 224
Menoetius 61
Mentor 66, 197
mercenaries 62, 63, 64, 67, 81, 85, 110,
　130, 148, 150, 151, 188, 195, 201
*meros* 151; *see also* Zeus
Merus, Mount 151; *see also* Zeus
Mesopotamia 51, 93

metamorphosis, metamorphic 1, 2, 3, 101–54 *passim*, 232; *see also* Alexander III; Dionysus; Pentheus
*Metaphysica* (Aristotle's) x
Metron 118
Midas, Gardens of 19–21
Midas, king 20, 71
Mieza 20–3, 58, 174
Miletus, Milesians 66, 67, 129, 130
Mithridates 63
Mithrines 65
Mnesitheus 239
Molossian(s) 12, 13, 17, 35, 39
Molossus 13
Moon 93
Mopsus 75
*Moralia* (Plutarch's): *see* Plutarch
Mosul 93
Muses 21, 55, 56
Myrtale: *see* Olympias
Mytilene 70, 102

Nabarzanes 112
naked philosophers: *see* Gymnosophists
Naoussa 20
Nautaca 140
Nearchus 32, 112, 163–4, 171, 180–1, 184, 189–90, 196, 197, 223, 226
Nectanebo II 86
Neoptolemus (actor) 36
Neoptolemus (father of Olympias) 13
Neoptolemus (son of Achilles) 13, 61
Nereids 61, 76, 171
Nereus 76
Nicaea 161–2, 170, 178; *see also* Athena
Nicanor (son of Parmenio) 123
Nicanor (son-in-law of Aristotle) 201
Nicesipolis (wife of Philip II) 17
Nicomachus (father of Aristotle) 19
Nicomachus (Macedonian aristocrat) 117, 118
Nike 134, 154
Nile, River 82, 86, 87, 91, 105, 162; Delta 87
Nymphs, Precinct of: *see* Midas, Gardens of; Mieza
Nysa, Nysaean(s) 15, 148, 151, 152, 153, 166; nymphs of 15

obeisance: *see* proskynesis
O'Brien, J. M. 233
Ocean (world-encircling river and

deity) 23, 114, 149, 162, 170, 171, 173, 179; Eastern 162; Okeanos 171
Ochus: *see* Artaxerxes III
*Odyssey* (Homer's) 87, 234, 236
Oedipus 54
*Oedipus Rex* (Sophocles') 235
Ohind (Udabhandapura) 155
*oinochoe* 231
*oinos*: *see* wine
Okeanos: *see* Ocean
oligarchs, oligarchy 65
Olympia 28, 62, 202, 210
Olympian gods, Olympians (Immortals, Twelve Immortals) 1, 36, 191, 194, 202
Olympias (mother of Alexander the Great) 12–19, 28–31, 35–42, 44, 49, 57, 58, 61, 64, 68, 69, 72, 74, 75, 86, 88, 90, 99, 115, 117, 126, 136, 140, 143, 167, 194, 209, 215, 218, 224
Olympic Games, Olympics 10, 13, 201
Olympus, Mount 15, 22, 46, 55, 186, 193
Olynthus, Olynthian(s) 6, 54, 55, 143
Omphis: *see* Taxiles
*On the Death of Alexander and Hephaestion* (Ephippus') 6
*On Drunkenness* (Aristotle's) 239
Onesicritus 156, 171, 184, 197
Opis 10, 204–10
Oreitae 181, 184
Orestis 34
*orgia*, orgiastic: *see* Dionysus
Orient: *see* Asia
orientalization: *see* Alexander III, orientalization
Orpheus 56
Orphic 15; *see also* Dionysus
Orsines 112, 192, 195
Osiris 224; *see also* Dionysus; Sarapis
Ossa, Mount 46
Oxathres 184–5
Oxus, River (Amu Darya) 129, 133; Valley 133
Oxyartes (father of Roxane) 140
Oxyathres 112
Oxydracae 170, 177
*oxyteros*: *see* Alexander III, *oxyteros*

*Paean* (Pindar's) 234, 235
Paeonian 93
page(s): *see* Royal Pages
Pages' Conspiracy: *see* Royal Pages
Pakistan 9, 116, 149, 150, 155

Pamphylia 70
Pan 232
Pangaeum, Mount 59, 106
Panhellenic: *see* Greece
Pantheia 78
Paphlagonia 73
Pareitacene 184
Paris 61
Parke, H. W. 130
Parmenio 31, 32, 33, 34, 39, 41, 44, 59,
    60, 63, 67, 69, 70, 74, 77, 81, 84, 91,
    94, 95, 96, 106, 107, 108, 110, 111,
    118–28, 130, 133, 147, 158, 186
Parysatis (wife of Alexander the
    Great) 197, 198
Pasargadae 194
Pasitigris, River 196
*pathos* 3, 105
Patroclus (Patroklos) 57, 58, 61, 172,
    197, 212, 213, 215, 221
Pattala 178, 180, 181
Paurava 155, 157, 161
Pausanias (Philip II's assassin) 34, 35,
    37, 38, 39, 41, 42, 126, 140, 225
Pausanias (Philip II's other lover) 34
Pausanias (writer) 40, 62
Peleus 10, 21, 77, 131, 132, 136–7, 143;
    *see also* Achilles
Pella 11, 17, 19, 24, 26, 28, 30, 35, 55,
    59, 60, 66, 112, 195
Pelopidas 54
Peloponnesus 69
Pentheus 2–4, 16, 56, 229, 230
*penthos* 3
Periander 102
Perdiccas 33, 41, 68, 119, 140, 146,
    150, 171, 174, 189, 197, 211, 218,
    224–5
Perdiccas I of Macedon 71
Perdiccas III of Macedon 44
Perinthus 23–4, 80, 83
Peritas 161
Persepolis 97, 98, 105–10, 111, 130,
    165, 191, 196, 229; Apadana 105;
    Hall of the Hundred Columns 105;
    Treasury 110; Tree of Life 105
Perses 114
Perseus 87, 88, 90, 114, 181
Persia(n)(s) 19, 24, 26, 27, 33, 35, 36,
    46, 47, 51, 52, 53, 57, 58, 59, 60, 61,
    62, 63, 64, 65, 66, 67, 68, 69, 70, 73,
    74, 75, 76, 77, 78, 79, 80, 81, 82, 83,
    86, 93, 94, 96, 97, 98, 99, 105, 107,
    108, 110, 111, 112, 113, 114, 115,
117, 129, 130, 135, 136, 142, 149,
    150, 155, 157, 159, 170, 180, 185,
    192, 193, 195, 196, 197, 198, 199,
    204, 205, 206, 207, 209, 210, 214;
    *see also* Achaemenian
Persian Empire ix, 11, 19, 31, 34, 51,
    65, 77, 111, 129, 130, 198, 202, 206;
    *see also* Achaemenian
Persian (Susian) Gates 105
Persian Gulf 184, 189, 196, 204
Persian Wars 59, 67
Persis 157, 192, 195
Peucestas 141, 171, 174, 189, 192, 197
phalanx 62, 77, 160
pharaoh: *see* Alexander III, pharaoh
    Nectanebo II
Pharasmanes 185
Pharnuches 132, 171, 211
Pharos 87
Phaselis 69–70
*phiale* 231
Phila (wife of Philip II) 17
Philinna (wife of Philip II) 17
Philip (the Acarnanian physician) 74,
    85, 122
Philip (the satrap) 188
Philip II of Macedon (father of
    Alexander the Great) 5–46 *passim*,
    49, 50, 52, 54, 55, 56, 58, 61, 64, 65,
    68, 69, 72, 73, 79, 80, 83, 84, 90, 91,
    92, 106, 119, 126, 127, 128, 135, 137,
    138, 139, 140, 141, 143, 145, 150,
    167, 171, 186, 197, 199, 201, 202,
    204, 205, 207, 218
Philip III (Arrhidaeus) of Macedon
    (half-brother of Alexander the
    Great) 5, 17, 31, 45
Philip Arrhidaeus: *see* Philip III of
    Macedon
Philippeum 28
Philippi 11, 49
Philippopolis (Plovdiv) 11, 24, 49
Philistus 27
Philochorus 102
*philoponia* 51
*philopotes* 7
Philotas 31, 32, 33, 53, 91, 93, 98,
    117–28, 135, 140, 146, 147, 202, 215,
    225
*Phobos* (Fear) 94, 114
Phoenicia, Phoenician 76, 79–82, 171,
    219, 222
*Phoenissae* (Euripides') 238
Phoenix 21

Phrada (Farah, Prophthasia) 117, 124, 126, 127, 128,
Phrygia, Phrygian(s) 62, 66, 70, 71, 73, 105, 149
Phthia 46
Pieria 55
Pillars of Heracles: *see* Heracles
Pinarus, River 76
Pindar 22, 54, 233–8
Pir-Sar: *see* Aornus
Pittacus 102
Pixodarus 31–3, 39, 40, 41, 45, 68, 91, 92, 119, 125
Plato 6, 19, 26, 103
Pleurias 34
Pliny the Elder 60, 66
Plovdiv: *see* Philippopolis
Plutarch 8–9, 9–10, 12, 13, 15, 16, 17, 18, 19, 20, 27, 28, 29, 30, 31, 32, 37, 38, 40, 41–2, 44, 45–7, 48, 54, 55, 57, 58, 59, 60, 62, 64, 66, 69–70, 72, 76, 78, 81, 83, 87, 93, 94, 95, 96, 101–3, 104, 107, 108–9, 113, 117, 123, 125, 133, 135–8, 140, 141, 143, 145, 148, 151, 155–6, 161, 172, 179, 184, 188, 190, 195, 196, 202, 214, 215, 217, 222, 223, 224, 225, 226; *Moralia* 44, 48, 66, 102–3, 202, 225, 230
Polemon 126
Polias: *see* Athena
*Politics* (Aristotle's) 202
Pollux: *see* Dioscuri
Polus 6
Polydamas 124
Polydeuces, Castor and: *see* Dioscuri
Polymachus 195
Polyperchon 208, 209
*pompe* 75
Pompeii 77
Porus (cousin of Porus of the Paurava) 162
Porus of the Paurava 155, 157–62, 166; medallions 203
Poseidon 60, 76, 171, 179, 190, 202
*pothos* 21, 50, 56, 88, 184; *see also* Alexander III, *pothos*
Priam 13, 61
Priapus 62
Priene 66–7
Prometheus 128–9
Prophthasia: *see* Phrada
*proskynesis* (obeisance) 142–3, 144, 147, 185, 202, 210, 215

Proteas 104, 135, 225–6
Protesilaus 60
Psychopompus 194
Ptolemy (later Ptolemy I) 32, 50, 91, 108, 126, 129, 140, 147, 148, 162, 165, 171, 177–8, 189, 196, 197, 205
Punjab 150, 153, 155, 161, 170, 195
Pura 183, 184
Pyrrhus 79
Pythagoras 220–1
Pythia 47, 48
Python 185
Pythonice 185

Ra 86
*Rauwolfia serpentina* 178
Ravi, River: *see* Hydraotes
Rawalpindi 155
Renault, M. 207
revel(s), reveler(s), revelry: *see* symposium
Rhodes 62, 96
Rhoesakes 63
Rome, Roman 189, 217
Roman historian: *see* Curtius
Roxane (Little Star, wife of Alexander the Great) 59, 140, 141, 144, 197
Royal Bodyguards (*somatophylakes*), personal bodyguards 33, 34, 36, 37, 41, 123, 126, 136, 137, 140, 171, 189, 197
Royal Companions (*hetairoi*) 61, 63, 64, 78, 94, 103, 112, 113, 141, 142, 148, 152, 160, 168, 169, 171, 188, 206, 214, 220, 223, 225, 226
*Royal Diaries* (*Ephemerides*) 210–11, 223–4, 225
Royal Pages, page(s) 78, 99, 118, 200; conspiracy 145–8
royal ring 112, 142, 224
Royal Seal 24
Royal Secretary: *see* Eumenes
Royal Squadron cavalry: 63, 75, 135; infantry 151
Royal Tombs: *see* Aegae
Royal Treasurer: *see* Harpalus
Rubinsohn, W. Z. 125

Sacred Band: *see* Thebes
Samaria, Samaritans 92
Samarkand: *see* Maracanda
Samothrace 13
Sangala 162–3
Sarapis 222, 223, 224

Sardanapalus (Ashurbanipal) 74
Sardis 65, 69
*sarissae* 200
Satibarzanes 117
satyr(s) (*satyros*) 83, 231
Satyrus 17, 28, 30, 39, 40
Schachermeyr, F. 90, 125, 163, 207, 227
Scylax 149, 180
Scythian(s) 24, 105, 130–1, 132, 134, 140, 217
Seistan, Lake 117
Seleucus 199
Seltman, C. 62
Semele (mother of Dionysus) 14–15, 49, 72, 149
Semiramis 181, 183
serpents: *see* snakes
Sestos 60
Sicily 27, 96, 217
Sidon 81
Silenus, Sileni 20, 231, 232
Sinai Desert 86
Sind (Hindu) 150, 153, 170
Sinope 46, 156
Siren's call 150
Sisygambis (mother of Darius III) 57, 58, 78, 79, 99
Sitalces 186
*situla* 231
Siwah 87–91, 121, 202
*skyphos* 28, 34, 225, 231
snake(s) (serpents), bites, handling 1, 13, 15, 23, 86, 152, 163–4, 170, 177–8, 182, 214
Snyder, J. W. 178
Sochi 75, 76
Socrates 26
*Socrates' Defense* (Xenophon's) 238
Sogdiana, Sogdian(s) 129, 130, 132, 140, 141, 148
Soli 74–5
*somatophylakes*: *see* Royal Bodyguards
Sophithes 163
Sophocles 27, 233–8
Spain 218
Sparta, Spartan(s) (Lacedaemonians) 18, 24, 64, 80, 81, 82, 99, 202, 209
Spitamenes 129, 132, 134, 140, 199
Spithridates 63, 135
Stagira 19, 143, 201
Stasanor 185

Stateira (wife of Alexander the Great) 197, 198
Stewart, A. 48
Strabo 51, 129, 163–4, 181, 182, 188, 218
Strymon, River 24
Styx, River 13
"Successors": *see Epigoni*
Suez, gulf of 149
"Sugar": *see* Glycera
Sun: *see* Helios
Susa, Susiana 19, 27, 76, 97, 98, 99, 103, 105, 130, 141, 184, 185, 187, 190, 196, 197–201, 204, 215
Susian Gates: *see* Persian Gates
Swat 150, 152
*Symposium* (Xenophon's) 235, 237
symposium, symposia(sts) (banquet, drinking party, feast, revel) 6–8, 15, 26, 28–9, 34, 36, 69–70, 78, 102, 103–4, 106–7, 119, 133–8, 142–3, 144–5, 146–7, 156, 178, 190, 197–8, 202, 210–11, 223, 225–6, 228, 232, 259; *see also* drinking; wine
*synedrion* of the Corinthian League 148
Syria, Syrian 74, 75, 93, 218
Syrian prophetess 146–7

*tagos* (president) of Thessaly 46
Tarn, W. W. 12, 101, 130, 151, 178, 198
Tarsus 73, 185
Taurus (mountains) 73
Taxila 150, 155, 156, 157, 161
Taxiles (Omphis) 150, 155–6, 157, 160, 161
Tell Gomel: *see* Gaugamela
Telmessus 56
Temenid 22
*temenos* 66
Tempe, vale of 46
Tent of a Hundred Couches 103
Teos 117
Thais 107, 108
Thapsacus 93
Thebes, Theban(s) 2, 3, 11, 24, 25, 46, 52–5, 57, 61, 81, 191, 226, 229; Sacred Band of 25
Theodectas 69
Theognis 102
Theophilus 96
Theophrastus 58
Theopompus 7, 8

Thermopylae 46, 52; battle of 18
Thersites 7
Thessalus 31–2, 92, 198
Thessaly, Thessalian(s) 8, 11, 17, 46, 52, 58, 60, 69, 96, 104, 110, 167, 223, 225
Thetis 13, 23, 76, 221
*tholos* 28, 202
Thrace, Thracian(s) 10, 11, 15, 24, 49, 80, 186, 209
Thracian Chersonese (Gallipoli peninsula) 59–60
Thrasymachus 26
*thymele* 188
thyrsus 15, 232
Tigris, River 93, 204
Timocleia 57
Titan(s), Titanic 16, 128, 163
tragedy, tragedians, tragic, 27, 32, 69, 101, 130, 133, 152, 182, 183, 198, 229, 230; "tragic hero" 229; "tragic pleasure" 27; *see also* Dionysus
Triballians 10, 24, 49, 52
trierarchs 171
Troad, Troy, Trojan, Trojan War 13, 19, 21, 27, 57, 60, 61, 66, 75; sacred shield of Troy 174
Trojan pass 49
Turbat 181
Twelve Immortals: *see* Olympian gods
Tyche (goddess of Fortune) 61, 146
Tyre, Tyrian(s) 82–5, 91, 92–3, 218

Udabhandapura: *see* Ohind
Una-Sar 153
Ura-Tyube: *see* Cyropolis

Uranus 219

Vergina: *see* Aegae
Victory: *see* Nicaea; Nike

Wadi Dalayeh 92
Wilcken, U. 70, 89, 204, 207
wine (fruit of the vine, gift of Dionysus) 1–2, 6–8, 15, 20, 23, 25, 34, 43, 48, 49, 55, 56, 68, 74, 93, 95, 102, 103, 104, 107, 134, 135, 142, 144, 179, 188, 190, 194, 196, 204, 208, 211, 213, 215, 223, 224, 226, 227, 228, 230, 231, 233–8, 239; utensils and vessels: *see* Aegae, specific items; vine(s), fruit of, grape(s) 149, 152, 188, 204; *see also* Aegae; Dionysus; drinking; symposium
wine god(s): *see* Dionysus; Priapus

Xenocrates 60
Xenophon 50, 51, 52, 60, 73, 77, 103, 233–8
Xerxes of Persia 27, 59, 60, 61, 97, 105, 107, 108, 129; as Great King 61

Zagros (mountains) 210, 215
Zeus 5, 12, 14, 15, 16, 21, 23, 38, 48, 66, 72, 79, 88, 89, 90, 91, 92, 96, 114, 128, 129, 133, 136, 137, 143, 149, 151, 156, 168, 190, 201, 202, 218; Apobaterios (Safe Landings) 61; Basileus 71; Herkeios (Enclosures) 61; Olympius 55, 65; Preserver 50; Saviour 190; thigh 14, *see also meros; see also* Ammon
ziggurat 97, 214